Development Centre Studies

The World Economy

HISTORICAL STATISTICS

by

Angus Maddison

OECD

DEVELOPMENT CENTRE OF THE ORGANISATION
FOR ECONOMIC CO-OPERATION AND DEVELOPMENT

✻ 534 65560

ORGANISATION FOR ECONOMIC CO-OPERATION AND DEVELOPMENT

Pursuant to Article 1 of the Convention signed in Paris on 14th December 1960, and which came into force on 30th September 1961, the Organisation for Economic Co-operation and Development (OECD) shall promote policies designed:

- to achieve the highest sustainable economic growth and employment and a rising standard of living in member countries, while maintaining financial stability, and thus to contribute to the development of the world economy;

- to contribute to sound economic expansion in member as well as non-member countries in the process of economic development; and

- to contribute to the expansion of world trade on a multilateral, non-discriminatory basis in accordance with international obligations.

The original member countries of the OECD are Austria, Belgium, Canada, Denmark, France, Germany, Greece, Iceland, Ireland, Italy, Luxembourg, the Netherlands, Norway, Portugal, Spain, Sweden, Switzerland, Turkey, the United Kingdom and the United States. The following countries became members subsequently through accession at the dates indicated hereafter: Japan (28th April 1964), Finland (28th January 1969), Australia (7th June 1971), New Zealand (29th May 1973), Mexico (18th May 1994), the Czech Republic (21st December 1995), Hungary (7th May 1996), Poland (22nd November 1996), Korea (12th December 1996) and the Slovak Republic (14th December 2000). The Commission of the European Communities takes part in the work of the OECD (Article 13 of the OECD Convention).

The Development Centre of the Organisation for Economic Co-operation and Development was established by decision of the OECD Council on 23rd October 1962 and comprises twenty-two member countries of the OECD: Austria, Belgium, Canada, the Czech Republic, Denmark, Finland, France, Germany, Greece, Iceland, Ireland, Italy, Korea, Luxembourg, Mexico, the Netherlands, Norway, Portugal, Slovak Republic, Spain, Sweden, Switzerland, as well as Argentina and Brazil from March 1994, Chile since November 1998 and India since February 2001. The Commission of the European Communities also takes part in the Centre's Advisory Board.

The purpose of the Centre is to bring together the knowledge and experience available in member countries of both economic development and the formulation and execution of general economic policies; to adapt such knowledge and experience to the actual needs of countries or regions in the process of development and to put the results at the disposal of the countries by appropriate means.

THE OPINIONS EXPRESSED AND ARGUMENTS EMPLOYED IN THIS PUBLICATION ARE THE SOLE RESPONSIBILITY OF THE AUTHOR AND DO NOT NECESSARILY REFLECT THOSE OF THE OECD, THE DEVELOPMENT CENTRE OR THE GOVERNMENTS OF THEIR MEMBER COUNTRIES.

*
* *

Publié en français sous le titre :
L'économie mondiale
STATISTIQUES HISTORIQUES

Foreword

This work cuts across the full range of the Development Centre's 2001–2002 Work Programme and responds to the Centre's mandate to " … bring together the knowledge and experience in Member countries of both economic development and the formulation and execution of general economic policies … and to put the results at the disposal of (developing) countries."

Table of Contents

List of Tables in Prologue and Source Notes

List of Basic Tables

HS-1

HS-2

HS-3A

HS–6

HS–7

HS–8

URL: http://www.theworldeconomy.org/

Username: historicalstatistics

Password: insight

Acknowledgements

I am indebted to Derek Blades for his encouragement and detailed comments on the tables and all of the text. Bart van Ark, Roger Brown, Ian Castles, Colm Foy, David Henderson and Eddy Szirmai gave me helpful comments on parts of it. Elizabeth Maddison helped advance my computer education. I am very grateful to Gerard Ypma for help in organising the basic statistical data in HS–1 to HS–7; and to Ly Na Tang Dollon for help with the tables in HS–8. Sheila Lionet put the manuscript into a form fit for publication. Alan Heston, David Roberts and Michael Ward answered many queries about PWT, OECD, and World Bank derivation of purchasing power parity converters. Steve Broadberry and Dirk Pilat were helpful in providing historical crosschecks on my measure of comparative GDP levels. Cathy Ward provided source material underlying IMF estimates of world GDP. Henk Jan Brinkman and Ian Kinniburgh provided access to UN material on world population and GDP. Nanno Mulder and Thomas Chalaux provided help in measurement of world population. Pierre van der Eng permitted me to use his estimates of Indonesian, Malaysian and Sri Lankan GDP. I received useful comments and research material from Maks Banens and Jean–Pascal Bassino on Vietnam, Luis Bertola on Uruguay, Claes Brundenius on Cuba, John Coatsworth, Stanley Engerman and Andre Hofman on Latin America, Thomas David on Switzerland, David Good and Max–Stephan Schulze on the successor states of the Austro–Hungarian Empire, Bryan Haig on Australia, Richard Hooley on the Philippines, Andrew Kamarck and J.R. McNeill on Africa, Debin Ma, Harry Wu and Xu Xianchun on China, Katya Maddison on the Middle East, Michelangelo van Meerten on Belgium, Patrick O'Brien on Egypt, Cormac O Grada and Mary O'Mahony on Ireland, Sevket Pamuk on Turkey and the successor states of the Ottoman Empire, Leandro Prados on Spain, Siva Sivasubramonian on India, Jean–Claude Toutain on France. Alan Bowman, Carol Kidwell and William McNeill gave me useful comments on chronology. Michèle Alkilic–Girard and Myriam Andrieux helped in locating bibliographic material. Since I did not always follow advice received, I do not suggest that those who gave it would endorse my judgement.

Preface

This is the eighth study by Angus Maddison published by the Development Centre since 1965. It is a companion volume to *The World Economy: A Millennial Perspective*, which appeared in 2001. This earlier work had an excellent reception from historians, economists and a broader public and has been a best–seller.

This book updates and supplements his earlier panoramic survey of the dynamics of growth, patterns of inequality and their deep–rooted causes. It provides fuller source notes and much more detailed estimates of population, GDP and per capita income. His rigorous handling of the data, systematic comparison and assessment of the reliability of sources and his suggestions about how gaps in the data should be filled are exemplary.

There is a closer scrutiny of the contours of African development over the past two millennia; and of Latin American experience since Columbus. It provides a critical review of the literature on macroeconomic measurement from its seventeenth century origins to the present, and is intended as a research guide for future comparisons of economic performance in space and time.

A comparative quantitative approach to the world's regions over a very long period is useful for policy formulation for several reasons. For developing countries, it augments the statistical information on which to base policy decisions in face of uncertainty. For OECD countries, it is a reminder of the key role of long–term processes such as demographic change, technological change and the operation of market forces in determining economic outcomes. It also provides an insightful account of the forces of convergence or divergence across economies and regions and is a valuable contribution to the complex debate about the benefits and costs of globalisation.

In order to facilitate access to the extensive data on which this book is based, a CD–Rom has been prepared by the OECD Statistics Directorate, under Chief Statistician Enrico Giovannini, to accompany this volume.

Louka T. Katseli
Director
OECD Development Centre

August 2003

Introduction

This book is intended as a quantitative reference work and guide to current and past research in macroeconomic history. It is a companion volume to *The World Economy: A Millennial Perspective*, published by OECD in 2001. The major purpose of that study was to provide an analytic survey of developments in the world economy over two millennia, and to explore the reasons for the great divergence in the momentum of advance in different regions. The analysis was underpinned by a comprehensive quantification of levels and movement in population, output, and per capita income. The statistical appendices provided annual estimates for 1950–1998, and for 8 benchmark years back to the first century. Annual estimates for 1870–1950 appeared in my earlier book *Monitoring the World Economy 1820–1992*.

The present work revises and updates the population estimates for 1950–2003, GDP and per capita GDP estimates for 1820–2001. It shows annual figures back to 1820 wherever possible and provides fuller source notes and explanations of proxy procedures for filling data gaps. For the period before 1820, there are fewer revisions, but detail is given for more countries and there is closer scrutiny of the contours of development in Latin America and Africa. Estimates of benchmark levels of output in 1990 international dollars are unchanged except for seven African countries.

The possibilities for extended annual coverage of population, GDP and per capita GDP were greatest for Europe and Western Offshoots. There were about 4 200 annual entries for individual countries in the 2001 volume and 15 200 here. For Latin America, Asia and Africa combined, there were about 15 300 entries in the earlier volume and 22 600 here.

The prologue provides a brief survey of the development of historical national accounts and demography from the 17th century to the present. It is based on some of the material I presented in the Kuznets lectures at Yale University in 1998. Sections HS–1 to HS–6 explain the sources and procedures used to derive the basic estimates for countries in the major regions. Section HS–7 summarises the procedures and problems involved in deriving the world totals for 1950–2003. HS–8 does the same for the estimates from the first century to 1950. Research on quantitative economic history has made great strides in the past quarter century, and the efforts of individual scholars have been reinforced by the creation of international networks as explained in HS–8. As a result we have a clearer notion of the range of growth experience, processes of catch–up, convergence and divergence, and underlying causal forces. Research has concentrated on the past two centuries of accelerated growth. Much less has been done on earlier centuries. As a consequence, there are conflicting views on relative levels of income in Europe and Asia around 1800. In my view, it is possible to resolve some of these differences by extending quantitative research further into the past. There were two reasons for indifference to or neglect of distant horizons. One is that quantitative evidence is scarcer the further back one goes in time, and earlier centuries were regarded as impenetrable to quantitative analysis. Another is that economic growth was much slower before the nineteenth century and therefore seemed irrelevant or uninteresting. There was a belief that the roots of modern growth lay in a sudden take–off (an industrial revolution) in the late eighteenth century, that agriculture originated eight thousand years ago and that there was a Malthusian torpor for most of the intervening interval. I disagree with this interpretation for reasons explained in HS–8.

Prologue: The Pioneers of Macromeasurement

National accounts are an indispensable tool for assessing the growth potential and performance of contemporary economies. They are fundamental in international comparison of development levels. They have become an important tool of analysis for quantitative economic historians. They are sometimes considered too "modern" to be applicable to the distant past. In fact, national accounting, international income comparisons, and historical demography originated in the seventeenth century, when "the art of reasoning by figures on things relating to government" was called Political Arithmetick.

The 17th Century Pioneers

The pioneer was **William Petty** (1623–87), a major figure in the scientific revolution of the seventeenth century. He was research assistant to the philosopher Thomas Hobbes in Paris in the 1640s, Professor of Anatomy in Oxford and organiser of the cadastral survey of Ireland after the Cromwellian conquest in the 1650s, one of the founders of the Royal Society in the 1660s, inventor, cartographer, economist, entrepreneur and founder of a wealthy dynasty. *Verbum Sapienti* (1665) presented his estimates of population, income, expenditure, stock of land, other physical assets and human capital in an integrated set of accounts for England and Wales. They were intended to provide a quantitative framework for effective implementation of fiscal policy and mobilisation of resources in time of war (the second Anglo–Dutch war of 1664–7).

Political Arithmetick (1676) was a comparative study of the economic performance of the Netherlands and France, using key indicators to demonstrate Dutch superiority. The French population was ten times the Dutch, but the Dutch merchant fleet was nine times as big, its foreign trade four times as big, its interest rate half the French level, its foreign assets large, those of France negligible. The Dutch economy was highly specialised, importing a large part of its food, hiring mercenaries to fight its wars, concentrating its labour force in high productivity sectors. High density of urban settlement, good ports and internal waterways reduced transport and infrastructure costs, cheapened government services and reduced the need for inventories. Property rights were clear and transfers facilitated by maintenance of registers. An efficient legal system and sound banking favoured economic enterprise. Taxes were high but levied on expenditure rather than income. This encouraged savings, frugality and hard work. The Dutch were a model of economic efficiency with obvious lessons for English policy, whereas popular notions of French power were greatly exaggerated.

Both these works were circulated in manuscript in Petty's lifetime, and published posthumously, in 1690 and 1691. Their publication sparked renewed interest in political arithmetic.

The second major contribution came from **Gregory King** (1648–1712), in reaction to Charles Davenant's (1694), *Essay upon Ways and Means of Supplying the War* (war of the League of Augsburg, 1688–97). **Davenant** (1656–1714) had literary talent as a clear expositor of economic issues (his father was poet laureate, and he was reputed by some to be the grandson of William Shakespeare). As former commissioner of excise when tax collection was taken out of the hands of tax farmers, he was able to present a first consolidated and transparent picture of the government's actual and potential revenues and expenditure. King was impressed by the possibilities of using fiscal information for macroeconomic analysis. He established a close relationship with Davenant who quoted his work in detail and called him "that wonderful genius and master in the art of computing". Publications on sensitive matters of public policy required an official license, and exposed the author to sanctions of official disapproval. King preferred to avoid this risk, circulated copies of his manuscript accounts for comment to Davenant, **Robert Harley** (1661–1724) and others, but did not publish them. Unlike Davenant who was a well connected member of parliament, King was a cautious public servant in course of moving from the antiquated world of heraldry to more lucrative employment as Commissioner of Public Accounts. Harley was later Chancellor of the Exchequer and effectively Prime Minister under Queen Anne.

King's work in this field was intense from 1695 to 1700. His *Natural and Political Observations and Conclusions on the State and Condition of England* (1696) presented his results in highly concentrated form, but his 300 page Notebook (published in facsimile form by Laslett, 1973) provides an understanding of his meticulous procedures and the sophistication of his analysis. King's *Observations* was first published in complete form by George Chalmers in 1802 as an annex to his book on the *Comparative Strength of Great Britain*. This sparked the interest of **Patrick Colquhoun** (1745–1820) who exploited new sources of information (the first two censuses and the first income tax accounts) to replicate King's income account, and provide a more comprehensive production account showing value added for 1812. However, King's *Notebook* did not surface until 1917, and was first explored by David Glass in 1965. It is a treasure trove which deserves to be mined more thoroughly by quantitative historians.

The modern standardised system of national accounts provides a coherent macroeconomic framework covering the whole economy, which can be crosschecked in three ways. From the income side, it is the total of wages, rents and profits. It is also the sum of final expenditures by consumers, investors and government. From the production side, it is the sum of value added in different sectors– agriculture, industry and services, net of duplication. The framework can be expanded to include measures of labour input and capital stock, labour and total factor productivity.

King had four dimensions to his accounts which anticipated this modern system of interrelated balances:

a) the best–known is his depiction of the 1688 social hierarchy, showing 26 types of household, their number, average size, income and expenditure, savings or dependency on social transfers, and type of economic activity. In constructing it, King drew on 30 years experience in the Herald's office, making visitations to various parts of England to examine credentials of succession to aristocratic titles, the status and social standing of people who accounted for about two–thirds of national income. As a commissioner for the graduated poll tax on births, deaths, and marriage which came into force in 1695, he had access to a great deal of new information on the structure of incomes. The hearth tax was a further guide to the number of households and their average size;

b) his second account showed government spending and consumer expenditure by type of product, based on information derived from land and excise taxes for food, drink and tobacco, and a special survey he made for clothing and textiles. In *Observations* this account is very summary, but it is clear from the *Notebook* that his aggregate was the fruit of detailed estimation, and contains enough information to provide an approximation to the modern notion of gross domestic product (see Table 1 where I augment his aggregate which had narrower boundaries than is now standard);

c) his production account was incomplete. It showed value added in farming (crops and livestock) and forestry. His *Notebook* provides detailed quantification of many other items–textiles, value added in the paper industry, a breakdown of material inputs and labour costs in construction and shipbuilding. It shows expenditure on furniture, ceramics, pottery, glass, tools and transport equipment which can be converted into production estimates, with adjustment to deduct material inputs, transport and distributive margins;

d) a fourth dimension was his consolidated wealth and income account for 1688, showing property and labour income, the capitalised value of physical assets and of human capital. This resembled Petty's account for 1665, though the techniques of capitalisation were different.

King had a fifth account which compared levels of per capita consumption, public expenditure and revenue in England, France and Holland in 1688 and in 1695 in order to demonstrate differences in capacity to mobilise resources for war. It also contained a forecast of English national income to 1698. The estimates for France and the Netherlands were in most respects very rough, and he did not discuss the problem of measuring changes in the volume of output over time or adjusting for differences in the purchasing power of currency in making international comparisons.

Table 1. **Gross Domestic Expenditure in England and Wales in 1688**
(£000 at market prices)

Food	**13 900**	**Education and Health**	**1 150**
Bread, Biscuits and Pastry	4 300	Schooling	250
Beef, Mutton and Pork	3 300	Paper, Books and Ink	500
Fish, Poultry and Eggs	1 700	Medical	400[a]
Dairy Products	2 300		
Fruits and Vegetables	1 200	**Personal and Professional Services**	**3 100**
Salt, Spices, Oil, and Sweetmeats	1 100	Domestic Servants	1 600[a]
		Recreation	500
Beverages and Tobacco	**7 350**	Legal, Financial, Hair-dressing,	
Beer and Ale	5 800	Inns and Taverns	1 000[a]
Wine and Brandy	1 300		
Tobacco, Pipes and Snuff	250[a]	**Passenger Transport**	**430**
		Passenger Transport by Road	280[a]
Clothing	**10 393**	Passenger Transport by Water	150[a]
Male Outerwear	2 390		
Shirts, Cravats, and Ruffles	1 300	**Government, Religion and Defence**	**4 844**
Male Underwear	100	Military Pay	1 530[a]
Male Accessories	85	Ecclesiastical Remuneration	514[a]
Female Outerwear	904	Civil Government Pay	1 800[a]
Female Underwear	1 400	Commodities	1 000[a]
Nightgowns and Aprons	500		
Female Accessories	335	**Gross Capital Formation**	**3 675**
Hats, Caps and Wigs	568	Structures	975[a]
Gloves, Mittens and Muffs	410	Transport Equipment	700[a]
Handkerchiefs	200	Other Equipment	2 000
Stockings and Socks	1 011		
Footwear	1 190	**Gross Domestic Expenditure**	**54 042**
		Gregory King's Total	41 643[b]
Household Operation	**9 200**	Additional Items	12 399[a]
Rent and Imputed Rent	2 200[a]		
Fire, Candles and Soap	2 000		
Beds and Bedding	1 500		
Sheets and Table Linen	1 500		
Brass and Pewterware	1 000		
Wood and Glassware	1 000		

a) Indicates items I added from *Notebook*.
b) Total of items shown in *Observations*.
Source: Gregory King's *Notebook* in Laslett (1973) and *Observations* in Barnett (1936).

Table 2. **Structure of British Gross Domestic Expenditure, 1688 and 1996**
(per cent of total)

	1688 *England and Wales*	*1996* *United Kingdom*
Food	25.7	6.5
Beverages and Tobacco	13.6	5.9
Clothing and Footwear	19.2	3.7
Light, Fuel and Power	3.7	2.2
Furniture, Furnishings and Household Equipment	9.3	4.0
Personal Services	3.0	1.2
Sub-total	**74.5**	**23.5**
Rent and Imputed Rent	4.1	10.0
Education	1.4	5.4
Health	0.7	6.7
Recreation and Entertainment	0.9	5.7
Transport and Communication	0.8	10.6
Other	1.9	11.5
Sub-total	**9.8**	**49.9**
Total Private Consumption (Total Items 1-12)	84.2	73.4
Government Consumption (except education and health)	9.0	10.9
Gross Capital Formation	6.8	15.8
Total Gross Domestic Expenditure	**100.0**	**100.0**
Level of Per Capita GDP (in 1990 international dollars)	1 411	17 891

Source: 1688 from Table 1; 1996 from OECD, *National Accounts 1984-1996*, Vol.2, Paris 1998.

Box 1. **Political arithmeticians were also pioneers of demography**

The first serious demographer was **John Graunt** (1620–74), a close friend of Petty. Graunt's *Observations on the Bills of Mortality* published in 1662 involved a meticulous assemblage and adjustment of a very large weekly and annual database on burials and christenings in London for 1603 onwards. For 20 years he had data on causes of death, broken down by 81 categories. He had access to returns of a partial census for 1631 which provided a benchmark for his growth estimates.

Graunt distinguished the regular pattern of chronic ailments from epidemics. Plague was endemic but recurred at irregular intervals. The worst year was 1603, when it caused 82 per cent of deaths. He had no direct information on age at death, but constructed a rough proxy by grouping illnesses which affected infants and children, and those associated with old age. He constructed a crude survival table which showed 36 per cent mortality for those aged 0–6, with only 3 per cent surviving beyond age 66. This was the ancestor of life tables, and attracted wide interest in England, France and Holland where life annuities and tontines (a lottery on life expectation invented by Lorenzo Tonti in 1652) were part of the public debt. **Edmond Halley** (1656–1742) improved on Graunt's crude analysis of life expectation and articulated the fundamental mathematical principles of life insurance in (1693) "Degrees of Mortality of Mankind; with an Attempt to ascertain the Price of Annuities", *Philosophical Transactions of the Royal Society*.

In confronting data on London burials and christenings, Graunt found that burials were bigger. By comparison of the average discrepancy between births and deaths, he concluded that there was net immigration from small towns and rural areas of about 6 000 persons a year. As a crosscheck, he analysed annual data for Romsey, a town near Southampton. Over 90 years there was a net increase of 1 059 persons, of which 300 remained in Romsey, 400 emigrated to the Americas and 300–400 emigrated to London. In the third edition, in 1665, Graunt extended the analysis of country towns to Tiverton in Devon and Cranbrook in Kent, which confirmed the Romsey/London differentials.

As births were rising substantially over time, it was clear that the population was growing, and the growth of the housing stock corroborated this. Using inferences about age structure and likely fertility in conjunction with his other material, he suggested that London had grown two and a half fold in the previous 56 years.

Graunt concluded that the population of England and Wales was 14 times as big as that of London. His multiplier was derived from several indicators, i.e. London's share of the tax burden; cartographic analysis of the area of different parts of the country, likely density of settlement, the average size of parishes.

Prior to Graunt, nobody had thought of using the mortality bills to reconstruct the demography of London. His meticulous inspection of data, adjustments for coverage, the caution and modesty with which he explained his carefully structured inferences and techniques of analysis are the foundation of modern historical demography, and he clearly belonged to the pantheon of seventeenth century science.

Gregory King made a significant improvement on Graunt's estimate of the population of England and Wales. He had much more information for areas outside London. He had the hearth tax returns on the number of houses (1 million rural and 300 000 urban). From Davenant (1694) he had evidence from the chimney tax on house occupancy. He organised mini–censuses for Lichfield, Harfield and Buckfastleigh as a crosscheck on household size. His estimate of family size was smaller than Graunt's. He found an average household of 4.23 persons, but this included domestic servants, apprentices and unmarried farm labourers who lived in. Deducting these the average family size was 3.8 persons.

King's estimate of the population of England and Wales in 1695 was 5.5 million, significantly lower than Graunt's 6.4 million, but virtually identical with the estimate of Wrigley *et al.* (1997) in their detailed reconstitution of English demographic history 1580–1837 using the sophisticated techniques and massive computing power of modern demography.

King also made an estimate of world population in 1695, based on a calculation of the surface area of the globe, the proportion of land in the total and the likely density of settlement on different types of land. His world total in the *Notebook* was 626 million, much closer to my 604 million for 1700 than Petty's estimate of 320 million in his day or Riccioli's (1672) estimate of 1 billion.

Between 1695 and 1707, there was interest in national income estimation in France. In 1695 **Pierre de Boisguilbert** (1646–1714), lieutenant–general (chief judge and president of the appeals court) in Rouen (capital of the province of Normandy), published anonymously *La France ruinée sous la règne de Louis XIV,* a very pessimistic assessment of the economic condition of France, the need to make its fiscal structure more effective and equitable and to be less dirigiste in economic policy. In 1697 another version appeared, still anonymous but with a less provocative title *Le détail de la France.* Boisguilbert was impressed by the hunger crises and population decline which hit France in the early 1690s. He asserted that the national income had fallen by a third since 1660, but in fact provided no detail. Boisguilbert's books attracted little notice but stimulated the interest of **Sebastien le Prestre de Vauban** (1633–1707), a military engineer, who designed and supervised the construction of fortifications on the Northern and Eastern frontiers, successfully besieged many enemy cities, and constructed ports and forts on the Atlantic coast. Marshal Vauban had experience in galvanising regional and local authorities and mobilising resources for construction projects in many parts of France over a period of decades, so it is not surprising that he developed aspirations as a social engineer at the end of his career. There is a striking difference in tone between the work of Boisguilbert and Vauban and the English school of political arithmetic. The French writers were both convinced that the economy of their country was in a parlous state and the English were much more upbeat about England.

In 1707 Vauban published *La dîme royale,* a detailed proposal to transform the tax structure, which included a detailed assessment of potential revenue under a new tax regime. He was encouraged in this endeavour by the success of a proposal he made to the king in January 1695 for a temporary wartime capitation tax. This was adopted in 1695 and terminated in 1697 when the war ended. It was similar to the English poll tax of 1695–1705. Its incidence was graduated by descending order in the social hierarchy for 22 classes of taxpayer from the Dauphin down; social position being a proxy for income assessment. It was reintroduced in 1701 as a regional supplement to the *taille* without the key feature of graduation by ability to pay (see Collins, 2001, pp. 133–4 and 165–7).

The French revenue system Boiguilbert and Vauban wanted to transform was highly inefficient and inequitable. The main direct tax, the *taille,* involved large exemptions for the nobility and office holders. Some of these were for individuals (*personnelle*), others exempted specified properties (*réelle*). Tax rates varied regionally, between the *pays d'élection* and the *pays d'état* (Brittany, Burgundy, Languedoc and Provence, where tax rates were largely determined by the regional authorities). There were internal transit duties (*traites*) on merchandise crossing regional frontiers, inhibiting the development of a national market. Collection of direct and indirect taxes was done mainly by tax farmers and *traitants,* who made advance payments to the authorities and kept what they could collect. At the bottom level, in the 36 000 parishes, tax liability was fixed collectively. A large proportion of public officials obtained their posts by purchase, or inherited them from relatives. Most of them paid an annual fee (*paulette*) to guarantee inheritability of their office. In fact their salaries (*gages*) were equivalent to interest on the money they paid for their post. As a result the bureaucracy was swollen by officials who were only partially employed. The major indirect tax (*gabelle*), was on salt; the rate of tax varied between regions, virtually zero in producing regions like Brittany, and high in Burgundy, where wine taxes were low. As a consequence, there was large–scale smuggling and expenditure on revenue police. In all these respects, England had a more efficient, transparent and equitable fiscal system. In 1694 it acquired a central bank and established effective foundations for a market in long–term government debt. In France the first attempt a national budget was Necker's *Compte Rendu au Roi* in 1781, and the Banque de France was not created until 1800.

Vauban proposed to abolish all the existing taxes on property, income and internal transit, and replace them with a single tax on income without exemptions or regional variation. He proposed to simplify the rate structure of the salt tax to reduce smuggling. He suggested new indirect taxes on luxuries and on liquor consumed in bars (*cabarets*).

In order to assess potential revenue from his new system he made estimates of national income, population and area. For area, he used a rough average of five different cartographic sources for 38 regions of France. His estimated total was the equivalent of 60 million hectares. This was an exaggeration. The present area is 55 million and at that time (before Lorraine and Savoie were incorporated) was about 50 million (see Le Roy Ladurie, 1992, p. 280). In fact, King's estimate of the area of France (51 million hectares) was much more exact. For population Vauban used estimates from 28 provincial officials for years between 1694–1700. His total was 19.1 million, which tallies fairly well with modern estimates for the area he covered (see Bardet and Dupaquier, 1997, p. 449). King's estimate for France (14 million) was much too low.

Vauban's estimates of national income were rough and hybrid. His measure for agriculture referred to gross output, with no deduction for feed, seed and upkeep of buildings and equipment. He did not distinguish between different categories of agricultural income, and did not cover non–agricultural activity in rural areas. He specified 10 types of non–agricultural income from property and labour. The sophistication of the analysis was greatly inferior to that of Gregory King, and he was dealing with a country where fiscal and other evidence for a coherent national analysis was much more exiguous than in England.

Vauban estimated agricultural output on the basis of a sample study of Normandy. For this he had help from an anonymous friend (possibly Boisguilbert). He assumed that 80 per cent of the land yielded income from crops, livestock, vineyards and forestry, with a third of cropland in fallow. He estimated the physical crop yield for wheat and its value per square league (20 square km.). He assumed this value yield per league was also valid for pastoral activities, vineyards and forestry. From this he estimated a tax yield about 24 per cent higher than the ecclesiastical tithe for Normandy. Nevertheless, he took the latter as representative and blew up it up by the ratio of the land area of France to that of Normandy. After a further conservative reduction of about 10 per cent, he concluded that the tax yield at the national level would be 60 million livres, assuming a 5 per cent levy (*vingtième*) on gross output. If we multiply his 5 per cent tax yield by 20, gross agricultural output for France would have been 1 200 million livres; his first estimate implied 1667 million livres. However, if we deduct inputs into agriculture, adjust for his overstatement of the area of France and the fact that Normandy was more densely populated than the country as a whole, it seems likely that he was overstating national income from agriculture substantially.

Vauban's estimate of non–rural income was 352 million livres. Rent and imputed rent (net of repair and maintenance) from 320 000 urban houses he estimated to be 32 million. Interest on government debt 20 million, mixed income from commerce, banking, fishing, shipping, and grain milling 58 million, pensions and emoluments of government officials 40 million, legal income 10 million. He assumed there were 1.5 million servants with emoluments of 30 million. 2 million non–agricultural labourers and artisans were assumed to earn 162 million–he derived this from their average daily wage, and assumed a working year of 185 days (deducting 52 Sundays, 38 days for public holidays, 50 for intemperate weather, 20 days attending fairs and markets, and 25 for illness). Except for the last three groups, he gave no indication of the number of people involved in rural and non–rural activity. He proposed the introduction of a Chinese–style household registration system to remedy this defect, and appended a form showing the type of detail by age, sex and occupation which should be garnered annually by local worthies. Vauban must have realised that his assessment of non–rural income was inadequate, as he started his analysis by asserting that it was bigger than rural income. However, he could have crosschecked his estimates more closely for consistency. His estimate of the number of non–rural houses (320 000) is manifestly too low for a non–rural labour force of more than 3.5 million and their families.

Vauban insisted that the costs of collection would be greatly reduced with his system and that the transition from the existing order would be painless. He felt that one could dispense with the sevices of tax farmers and traitants whom he classified as bloodsuckers (*Sang-suës d'État*). He felt that there could be a smooth tansition to collection of agricultural levies in kind to be stored in government warehouses. He did not explain how the government would dispose of these commodities. He was also insouciant about the protests of the elite who would lose their tax–exempt status. In chapter VIII he identified all the groups who might oppose his proposition and suggested that with 200 000 armed men at his disposal the king could easily quell any opposition. Politically his proposition was both naïve and provocative. In February 1707, a month before Vauban's death, the book was officially condemned and the remaining copies were destroyed.

The 18th Century Onwards

From the beginning of the eighteenth century to the 1940s, there were about thirty attempts to measure national income in Britain. There were significant differences in their coverage and methodology. Most concentrated on the income dimension without crosschecks from the expenditure or production side. Most were spot estimates for a given point of time and it was difficult to link them to measure economic growth, as there was only a limited and belated effort to develop appropriate price deflators (see Colin Clark, 1937). Nevertheless, these estimates are still very useful to quantitative economic historians. Thanks to detailed scrutiny by Phyllis Deane (1955–7) they provided a starting point and inspiration for pioneering studies of British economic growth by Deane and Cole (1964), Feinstein (1972), Matthews, Feinstein and Odling–Smee (1982) and Crafts (1985). The retrospective estimates of this new generation of quantitative historians are generally based on the modern international standardised system of national accounts.

Studenski (1958) cites nine attempts to measure French national income later in the 18th century. Some of these were an improvement on Vauban, notably Lavoisier's *De la richesse territoriale du royaume de France* (1791), and Arthur Young's (1794, chapter 15) detailed estimates of French agricultural output for 1787–9. Young found that land productivity in Normandy was much higher than in the rest of France, which strengthens the impression that Vauban overstated agricultural output.

Between 1800 and the first world war, the statistical basis for macroeconomic measurement improved a good deal in Europe, North America and the Antipodes. Population censuses provided a much better basis for demographic analysis. Statistical offices collected data on trade, transport, fiscal and monetary matters, employment, wages and prices. There was an increasing array of information on commodity output in agriculture, mining and manufacturing. Index number techniques were developed which would have made it possible to measure temporal change and inter–spatial variance of complex aggregates.

Although there was a proliferation of national income estimates, there was little improvement in their quality or comparability. They provided little help for serious analysis of economic growth, and there were significant differences in their coverage and methodology.

Michael Mulhall (1836–1900) made a serious contribution to international comparison of levels of performance.

Mulhall was Irish, educated in Rome, and spent his early working life as a journalist in Argentina. He published four major books between 1880 and 1896, drawing on census, trade, and commercial information to demonstrate developments in the world economy. His *Industry and Wealth of Nations* (1896) was devoted entirely to providing consistent comparisons of national output and wealth. He gave detailed sources and a mass of carefully structured statistical material in comparative form for 22 countries representing about 60 per cent of world product in 1894–5. He referred to other national income estimates where available, but used his own standard rules of thumb to assess value added for all countries. He also provided standard guidelines for his measures of national wealth. His methods were simple and described transparently. To determine total value added, he divided each national economy into 9 sectors, estimated gross output in each sector, and to avoid double counting, deducted inputs as specified below.

His coverage of Europe and Western offshoots was pretty comprehensive, but for the rest of the world was confined to Argentina and South Africa. He provided current price estimates of the level in income in eight countries at dates ranging from 1812 to 1895. His cross–country comparison for 1894 was at current prices (in £ sterling) using exchange rates.

Mulhall had a powerful influence on Timothy Coghlan, the government statistician for New South Wales who made the first official estimates of national income for the *Seven Colonies of Australasia* which were published regularly from 1886–1905.

Table 3. **Mulhall's 1896 Guidelines for Estimating Value Added by Sector of Economic Activity**

Economic Sector	*Value Added*
Agriculture	60 per cent of gross product
Manufacturing	50 per cent of gross product
Minerals, forestry and fisheries	100 per cent of gross product
Commerce	10 per cent of aggregate domestic sales
Transport	10.5 per cent of aggregate domestic sales
House-rent	6 per cent of the value of the housing stock
Domestic servants	two-thirds of house rent
Public service	50 per cent of tax revenue
Professional services	10 per cent of the sum of 8 items above

Colin Clark (1905–89) took a major step towards world accounts in his *Conditions of Economic Progress* in 1940. He assembled income estimates for 30 countries (pp. 40–1). He adjusted them to mitigate national idiosyncrasies of measurement and made rough proxies for another 20 countries (based on indicators of real wages) to make a rough estimate of world income for 1925–34 (p. 56). He constructed a crude PPP measure to make the individual country estimates additive in terms of his "international unit" (US dollars with average purchasing power of 1925–34). Unlike Mulhall, who made his own multicountry estimates on a standardised basis, Clark was in large degree a compiler of other people's estimates, seeking maximalist coverage. To measure economic growth, he made time series comparisons in real terms for 15 countries for disparate years between 1850 and the 1930s (pp. 146–148), but in many cases these were weak because he was willing to make crude links between different and not always comparable "spot" estimates, and to make use of some dubious deflators.

All of Clark's 1940 estimates have now been superseded, but his work is still of substantial historical interest, because he made an exhaustive survey of the work of virtually all the economists and statisticians who had published in his field in the nineteenth and twentieth centuries and had extensive correspondance with the statisticians of his day who were engaged in such work. He never hesitated to adjust these estimates to conform to his own ideas about the appropriate coverage of the accounts or methods of treatment of particular items. He also used the estimates analytically. Systematic comparative confrontation is a particularly good way of testing the plausibility and consistency of estimates and may well induce careful scrutiny of "outlier countries". In 1940, however, there was no agreement on the coverage and methodology of national accounts, and the comparability of the different estimates was therefore restricted.

The Modern Era

The first official estimates for the United States were made by **Simon Kuznets** (1901–85) in 1934, at a time when the economy was in deep depression. The accounts were felt to be an important tool for improving public policy. In the United Kingdom, the outbreak of war in 1939 led to a replication of the Davenant–King partnership of the 1690s. In February 1940, Maynard Keynes published *How to Pay for the War: A Radical Plan for the Chancellor of the Exchequer*. The structure of his argument was butressed by national accounts developed by Colin Clark (they were already closely associated in 1931–7, when Keynes was analysing the causes and cure for unemployment). Keynes persuaded the chancellor to include a first official set of accounts in his 1941 budget. The accounts were an important tool in Whitehall strategy for winning the war. The integrated statistical perspective led to much more effective resource mobilisatiton than in Germany (see Kaldor, 1946).

In 1944 there were consultations between British, Canadian and US statisticians with a view to standardisation of their concepts and procedures (see Denison, 1947). In the postwar years, comparable accounts were felt to be a political necessity to facilitate assessment of needs for Marshall Aid and burden–sharing in NATO.

The standardised system was designed in large part by **Richard Stone** (1913–1991), who together with James Meade made the first official estimates of national income for the United Kingdom in 1941. He also produced guidelines for OEEC and OECD on *Quantity and Price Indexes* (1956), *Input–Output and National Accounts* (1961) and *Demographic Accounting and Model Building* (1971). His magnum opus was his posthumously published (1997) *Some British Empiricists in the Social Sciences, 1650-1900*. Stone and Milton Gilbert (chief of US national income accounts until 1951 and Director of the OEEC Economics and Statistics Department until 1960) were very active in the 1950s in seeing that the 1952 standardised system was implemented in OEEC countries. Shortly after, the OEEC system was merged with that of the UN which was applied by official statisticians in most countries in the postwar years, except in communist countries whose accounts excluded many service activities, and involved some duplication. **Milton Gilbert** (1909–79) and **Irving Kravis** (1916–92) pioneered the first official measures of the purchasing power parity of currencies, published by OEEC in 1954. Kravis greatly expanded the scope of the PPP measures by starting the International Comparison Project (ICP) in 1968, and in 1978, together with his colleagues Robert Summers and Alan Heston inaugurated the Penn World Tables (PWT) to fill gaps in ICP coverage.

Thanks to these pioneering efforts, there are now official estimates of GDP growth for years since 1950 for 179 countries, and purchasing power parity measures which permit comparison of levels of performance. They have become a major instrument of economic policy in virtually all countries.

HS–1: Western Europe, 1500–2001

Population 1500-1700 and GDP growth rates 1500-1820 (except for France) from Appendix B of Maddison (2001), *The World Economy: A Millennial Perspective*; 1820 onwards as described below.

Population: Sources for the annual estimates, 1820–1950, are described in the country notes below. 1950 onwards from International Programs Center, US Bureau of the Census, October 2002.

GDP: Annual estimates, 1820–1950, as described below. In most cases, the country source notes are abbreviated versions of those in Maddison (1995), *Monitoring the World Economy, 1820–1992*, pp. 126–139, but there are revised estimates for France, the Netherlands, Portugal, Switzerland and Spain. I also comment on new estimates for Austria and Greece which I have not adopted. 1950 onwards from Appendix C of Maddison (2001), *The World Economy: A Millennial Perspective*, updated as follows: GDP volume movement 1995–2001 from OECD, *National Accounts of OECD Countries, 1989–2000*, vol. 1, and OECD, *Quarterly National Accounts Statistics*, 2/2002; Maddison (2001), pp.171–4 and 189–90 explain the derivation of the benchmark 1990 GDP levels. Except for Germany and the United Kingdom, the estimates are adjusted to eliminate the impact of frontier change.

Austria: GDP by industry of origin in 1913 prices for 1830, 1840, 1850, 1860 and annual estimates 1870–1913, from A. Kausel, "Österreichs Volkseinkommen 1830 bis 1913" in *Geschichte und Ergebnisse der zentralen amtlichen Statistik in Österreich 1829–1979, Beitrage zur österreichischen Statistik*, Heft 550, Vienna, 1979, pp. 692–3. 1820–30 per capita movement assumed to be the same as that for 1830–40 (see Kausel, p. 701). 1913–50 gross national product in 1937 prices by expenditure and industry of origin, from A. Kausel, N. Nemeth, and H. Seidel, "Österreichs Volkseinkommen, 1913–63", *Monatsberichte des Österreichischen Institutes für Wirtschaftsforschung*, 14th Sonderheft, Vienna, August 1965, p. 38 and 42; 1937–45 from F. Butschek, *Die Österreichische Wirtschaft 1938 bis 1945*, Fischer, Stuttgart, 1979, p. 65. 1950 onwards from OECD sources. Kausel's estimates are corrected for territorial change, and refer to population and product within the present boundaries of Austria. Kausel (1979) also presented 1830–1913 estimates for Cisleithenia (the Austrian half of the Austro–Hungarian Empire). Other Cisleithenia included Bohemia, Moravia, Galicia, Bukowina, the Trieste region, and Dalmatia (subsequently parts of Czechoslavakia, Poland and Yugoslavia). Kausel was head of the national accounts division and subsequently Vice President of the Austrian Central Statistical Office. His 1979 article was part of a large–scale exercise in quantitative economic history to celebrate the 150th anniversary of the Statistical Office. The anniversary volume contained many other papers, including a comprehensive demographic analysis of the different components of the Austro–Hungarian Empire("Die Bevölkerung Österrreich–Ungarns", by H. Helczmanovszki).

David Good and Tongshu Ma (1999), "The Economic Growth of Central and Eastern Europe in Comparative Perspective, 1870–1989", *European Review of Economic History*, vol. 3, Part 2, pp. 105 and 107 reject the Kausel (1979) estimates as "back–of–the envelope" calculations. They suggest a "more plausible" alternative with "firmer foundations". In fact, it is derived from regression and three proxy measures: letters posted per capita, crude birth rate, and share of non–agricultural employment in the labour force. Their estimate refers to 1870–1910 and shows slower growth than Kausel. In an earlier estimate, using five proxies and a different estimating procedure, Good (1994) appeared satisfied to have found growth "almost identical to that of Kausel". The Good and Ma characterisation of Kausel's direct estimate is inaccurate and there is no justification for dropping it in favour of their proxy for Austria. However, their other proxies are useful as they cover countries and periods for which direct estimates are not available (see HS–2 below).

Max–Stephan Schulze, "Patterns of Growth and Stagnation in the Late Nineteenth Century Habsburg Economy", *European Review of Economic History*, December 2000, pp. 311–40 provides well–documented annual GDP and per capita GDP estimates for 1870–1913 for Cisleithenia and Transleithenia (the Hungarian half of the Habsburg Empire). He made no estimate for present–day Austria, but used Good and Ma results. He shows slower growth for present–day Austria than for Cisleithenia, whereas Kausel showed the opposite. Kausel's 1913 per capita GDP was more than 60 per cent higher than he found for Cisleithenia. The Schulze differential is 29 per cent. Table 1–1 shows my estimates for 1830, 1870 and 1913 derived from Kausel; the bottom panel shows those of Schulze.

Table 1-1. **Population and GDP in Modern and Habsburg Austria, 1830-1913**

	Modern Austria	*Other Cisleithenia*	*Total Cisleithenia*
	Population (000s)		
1830	3 538	12 292	15 830
1870	4 520	16 028	20 248
1913	6 767	22 572	29 339
	GDP (million 1990 international Geary-Khamis $)		
1830	4 937	11 150	16 087
1870	8 429	16 574	25 003
1913	23 451	39 187	62 638
	GDP per capita (1990 international Geary-Khamis $)		
1830	1 395	907	1 016
1870	1 865	1 034	1 235
1913	3 465	1 736	2 135
	Schulze GDP per capita estimates		
1870	1 856	n.a.	1 421
1913	2 871	n.a.	2 222

Belgium: 1820–46 movement in agricultural output from Martine Goossens, *De Economische Ontwikkeling van de Belgische Landbouw in Regional Perspectief, 1812–1846*, Leuven 1989. 1831–46 industrial output estimates supplied by Jean Gadisseur (1820–31 assumed to increase at same pace as in 1831–42). Service output 1820–46 assumed to move with population. 1846–1913 GDP derived from movements in agricultural and industrial output from J. Gadisseur, "Contribution à l'étude de la production agricole en Belgique de 1846 à 1913", *Revue belge d'histoire contemporaine*, vol. IV, 1–2, 1973. Service output is from the same source and was assumed to move with service employment (derived for census years from P. Bairoch, *La Population active et sa structure*, Brussels, 1968, pp. 87–8). 1913 weights and 1913–50 GDP from C. Carbonnelle, "Recherches sur l'évolution de la production en Belgique de 1900 à 1957", *Cahiers Économiques de Bruxelles*, no. 3, April 1959, p. 358. Carbonnelle gives GDP figures for only a few benchmark years but gives a commodity production series for many more years. Interpolations were made for the service sector to arrive at a figure for GDP for all the years for which Carbonnelle shows total commodity production. GDP movement 1914–19 and 1939–47 are interpolations between the 1913 and 1920 estimates and those for 1938 and 1948 respectively, assuming the same pattern of movement as in France. Population 1820–1950 from *Annuaire statistique de la Belgique et du Congo Belge*, 1955. Figures adjusted to exclude the impact of the cession by Germany of Eupen and Malmedy in 1925, which added 0.81 per cent to population and was assumed to have added the same proportion to output.

Denmark: 1820–1947 GDP at 1929 factor cost by industry of origin from S.A. Hansen, *Økonomisk vaekst i Danmark*, vol. II, Institute of Economic History, Copenhagen, 1974, pp. 229–32. 1947–60 GDP at 1955 factor cost from Søren Larsen, "Reviderede tidsserier for produktionsvaerdi og bruttofaktorindkomst for perioden 1947–65", CBS, Copenhagen, 1992. 1820–1950 population from Hansen (1974). Estimates are adjusted to eliminate the impact of the acquisition of North Schleswig in 1921, which added 5.3 per cent to population, and 4.5 per cent to GDP.

Finland: 1860–1960 GDP by industry of origin at market prices from R. Hjerppe, *The Finnish Economy 1860–1985: Growth and Structural Change*, Bank of Finland, Helsinki, 1989, pp. 198–200. 1820–60 per capita GDP assumed to increase by 22.5 per cent, as indicated in S. Heikkinen, R. Hjerppe, Y. Kaukiainen, E. Markkanen and I. Nummela, "Förändringar i levnadsstandarden i Finland, 1750–1913" in G. Karlson, ed., *Levestandarden i Norden 1750–1914*, Reykjavik, 1987, p. 74. Population 1820–1950 from O. Turpeinen, *Ikaryhmittainen kuolleisuus Suomessa vv. 1751–1970*, (Mortality by Age-group in Finland, 1751-1970), Helsinki, 1973. The 1940 and 1944 treaties which ceded territory to the USSR had no impact on population as all inhabitants were moved to Finland.

France: GDP estimates for 1820–70 in Maddison (1995) have been revised. I used J–C. Toutain's volume movement for agriculture and services, but not for industry where he showed much faster growth than other scholars (see Toutain, *Le produit intérieur de la France de 1789 à 1982*, Presses Universitaires de Grenoble, 1987). Instead I used the industrial index of M. Levy–Leboyer and F. Bourguignon (1984) *L'économie Francaise au XIXe siècle*, using Toutain's sector weights for 1870. Toutain has revised his 1820–70 estimates significantly (see J.–C. Toutain, "Le produit intérieur brut de la France, 1789–1990", ISMEA, *Histoire et Sociétés, histoire économique et quantitative*, 1, no. 11, 1997, pp. 5–136 Presses Universitaires de Grenoble), showing faster growth for services. I now use his new estimates for agriculture and services, together with the Levy–Leboyer/Bouguignon estimate for industry. Sources for 1870 onwards are unchanged–see Maddison (1995), pp.127–130.

Growth rates of per capita GDP for 1500-1600 and 1700-1820 are unchanged, but modified for 1600-1700. For the second half of the seventeenth century I assume stagnant per capita income because of hunger crises and the depressing impact of more or less continuous warfare as noted by Boisguilbert and Vauban.

Population and GDP estimates refer to the present territory of France, excluding the impact of the loss of Alsace–Lorraine 1871–1918 and acquisition of territory in 1861 (Savoie, Haute Savoie, Nice and surrounding parts of the Alpes Maritimes), which represented 600 000 of the 37 390 000 population of 1861. Population 1820–1860 from L. Henry and Y. Blayo, "La population de la France de 1740 à 1860", *Population*, November 1975, pp. 97–9; 1861–1950 from *Annuaire statistique de la France*, 1966, pp. 66–72.

Germany: The present estimates refer to GDP and population within 1870 frontiers until 1918, 1936 frontiers for 1919–45, and present frontiers from 1946 onwards. Maddison 1995 provided estimates for 1820–1992 adjusted to exclude the impact of territorial change for the area of the Federal republic within its 1989 boundaries. As frontier changes have been very complicated it is difficult to make adjusted estimates at this stage for the whole period for reunified Germany.

a)   In 1871 Germany took Alsace–Lorraine from France. This increased its population and GDP by 4 per cent;

b)   between 1918 and 1922 Germany lost Alsace–Lorraine, Memel, Danzig, Eupen and Malmedy, Saarland, North Schleswig and Eastern Upper Silesia. These territories had a population of 7 330 000 in 1918 out of a total of 66 811 000 within the 1918 Reich frontiers, i.e. the old Reich was 12.3 per cent bigger in terms of population. However, as 1913 per capita income in the truncated area was 2.4 per cent higher than in the former Reich, the total income loss due to these changes was 9.7 per cent (for the population changes see A. Maddison, *Dynamic Forces in Capitalist Development*, 1991, pp. 232–5; for the per capita income difference see F. Grünig, "Die Anfänge der volkswirtschaftlichen Gesamtrechnung in Deutschland", *Beitrage zur empirischen Konjunkturforschung*, Berlin, 1950, p. 76);

c)   in 1935, Germany regained the Saarland which added 1.79 per cent to population and income;

d)   in 1938, Germany incorporated Austria and took the Sudetenland from Czechoslovakia. Later it took Alsace–Lorraine and parts of Poland and Yugoslavia. In 1941 these areas added 22.4 per cent to the GDP generated with the 1937 frontiers;

e)   after the second world war, Germany within its 1936 frontiers was effectively split between the Federal Republic, the DDR (East Germany) and the territory East of the Oder–Neisse which went to Poland, and to the USSR (Koenigsberg became Kaliningrad);

f)   in 1991, East German territory became part of the Federal Republic.

A detailed account of German border changes and their impact on GDP can be found in Maddison (1977), "Phases of Capitalist Development", *Banca Nazionale del Lavoro Quarterly Review*, no. 121, pp. 134 and Maddison (1995), p. 130–33. For the impact of territorial change on population see Maddison (1991), *Dynamic Forces in Capitalist Development*, pp.226–237. Maddison (2001), p. 178 provides a summary presentation of the impact of frontier change on population and GDP.

Sources for GDP 1820–2001 were as follows: 1820, 1830 and 1850 derived from Tilly's estimates for Prussia–see R.H. Tilly, "Capital Formation in Germany in the Nineteenth Century", in P. Mathias and M.M. Postan (eds.), *Cambridge Economic History of Europe*, vol. VII, I, 1978, pp. 395, 420, and 441. Prussian per capita output in agriculture and industry were multiplied by population in Germany as a whole. Output in services was assumed to move with population. GDP aggregate estimated with 1850 weights for the three sectors from W.G. Hoffmann, F. Grumbach and H. Hesse, *Das Wachstum der deutschen Wirtschaft seit der Mitte des 19. Jahrhunderts*, Springer, Berlin, 1965, p. 454.

1850–1938 annual GDP volume movement and link to 1950 derived from Hoffmann, Grumbach and Hesse, *op. cit.*, pp. 454–5. As Hoffmann *et al.* omit 1914–24, the pattern of movement in these years in industry and agriculture was derived from the output estimates of J. Dessirier, "Indices comparés de la production industrielle et production agricole en divers pays de 1870 à 1928", *Bulletin de la statistique générale de la France, Études spéciales*, October–December 1928. Service output was interpolated between the 1913 and 1925 estimates of Hoffmann *et al.* for this sector.

1938–44 GNP in 1939 prices (from the expenditure side) for the 1938 territory (including Austria and Sudetenland) from W.C. Haraldson and E.F. Denison, "The Gross National Product of Germany 1936–1944", *Special Paper 1* (mimeographed) in J.K. Galbraith (ed.), *The Effects of Strategic Bombing on the German War Economy*, US Strategic Bombing Survey, 1945. 1946 (linked to 1936) from *Wirtschaftsproblemen der Besatzungszonen*, D.I.W. Duncker and Humblot, Berlin, 1948, p. 135; 1945 onwards, the derivation of GDP for West Germany (Federal Republic) and East Germany (DDR) is explained in Maddison (1995), pp. 131-2 and Maddison (2001), p. 178. Table 1-2 shows the impact of frontier changes 1870-1991.

Table 1-2. **The Impact of Frontier Changes on German GDP, 1870-1991**

	West Germany (1990 frontiers)	*East Germany (1990 frontiers)*	*Germany within 1991 boundaries*	*Germany within 1936 boundaries*	*Germany within 1913 frontiers (ex. Alsace–Lorraine)*
	GDP in million 1990 international dollars				
1820	16 390				26 819
1870	44 094				72 149
1913	145 045			225 008	237 332
1936	192 910	74 652	267 562	299 753	
1950	213 942	51 412	265 354		
1973	814 786	129 969	944 755		
1990	1 182 261	82 177	1 264 438		
1991	1 242 096	85 961	1 328 057		

Greece: 1913–29 real product in international units from C. Clark, *Conditions of Economic Progress*, 3rd edition, Macmillan, London, 1957, pp. 148–9; 1929–38 GNP at factor cost from *Ekonomikos Tachydromos*, 22 May 1954; 1938–50 from OEEC, *Europe and the World Economy*, Paris 1960, p.116. 1950 onwards from OECD, *National Accounts*, various issues. 1820–1913 per capita GDP assumed to move with the aggregate for Eastern Europe. 1820–1900 population derived, with interpolation, from B.R. Mitchell *European Historical Statistics 1750–1970*, Macmillan, London, 1975, p. 21, 1900–40 from I. Svennilson, *Growth and Stagnation in the European Economy*, ECE, Geneva, 1954, pp. 236–7, 1941–9 from UN, *Demographic Yearbook 1951*, New York, 1952 pp. 124–5. Figures are adjusted to offset territorial change. Greece gained independence from Turkey in the 1820s, and gradually extended its area to include the Ionian Islands in 1864, Thessaly in 1881, Crete (*de facto*) in 1898, Epirus, Macedonia, Thrace and the Aegean Islands in 1913, Rhodes and the rest of the Dodecanese in 1947.

George Kostelenos, *Money and Output in Modern Greece*, Centre of Planning and Economic Research, Athens, 1995 provides annual estimates of output in current prices for primary, secondary and tertiary activity for 1858–1938. He does not estimate the volume of sector output, but constructs an aggregate deflator to derive a GDP estimate at 1914 prices (pp. 457–9). He measures growth of the money supply for the same period and uses the apparent velocity of circulation as a crosscheck on his GDP estimates (leading him to modify the results for 1858–9). Although Kostelenos throws more light on the available evidence than was previously available, there are three problems with his direct measure: *a)* his GDP deflator is very crude; with prices of only 11 items (6 for the whole period). All are agricultural or mining products, and the weights are gross output of the same items (in 1860, 1875, 1899, and 1914). The acceptibility of the GDP measure would be enhanced by construction of sectoral volume indices. I am not clear whether this is feasible, but it is certainly desirable. *b)* the second problem is territorial change. Kostelenos refers to Greece within the boundaries of the years he covers. His population figures show the impact of change very clearly. There were four major breaks: population jumped by 21 per cent in 1864, by 18 per cent in 1881, 77 per cent in 1913, and 15 per cent in 1920, but he does not discuss the problems this created in finding appropriate data on output, adjusting for differences in level between old and new territories, etc. His estimates suggest that these problems were difficult to resolve. For 1910–12 he shows a rise in per capita income of 63 per cent, a drop of a quarter in 1913, and a rise of a quarter in 1914. There is a similar problem for 1883–87 where his per capita GDP rises by nearly 90 per cent. It is not clear whether it is possible to accommodate these problems successfully, and one cannot criticise Kostelenos for attempting to overcome such an inherently difficult challenge. The third problem is that Kostelenos shows a very stagnant economy in the nineteenth century, with per capita income 6 per cent lower in 1910 than in 1860. If his estimates were linked to mine at 1938, per capita GDP in 1858 would be 1550 international 1990 dollars–a level similar to that in Germany and Sweden and about 70 per cent higher than the average for Eastern Europe. This seeems highly improbable. Recently, Kostelenos has revised his estimates, and his new results (in cooperation with Petmezas and others), show much faster and smoother growth, and are carried back to 1833. The main reason for faster growth is the use of a new deflator — a "rolling index" with a moving base, merging segments with weights of 1860, 1886 and 1914 respectively. The results are more plausible, but are still tentative. They will be more fully explained in a forthcoming publication of the National Bank of Greece. See Kostelenos (2001), "Economic Growth and Inequality in Greece in the 19th and 20th Century: A Tentative Approach", available on the Groningen website: www.eco.rug.nl/ggdc.

Ireland: For Ireland before 1920, see note below for the United Kingdom. 1920 per capita GDP level taken to be 54 per cent of that in the UK (excluding Southern Ireland) as estimated by C.H. Feinstein, *National Income, Expenditure and Output of the United Kingdom 1855–1965*, Cambridge University Press, 1972, Table 6. 1926–50 from K.A. Kennedy, *Productivity and Industrial Growth: The Irish Experience*, Oxford University Press, 1971, p. 3. Population, 1921–49, from UN, *Demographic Yearbook 1960*, New York.

Italy: 1820 and annual 1861–1970 GDP movement from A. Maddison, "A Revised Estimate of Italian Economic Growth 1861–1989", *Banca Nazionale del Lavoro Quarterly Review*, June 1991. The official ISTAT estimates I used for 1970 onwards have a more complete coverage of the underground economy than is the case in other countries (20.2 per cent of total GDP). In other countries, underground activities which escape the net of official national accounts statisticians are typically about 3 per cent of GDP (see D. Blades, "The Hidden Economy and the National Accounts", OECD, *Occasional Studies*, June 1982, p. 39). I therefore made a 3 per cent downward adjustment to the benchmark level of GDP to enhance international comparability. This has no effect on GDP volume movement, but reduces the level for all years.

1820 population derived from K.J. Beloch, *Bevölkerungsgeschichte Italiens*, de Gruyter, Berlin, 1961, pp. 351–4; annual change in resident population, 1861–1950 from *Sommario di statistiche storiche dell Italia, 1861–1975*, Istat, Rome, 1976, adjusted to midyear. Annual estimates for 1821–61 derived by logarithmic interpolation; average annual growth was 0.644 per cent. Galloway's estimates for Northern Italy show an annual growth rate of 0.703 per cent for the period I interpolated (see P.R. Galloway, "A Reconstruction of the Population of Northern Italy from 1650 to 1881 using Annual Inverse Projection", *European Journal of Population*, 10, 1994, pp. 223–274). Population and GDP are adjusted to eliminate the impact of territorial change. In 1866, after the war with Austria, the Venetian territories became part of Italy, and after 1870 the Papal states were added. In 1919 South Tirol, the old Austrian Kustenland provinces and the port of Zara were acquired. Fiume was added in 1922. In 1945, Zara, Fiume and part of Venezia–Giulia were ceded to Yugoslavia. Until the settlement of 1954 Trieste was in dispute and under international occupation; thereafter the city and a strip of coast went to Italy and the hinterland to Yugoslavia. In 1947, Tenda and Briga were added to France. The impact of these changes can be seen in Maddison (1995), p. 231.

Netherlands: annual estimates of population and GDP, 1820–1913 from J.–P. Smits, E. Horlings and J.L.van Zanden, *Dutch GDP and Its Components, 1800–1913*, Groningen, 2000, which Edwin Horlings kindly adjusted to a midyear basis. GDP, 1913–60, from C.A. van Bochove and T.A. Huitker, "Main National Accounting Series, 1900–1986", *CBS Occasional Paper*, No. 17, The Hague, 1987. 1960 onwards from OECD, *National Accounts*. Population 1913–50 from *Zeventig jaren statistiek in tijdreeksen*, CBS, The Hague, 1970, p. 14, adjusted to a midyear basis.

Norway: 1865–1950 GDP by category of expenditure at constant market prices from *National Accounts 1865–1960*, Central Bureau of Statistics, Oslo, 1965, pp. 348–59, with gross fixed investment adjusted downwards by a third to eliminate repairs and maintenance. For the 1939–44 gap in these estimates, I used the movement in national income (excluding shipping and whaling operations carried out from Allied bases 1940–4) from O. Aukrust and P.J. Bjerve, *Hva krigen kostet Norge*, Dreyers, Oslo, 1945, p. 45. 1945 assumed to be midway between 1944 and 1946. For 1820–65 I assume per capita GDP movement was the same as in Sweden.

There are interesting estimates of GDP back to 1835 in F. Hodne and O. H. Grytten, "Gross Domestic Product of Norway 1835-1915", *Occasional Papers in Economic History*, Umeå University, 1994. They adjust and link three nineteenth century spot estimates for 1835, 1845 and 1850 with the official estimate for 1865. They show faster growth than I have assumed (their per capita estimate for 1850 is about one fifth lower than mine). A more definitive estimate for 1820-65 will probably emerge when the Nordic Group complete their review of estimates for Scandinavia. Annual mid–year population estimates 1770–1950 from *Historical Statistics, 1968*, CBS, Oslo, 1969, pp.44–47.

Portugal: Annual GDP movement 1851–1910 derived from C. Bardini, A. Carreras and Pedro Lains, "The National Accounts for Italy, Spain and Portugal", *Scandinavian Economic History Review*, 1, 1995, p.135. They estimate agricultural and industrial output and use the combined movement in these two sectors to measure aggregate physical output, which they use as a proxy for GDP movement. I used their estimates for agriculture and industry, and derived a crude measure of GDP, using sector weights for 1910 and assuming that half of output in the rest of the economy (trade, transport and services) moved parallel to population and half parallel to aggregate physical ouput. GDP 1910–58 and 1910 sector weights from D. Batista, C. Martins, M. Pinheiro, and J. Reis, "New Estimates for Portugal's GDP, 1910–1958", Bank of Portugal and European University Institute, October, 1997. There are annual estimates of GDP movement 1834–1946 in A.B. Nunes, E. Mata, and N. Valerio, "Portuguese Economic Growth, 1833–1985", *Journal of European Economic History*, Fall, 1989, They were derived by regression, using three proxy indicators (exports, fiscal receipts and public expenditure) and their relationship to GDP movement for 1947–85. For 1834–51 they show a bumpy trajectory, without much indication of growth. This was a period of political and economic instability, following the upheavals of the Napoleonic wars and loss of the Brazilian Empire. I used their estimate of the 1850–51 movement and assumed that the per capita GDP level in 1820 was the same as in 1850.

Population: 1820 and annual movement 1833–64 from Nunes, Mata and Valerio (1989), p. 292, interpolation for 1821–32. 1865–1949 from Nuno Valerio, *Portuguese Historical Statistics,* INE, Lisbon, 2001, vol. 1, pp.52–3. Population estimates are adjusted to a midyear basis.

Spain: 1820-50 GDP volume movement derived from Prados (1982) as explained in Maddison (1995), p.138; 1850–1990 from Leandro Prados, *El Progreso Economico de Espana, 1850–2000,* Universidad Carlos III, Madrid, 2002. Population 1820 and 1850 from A. Carreras, ed. *Estadisticas Historicas de Espana: Siglos XIX–XX,* Fundacion Banco Exterior, Madrid, 1989, pp. 68–72; 1821–49 interpolated, 1850–1949 from Prados (2002).

Sweden: 1820–1950 population and provisional estimates of GDP 1820-1960 by industry of origin were kindly supplied by Olle Krantz. His procedures are explained in Olle Krantz, "New Estimates of Swedish Historical GDP Since the Beginning of the Nineteenth Century", *Review of Income and Wealth,* June l988. He has revised these estimates and will present a final version fairly soon.

Switzerland: 1820–51 per capita GDP movement assumed equal to average for France and Germany. 1851–1913 annual estimates of real GDP, average of two alternatively deflated series from H. Ritzmann–Blickenstorfer, *Historical Statistics of Switzerland,* Chronos, Zürich, 1996, pp. 859–79. Real product in international units, 1913, and annual estimates 1924–50 from C. Clark, *Conditions of Economic Progress* (3rd ed.), Macmillan, London, 1957, pp. 188–9. Annual percentage GDP movement, 1913–24, derived from economic activity estimates of F. Andrist, R.G. Anderson, and M.M. Williams, "Real Output in Switzerland: New Estimates for 1914–47", *Federal Reserve Bank of St. Louis Review,* May/June 2000, adjusted to fit 1913–24 movement shown by Clark (1957). 1950 onwards from OECD sources. Population, 1830, 1840 and 1850 from A. Kausel, *150 Jahre Wirtschaftswachstum,* Staatsdruckerei, Vienna, 1985, p.12. 1820–30 assumed to grow at same pace as 1830–40. Annual movement 1851–70 from Ritzmann, *op. cit.*; 1871–1949 from *Annuaire statistique de la Suisse 1952,* Federal Statistical Office, Bern 1953, pp. 42–3.

United Kingdom: 1801–31 GDP movement from N.F.R. Crafts and C.K. Harley, "Output Growth and the British Industrial Revolution: A Restatement of the Crafts–Harley View", *Economic History Review,* November 1992, p. 715 for England, Wales and Scotland, adjusted to a UK basis assuming Irish output per head of population in 1831 to have been half of that in Great Britain (hypothesis of P. Deane, "New Estimates of Gross National Product for the United Kingdom 1830–1914", *Review of Income and Wealth,* June 1968) and to have grown at half the pace from 1801. 1830–1855 annual movement in real gross national product from P. Deane (1968), p. 106. 1855–1960 annual movement of GDP at factor cost (average of real expenditure, output and income estimates) from C.H. Feinstein, *National Income Expenditure and Output of the United Kingdom 1855–1965,* Cambridge, 1972, pp. T18–20.

Population 1815–71 for England, excluding Monmouth, from E.A. Wrigley, R.S. Davies, J.E. Oeppen and R. S. Schofield (1997), *English Population History from Family Reconstitution 1580–1837,* Cambridge, p. 614 derived by interpolation of their quinnquennial estimates. Monmouth and Wales 1811–71 interpolation of the decennial census results shown in B.R. Mitchell, *Abstract of British*

Table 1-3. **Economic Growth in Ireland/Irish Republic and the United Kingdom, 1820-2001**

	United Kingdom	Ireland	E+W+S	Northern Ireland
		Population (000)		
1820	21 239	7 101	14 138	
1840	26 745	8 348	18 396	
1870	31 400	5 419	25 981	
1913	45 649	4 346	41 303	
1920	46 821	4 361	42 460	
1920	43 718	**3 103**	42 460	1 258
1950	50 363	**2 969**	48 986	1 377
1973	56 223	**3 072**		1 530
2001	59 905	**3 839**		1 689
		GDP (million 1990 Geary-Khamis international $)		
1820	36 232	6 231	30 001	
1840	53 234	8 638	44 596	
1870	100 179	9 619	90 560	
1913	224 618	11 891	212 727	
1920	212 938	11 078	201 860	
1920	205 056	**7 882**	201 860	3 196
1950	347 850	**10 231**		
1973	675 941	**21 103**		
2001	1 202 074	**89 113**		
		Per Capita GDP (1990 Geary-Khamis international $		
1820	1 707	880	2 121	
1840	1 990	1 035	2 424	
1870	3 191	1 775	3 487	
1913	4 921	2 736	5 150	
1920	4 568	2 540	4 754	2 540
1920	4 690	**2 540**		
1950	6 907	**3 446**		
1973	12 022	**6 867**		
2001	20 066	**23 201**		

Note: E+W+S means England, Wales and Scotland.
Source: Maddison (2001), p. 247. Figures in **bold** refer to Irish Republic.

Historical Statistics, 1962, p. 20. Scotland, 1815–71 from Mitchell, pp. 8–9. Ireland 1791–1821 from D. Dickson, C. O Grada and S. Daultry, "Hearth Tax, Household Size and Irish Population Change 1672–1821", *Proceedings of the Royal Irish Academy*, vol. 82, C, no. 6, Dublin, 1982, p. 156. Ireland 1821–41 from J. Lee, "On the Accuracy of the Pre–Famine Irish Censuses", in J.M. Goldstrom and I.A. Clarkson (1981), *Irish Population, Economy and Society*, Oxford, p. 54; 1842–1920 from Mitchell, *op. cit.*, pp. 8–9, with 2.44 per cent upward adjustment of his 1842–7 figures to link with those of Lee. 1871–1949 UK population from Feinstein (1972), pp. T120–1.

The population and GDP estimates for 1920 and earlier years include the whole of Ireland.

Table 1–3 gives a geographic breakdown for benchmark years 1820–2001. Until the 1990s, Irish per capita income levels were well below those in Great Britain, but have now surged ahead.

Table 1-4. **Population and GDP: 13 Small West European Countries, 1950-2001**

	1950	*1973*	*1990*	*2001*
Population (000 at mid-year)				
Iceland	143	212	255	278
Luxembourg	296	350	382	443
Cyprus	494	634	681	763
Malta	312	322	359	395
9 Other	285	389	482	516
13 Country Total	1 529	1 907	2 159	2 595
GDP (million 1990 international dollars)				
Iceland	762	2 435	4 596	6 131
Luxembourg	2 481	5 237	8 819	16 452
Cyprus	930	3 207	6 651	9 823
Malta	278	855	2 987	4 790
9 Other	1 429	4 718	8 152	10 357
13 Country Total	5 880	16 452	31 205	47 553
Per capita GDP (1990 international dollars)				
Iceland	5 336	11 472	18 024	22 054
Luxembourg	8 382	14 963	23 086	37 138
Cyprus	1 883	5 058	9 767	12 874
Malta	894	2 655	8 320	12 127
9 Other	5 013	12 129	16 913	20 077
13 Country Average	3 846	8 627	14 453	19 855

13 Small Countries: Estimates of GDP movement for Iceland and Luxembourg 1950–2001 from OECD National Accounts, various issues; Cyprus and Malta 1950–90 from Maddison (1995) updated from IMF. Per capita GDP in 9 smaller countries (Andorra, Channel Islands, Faeroe Islands, Gibraltar, Greenland, Isle of Man, Liechtenstein, Monaco and San Marino) assumed to be the same as the average for 12 West European countries. Pre–1950 population and GDP per capita levels for the 13–country group assumed to move parallel to the total/average for 12 West European countries.

Table 1a. **Population of 12 West European Countries, 1500-1868**
(000 at mid-year)

	Austria	Belgium	Denmark	Finland	France	Germany	Italy
1500	2 000	1 400	600	300	15 000	12 000	10 500
1600	2 500	1 600	650	400	18 500	16 000	13 100
1700	2 500	2 000	700	400	21 471	15 000	13 300
1820	3 369	3 434	1 155	1 169	31 250	24 905	20 176
1821	3 386	3 464	1 167	1 186	31 460	25 260	20 306
1822	3 402	3 495	1 179	1 202	31 685	25 620	20 437
1823	3 419	3 526	1 196	1 219	31 905	25 969	20 568
1824	3 436	3 557	1 213	1 235	32 127	26 307	20 701
1825	3 452	3 589	1 228	1 252	32 350	26 650	20 834
1826	3 469	3 620	1 243	1 268	32 538	26 964	20 968
1827	3 486	3 652	1 255	1 310	32 727	27 249	21 103
1828	3 504	3 685	1 265	1 326	32 917	27 540	21 239
1829	3 521	3 717	1 270	1 343	33 108	27 807	21 376
1830	3 538	3 750	1 273	1 364	33 300	28 045	21 513
1831	3 555	3 782	1 275	1 374	33 439	28 283	21 652
1832	3 573	3 814	1 276	1 378	33 598	28 535	21 791
1833	3 590	3 846	1 284	1 383	33 718	28 801	21 932
1834	3 608	3 879	1 295	1 387	33 859	29 071	22 073
1835	3 626	3 912	1 306	1 391	34 000	29 390	22 215
1836	3 614	3 945	1 315	1 399	34 178	29 702	22 358
1837	3 662	3 978	1 325	1 409	34 357	30 013	22 502
1838	3 680	4 012	1 335	1 420	34 537	30 365	22 647
1839	3 698	4 046	1 347	1 430	34 718	30 746	22 793
1840	3 716	4 080	1 357	1 441	34 900	31 126	22 939
1841	3 739	4 115	1 371	1 456	35 059	31 475	23 087
1842	3 762	4 151	1 385	1 476	35 218	31 787	23 236
1843	3 785	4 187	1 392	1 495	35 378	32 086	23 385
1844	3 808	4 223	1 414	1 516	35 539	32 394	23 536
1845	3 831	4 259	1 430	1 536	35 700	32 743	23 687
1846	3 855	4 296	1 444	1 555	35 829	33 059	23 840
1847	3 878	4 333	1 456	1 573	35 959	33 231	23 993
1848	3 902	4 371	1 470	1 591	36 089	33 289	24 148
1849	3 926	4 408	1 484	1 610	36 219	33 452	24 303
1850	3 950	4 449	1 499	1 628	36 350	33 746	24 460
1851	3 978	4 477	1 517	1 642	36 479	34 055	24 617
1852	4 006	4 506	1 536	1 652	36 609	34 290	24 776
1853	4 035	4 534	1 552	1 663	36 739	34 422	24 935
1854	4 063	4 563	1 569	1 673	36 869	34 531	25 096
1855	4 092	4 592	1 590	1 683	37 000	34 586	25 257
1856	4 120	4 621	1 612	1 692	37 060	34 715	25 420
1857	4 150	4 651	1 634	1 703	37 120	34 979	25 584
1858	4 178	4 680	1 653	1 715	37 180	35 278	25 748
1859	4 206	4 710	1 674	1 726	37 240	35 633	25 914
1860	4 235	4 740	1 696	1 738	37 300	36 049	26 081
1861	4 263	4 774	1 717	1 754	37 390	36 435	26 249
1862	4 292	4 809	1 739	1 774	37 520	36 788	26 418
1863	4 321	4 844	1 761	1 794	37 710	37 184	26 610
1864	4 350	4 879	1 777	1 813	37 860	37 602	26 814
1865	4 380	4 915	1 799	1 833	38 020	37 955	27 023
1866	4 409	4 950	1 814	1 840	38 080	38 193	27 256
1867	4 439	4 986	1 833	1 831	38 230	38 440	27 411
1868	4 469	5 023	1 852	1 776	38 330	38 637	27 501

Table 1a. **Population of 12 West European Countries, 1500-1868**
(000 at mid-year)

	Netherlands	Norway	Sweden	Switzerland	United Kingdom	12 WEC
1500	950	300	550	650	3 942	**48 192**
1600	1 500	400	760	1 000	6 170	**62 580**
1700	1 900	500	1 260	1 200	8 565	**68 796**
1820	2 333	970	2 585	1 986	21 239	**114 571**
1821	2 365	984	2 611	1 998	21 551	**115 738**
1822	2 400	998	2 646	2 008	21 832	**116 904**
1823	2 435	1 013	2 689	2 020	22 117	**118 076**
1824	2 474	1 028	2 727	2 031	22 407	**119 243**
1825	2 514	1 044	2 771	2 042	22 698	**120 424**
1826	2 543	1 062	2 805	2 054	22 996	**121 530**
1827	2 561	1 079	2 828	2 065	23 275	**122 590**
1828	2 585	1 093	2 847	2 077	23 560	**123 638**
1829	2 610	1 108	2 863	2 088	23 847	**124 658**
1830	2 633	1 124	2 888	2 100	24 139	**125 667**
1831	2 653	1 137	2 901	2 112	24 433	**126 596**
1832	2 665	1 150	2 923	2 123	24 684	**127 510**
1833	2 683	1 163	2 959	2 135	24 937	**128 431**
1834	2 707	1 174	2 983	2 147	25 194	**129 377**
1835	2 732	1 188	3 025	2 159	25 452	**130 396**
1836	2 762	1 202	3 059	2 171	25 715	**131 420**
1837	2 791	1 214	3 076	2 183	25 968	**132 478**
1838	2 821	1 224	3 090	2 195	26 223	**133 549**
1839	2 853	1 233	3 106	2 208	26 483	**134 661**
1840	2 886	1 241	3 139	2 220	26 745	**135 790**
1841	2 921	1 254	3 173	2 235	27 004	**136 889**
1842	2 952	1 271	3 207	2 251	27 277	**137 973**
1843	2 981	1 286	3 237	2 266	27 511	**138 989**
1844	3 014	1 302	3 275	2 282	27 785	**140 088**
1845	3 047	1 319	3 317	2 298	28 040	**141 207**
1846	3 069	1 337	3 343	2 314	28 272	**142 213**
1847	3 071	1 351	3 362	2 330	28 118	**142 655**
1848	3 069	1 363	3 397	2 346	27 683	**142 718**
1849	3 076	1 377	3 441	2 363	27 429	**143 088**
1850	3 098	1 392	3 483	2 379	27 181	**143 615**
1851	3 133	1 409	3 517	2 399	26 945	**144 168**
1852	3 167	1 425	3 540	2 406	27 076	**144 989**
1853	3 194	1 440	3 563	2 412	27 248	**145 737**
1854	3 218	1 457	3 608	2 427	27 446	**146 520**
1855	3 235	1 479	3 641	2 442	27 697	**147 294**
1856	3 253	1 501	3 673	2 457	27 978	**148 102**
1857	3 277	1 521	3 688	2 471	28 186	**148 964**
1858	3 294	1 543	3 734	2 484	28 422	**149 909**
1859	3 304	1 570	3 788	2 497	28 660	**150 922**
1860	3 318	1 596	3 860	2 510	28 888	**152 011**
1861	3 340	1 614	3 917	2 524	29 128	**153 105**
1862	3 366	1 627	3 966	2 538	29 401	**154 238**
1863	3 397	1 646	4 023	2 552	29 630	**155 472**
1864	3 431	1 668	4 070	2 566	29 842	**156 672**
1865	3 460	1 690	4 114	2 579	30 089	**157 857**
1866	3 484	1 707	4 161	2 593	30 315	**158 802**
1867	3 510	1 716	4 196	2 607	30 572	**159 771**
1868	3 543	1 724	4 173	2 623	30 845	**160 496**

Table 1a. **Population of 12 West European Countries, 1869-1918**
(000 at mid-year)

	Austria	*Belgium*	*Denmark*	*Finland*	*France*	*Germany*	*Italy*
1869	4 499	5 029	1 871	1 734	38 890	38 914	27 681
1870	4 520	5 096	1 888	1 754	38 440	39 231	27 888
1871	4 562	5 137	1 903	1 786	37 731	39 456	28 063
1872	4 604	5 178	1 918	1 819	37 679	39 691	28 233
1873	4 646	5 219	1 935	1 847	37 887	40 017	28 387
1874	4 688	5 261	1 954	1 873	38 044	40 450	28 505
1875	4 730	5 303	1 973	1 899	38 221	40 897	28 630
1876	4 772	5 345	1 994	1 928	38 398	41 491	28 837
1877	4 815	5 394	2 019	1 957	38 576	42 034	29 067
1878	4 857	5 442	2 043	1 983	38 763	42 546	29 252
1879	4 899	5 492	2 064	2 014	38 909	43 052	29 425
1880	4 941	5 541	2 081	2 047	39 045	43 500	29 534
1881	4 985	5 606	2 101	2 072	39 191	43 827	29 672
1882	5 030	5 673	2 120	2 098	39 337	44 112	29 898
1883	5 075	5 740	2 137	2 130	39 472	44 404	30 113
1884	5 121	5 807	2 160	2 164	39 629	44 777	30 366
1885	5 166	5 876	2 186	2 195	39 733	45 084	30 644
1886	5 212	5 919	2 213	2 224	39 858	45 505	30 857
1887	5 257	5 962	2 237	2 259	39 889	46 001	31 049
1888	5 303	6 007	2 257	2 296	39 920	46 538	31 243
1889	5 348	6 051	2 276	2 331	40 004	47 083	31 468
1890	5 394	6 096	2 294	2 364	40 014	47 607	31 702
1891	5 446	6 164	2 311	2 394	39 983	48 129	31 892
1892	5 504	6 231	2 327	2 451	39 993	48 633	32 091
1893	5 563	6 300	2 344	2 430	40 014	49 123	32 303
1894	5 622	6 370	2 367	2 511	40 056	49 703	32 513
1895	5 680	6 439	2 397	2 483	40 098	50 363	32 689
1896	5 739	6 494	2 428	2 515	40 192	51 111	32 863
1897	5 798	6 548	2 462	2 549	40 348	51 921	33 078
1898	5 856	6 604	2 497	2 589	40 473	52 753	33 285
1899	5 915	6 662	2 530	2 624	40 546	53 592	33 487
1900	5 973	6 719	2 561	2 646	40 598	54 388	33 672
1901	6 035	6 801	2 594	2 667	40 640	55 214	33 877
1902	6 099	6 903	2 623	2 686	40 713	56 104	34 166
1903	6 164	6 997	2 653	2 706	40 786	56 963	34 436
1904	6 228	7 086	2 681	2 735	40 859	57 806	34 715
1905	6 292	7 175	2 710	2 762	40 890	58 644	35 011
1906	6 357	7 258	2 741	2 788	40 942	59 481	35 297
1907	6 421	7 338	2 775	2 821	40 942	60 341	35 594
1908	6 485	7 411	2 809	2 861	41 046	61 187	35 899
1909	6 550	7 478	2 845	2 899	41 109	62 038	36 213
1910	6 614	7 498	2 882	2 929	41 224	62 884	36 572
1911	6 669	7 517	2 917	2 962	41 307	63 852	36 917
1912	6 724	7 590	2 951	2 998	41 359	64 457	37 150
1913	6 767	7 666	2 983	3 027	41 463	65 058	37 248
1914	6 806	7 723	3 018	3 053	41 476	66 096	37 526
1915	6 843	7 759	3 055	3 083	40 481	66 230	37 982
1916	6 825	7 762	3 092	3 105	39 884	66 076	38 142
1917	6 785	7 729	3 130	3 124	39 288	65 763	37 981
1918	6 727	7 660	3 165	3 125	38 542	65 237	37 520

Table 1a. **Population of 12 West European Countries, 1869-1918**
(000 at mid-year)

	Netherlands	Norway	Sweden	Switzerland	United Kingdom	12 WEC
1869	3 575	1 729	4 159	2 639	31 127	**161 847**
1870	3 610	1 735	4 169	2 655	31 400	**162 386**
1871	3 636	1 745	4 186	2 680	31 685	**162 570**
1872	3 662	1 755	4 227	2 697	31 874	**163 337**
1873	3 670	1 767	4 274	2 715	32 177	**164 541**
1874	3 745	1 783	4 320	2 733	32 501	**165 857**
1875	3 788	1 803	4 362	2 750	32 839	**167 195**
1876	3 832	1 829	4 407	2 768	33 200	**168 801**
1877	3 883	1 852	4 457	2 786	33 576	**170 416**
1878	3 834	1 877	4 508	2 803	33 932	**171 840**
1879	3 986	1 902	4 555	2 821	34 304	**173 423**
1880	4 043	1 919	4 572	2 839	34 623	**174 685**
1881	4 079	1 923	4 569	2 853	34 935	**175 813**
1882	4 130	1 920	4 576	2 863	35 206	**176 963**
1883	4 180	1 919	4 591	2 874	35 450	**178 085**
1884	4 226	1 929	4 624	2 885	35 724	**179 412**
1885	4 276	1 944	4 664	2 896	36 015	**180 679**
1886	4 326	1 958	4 700	2 907	36 313	**181 992**
1887	4 378	1 970	4 726	2 918	36 598	**183 244**
1888	4 432	1 977	4 742	2 929	36 881	**184 525**
1889	4 485	1 984	4 761	2 940	37 178	**185 909**
1890	4 535	1 997	4 780	2 951	37 485	**187 219**
1891	4 585	2 013	4 794	2 965	37 802	**188 478**
1892	4 632	2 026	4 805	3 002	38 134	**189 829**
1893	4 684	2 038	4 816	3 040	38 490	**191 145**
1894	4 743	2 057	4 849	3 077	38 859	**192 727**
1895	4 803	2 083	4 896	3 114	39 221	**194 266**
1896	4 866	2 112	4 941	3 151	39 599	**196 011**
1897	4 935	2 142	4 986	3 188	39 987	**197 942**
1898	5 003	2 174	5 036	3 226	40 381	**199 877**
1899	5 070	2 204	5 080	3 263	40 773	**201 746**
1900	5 142	2 230	5 117	3 300	41 155	**203 501**
1901	5 221	2 255	5 156	3 341	41 538	**205 339**
1902	5 305	2 275	5 187	3 384	41 893	**207 338**
1903	5 389	2 288	5 210	3 428	42 246	**209 266**
1904	5 470	2 297	5 241	3 472	42 611	**211 201**
1905	5 551	2 309	5 278	3 461	42 981	**213 064**
1906	5 632	2 319	5 316	3 560	43 361	**215 052**
1907	5 710	2 329	5 357	3 604	43 737	**216 969**
1908	5 786	2 346	5 404	3 647	44 124	**219 005**
1909	5 862	2 367	5 453	3 691	44 520	**221 025**
1910	5 922	2 384	5 449	3 735	44 916	**223 009**
1911	5 984	2 401	5 542	3 776	45 268	**225 112**
1912	6 068	2 423	5 583	3 819	45 426	**226 548**
1913	6 164	2 447	5 621	3 864	45 649	**227 957**
1914	6 277	2 472	5 659	3 897	46 049	**230 052**
1915	6 395	2 498	5 696	3 883	46 340	**230 245**
1916	6 516	2 522	5 735	3 883	46 514	**230 056**
1917	6 654	2 551	5 779	3 888	46 614	**229 286**
1918	6 752	2 578	5 807	3 880	46 575	**227 568**

Table 1a. **Population of 12 West European Countries, 1919-1969**
(000 at mid-year)

	Austria	Belgium	Denmark	Finland	France	Germany	Italy
1919	6 420	7 628	3 202	3 117	38 700	60 547	37 250
1920	6 455	7 552	3 242	3 133	39 000	60 894	37 398
1921	6 504	7 504	3 285	3 170	39 240	61 573	37 691
1922	6 528	7 571	3 322	3 210	39 420	61 900	38 086
1923	6 543	7 635	3 356	3 243	39 880	62 307	38 460
1924	6 562	7 707	3 389	3 272	40 310	62 697	38 810
1925	6 582	7 779	3 425	3 304	40 610	63 166	39 165
1926	6 603	7 844	3 452	3 339	40 870	63 630	39 502
1927	6 623	7 904	3 475	3 368	40 940	64 023	39 848
1928	6 643	7 968	3 497	3 396	41 050	64 393	40 186
1929	6 664	8 032	3 518	3 424	41 230	64 739	40 469
1930	6 684	8 076	3 542	3 449	41 610	65 084	40 791
1931	6 705	8 126	3 569	3 476	41 860	65 423	41 132
1932	6 725	8 186	3 603	3 503	41 860	65 716	41 431
1933	6 746	8 231	3 633	3 526	41 890	66 027	41 753
1934	6 760	8 262	3 666	3 549	41 950	66 409	42 093
1935	6 761	8 288	3 695	3 576	41 940	66 871	42 429
1936	6 758	8 315	3 722	3 601	41 910	67 349	42 750
1937	6 755	8 346	3 749	3 626	41 930	67 831	43 068
1938	6 753	8 374	3 777	3 656	41 960	68 558	43 419
1939	6 653	8 392	3 805	3 686	41 900	69 286	43 865
1940	6 705	8 346	3 832	3 698	41 000	69 835	44 341
1941	6 745	8 276	3 863	3 702	39 600	70 244	44 734
1942	6 783	8 247	3 903	3 708	39 400	70 834	45 004
1943	6 808	8 242	3 949	3 721	39 000	70 411	45 177
1944	6 834	8 291	3 998	3 735	38 900	69 865	45 290
1945	6 799	8 339	4 045	3 758	39 700	67 000	45 442
1946	7 000	8 367	4 101	3 806	40 290	64 678	45 725
1947	6 971	8 450	4 146	3 859	40 680	66 094	46 040
1948	6 956	8 557	4 190	3 912	41 110	67 295	46 381
1949	6 943	8 614	4 230	3 963	41 480	67 991	46 733
1950	6 935	8 639	4 271	4 009	41 829	68 375	47 105
1951	6 935	8 678	4 304	4 047	42 156	68 876	47 418
1952	6 928	8 730	4 334	4 091	42 460	69 146	47 666
1953	6 932	8 778	4 369	4 139	42 752	69 550	47 957
1954	6 940	8 819	4 406	4 187	43 057	69 868	48 299
1955	6 947	8 868	4 439	4 235	43 428	70 196	48 633
1956	6 952	8 924	4 466	4 282	43 843	70 603	48 921
1957	6 966	8 989	4 488	4 324	44 311	71 019	49 182
1958	6 987	9 053	4 515	4 360	44 789	71 488	49 476
1959	7 014	9 104	4 547	4 395	45 240	72 014	49 832
1960	7 047	9 119	4 581	4 430	45 670	72 481	50 198
1961	7 086	9 166	4 610	4 461	46 189	73 123	50 523
1962	7 130	9 218	4 647	4 491	47 124	73 739	50 843
1963	7 176	9 283	4 684	4 523	47 808	74 340	51 198
1964	7 224	9 367	4 720	4 549	48 340	74 954	51 600
1965	7 271	9 448	4 758	4 564	48 763	75 639	51 987
1966	7 322	9 508	4 798	4 581	49 194	76 206	52 332
1967	7 377	9 557	4 839	4 606	49 569	76 368	52 667
1968	7 415	9 590	4 867	4 626	49 934	76 584	52 987
1969	7 441	9 613	4 891	4 624	50 353	77 144	53 317

Table 1a. **Population of 12 West European Countries, 1919-1969**
(000 at mid-year)

	Netherlands	Norway	Sweden	Switzerland	United Kingdom	12 WEC
1919	6 805	2 603	5 830	3 869	46 534	222 505
1920	6 848	2 635	5 876	3 877	46 821	223 731
1921	6 921	2 668	5 929	3 876	44 072	222 433
1922	7 032	2 695	5 971	3 874	44 372	223 981
1923	7 150	2 713	5 997	3 883	44 596	225 763
1924	7 264	2 729	6 021	3 896	44 915	227 572
1925	7 366	2 747	6 045	3 910	45 059	229 158
1926	7 471	2 763	6 064	3 932	45 232	230 702
1927	7 576	2 775	6 081	3 956	45 389	231 958
1928	7 679	2 785	6 097	3 988	45 578	233 260
1929	7 782	2 795	6 113	4 022	45 672	234 460
1930	7 884	2 807	6 131	4 051	45 866	235 975
1931	7 999	2 824	6 152	4 080	46 074	237 420
1932	8 123	2 842	6 176	4 102	46 335	238 602
1933	8 237	2 858	6 201	4 122	46 520	239 744
1934	8 341	2 874	6 222	4 140	46 666	240 932
1935	8 434	2 889	6 242	4 155	46 868	242 148
1936	8 516	2 904	6 259	4 168	47 081	243 333
1937	8 599	2 919	6 276	4 180	47 289	244 568
1938	8 685	2 936	6 298	4 192	47 494	246 102
1939	8 782	2 954	6 326	4 206	47 991	247 846
1940	8 879	2 973	6 356	4 226	48 226	248 417
1941	8 966	2 990	6 389	4 254	48 216	247 979
1942	9 042	3 009	6 432	4 286	48 400	249 048
1943	9 103	3 032	6 491	4 323	48 789	249 046
1944	9 175	3 060	6 560	4 364	49 016	249 088
1945	9 262	3 091	6 636	4 412	49 182	247 666
1946	9 424	3 127	6 719	4 467	49 217	246 921
1947	9 630	3 165	6 803	4 524	49 519	249 881
1948	9 800	3 201	6 884	4 582	50 014	252 882
1949	9 956	3 234	6 956	4 640	50 312	255 052
1950	10 114	3 265	7 014	4 694	50 127	256 376
1951	10 264	3 296	7 073	4 749	50 290	258 086
1952	10 382	3 328	7 125	4 815	50 430	259 434
1953	10 493	3 361	7 171	4 878	50 593	260 975
1954	10 615	3 394	7 213	4 929	50 765	262 493
1955	10 751	3 427	7 262	4 980	50 946	264 112
1956	10 889	3 460	7 315	5 045	51 184	265 884
1957	11 026	3 492	7 364	5 126	51 430	267 717
1958	11 187	3 523	7 409	5 199	51 652	269 638
1959	11 348	3 553	7 446	5 259	51 956	271 707
1960	11 486	3 581	7 480	5 362	52 372	273 807
1961	11 639	3 610	7 520	5 512	52 807	276 246
1962	11 806	3 639	7 562	5 666	53 292	279 157
1963	11 966	3 667	7 604	5 789	53 625	281 663
1964	12 127	3 694	7 661	5 887	53 991	284 115
1965	12 292	3 723	7 734	5 943	54 350	286 472
1966	12 455	3 754	7 808	5 996	54 643	288 595
1967	12 597	3 786	7 868	6 063	54 959	290 255
1968	12 725	3 819	7 912	6 132	55 214	291 806
1969	12 873	3 851	7 968	6 212	55 461	293 747

Table 1a. **Population of 12 West European Countries, 1970-2003**
(000 at mid-year)

	Austria	Belgium	Denmark	Finland	France	Germany	Italy
1970	7 467	9 638	4 929	4 606	50 787	77 783	53 661
1971	7 500	9 673	4 963	4 612	51 285	78 355	54 006
1972	7 544	9 709	4 992	4 640	51 732	78 717	54 366
1973	7 586	9 738	5 022	4 666	52 157	78 950	54 797
1974	7 599	9 768	5 045	4 691	52 503	78 966	55 226
1975	7 579	9 795	5 060	4 711	52 758	78 682	55 572
1976	7 566	9 811	5 073	4 726	52 954	78 299	55 839
1977	7 568	9 822	5 088	4 739	53 165	78 161	56 059
1978	7 562	9 830	5 104	4 753	53 381	78 066	56 240
1979	7 549	9 837	5 117	4 765	53 606	78 081	56 368
1980	7 549	9 847	5 123	4 780	53 870	78 298	56 451
1981	7 565	9 852	5 122	4 800	54 147	78 402	56 502
1982	7 574	9 856	5 118	4 827	54 434	78 335	56 536
1983	7 552	9 856	5 114	4 856	54 650	78 122	56 630
1984	7 553	9 855	5 112	4 882	54 947	77 855	56 697
1985	7 558	9 858	5 114	4 902	55 171	77 685	56 731
1986	7 566	9 862	5 121	4 917	55 387	77 713	56 734
1987	7 576	9 870	5 127	4 932	55 630	77 718	56 730
1988	7 596	9 884	5 130	4 947	55 873	78 031	56 734
1989	7 624	9 938	5 133	4 962	56 417	78 645	56 738
1990	7 718	9 969	5 141	4 986	56 735	79 380	56 743
1991	7 813	10 004	5 154	5 014	57 055	79 984	56 747
1992	7 910	10 045	5 171	5 041	57 374	80 598	56 841
1993	7 983	10 084	5 188	5 065	57 658	81 132	57 027
1994	8 022	10 116	5 206	5 087	57 907	81 414	57 179
1995	8 042	10 137	5 233	5 106	58 150	81 654	57 275
1996	8 056	10 157	5 262	5 122	58 388	81 891	57 367
1997	8 072	10 181	5 284	5 136	58 623	82 011	57 479
1998	8 092	10 203	5 302	5 148	58 866	82 024	57 550
1999	8 111	10 223	5 320	5 158	59 116	82 075	57 604
2000	8 131	10 242	5 336	5 167	59 382	82 188	57 719
2001	8 151	10 259	5 353	5 176	59 658	82 281	57 845
2002	8 170	10 275	5 369	5 184	59 925	82 351	57 927
2003	8 188	10 289	5 384	5 191	60 181	82 398	57 998

Table 1a. **Population of 12 West European Countries, 1970-2003**
(000 at mid-year)

	Netherlands	Norway	Sweden	Switzerland	United Kingdom	12 WEC
1970	13 032	3 877	8 043	6 267	55 632	295 723
1971	13 194	3 903	8 098	6 343	55 907	297 839
1972	13 330	3 933	8 122	6 401	56 079	299 565
1973	13 438	3 961	8 137	6 441	56 210	301 103
1974	13 541	3 985	8 161	6 460	56 224	302 169
1975	13 653	4 007	8 193	6 404	56 215	302 629
1976	13 770	4 026	8 222	6 333	56 206	302 824
1977	13 853	4 043	8 252	6 316	56 179	303 246
1978	13 937	4 059	8 276	6 333	56 167	303 706
1979	14 030	4 073	8 294	6 351	56 228	304 298
1980	14 144	4 086	8 310	6 385	56 314	305 157
1981	14 246	4 100	8 320	6 425	56 383	305 864
1982	14 310	4 115	8 325	6 468	56 340	306 238
1983	14 362	4 128	8 329	6 501	56 383	306 483
1984	14 420	4 140	8 343	6 530	56 462	306 795
1985	14 491	4 152	8 356	6 565	56 620	307 204
1986	14 572	4 167	8 376	6 604	56 796	307 815
1987	14 665	4 186	8 405	6 651	56 982	308 472
1988	14 761	4 209	8 445	6 705	57 160	309 474
1989	14 849	4 226	8 493	6 765	57 324	311 113
1990	14 952	4 242	8 559	6 838	57 493	312 757
1991	15 066	4 262	8 617	6 923	57 666	314 306
1992	15 174	4 286	8 676	7 001	57 866	315 984
1993	15 275	4 312	8 722	7 064	58 027	317 539
1994	15 382	4 337	8 769	7 120	58 213	318 750
1995	15 459	4 359	8 825	7 166	58 426	319 831
1996	15 533	4 381	8 859	7 198	58 619	320 832
1997	15 613	4 406	8 865	7 213	58 808	321 691
1998	15 705	4 433	8 868	7 225	59 036	322 451
1999	15 800	4 458	8 871	7 242	59 293	323 271
2000	15 892	4 481	8 873	7 262	59 522	324 197
2001	15 981	4 503	8 875	7 283	59 723	325 088
2002	16 068	4 525	8 877	7 302	59 912	325 884
2003	16 151	4 546	8 878	7 319	60 095	326 618

Table 1a. **Population of 4 West European Countries and Total WEC, 1500-1868**
(000 at mid-year)

	Ireland[a]	Greece	Portugal	Spain	13 small WEC	29 WEC
1500	800	1 000	1 000	6 800	276	57 268
1600	1 000	1 500	1 100	8 240	358	73 778
1700	1 925	1 500	2 000	8 770	394	81 460
1820	7 101	2 312	3 297	12 203	657	133 040
1821	7 200	2 333	3 316	12 284	665	134 336
1822	7 267	2 355	3 335	12 366	672	135 632
1823	7 335	2 376	3 354	12 449	678	136 933
1824	7 403	2 398	3 373	12 532	685	138 231
1825	7 472	2 420	3 393	12 615	692	139 544
1826	7 542	2 443	3 412	12 699	698	140 782
1827	7 612	2 465	3 432	12 784	704	141 975
1828	7 683	2 488	3 452	12 869	710	143 157
1829	7 755	2 511	3 472	12 955	716	144 312
1830	7 827	2 534	3 491	13 041	722	145 455
1831	7 900	2 557	3 512	12 128	727	145 520
1832	7 949	2 581	3 532	13 216	733	147 572
1833	7 998	2 605	3 552	13 304	738	148 630
1834	8 047	2 629	3 475	13 392	743	149 616
1835	8 096	2 653	3 595	13 482	749	150 875
1836	8 146	2 677	3 617	13 571	755	152 040
1837	8 196	2 702	3 639	13 662	761	153 242
1838	8 247	2 727	3 661	13 753	767	154 457
1839	8 298	2 752	3 683	13 845	774	155 715
1840	8 349	2 777	3 704	13 937	780	156 988
1841	8 400	2 803	3 715	14 030	787	158 224
1842	8 422	2 829	3 726	14 123	793	159 444
1843	8 441	2 855	3 738	14 217	799	160 598
1844	8 479	2 881	3 749	14 312	805	161 835
1845	8 497	2 908	3 760	14 407	811	163 093
1846	8 490	2 934	3 771	14 503	817	164 238
1847	8 205	2 961	3 783	14 600	820	164 819
1848	7 640	2 989	3 794	14 697	820	165 018
1849	7 256	3 016	3 804	14 795	822	165 525
1850	6 878	3 044	3 816	14 894	825	166 194
1851	6 514	3 072	3 827	14 974	828	166 869
1852	6 337	3 100	3 839	15 055	833	167 816
1853	6 199	3 129	3 850	15 136	837	168 689
1854	6 083	3 158	3 858	15 217	842	169 595
1855	6 015	3 187	3 867	15 299	846	170 493
1856	5 973	3 216	3 875	15 381	851	171 425
1857	5 919	3 246	3 889	15 455	856	172 410
1858	5 891	3 273	3 925	15 526	861	173 494
1859	5 862	3 306	3 963	15 584	867	174 642
1860	5 821	3 336	4 000	15 642	873	175 862
1861	5 788	3 367	4 074	15 699	880	177 125
1862	5 776	3 398	4 113	15 754	886	178 389
1863	5 718	3 430	4 131	15 809	893	179 735
1864	5 641	3 461	4 176	15 864	900	181 073
1865	5 595	3 493	4 201	15 920	907	182 378
1866	5 523	3 525	4 226	15 976	912	183 441
1867	5 487	3 558	4 251	16 032	918	184 530
1868	5 466	3 591	4 276	16 088	922	185 373

Table 1a. **Population of 4 West European Countries and Total WEC, 1869-1918**
(000 at mid-year)

	Ireland	Greece	Portugal	Spain	13 small WEC	29 WEC
1869	5 449	3 621	4 302	16 144	930	186 844
1870	5 419	3 657	4 327	16 201	933	187 504
1871	5 398	3 694	4 353	16 258	941	187 816
1872	5 373	3 732	4 379	16 315	949	188 712
1873	5 328	3 770	4 405	16 372	958	190 046
1874	5 299	3 809	4 431	16 429	966	191 492
1875	5 279	3 848	4 458	16 487	975	192 963
1876	5 278	3 887	4 484	16 545	983	194 700
1877	5 286	3 927	4 511	16 603	992	196 449
1878	5 282	3 967	4 538	16 677	1 000	198 022
1879	5 266	4 008	4 571	16 768	1 009	199 779
1880	5 203	4 049	4 610	16 859	1 018	201 221
1881	5 146	4 090	4 651	16 951	1 027	202 532
1882	5 101	4 132	4 691	17 043	1 036	203 865
1883	5 024	4 174	4 732	17 136	1 045	205 172
1884	4 975	4 217	4 773	17 230	1 054	206 686
1885	4 939	4 260	4 815	17 323	1 064	208 141
1886	4 906	4 303	4 857	17 418	1 073	209 643
1887	4 857	4 347	4 899	17 513	1 082	211 085
1888	4 801	4 392	4 942	17 600	1 092	212 551
1889	4 757	4 437	4 985	17 678	1 101	214 110
1890	4 718	4 482	5 028	17 757	1 111	215 597
1891	4 680	4 528	5 068	17 836	1 121	217 031
1892	4 634	4 574	5 104	17 916	1 131	218 554
1893	4 607	4 621	5 141	17 996	1 140	220 043
1894	4 589	4 668	5 178	18 076	1 150	221 799
1895	4 560	4 716	5 215	18 157	1 161	223 515
1896	4 542	4 764	5 252	18 238	1 171	225 436
1897	4 530	4 813	5 290	18 320	1 181	227 546
1898	4 518	4 862	5 327	18 402	1 191	229 659
1899	4 502	4 912	5 366	18 484	1 202	231 710
1900	4 469	4 962	5 404	18 566	1 212	233 645
1901	4 447	4 997	5 447	18 659	1 223	235 665
1902	4 435	5 032	5 494	18 788	1 234	237 886
1903	4 418	5 067	5 541	18 919	1 244	240 037
1904	4 408	5 102	5 589	19 050	1 255	242 197
1905	4 399	5 138	5 637	19 133	1 266	244 238
1906	4 398	5 174	5 686	19 316	1 277	246 505
1907	4 388	5 210	5 735	19 450	1 289	248 653
1908	4 385	5 246	5 784	19 585	1 300	250 920
1909	4 387	5 283	5 834	19 721	1 311	253 174
1910	4 385	5 320	5 884	19 858	1 323	255 394
1911	4 381	5 355	5 935	19 994	1 334	257 730
1912	4 368	5 390	5 964	20 128	1 346	259 376
1913	4 346	5 425	5 972	20 263	1 358	260 975
1914	4 334	5 463	5 980	20 398	1 362	263 255
1915	4 278	5 502	5 988	20 535	1 367	263 637
1916	4 273	5 541	5 996	20 673	1 371	263 637
1917	4 273	5 580	6 005	20 811	1 376	263 058
1918	4 280	5 620	6 013	20 950	1 380	261 531

a.   Figures are shown here for Ireland 1500-1920 for information. They are not included in the total because the UK figures already include the whole of Ireland for 1500-1920, thereafter only the Northern Ireland province.

Table 1a. **Population of 4 West European Countries and Total WEC, 1919-1969**
(000 at mid-year)

	Ireland [b]	Greece	Portugal	Spain	13 small WEC	29 WEC
1919	4 352	5 660	6 021	21 091	1 384	**256 661**
1920	4 361	5 700	6 029	21 232	1 389	**258 081**
1921	3 096	5 837	6 071	21 411	1 393	**260 241**
1922	3 002	5 890	6 146	21 628	1 398	**262 045**
1923	3 014	6 010	6 223	21 847	1 402	**264 259**
1924	3 005	6 000	6 300	22 069	1 407	**266 353**
1925	2 985	5 958	6 378	22 292	1 411	**268 182**
1926	2 971	6 042	6 457	22 518	1 416	**270 106**
1927	2 957	6 127	6 538	22 747	1 420	**271 747**
1928	2 944	6 205	6 619	22 977	1 425	**273 430**
1929	2 937	6 275	6 701	23 210	1 429	**275 012**
1930	2 927	6 351	6 784	23 445	1 434	**276 916**
1931	2 933	6 440	6 869	23 675	1 439	**278 776**
1932	2 949	6 516	6 954	23 897	1 443	**280 361**
1933	2 962	6 591	7 040	24 122	1 448	**281 907**
1934	2 971	6 688	7 127	24 349	1 453	**283 520**
1935	2 971	6 793	7 216	24 579	1 457	**285 164**
1936	2 967	6 886	7 305	23 810	1 462	**285 763**
1937	2 948	6 973	7 396	25 043	1 467	**288 395**
1938	2 937	7 061	7 488	25 279	1 471	**290 338**
1939	2 934	7 156	7 581	25 517	1 476	**292 510**
1940	2 958	7 280	7 675	25 757	1 481	**293 568**
1941	2 993	7 362	7 757	25 979	1 485	**293 555**
1942	2 963	7 339	7 826	26 182	1 490	**294 848**
1943	2 946	7 297	7 896	26 387	1 495	**295 067**
1944	2 944	7 284	7 967	26 594	1 500	**295 377**
1945	2 952	7 322	8 038	26 802	1 505	**294 285**
1946	2 957	7 418	8 110	27 012	1 510	**293 928**
1947	2 974	7 529	8 183	27 223	1 514	**297 304**
1948	2 985	7 749	8 256	27 437	1 519	**300 828**
1949	2 981	7 856	8 329	27 651	1 524	**303 393**
1950	2 963	7 566	8 443	28 063	1 529	**304 940**
1951	2 959	7 646	8 490	28 298	1 544	**307 024**
1952	2 952	7 733	8 526	28 550	1 559	**308 754**
1953	2 947	7 817	8 579	28 804	1 574	**310 696**
1954	2 937	7 893	8 632	29 060	1 591	**312 607**
1955	2 916	7 966	8 693	29 319	1 600	**314 605**
1956	2 895	8 031	8 756	29 579	1 613	**316 758**
1957	2 878	8 096	8 818	29 842	1 636	**318 987**
1958	2 852	8 173	8 889	30 106	1 661	**321 318**
1959	2 843	8 258	8 962	30 373	1 682	**323 824**
1960	2 832	8 327	9 037	30 641	1 701	**326 346**
1961	2 818	8 398	9 031	30 904	1 717	**329 115**
1962	2 830	8 448	9 020	31 158	1 729	**332 342**
1963	2 850	8 480	9 082	31 430	1 747	**335 251**
1964	2 864	8 510	9 123	31 741	1 759	**338 111**
1965	2 876	8 550	9 129	32 085	1 773	**340 884**
1966	2 884	8 614	9 109	32 452	1 787	**343 440**
1967	2 900	8 716	9 103	32 850	1 803	**345 628**
1968	2 913	8 741	9 115	33 239	1 819	**347 633**
1969	2 926	8 773	9 097	33 566	1 837	**349 946**

Table 1a. **Population of 4 West European Countries and Total WEC, 1970-2003**
(000 at mid-year)

	Ireland [b]	Greece	Portugal	Spain	13 small WEC	29 WEC
1970	2 950	8 793	9 044	33 876	1 853	**352 240**
1971	2 978	8 831	8 990	34 195	1 869	**354 702**
1972	3 024	8 889	8 970	34 513	1 883	**356 845**
1973	3 073	8 929	8 976	34 837	1 907	**358 825**
1974	3 124	8 962	9 098	35 184	1 929	**360 466**
1975	3 177	9 047	9 411	35 564	1 915	**361 743**
1976	3 228	9 167	9 622	35 997	1 914	**362 752**
1977	3 272	9 308	9 663	36 439	1 922	**363 850**
1978	3 314	9 430	9 699	36 861	1 939	**364 949**
1979	3 368	9 548	9 725	37 200	1 957	**366 096**
1980	3 401	9 643	9 778	37 488	1 990	**367 457**
1981	3 443	9 729	9 850	37 751	2 009	**368 647**
1982	3 480	9 790	9 860	37 983	2 020	**369 371**
1983	3 504	9 847	9 872	38 184	2 030	**369 920**
1984	3 529	9 896	9 885	38 363	2 040	**370 509**
1985	3 540	9 936	9 897	38 535	2 050	**371 162**
1986	3 541	9 967	9 907	38 708	2 064	**372 001**
1987	3 540	9 993	9 915	38 881	2 086	**372 887**
1988	3 530	10 004	9 921	39 054	2 110	**374 092**
1989	3 513	10 056	9 923	39 215	2 131	**375 950**
1990	3 508	10 158	9 923	39 351	2 159	**377 856**
1991	3 531	10 283	9 919	39 461	2 188	**379 688**
1992	3 557	10 357	9 915	39 549	2 218	**381 580**
1993	3 577	10 415	9 931	39 628	2 245	**383 334**
1994	3 594	10 462	9 955	39 691	2 268	**384 719**
1995	3 611	10 489	9 969	39 750	2 285	**385 936**
1996	3 633	10 511	9 980	39 804	2 303	**387 063**
1997	3 669	10 533	9 995	39 855	2 322	**388 065**
1998	3 711	10 556	10 012	39 906	2 340	**388 977**
1999	3 754	10 579	10 030	39 953	2 359	**389 945**
2000	3 797	10 602	10 048	40 016	2 377	**391 036**
2001	3 841	10 624	10 066	40 087	2 395	**392 101**
2002	3 883	10 645	10 084	40 153	2 412	**393 061**
2003	3 924	10 666	10 102	40 217	2 429	**393 957**

b.   From 1921 the figures refer to the Irish Republic.

Table 1b. **GDP Levels in 12 West European Countries, 1500-1868**
(million 1990 international Geary-Khamis dollars)

	Austria	Belgium	Denmark	Finland	France	Germany	Italy
1500	1 414	1 225	443	136	10 912	8 256	11 550
1600	2 093	1 561	569	215	15 559	12 656	14 410
1700	2 483	2 288	727	255	19 539	13 650	14 630
1820	4 104	4 529	1 471	913	35 468	26 819	22 535
1821			1 541		38 524		
1822			1 564		37 267		
1823			1 564		38 706		
1824			1 611		40 025		
1825			1 623		38 526		
1826			1 646		39 783		
1827			1 693		39 179		
1828			1 716		39 158		
1829			1 681		40 415		
1830	4 948	5 078	1 693		39 655	37 250	
1831			1 681		40 378		
1832			1 728		44 090		
1833			1 716		43 416		
1834			1 809		43 663		
1835			1 798		45 312		
1836			1 798		44 803		
1837			1 844		45 669		
1838			1 856		47 899		
1839			1 879		46 367		
1840	5 628		1 938		49 828		
1841			1 938		51 045		
1842			1 949		49 933		
1843			2 054		52 595		
1844			2 159		54 497		
1845			2 218		52 833		
1846		7 277	2 265		52 965		
1847		7 633	2 253		58 806		
1848		7 665	2 370		55 198		
1849		7 892	2 510		56 933		
1850	6 519	8 216	2 649	1 483	58 039	48 178	33 019
1851		8 442	2 521		57 188	47 941	
1852		8 668	2 615		60 931	48 890	
1853		8 894	2 626		57 969	48 653	
1854		9 444	2 638		60 763	49 840	
1855		9 509	2 930		59 842	49 128	
1856		10 026	2 766		62 469	53 162	
1857		10 285	2 813		66 038	55 773	
1858		10 350	2 790		70 645	55 536	
1859		10 350	2 977		66 046	55 773	
1860	7 528	10 867	2 953	1 667	70 577	59 096	
1861		11 029	3 000	1 680	66 154	57 672	37 995
1862		11 320	3 093	1 590	71 812	60 520	39 141
1863		11 644	3 292	1 718	74 416	65 029	38 377
1864		12 032	3 257	1 756	75 256	66 928	39 523
1865		12 032	3 373	1 744	73 157	67 165	40 503
1866		12 388	3 373	1 763	73 651	67 640	42 482
1867		12 452	3 373	1 622	69 308	67 877	38 950
1868		12 905	3 432	1 782	75 958	71 912	40 668

Table 1b. **GDP Levels in 12 West European countries, 1500-1868**
(million 1990 international Geary-Khamis dollars)

	Netherlands	Norway	Sweden	Switzerland	United Kingdom	12 WEC
1500	723	192	382	411	2 815	**38 459**
1600	2 072	304	626	750	6 007	**56 822**
1700	4 047	450	1 231	1 068	10 709	**71 077**
1820	4 288	1 071	3 098	2 165	36 232	**142 693**
1821	4 458		3 255			
1822	4 498		3 220			
1823	4 702		3 342			
1824	4 871		3 463			
1825	4 871		3 498			
1826	4 902		3 185			
1827	5 125		3 307			
1828	5 373		3 603			
1829	5 492		3 463			
1830	5 300		3 394		42 228	
1831	5 298		3 255		44 249	
1832	5 638		3 463		43 800	
1833	5 742		3 638		44 249	
1834	5 750		3 638		46 046	
1835	5 823		3 725		48 517	
1836	5 980		3 777		50 314	
1837	6 205		3 638		49 640	
1838	6 380		3 429		52 336	
1839	6 485		3 777		54 806	
1840	6 588		3 864		53 234	
1841	6 734		3 742		52 111	
1842	6 756		3 742		50 988	
1843	6 680		3 899		51 886	
1844	6 723		4 247		55 031	
1845	6 807		4 020		57 951	
1846	6 837		3 933		61 770	
1847	6 869		4 177		62 219	
1848	6 938		4 438		62 893	
1849	7 119		4 595		64 016	
1850	7 345	1 653	4 490	3 541	63 342	**238 474**
1851	7 551		4 334	3 633	66 037	
1852	7 642		4 351	3 863	67 160	
1853	7 578		4 334	3 729	69 631	
1854	7 790		4 769	3 314	71 428	
1855	7 941		5 013	3 873	71 203	
1856	8 036		4 856	3 869	76 370	
1857	8 179		4 995	4 200	77 717	
1858	8 039		5 395	5 298	77 942	
1859	7 810		5 656	5 035	79 964	
1860	7 887		5 743	4 379	81 760	
1861	8 007		5 413	4 691	84 007	
1862	8 123		5 709	5 049	84 680	
1863	8 427		5 918	5 047	85 354	
1864	8 760		6 283	4 778	87 600	
1865	9 015	2 301	6 057	5 183	90 296	
1866	9 255	2 344	6 109	5 135	91 644	
1867	9 335	2 405	6 005	4 514	90 745	
1868	9 286	2 393	6 161	5 333	93 665	

Table 1b. **GDP Levels in 12 West European Countries, 1869-1918**
(million 1990 international Geary-Khamis dollars)

	Austria	Belgium	Denmark	Finland	France	Germany	Italy
1869		13 390	3 630	1 910	78 029	72 386	41 146
1870	8 419	13 716	3 782	1 999	72 100	72 149	41 814
1871	9 029	13 780	3 793	2 013	71 667	71 674	42 272
1872	9 099	14 621	4 003	2 083	78 313	76 658	41 647
1873	8 888	14 718	3 979	2 204	72 822	79 981	43 274
1874	9 287	15 203	4 096	2 255	82 070	85 914	43 130
1875	9 333	15 171	4 166	2 300	84 815	86 389	44 365
1876	9 545	15 365	4 248	2 428	77 880	85 914	43 431
1877	9 873	15 559	4 131	2 370	82 070	85 440	43 409
1878	10 201	16 012	4 295	2 326	81 058	89 474	44 051
1879	10 131	16 174	4 435	2 351	76 001	87 338	44 561
1880	10 272	16 982	4 540	2 364	82 792	86 626	46 690
1881	10 694	17 209	4 586	2 300	85 971	88 762	43 541
1882	10 764	17 791	4 750	2 524	90 017	90 186	47 354
1883	11 210	18 050	4 913	2 619	90 306	95 170	47 218
1884	11 514	18 211	4 936	2 639	89 294	97 543	47 556
1885	11 444	18 438	4 971	2 703	87 705	99 917	48 542
1886	11 819	18 664	5 170	2 837	89 150	100 629	50 695
1887	12 640	19 376	5 357	2 881	89 728	104 663	52 090
1888	12 617	19 505	5 392	2 990	90 595	108 935	51 920
1889	12 499	20 443	5 462	3 092	92 906	112 021	49 686
1890	13 179	20 896	5 788	3 265	95 074	115 581	52 863
1891	13 648	20 929	5 905	3 233	97 241	115 343	52 648
1892	13 953	21 446	6 045	3 137	99 697	120 090	49 688
1893	14 047	21 770	6 162	3 258	101 431	126 023	51 967
1894	14 868	22 093	6 290	3 514	105 188	129 109	51 235
1895	15 267	22 611	6 640	3 706	103 021	135 279	52 027
1896	15 501	23 063	6 885	3 948	107 933	140 026	53 456
1897	15 829	23 484	7 049	4 140	106 488	144 061	51 091
1898	16 721	23 872	7 165	4 319	111 690	150 231	55 646
1899	17 072	24 357	7 469	4 217	118 048	155 690	56 944
1900	17 213	25 069	7 726	4 415	116 747	162 335	60 114
1901	17 283	25 295	8 052	4 364	114 869	158 538	64 016
1902	17 963	25 813	8 239	4 274	112 990	162 335	62 231
1903	18 128	26 395	8 729	4 562	115 447	171 354	65 196
1904	18 409	27 074	8 916	4 734	116 314	178 236	65 805
1905	19 441	27 851	9 068	4 811	118 336	182 034	69 477
1906	20 191	28 433	9 324	5 003	120 504	187 492	72 087
1907	21 434	28 854	9 674	5 175	125 705	195 799	80 214
1908	21 528	29 145	9 978	5 233	124 983	199 122	82 149
1909	21 458	29 695	10 363	5 463	130 185	203 156	88 494
1910	21 763	30 471	10 678	5 584	122 238	210 513	85 285
1911	22 443	31 183	11 250	5 744	134 230	217 633	90 839
1912	23 568	31 926	11 250	6 063	145 356	227 127	91 574
1913	23 451	32 347	11 670	6 389	144 489	237 332	95 487
1914	19 572	30 300	12 405	6 108	134 230	202 207	95 413
1915	18 154	29 935	11 542	5 801	131 485	192 002	106 730
1916	17 933	31 672	12 032	5 878	138 131	193 900	119 746
1917	17 548	27 199	11 320	4 939	117 036	194 138	125 383
1918	17 186	21 917	10 946	4 281	92 328	194 612	127 249

Table 1b. **GDP Levels in 12 West European Countries, 1869-1918**
(million 1990 international Geary-Khamis dollars)

	Netherlands	Norway	Sweden	Switzerland	United Kingdom	12 WEC
1869	9 552	2 491	6 474	5 836	94 339	
1870	9 952	2 485	6 927	5 581	100 180	**339 103**
1871	9 942	2 521	7 048	5 964	105 570	**345 273**
1872	10 146	2 680	7 379	5 684	105 795	**358 108**
1873	10 472	2 735	8 058	5 844	108 266	**361 242**
1874	10 213	2 827	8 371	6 550	110 063	**379 979**
1875	10 908	2 913	8 005	7 275	112 758	**388 398**
1876	11 074	2 998	8 527	7 109	113 881	**382 400**
1877	11 364	3 011	8 249	6 416	115 004	**386 896**
1878	11 468	2 919	8 197	6 535	115 454	**391 988**
1879	11 058	2 955	8 058	6 517	115 004	**384 599**
1880	12 313	3 047	8 440	6 955	120 395	**401 416**
1881	12 540	3 072	8 458	7 078	124 663	**408 873**
1882	12 875	3 060	8 806	6 870	128 257	**423 253**
1883	13 816	3 047	8 893	6 887	129 155	**431 284**
1884	14 065	3 108	9 137	7 666	129 380	**435 051**
1885	14 378	3 145	9 102	8 268	128 706	**437 319**
1886	14 594	3 164	9 067	8 593	130 728	**445 109**
1887	15 178	3 200	9 102	8 554	135 894	**458 663**
1888	15 707	3 341	9 345	8 757	141 959	**471 062**
1889	15 707	3 457	9 833	8 766	149 596	**483 468**
1890	15 070	3 549	9 972	9 389	150 269	**494 895**
1891	14 783	3 580	10 094	8 856	150 269	**496 530**
1892	15 006	3 659	10 303	9 627	146 676	**499 328**
1893	15 157	3 757	10 320	10 014	146 676	**510 582**
1894	15 524	3 769	10 529	9 783	156 559	**528 460**
1895	16 015	3 806	11 051	10 861	161 500	**541 783**
1896	15 405	3 922	11 695	11 142	168 239	**561 217**
1897	16 959	4 118	12 112	11 716	170 485	**567 533**
1898	17 310	4 130	12 374	11 927	178 796	**594 181**
1899	17 566	4 247	12 652	12 513	186 208	**616 982**
1900	17 604	4 320	13 104	12 649	184 861	**626 156**
1901	17 958	4 436	12 965	12 511	184 861	**625 148**
1902	18 796	4 528	12 948	12 801	189 578	**632 497**
1903	19 197	4 510	13 905	12 554	187 556	**647 532**
1904	19 334	4 504	14 044	13 223	188 679	**659 273**
1905	19 953	4 559	14 201	13 543	194 295	**677 567**
1906	20 661	4 724	15 123	14 972	200 808	**699 323**
1907	20 679	4 901	15 454	15 110	204 627	**727 627**
1908	20 694	5 060	15 419	14 873	196 316	**724 500**
1909	21 457	5 195	15 315	15 648	200 808	**747 235**
1910	22 438	5 379	16 237	16 177	207 098	**753 860**
1911	23 263	5 544	16 637	16 530	213 162	**788 458**
1912	23 998	5 795	17 107	16 701	216 307	**816 772**
1913	24 955	6 119	17 403	16 483	224 618	**840 743**
1914	24 281	6 254	17 246	16 496	226 864	**791 376**
1915	25 105	6 523	17 246	16 658	245 058	**806 239**
1916	25 779	6 731	17 020	16 606	250 449	**835 878**
1917	24 131	6 119	14 932	14 790	252 695	**810 230**
1918	22 634	5 893	14 706	14 737	254 268	**780 758**

Table 1b. GDP Levels in 12 West European Countries, 1919-1969
(million 1990 international Geary-Khamis dollars)

	Austria	Belgium	Denmark	Finland	France	Germany	Italy
1919	14 503	25 854	12 359	5 169	108 800	156 591	105 980
1920	15 571	29 921	12 942	5 782	125 850	170 235	96 757
1921	17 236	30 439	12 569	5 974	120 648	189 511	95 287
1922	18 784	33 414	13 841	6 606	142 322	206 188	100 210
1923	18 597	34 611	15 299	7 092	149 691	171 318	106 266
1924	20 754	35 743	15 346	7 277	168 474	200 557	107 312
1925	22 161	36 293	14 996	7 692	169 197	223 082	114 397
1926	22 536	37 523	15 871	7 986	173 676	229 363	115 595
1927	23 216	38 913	16 186	8 612	170 064	252 321	113 094
1928	24 295	40 951	16 735	9 194	181 912	263 367	121 182
1929	24 647	40 595	17 855	9 302	194 193	262 284	125 180
1930	23 967	40 207	18 917	9 194	188 558	258 602	119 014
1931	22 044	39 496	19 127	8 970	177 288	238 893	118 323
1932	19 769	37 717	18 625	8 932	165 729	220 916	122 140
1933	19 113	38 525	19 220	9 526	177 577	234 778	121 317
1934	19 277	38 202	19 804	10 606	175 843	256 220	121 826
1935	19 652	40 563	20 247	11 059	171 364	275 496	133 559
1936	20 238	40 854	20 749	11 807	177 866	299 753	133 792
1937	21 317	41 404	21 251	12 478	188 125	317 783	142 954
1938	24 037	40 466	21 765	13 123	187 402	342 351	143 981
1939	27 250	43 216	22 803	12 561	200 840	374 577	154 470
1940	26 547	38 072	19 606	11 909	165 729	377 284	155 424
1941	28 446	36 067	17 668	12 299	131 052	401 174	153 517
1942	27 016	32 962	18 065	12 337	117 470	406 582	151 610
1943	27 672	32 198	20 061	13 756	111 546	414 696	137 307
1944	28 376	34 094	22 161	13 762	94 207	425 041	111 562
1945	11 726	36 132	20 493	12 963	102 154	302 457	87 342
1946	13 695	38 267	23 690	14 017	155 326	143 381	114 422
1947	15 102	40 563	25 020	14 343	168 330	161 011	134 446
1948	19 230	42 989	25 697	15 481	180 611	190 695	142 074
1949	22 865	44 736	27 471	16 420	205 174	223 178	152 563
1950	25 702	47 190	29 654	17 051	220 492	265 354	164 957
1951	27 460	49 874	29 852	18 501	234 074	289 679	177 272
1952	27 484	49 486	30 144	19 121	240 287	314 794	190 541
1953	28 680	51 071	31 859	19 255	247 223	341 150	204 288
1954	31 611	53 173	32 478	20 941	259 215	366 584	214 884
1955	35 105	55 696	32 828	22 008	274 098	406 922	227 389
1956	37 520	57 313	33 225	22 673	287 969	436 086	237 699
1957	39 818	58 381	35 746	23 739	305 308	461 071	251 732
1958	41 272	58 316	36 551	23 867	312 966	481 599	265 192
1959	42 445	60 160	39 270	25 285	321 924	516 821	281 707
1960	45 939	63 394	40 367	27 598	344 609	558 482	296 981
1961	48 378	66 478	42 926	29 701	363 754	581 487	321 992
1962	49 550	69 904	45 295	30 627	387 937	606 292	347 098
1963	51 567	72 988	45 579	31 636	408 090	623 382	371 822
1964	54 662	78 128	49 843	33 235	435 296	661 273	386 333
1965	56 234	80 870	52 117	35 002	456 456	695 798	395 020
1966	59 399	83 440	53 539	35 843	479 631	715 393	415 639
1967	61 205	86 695	55 339	36 600	501 799	717 610	445 232
1968	63 925	90 293	57 613	37 442	523 967	755 463	482 462
1969	67 945	96 302	61 283	41 048	560 280	805 410	510 051

Table 1b. **GDP Levels in 12 West European Countries, 1919-1969**
(million 1990 international Geary-Khamis dollars)

	Netherlands	Norway	Sweden	Switzerland	United Kingdom	12 WEC
1919	28 049	6 890	15 558	15 707	226 640	**722 099**
1920	28 898	7 324	16 463	16 726	212 938	**739 408**
1921	30 670	6 719	15 854	16 311	195 642	**736 859**
1922	32 342	7 502	17 351	17 890	205 750	**802 200**
1923	33 140	7 667	18 273	18 925	212 264	**793 144**
1924	35 561	7 630	18 847	19 631	221 024	**858 158**
1925	37 058	8 102	19 544	21 065	231 806	**905 392**
1926	40 028	8 279	20 640	22 120	223 270	**916 887**
1927	41 700	8 597	21 284	23 307	241 240	**958 535**
1928	43 921	8 879	22 293	24 609	244 160	**1 001 498**
1929	44 270	9 705	23 651	25 466	251 348	**1 028 497**
1930	44 170	10 421	24 138	25 301	249 551	**1 012 040**
1931	41 475	9 613	23 268	24 246	236 747	**959 491**
1932	40 901	10 255	22 641	23 422	238 544	**929 593**
1933	40 826	10 500	23 076	24 593	245 507	**964 560**
1934	40 078	10 837	24 834	24 642	261 680	**1 003 848**
1935	41 575	11 302	26 418	24 543	271 788	**1 047 566**
1936	44 195	11 993	27 949	24 626	284 142	**1 097 965**
1937	46 716	12 422	29 272	25 796	294 025	**1 153 541**
1938	45 593	12 734	29 759	26 785	297 619	**1 185 615**
1939	48 687	13 339	31 813	26 752	300 539	**1 256 847**
1940	42 898	12 152	30 873	27 032	330 638	**1 238 163**
1941	40 627	12 446	31 395	26 851	360 737	**1 252 277**
1942	37 133	11 963	33 309	26 175	369 721	**1 244 342**
1943	36 235	11 724	34 789	25 944	377 807	**1 243 734**
1944	24 306	11 112	35 972	26 571	362 983	**1 190 146**
1945	24 880	12 452	36 947	34 202	347 035	**1 028 782**
1946	41 999	13 786	41 001	36 543	331 985	**968 114**
1947	48 613	15 365	42 011	40 944	327 044	**1 032 793**
1948	53 804	16 589	43 316	41 768	337 376	**1 109 630**
1949	58 546	16 913	44 900	40 631	349 955	**1 203 351**
1950	60 642	17 838	47 269	42 545	347 850	**1 286 544**
1951	61 914	18 665	49 148	45 990	358 234	**1 360 663**
1952	63 162	19 332	49 845	46 369	357 585	**1 408 150**
1953	68 652	20 225	51 237	48 001	371 646	**1 483 287**
1954	73 319	21 229	53 395	50 705	386 789	**1 564 323**
1955	78 759	21 639	54 944	54 117	400 850	**1 664 355**
1956	81 654	22 771	57 032	57 710	405 825	**1 737 477**
1957	83 950	23 432	59 591	60 002	412 315	**1 815 085**
1958	83 701	23 218	59 887	58 732	411 450	**1 856 751**
1959	87 793	24 411	61 714	62 425	428 107	**1 952 062**
1960	95 180	25 813	64 986	66 793	452 768	**2 082 910**
1961	95 455	27 377	68 710	72 200	467 694	**2 186 152**
1962	101 993	28 159	71 599	75 661	472 454	**2 286 569**
1963	105 686	29 254	75 411	79 370	490 625	**2 385 410**
1964	114 446	30 662	80 562	83 541	516 584	**2 524 565**
1965	120 435	32 305	83 643	86 195	529 996	**2 624 071**
1966	123 754	33 556	85 383	88 305	540 163	**2 714 045**
1967	130 267	35 690	88 272	91 008	552 277	**2 801 994**
1968	138 627	36 498	91 475	94 272	574 775	**2 946 812**
1969	147 552	38 140	96 056	99 584	585 207	**3 108 858**

Table 1b. **GDP Levels in 12 West European Countries, 1970-2001**
(million 1990 international Geary-Khamis dollars)

	Austria	Belgium	Denmark	Finland	France	Germany	Italy
1970	72 785	102 265	62 524	44 114	592 389	843 103	521 506
1971	76 506	106 103	64 191	45 036	621 055	867 917	531 385
1972	81 256	111 679	67 578	48 473	648 668	903 739	546 933
1973	85 227	118 516	70 032	51 724	683 965	944 755	582 713
1974	88 588	123 494	69 379	53 291	704 012	952 571	610 040
1975	88 267	121 855	68 921	53 905	699 106	947 383	596 946
1976	92 307	128 743	73 382	53 676	729 326	993 132	635 737
1977	96 624	129 549	74 573	53 808	756 545	1 021 710	654 108
1978	96 273	133 231	75 674	54 934	777 544	1 050 404	678 494
1979	101 525	136 350	78 356	58 756	802 491	1 092 615	716 984
1980	103 874	142 458	78 010	61 890	813 763	1 105 099	742 299
1981	103 771	140 680	77 316	63 043	822 116	1 109 276	745 816
1982	105 750	142 665	79 650	65 090	842 787	1 099 799	749 233
1983	108 716	142 648	81 656	66 849	852 644	1 119 394	758 360
1984	109 077	146 180	85 241	68 866	865 172	1 150 951	777 841
1985	111 525	147 650	88 897	71 184	877 305	1 176 131	799 697
1986	114 135	149 854	92 135	72 873	898 129	1 202 151	822 404
1987	116 053	153 392	92 406	75 861	920 822	1 220 284	847 870
1988	119 730	160 632	93 482	79 581	961 287	1 260 983	880 671
1989	124 791	166 396	93 728	84 092	1 000 286	1 302 212	906 053
1990	130 476	171 442	94 863	84 103	1 026 491	1 264 438	925 654
1991	134 944	174 880	96 184	78 841	1 036 379	1 328 057	938 522
1992	136 754	177 695	97 413	76 222	1 051 689	1 357 825	945 660
1993	137 455	175 072	98 232	75 347	1 041 232	1 343 060	937 303
1994	140 949	180 312	103 884	78 327	1 061 556	1 374 575	957 993
1995	143 849	185 047	107 713	81 311	1 079 157	1 398 310	986 004
1996	146 726	187 268	110 406	84 563	1 091 028	1 409 496	996 850
1997	149 028	193 929	113 745	89 930	1 111 532	1 429 073	1 016 570
1998	154 350	198 370	116 545	94 727	1 150 381	1 457 039	1 035 304
1999	158 665	204 292	119 238	98 549	1 188 152	1 483 607	1 052 066
2000	163 412	212 434	122 793	104 566	1 235 635	1 528 353	1 081 646
2001	164 851	214 655	123 978	105 298	1 258 297	1 536 743	1 101 366

Table 1b. **GDP Levels in 12 West European Countries, 1970-2001**
(million 1990 international Geary-Khamis dollars)

	Netherlands	*Norway*	*Sweden*	*Switzerland*	*United Kingdom*	*12 WEC*
1970	155 955	38 902	102 275	105 935	599 016	**3 240 769**
1971	162 539	40 683	103 241	110 253	611 705	**3 340 614**
1972	167 919	42 785	105 604	113 781	633 352	**3 471 767**
1973	175 791	44 544	109 794	117 251	675 941	**3 660 253**
1974	182 763	46 858	113 306	118 957	666 755	**3 730 014**
1975	182 596	48 811	116 198	110 294	665 984	**3 700 266**
1976	191 194	52 135	117 428	108 745	680 933	**3 856 738**
1977	196 392	54 002	115 553	111 392	695 699	**3 959 955**
1978	201 024	56 453	117 577	111 847	720 501	**4 073 956**
1979	205 501	58 894	122 092	114 634	740 370	**4 228 568**
1980	207 979	61 811	124 130	119 909	728 224	**4 289 446**
1981	206 925	62 406	124 113	121 802	718 733	**4 295 997**
1982	204 517	62 514	125 358	120 051	729 861	**4 327 275**
1983	208 014	64 729	127 555	120 659	755 779	**4 407 003**
1984	214 854	68 530	132 717	124 311	774 665	**4 518 405**
1985	221 470	72 105	135 277	128 561	802 000	**4 631 802**
1986	227 570	74 687	138 381	130 653	837 280	**4 760 252**
1987	230 788	76 203	142 733	131 614	877 143	**4 885 169**
1988	236 824	76 117	145 946	135 709	920 841	**5 071 803**
1989	247 906	76 818	149 415	141 599	940 908	**5 234 204**
1990	258 094	78 333	151 451	146 900	944 610	**5 276 855**
1991	263 950	80 774	149 760	145 724	930 493	**5 358 508**
1992	269 298	83 413	147 631	145 540	930 975	**5 420 115**
1993	271 347	85 694	144 353	144 839	952 554	**5 406 488**
1994	280 094	90 400	150 296	145 610	994 384	**5 558 380**
1995	286 416	93 879	155 843	146 345	1 022 172	**5 686 046**
1996	295 008	98 479	157 557	146 784	1 048 748	**5 772 913**
1997	306 465	103 079	160 830	149 272	1 085 547	**5 909 000**
1998	319 640	105 614	166 596	152 784	1 117 234	**6 068 584**
1999	331 670	106 740	174 077	155 272	1 143 810	**6 216 138**
2000	343 126	109 181	180 310	159 955	1 179 586	**6 420 997**
2001	347 136	110 683	182 492	162 150	1 202 074	**6 509 723**

Table 1b. GDP Levels in 4 West European Countries and Total WEC, 1500-1868
(million 1990 international Geary-Khamis dollars)

	Ireland [a]	Greece	Portugal	Spain	13 small WEC	29 WEC
1500	421	433	606	4 495	169	**44 162**
1600	615	725	814	7 029	250	**65 640**
1700	1 377	795	1 638	7 481	311	**81 302**
1820	6 231	1 482	3 043	12 299	628	**160 145**
1821						
1822						
1823						
1824						
1825						
1826						
1827						
1828						
1829						
1830						
1831						
1832						
1833						
1834						
1835						
1836						
1837						
1838						
1839						
1840						
1841						
1842						
1843						
1844						
1845						
1846						
1847						
1848						
1849						
1850		2 484	3 524	16 066	1 050	**261 598**
1851			3 793	16 311		
1852				17 053		
1853				17 192		
1854				17 506		
1855			3 552	18 391		
1856				17 892		
1857				17 489		
1858				17 902		
1859				18 700		
1860				19 336		
1861			3 597	19 595		
1862				19 729		
1863				20 190		
1864				20 206		
1865			3 745	19 586		
1866			3 887	20 612		
1867			4 000	20 566		
1868			4 042	18 490		

Table 1b. **GDP Levels in 4 West European Countries and Total WEC, 1869-1918**
(million 1990 international Geary-Khamis dollars)

	Ireland [a]	Greece	Portugal	Spain	13 small WEC	29 WEC
1869			4 148	19 073		
1870	9 619	3 218	4 219	19 556	1 495	**367 591**
1871			4 061	21 104		
1872			4 179	24 034		
1873			4 353	26 156		
1874			4 282	23 968		
1875			4 277	24 670		
1876			4 177	25 136		
1877			4 372	27 701		
1878			4 375	26 982		
1879			4 384	25 492		
1880			4 367	27 750		
1881			4 513	28 462		
1882			4 655	28 831		
1883			4 770	29 480		
1884			4 934	29 561		
1885			5 064	28 774		
1886			5 343	28 157		
1887			5 457	27 765		
1888			5 523	28 890		
1889			5 425	28 823		
1890		5 280	5 671	28 839	2 253	**536 938**
1891			5 572	29 495		
1892			5 548	31 707		
1893			5 660	30 597		
1894			5 587	30 939		
1895			5 827	30 668		
1896			5 908	28 224		
1897			6 251	29 659		
1898			6 469	31 945		
1899			6 701	32 457		
1900		6 704	7 037	33 164	2 862	**675 923**
1901			6 914	35 471		
1902			6 954	34 440		
1903			7 054	34 600		
1904			7 148	34 485		
1905			6 950	34 005		
1906			6 997	35 760		
1907			7 165	36 885		
1908			7 052	38 331		
1909			7 048	38 998		
1910			7 225	37 633		
1911			7 369	40 332		
1912			7 494	40 028		
1913	11 891	8 635	7 467	41 653	3 843	**902 341**
1914			7 520	41 075	3 594	
1915			7 352	41 746	3 673	
1916			7 397	43 687	3 822	
1917			7 281	43 150	3 732	
1918			6 913	42 844	3 634	

a. Figures are shown here for Ireland 1500-1920 for information. They are not included in the total because the UK figures already include the whole of Ireland for 1500-1920, thereafter only the Northern Ireland province.

Table 1b. **GDP Levels in 4 West European Countries and Total WEC, 1919-1969**
(million 1990 international Geary-Khamis dollars)

	Ireland [b]	Greece	Portugal	Spain	13 small WEC	29 WEC
1919			7 064	43 112	3 446	
1920			7 411	46 226	3 523	
1921	7 841	11 196	7 831	47 370	3 346	814 443
1922	7 800	11 565	8 788	49 390	3 843	883 586
1923	7 760	11 947	9 169	50 028	3 780	875 828
1924	7 720	12 341	8 828	51 443	4 072	942 562
1925	7 680	12 748	9 223	54 627	4 278	993 948
1926	7 640	13 169	9 163	54 424	4 317	1 005 600
1927	7 845	13 603	10 772	59 140	4 503	1 054 398
1928	8 058	13 864	9 732	59 371	4 694	1 097 217
1929	8 294	14 696	10 789	63 570	4 810	1 130 656
1930	8 480	14 342	10 656	61 435	4 719	1 111 672
1931	8 716	13 746	11 204	59 871	4 462	1 057 490
1932	8 508	14 912	11 422	61 163	4 615	1 030 213
1933	8 294	15 784	12 194	59 966	4 470	1 065 268
1934	8 562	16 173	12 714	62 231	4 647	1 108 175
1935	8 812	16 846	12 041	63 482	4 837	1 153 584
1936	9 056	16 907	11 124	49 343	5 061	1 189 456
1937	8 716	19 307	12 997	45 272	5 311	1 245 144
1938	8 965	18 901	13 084	45 255	5 438	1 277 258
1939	8 955	18 875	13 259	48 856	5 743	1 352 535
1940	9 028	16 183	12 396	53 585	5 663	1 335 018
1941	9 135	13 796	13 551	52 726	5 753	1 347 238
1942	9 043	11 588	13 369	55 670	5 713	1 339 725
1943	8 991	9 683	14 263	57 724	5 729	1 340 124
1944	8 985	8 129	15 079	60 407	5 499	1 288 245
1945	8 912	6 865	14 497	56 326	4 798	1 120 180
1946	9 025	10 284	15 635	58 854	4 544	1 066 456
1947	9 196	13 272	16 943	59 823	4 801	1 136 828
1948	9 643	13 936	16 894	59 970	5 114	1 215 187
1949	10 148	14 679	17 129	59 583	5 517	1 310 407
1950	10 231	14 489	17 615	61 429	5 880	1 396 188
1951	10 488	15 765	18 404	67 533	5 746	1 478 599
1952	10 753	15 878	18 428	73 044	6 180	1 532 433
1953	11 043	18 053	19 714	72 806	6 436	1 611 339
1954	11 142	18 615	20 660	78 335	6 647	1 699 722
1955	11 432	20 022	21 512	81 457	7 001	1 805 779
1956	11 283	21 731	22 451	88 083	7 427	1 888 452
1957	11 266	23 147	23 445	90 901	7 752	1 971 596
1958	11 034	24 218	23 753	94 829	7 966	2 018 551
1959	11 481	25 107	25 039	92 651	8 279	2 114 619
1960	12 127	26 195	26 711	94 119	8 487	2 250 549
1961	12 706	28 492	28 170	106 187	8 876	2 370 583
1962	13 120	29 562	30 040	118 386	9 269	2 486 946
1963	13 741	32 567	31 823	130 477	9 756	2 603 774
1964	14 279	35 243	33 921	143 308	10 165	2 761 481
1965	14 528	38 553	36 446	152 794	10 877	2 877 269
1966	14 652	40 907	37 929	164 199	11 398	2 983 130
1967	15 521	43 152	40 792	175 227	11 862	3 088 548
1968	16 804	46 027	44 421	185 747	12 261	3 252 072
1969	17 815	50 585	45 364	202 472	13 144	3 438 238

b.   From 1921 the figures refer to the Irish Republic.

Table 1b. **GDP Levels in 4 West European Countries and Total WEC, 1970-2001**
(1990 international Geary-Khamis dollars)

	Ireland	Greece	Portugal	Spain	13 small WEC	29 WEC
1970	18 289	54 609	49 498	214 070	13 713	3 590 948
1971	18 923	58 496	52 781	226 319	14 651	3 711 784
1972	20 151	65 775	57 011	245 019	15 548	3 875 271
1973	21 103	68 355	63 397	266 896	16 452	4 096 456
1974	22 002	65 868	64 122	286 732	16 510	4 185 248
1975	23 246	69 853	61 334	296 824	16 005	4 167 528
1976	23 571	74 296	65 566	309 546	17 038	4 346 755
1977	25 506	76 843	69 239	321 868	18 095	4 471 506
1978	27 340	81 989	71 189	332 597	19 058	4 606 129
1979	28 180	85 015	75 203	337 333	20 007	4 774 306
1980	29 047	86 505	78 655	344 987	20 768	4 849 408
1981	30 013	86 553	79 928	346 768	21 257	4 860 516
1982	30 698	86 895	81 634	352 979	21 886	4 901 367
1983	30 624	87 244	81 492	361 902	22 385	4 990 650
1984	31 957	89 645	79 961	367 170	23 512	5 110 650
1985	32 943	92 442	82 206	374 627	24 313	5 238 333
1986	32 802	93 941	85 610	386 998	25 556	5 385 159
1987	34 331	93 507	91 073	409 027	26 754	5 539 861
1988	36 123	97 670	97 894	431 389	28 385	5 763 264
1989	38 223	101 425	102 922	454 166	30 000	5 960 940
1990	41 459	101 452	107 427	474 366	31 205	6 032 764
1991	42 259	104 597	110 047	485 126	32 342	6 132 879
1992	43 672	105 329	112 134	488 459	33 161	6 202 870
1993	44 848	103 644	110 593	482 776	34 633	6 182 982
1994	47 429	105 717	113 328	493 643	35 838	6 354 335
1995	52 163	107 937	116 640	507 054	36 899	6 506 739
1996	56 207	110 482	120 722	519 223	38 136	6 617 683
1997	62 295	114 500	125 505	540 520	39 918	6 791 738
1998	67 658	118 351	131 220	563 844	41 769	6 991 426
1999	74 999	122 405	135 886	587 169	43 639	7 180 236
2000	83 596	127 681	140 901	611 000	46 112	7 430 287
2001	89 113	132 916	143 234	627 733	47 553	7 550 272

Table 1c. **Per Capita GDP in 12 West European Countries, 1500-1868**
(1990 international Geary-Khamis dollars)

	Austria	Belgium	Denmark	Finland	France	Germany	Italy
1500	707	875	738	453	727	688	1 100
1600	837	976	875	538	841	791	1 100
1700	993	1 144	1 039	638	910	910	1 100
1820	1 218	1 319	1 274	781	1 135	1 077	1 117
1821			1 320		1 225		
1822			1 327		1 176		
1823			1 308		1 213		
1824			1 328		1 246		
1825			1 322		1 191		
1826			1 324		1 223		
1827			1 349		1 197		
1828			1 357		1 190		
1829			1 324		1 221		
1830	1 399	1 354	1 330		1 191	1 328	
1831			1 318		1 208		
1832			1 354		1 312		
1833			1 336		1 288		
1834			1 397		1 290		
1835			1 377		1 333		
1836			1 367		1 311		
1837			1 392		1 329		
1838			1 390		1 387		
1839			1 395		1 336		
1840	1 515		1 428		1 428		
1841			1 414		1 456		
1842			1 407		1 418		
1843			1 476		1 487		
1844			1 527		1 533		
1845			1 551		1 480		
1846		1 694	1 569		1 478		
1847		1 762	1 547		1 635		
1848		1 754	1 612		1 529		
1849		1 790	1 691		1 572		
1850	1 650	1 847	1 767	911	1 597	1 428	1 350
1851		1 886	1 662		1 568	1 408	
1852		1 924	1 702		1 664	1 426	
1853		1 962	1 692		1 578	1 413	
1854		2 070	1 681		1 648	1 443	
1855		2 071	1 843		1 617	1 420	
1856		2 170	1 716		1 686	1 531	
1857		2 211	1 722		1 779	1 594	
1858		2 212	1 688		1 900	1 574	
1859		2 197	1 778		1 774	1 565	
1860	1 778	2 293	1 741	959	1 892	1 639	
1861		2 310	1 747	958	1 769	1 583	1 447
1862		2 354	1 779	896	1 914	1 645	1 482
1863		2 404	1 869	958	1 973	1 749	1 442
1864		2 466	1 833	969	1 988	1 780	1 474
1865		2 448	1 875	951	1 924	1 770	1 499
1866		2 503	1 859	958	1 934	1 771	1 559
1867		2 497	1 840	886	1 813	1 766	1 421
1868		2 569	1 853	1 003	1 982	1 861	1 479

Table 1c. **Per Capita GDP in 12 West European Countries, 1500-1868**
(1990 international Geary-Khamis dollars)

	Netherlands	Norway	Sweden	Switzerland	United Kingdom	12 WEC
1500	761	640	695	632	714	**798**
1600	1 381	760	824	750	974	**908**
1700	2 130	900	977	890	1 250	**1 033**
1820	1 838	1 104	1 198	1 090	1 706	**1 245**
1821	1 885		1 247			
1822	1 874		1 217			
1823	1 931		1 243			
1824	1 969		1 270			
1825	1 938		1 262			
1826	1 928		1 135			
1827	2 001		1 169			
1828	2 079		1 266			
1829	2 104		1 210			
1830	2 013		1 175		1 749	
1831	1 997		1 122		1 811	
1832	2 116		1 185		1 774	
1833	2 140		1 229		1 774	
1834	2 124		1 220		1 828	
1835	2 131		1 231		1 906	
1836	2 165		1 235		1 957	
1837	2 223		1 183		1 912	
1838	2 262		1 110		1 996	
1839	2 273		1 216		2 069	
1840	2 283		1 231		1 990	
1841	2 305		1 179		1 930	
1842	2 289		1 167		1 869	
1843	2 241		1 205		1 886	
1844	2 231		1 297		1 981	
1845	2 234		1 212		2 067	
1846	2 228		1 176		2 185	
1847	2 237		1 242		2 213	
1848	2 261		1 306		2 272	
1849	2 314		1 335		2 334	
1850	2 371	1 188	1 289	1 488	2 330	**1 661**
1851	2 410		1 232	1 514	2 451	
1852	2 413		1 229	1 606	2 480	
1853	2 373		1 216	1 546	2 555	
1854	2 421		1 322	1 365	2 602	
1855	2 455		1 377	1 586	2 571	
1856	2 470		1 322	1 575	2 730	
1857	2 496		1 354	1 700	2 757	
1858	2 440		1 445	2 133	2 742	
1859	2 364		1 493	2 016	2 790	
1860	2 377		1 488	1 745	2 830	
1861	2 397		1 382	1 859	2 884	
1862	2 413		1 439	1 989	2 880	
1863	2 481		1 471	1 978	2 881	
1864	2 553		1 544	1 862	2 935	
1865	2 605	1 362	1 472	2 010	3 001	
1866	2 656	1 373	1 468	1 980	3 023	
1867	2 660	1 402	1 431	1 731	2 968	
1868	2 621	1 388	1 476	2 033	3 037	

Table 1c. **Per Capita GDP in 12 West European Countries, 1869-1918**
(1990 international Geary-Khamis dollars)

	Austria	*Belgium*	*Denmark*	*Finland*	*France*	*Germany*	*Italy*
1869		2 663	1 940	1 101	2 006	1 860	1 486
1870	1 863	2 692	2 003	1 140	1 876	1 839	1 499
1871	1 979	2 682	1 993	1 127	1 899	1 817	1 506
1872	1 976	2 824	2 087	1 145	2 078	1 931	1 475
1873	1 913	2 820	2 057	1 193	1 922	1 999	1 524
1874	1 981	2 890	2 096	1 204	2 157	2 124	1 513
1875	1 973	2 861	2 112	1 211	2 219	2 112	1 550
1876	2 000	2 875	2 130	1 259	2 028	2 071	1 506
1877	2 050	2 884	2 046	1 211	2 127	2 033	1 493
1878	2 100	2 942	2 102	1 173	2 091	2 103	1 506
1879	2 068	2 945	2 149	1 167	1 953	2 029	1 514
1880	2 079	3 065	2 181	1 155	2 120	1 991	1 581
1881	2 145	3 070	2 183	1 110	2 194	2 025	1 467
1882	2 140	3 136	2 240	1 203	2 288	2 044	1 584
1883	2 209	3 145	2 299	1 230	2 288	2 143	1 568
1884	2 248	3 136	2 285	1 219	2 253	2 178	1 566
1885	2 215	3 138	2 274	1 231	2 207	2 216	1 584
1886	2 268	3 153	2 336	1 276	2 237	2 211	1 643
1887	2 404	3 250	2 395	1 276	2 249	2 275	1 678
1888	2 379	3 247	2 389	1 302	2 269	2 341	1 662
1889	2 337	3 379	2 400	1 327	2 322	2 379	1 579
1890	2 443	3 428	2 523	1 381	2 376	2 428	1 667
1891	2 506	3 395	2 555	1 350	2 432	2 397	1 651
1892	2 535	3 442	2 598	1 280	2 493	2 469	1 548
1893	2 525	3 455	2 629	1 341	2 535	2 565	1 609
1894	2 645	3 468	2 657	1 399	2 626	2 598	1 576
1895	2 688	3 512	2 770	1 492	2 569	2 686	1 592
1896	2 701	3 551	2 836	1 570	2 685	2 740	1 627
1897	2 730	3 586	2 863	1 624	2 639	2 775	1 545
1898	2 855	3 615	2 870	1 668	2 760	2 848	1 672
1899	2 886	3 656	2 952	1 607	2 911	2 905	1 700
1900	2 882	3 731	3 017	1 668	2 876	2 985	1 785
1901	2 864	3 719	3 104	1 636	2 826	2 871	1 890
1902	2 945	3 739	3 141	1 591	2 775	2 893	1 821
1903	2 941	3 772	3 290	1 686	2 831	3 008	1 893
1904	2 956	3 821	3 326	1 731	2 847	3 083	1 896
1905	3 090	3 882	3 346	1 742	2 894	3 104	1 984
1906	3 176	3 917	3 402	1 794	2 943	3 152	2 042
1907	3 338	3 932	3 486	1 834	3 070	3 245	2 254
1908	3 320	3 933	3 552	1 829	3 045	3 254	2 288
1909	3 276	3 971	3 643	1 884	3 167	3 275	2 444
1910	3 290	4 064	3 705	1 906	2 965	3 348	2 332
1911	3 365	4 148	3 857	1 939	3 250	3 408	2 461
1912	3 505	4 206	3 812	2 022	3 514	3 524	2 465
1913	3 465	4 220	3 912	2 111	3 485	3 648	2 564
1914	2 876	3 923	4 110	2 001	3 236	3 059	2 543
1915	2 653	3 858	3 778	1 882	3 248	2 899	2 810
1916	2 628	4 080	3 891	1 893	3 463	2 935	3 139
1917	2 586	3 519	3 617	1 581	2 979	2 952	3 301
1918	2 555	2 861	3 459	1 370	2 396	2 983	3 392

Table 1b. **Per Capita GDP in 12 West European Countries, 1869-1918**
(1990 international Geary-Khamis dollars)

	Netherlands	Norway	Sweden	Switzerland	United Kingdom	12 WEC
1869	2 672	1 441	1 557	2 211	3 031	
1870	2 757	1 432	1 662	2 102	3 190	2 088
1871	2 734	1 445	1 684	2 225	3 332	2 124
1872	2 771	1 527	1 746	2 108	3 319	2 192
1873	2 853	1 548	1 885	2 152	3 365	2 195
1874	2 727	1 586	1 938	2 397	3 386	2 291
1875	2 880	1 615	1 835	2 645	3 434	2 323
1876	2 890	1 639	1 935	2 568	3 430	2 265
1877	2 927	1 626	1 851	2 303	3 425	2 270
1878	2 991	1 555	1 818	2 331	3 403	2 281
1879	2 778	1 554	1 769	2 310	3 353	2 218
1880	3 046	1 588	1 846	2 450	3 477	2 298
1881	3 074	1 597	1 851	2 481	3 568	2 326
1882	3 117	1 593	1 924	2 400	3 643	2 392
1883	3 305	1 588	1 937	2 396	3 643	2 422
1884	3 328	1 611	1 976	2 657	3 622	2 425
1885	3 362	1 618	1 951	2 855	3 574	2 420
1886	3 374	1 616	1 929	2 956	3 600	2 446
1887	3 467	1 624	1 926	2 931	3 713	2 503
1888	3 544	1 690	1 971	2 990	3 849	2 553
1889	3 502	1 743	2 065	2 982	4 024	2 601
1890	3 323	1 777	2 086	3 182	4 009	2 643
1891	3 224	1 778	2 105	2 987	3 975	2 634
1892	3 240	1 806	2 144	3 207	3 846	2 630
1893	3 236	1 844	2 143	3 294	3 811	2 671
1894	3 273	1 832	2 171	3 179	4 029	2 742
1895	3 334	1 827	2 257	3 488	4 118	2 789
1896	3 166	1 857	2 367	3 536	4 249	2 863
1897	3 436	1 923	2 429	3 675	4 264	2 867
1898	3 460	1 900	2 457	3 697	4 428	2 973
1899	3 465	1 927	2 491	3 835	4 567	3 058
1900	3 424	1 937	2 561	3 833	4 492	3 077
1901	3 440	1 967	2 515	3 745	4 450	3 044
1902	3 543	1 990	2 496	3 783	4 525	3 051
1903	3 562	1 971	2 669	3 662	4 440	3 094
1904	3 535	1 961	2 680	3 808	4 428	3 122
1905	3 594	1 974	2 691	3 913	4 520	3 180
1906	3 669	2 037	2 845	4 206	4 631	3 252
1907	3 622	2 104	2 885	4 193	4 679	3 354
1908	3 577	2 157	2 853	4 078	4 449	3 308
1909	3 660	2 195	2 808	4 240	4 511	3 381
1910	3 789	2 256	2 980	4 331	4 611	3 380
1911	3 888	2 309	3 002	4 378	4 709	3 503
1912	3 955	2 392	3 064	4 373	4 762	3 605
1913	4 049	2 501	3 096	4 266	4 921	3 688
1914	3 868	2 530	3 048	4 233	4 927	3 440
1915	3 926	2 611	3 028	4 290	5 288	3 502
1916	3 956	2 669	2 968	4 277	5 384	3 633
1917	3 627	2 399	2 584	3 804	5 421	3 534
1918	3 352	2 286	2 532	3 798	5 459	3 431

Table 1c. **Per Capita GDP in 12 West European Countries, 1919-1969**
(1990 international Geary-Khamis dollars)

	Austria	Belgium	Denmark	Finland	France	Germany	Italy
1919	2 259	3 389	3 860	1 658	2 811	2 586	2 845
1920	2 412	3 962	3 992	1 846	3 227	2 796	2 587
1921	2 650	4 056	3 826	1 884	3 075	3 078	2 528
1922	2 877	4 413	4 166	2 058	3 610	3 331	2 631
1923	2 842	4 533	4 559	2 187	3 754	2 750	2 763
1924	3 163	4 638	4 528	2 224	4 179	3 199	2 765
1925	3 367	4 666	4 378	2 328	4 166	3 532	2 921
1926	3 413	4 784	4 598	2 392	4 249	3 605	2 926
1927	3 505	4 923	4 658	2 557	4 154	3 941	2 838
1928	3 657	5 139	4 785	2 707	4 431	4 090	3 016
1929	3 699	5 054	5 075	2 717	4 710	4 051	3 093
1930	3 586	4 979	5 341	2 666	4 532	3 973	2 918
1931	3 288	4 860	5 359	2 581	4 235	3 652	2 877
1932	2 940	4 607	5 169	2 550	3 959	3 362	2 948
1933	2 833	4 681	5 291	2 702	4 239	3 556	2 906
1934	2 852	4 624	5 402	2 988	4 192	3 858	2 894
1935	2 907	4 894	5 480	3 093	4 086	4 120	3 148
1936	2 995	4 913	5 575	3 279	4 244	4 451	3 130
1937	3 156	4 961	5 668	3 441	4 487	4 685	3 319
1938	3 559	4 832	5 762	3 589	4 466	4 994	3 316
1939	4 096	5 150	5 993	3 408	4 793	5 406	3 521
1940	3 959	4 562	5 116	3 220	4 042	5 403	3 505
1941	4 217	4 358	4 574	3 322	3 309	5 711	3 432
1942	3 983	3 997	4 629	3 327	2 981	5 740	3 369
1943	4 065	3 907	5 080	3 697	2 860	5 890	3 039
1944	4 152	4 112	5 543	3 685	2 422	6 084	2 463
1945	1 725	4 333	5 066	3 450	2 573	4 514	1 922
1946	1 956	4 574	5 777	3 683	3 855	2 217	2 502
1947	2 166	4 800	6 035	3 717	4 138	2 436	2 920
1948	2 764	5 024	6 133	3 957	4 393	2 834	3 063
1949	3 293	5 193	6 494	4 143	4 946	3 282	3 265
1950	3 706	5 462	6 943	4 253	5 271	3 881	3 502
1951	3 959	5 747	6 936	4 571	5 553	4 206	3 738
1952	3 967	5 668	6 955	4 674	5 659	4 553	3 997
1953	4 137	5 818	7 292	4 652	5 783	4 905	4 260
1954	4 555	6 029	7 371	5 002	6 020	5 247	4 449
1955	5 053	6 280	7 395	5 197	6 312	5 797	4 676
1956	5 397	6 422	7 439	5 295	6 568	6 177	4 859
1957	5 716	6 495	7 965	5 490	6 890	6 492	5 118
1958	5 907	6 442	8 095	5 474	6 988	6 737	5 360
1959	6 051	6 608	8 637	5 754	7 116	7 177	5 653
1960	6 519	6 952	8 812	6 230	7 546	7 705	5 916
1961	6 827	7 253	9 312	6 658	7 875	7 952	6 373
1962	6 950	7 583	9 747	6 819	8 232	8 222	6 827
1963	7 186	7 862	9 732	6 994	8 536	8 386	7 262
1964	7 567	8 341	10 560	7 307	9 005	8 822	7 487
1965	7 734	8 559	10 953	7 670	9 361	9 199	7 598
1966	8 112	8 776	11 160	7 824	9 750	9 388	7 942
1967	8 297	9 072	11 437	7 947	10 123	9 397	8 454
1968	8 621	9 416	11 837	8 093	10 493	9 864	9 105
1969	9 131	10 018	12 531	8 878	11 127	10 440	9 566

Table 1c. **Per Capita GDP in 12 West European Countries, 1919-1969**
(1990 international Geary-Khamis dollars)

	Netherlands	Norway	Sweden	Switzerland	United Kingdom	12 WEC
1919	4 122	2 647	2 669	4 060	4 870	**3 245**
1920	4 220	2 780	2 802	4 314	4 548	**3 305**
1921	4 431	2 518	2 674	4 208	4 439	**3 313**
1922	4 599	2 784	2 906	4 618	4 637	**3 582**
1923	4 635	2 826	3 047	4 874	4 760	**3 513**
1924	4 895	2 796	3 130	5 039	4 921	**3 771**
1925	5 031	2 949	3 233	5 388	5 144	**3 951**
1926	5 358	2 996	3 404	5 626	4 936	**3 974**
1927	5 504	3 098	3 500	5 892	5 315	**4 132**
1928	5 720	3 188	3 656	6 171	5 357	**4 293**
1929	5 689	3 472	3 869	6 332	5 503	**4 387**
1930	5 603	3 712	3 937	6 246	5 441	**4 289**
1931	5 185	3 404	3 782	5 943	5 138	**4 041**
1932	5 035	3 609	3 666	5 710	5 148	**3 896**
1933	4 956	3 674	3 721	5 966	5 277	**4 023**
1934	4 805	3 771	3 991	5 952	5 608	**4 167**
1935	4 929	3 912	4 232	5 907	5 799	**4 326**
1936	5 190	4 130	4 465	5 908	6 035	**4 512**
1937	5 433	4 255	4 664	6 171	6 218	**4 717**
1938	5 250	4 337	4 725	6 390	6 266	**4 818**
1939	5 544	4 516	5 029	6 360	6 262	**5 071**
1940	4 831	4 088	4 857	6 397	6 856	**4 984**
1941	4 531	4 163	4 914	6 312	7 482	**5 050**
1942	4 107	3 976	5 179	6 107	7 639	**4 996**
1943	3 981	3 867	5 360	6 001	7 744	**4 994**
1944	2 649	3 631	5 484	6 089	7 405	**4 778**
1945	2 686	4 029	5 568	7 752	7 056	**4 154**
1946	4 457	4 409	6 102	8 181	6 745	**3 921**
1947	5 048	4 855	6 175	9 050	6 604	**4 133**
1948	5 490	5 182	6 292	9 116	6 746	**4 388**
1949	5 880	5 230	6 455	8 757	6 956	**4 718**
1950	5 996	5 463	6 739	9 064	6 939	**5 018**
1951	6 032	5 663	6 949	9 684	7 123	**5 272**
1952	6 084	5 809	6 996	9 630	7 091	**5 428**
1953	6 543	6 018	7 145	9 840	7 346	**5 684**
1954	6 907	6 254	7 402	10 287	7 619	**5 959**
1955	7 326	6 314	7 566	10 867	7 868	**6 302**
1956	7 499	6 581	7 797	11 439	7 929	**6 535**
1957	7 614	6 710	8 092	11 705	8 017	**6 780**
1958	7 482	6 590	8 083	11 297	7 966	**6 886**
1959	7 737	6 871	8 288	11 870	8 240	**7 184**
1960	8 287	7 208	8 688	12 457	8 645	**7 607**
1961	8 202	7 584	9 137	13 099	8 857	**7 914**
1962	8 639	7 738	9 469	13 354	8 865	**8 191**
1963	8 832	7 979	9 917	13 710	9 149	**8 469**
1964	9 437	8 300	10 515	14 191	9 568	**8 886**
1965	9 798	8 677	10 815	14 504	9 752	**9 160**
1966	9 936	8 940	10 936	14 727	9 885	**9 404**
1967	10 341	9 427	11 219	15 010	10 049	**9 654**
1968	10 894	9 557	11 561	15 374	10 410	**10 099**
1969	11 462	9 904	12 055	16 031	10 552	**10 583**

Table 1c. **Per Capita GDP in 12 West European Countries, 1970-2001**
(1990 international Geary-Khamis dollars)

	Austria	Belgium	Denmark	Finland	France	Germany	Italy
1970	9 747	10 611	12 686	9 577	11 664	10 839	9 719
1971	10 200	10 970	12 934	9 765	12 110	11 077	9 839
1972	10 771	11 503	13 538	10 448	12 539	11 481	10 060
1973	11 235	12 170	13 945	11 085	13 114	11 966	10 634
1974	11 658	12 643	13 751	11 361	13 409	12 063	11 046
1975	11 646	12 441	13 621	11 441	13 251	12 041	10 742
1976	12 201	13 122	14 466	11 358	13 773	12 684	11 385
1977	12 767	13 190	14 655	11 355	14 230	13 072	11 668
1978	12 731	13 554	14 826	11 559	14 566	13 455	12 064
1979	13 448	13 861	15 313	12 332	14 970	13 993	12 720
1980	13 759	14 467	15 227	12 949	15 106	14 114	13 149
1981	13 718	14 279	15 096	13 134	15 183	14 149	13 200
1982	13 962	14 474	15 563	13 485	15 483	14 040	13 252
1983	14 396	14 474	15 966	13 767	15 602	14 329	13 391
1984	14 442	14 833	16 676	14 107	15 746	14 783	13 719
1985	14 757	14 977	17 384	14 522	15 901	15 140	14 096
1986	15 086	15 195	17 993	14 819	16 215	15 469	14 496
1987	15 319	15 541	18 023	15 382	16 553	15 701	14 946
1988	15 762	16 252	18 224	16 088	17 205	16 160	15 523
1989	16 369	16 744	18 261	16 946	17 730	16 558	15 969
1990	16 905	17 197	18 452	16 866	18 093	15 929	16 313
1991	17 272	17 480	18 661	15 725	18 164	16 604	16 539
1992	17 290	17 690	18 837	15 120	18 330	16 847	16 637
1993	17 218	17 361	18 933	14 876	18 059	16 554	16 436
1994	17 570	17 825	19 956	15 398	18 332	16 884	16 754
1995	17 887	18 255	20 585	15 925	18 558	17 125	17 215
1996	18 213	18 438	20 981	16 511	18 686	17 212	17 377
1997	18 462	19 048	21 528	17 511	18 961	17 425	17 686
1998	19 075	19 443	21 981	18 401	19 542	17 764	17 990
1999	19 561	19 984	22 415	19 105	20 099	18 076	18 264
2000	20 097	20 742	23 010	20 235	20 808	18 596	18 740
2001	20 225	20 924	23 161	20 344	21 092	18 677	19 040

Table 1c. **Per Capita GDP in 12 West European Countries, 1970-2001**
(1990 international Geary-Khamis dollars)

	Netherlands	Norway	Sweden	Switzerland	United Kingdom	12 WEC
1970	11 967	10 033	12 716	16 904	10 767	**10 959**
1971	12 319	10 423	12 748	17 381	10 941	**11 216**
1972	12 597	10 878	13 002	17 774	11 294	**11 589**
1973	13 081	11 247	13 494	18 204	12 025	**12 156**
1974	13 497	11 758	13 885	18 414	11 859	**12 344**
1975	13 374	12 180	14 183	17 224	11 847	**12 227**
1976	13 885	12 949	14 282	17 170	12 115	**12 736**
1977	14 177	13 356	14 004	17 635	12 384	**13 059**
1978	14 424	13 909	14 207	17 662	12 828	**13 414**
1979	14 647	14 461	14 721	18 050	13 167	**13 896**
1980	14 705	15 129	14 937	18 779	12 931	**14 057**
1981	14 525	15 222	14 917	18 956	12 747	**14 045**
1982	14 291	15 193	15 058	18 560	12 955	**14 130**
1983	14 483	15 679	15 315	18 559	13 404	**14 379**
1984	14 900	16 553	15 908	19 036	13 720	**14 728**
1985	15 283	17 365	16 189	19 584	14 165	**15 077**
1986	15 617	17 925	16 521	19 784	14 742	**15 465**
1987	15 737	18 204	16 982	19 788	15 393	**15 837**
1988	16 044	18 086	17 283	20 239	16 110	**16 388**
1989	16 695	18 177	17 593	20 931	16 414	**16 824**
1990	17 262	18 466	17 695	21 482	16 430	**16 872**
1991	17 519	18 953	17 379	21 051	16 136	**17 049**
1992	17 747	19 460	17 017	20 788	16 088	**17 153**
1993	17 764	19 874	16 550	20 504	16 416	**17 026**
1994	18 209	20 846	17 139	20 452	17 082	**17 438**
1995	18 527	21 536	17 658	20 421	17 495	**17 778**
1996	18 992	22 477	17 785	20 393	17 891	**17 994**
1997	19 629	23 397	18 143	20 696	18 459	**18 369**
1998	20 353	23 826	18 787	21 145	18 925	**18 820**
1999	20 992	23 942	19 624	21 440	19 291	**19 229**
2000	21 591	24 364	20 321	22 025	19 817	**19 806**
2001	21 721	24 577	20 562	22 263	20 127	**20 024**

Table 1c. **Per Capita GDP in 4 West European Countries and Average WEC, 1500-1868**
(1990 international Geary-Khamis dollars)

	Ireland[a]	Greece	Portugal	Spain	13 small WEC	29 WEC
1500	526	433	606	661	612	**771**
1600	615	483	740	853	698	**890**
1700	715	530	819	853	789	**998**
1820	877	641	923	1 008	956	**1 204**
1821						
1822						
1823						
1824						
1825						
1826						
1827						
1828						
1829						
1830						
1831						
1832						
1833						
1834						
1835						
1836						
1837						
1838						
1839						
1840						
1841						
1842						
1843						
1844						
1845						
1846						
1847						
1848						
1849						
1850		816	923	1 079	1 273	**1 574**
1851			991	1 089		
1852				1 133		
1853				1 136		
1854				1 150		
1855			919	1 202		
1856				1 163		
1857				1 132		
1858				1 153		
1859				1 200		
1860				1 236		
1861			883	1 248		
1862				1 252		
1863				1 277		
1864				1 274		
1865			891	1 230		
1866			920	1 290		
1867			941	1 283		
1868			945	1 149		

Table 1c. **Per Capita GDP in 4 West European Countries and Average WEC, 1869-1918**
(1990 international Geary-Khamis dollars)

	Ireland[a]	Greece	Portugal	Spain	13 small WEC	29 WEC
1869			964	1 181		
1870	1 775	880	975	1 207	1 602	**1 960**
1871			933	1 298		
1872			954	1 473		
1873			988	1 598		
1874			966	1 459		
1875			959	1 496		
1876			932	1 519		
1877			969	1 668		
1878			964	1 618		
1879			959	1 520		
1880			947	1 646		
1881			970	1 679		
1882			992	1 692		
1883			1 008	1 720		
1884			1 034	1 716		
1885			1 052	1 661		
1886			1 100	1 617		
1887			1 114	1 585		
1888			1 118	1 641		
1889			1 088	1 630		
1890		1 178	1 128	1 624	2 028	**2 490**
1891			1 099	1 654		
1892			1 087	1 770		
1893			1 101	1 700		
1894			1 079	1 712		
1895			1 117	1 689		
1896			1 125	1 548		
1897			1 182	1 619		
1898			1 214	1 736		
1899			1 249	1 756		
1900		1 351	1 302	1 786	2 361	**2 893**
1901			1 269	1 901		
1902			1 266	1 833		
1903			1 273	1 829		
1904			1 279	1 810		
1905			1 233	1 777		
1906			1 231	1 851		
1907			1 249	1 896		
1908			1 219	1 957		
1909			1 208	1 977		
1910			1 228	1 895		
1911			1 242	2 017		
1912			1 257	1 989		
1913	2 736	1 592	1 250	2 056	2 830	**3 458**
1914			1 258	2 014	2 639	
1915			1 228	2 033	2 687	
1916			1 234	2 113	2 788	
1917			1 212	2 073	2 712	
1918			1 150	2 045	2 633	

a.   Figures are shown here for Ireland 1500-1920 for information. They are not included in the total because the UK figures already include the whole of Ireland for 1500-1920, thereafter only the Northern Ireland province.

Table 1c. **Per Capita GDP in 4 West European Countries and Average WEC, 1919-1969**
(1990 international Geary-Khamis dollars)

	Ireland [b]	Greece	Portugal	Spain	13 small WEC	29 WEC
1919			1 173	2 044	2 490	
1920			1 229	2 177	2 536	
1921	2 533	1 918	1 290	2 212	2 402	3 130
1922	2 598	1 963	1 430	2 284	2 749	3 372
1923	2 575	1 988	1 473	2 290	2 696	3 314
1924	2 569	2 057	1 401	2 331	2 894	3 539
1925	2 573	2 140	1 446	2 451	3 032	3 706
1926	2 572	2 180	1 419	2 417	3 049	3 723
1927	2 653	2 220	1 648	2 600	3 171	3 880
1928	2 737	2 234	1 470	2 584	3 294	4 013
1929	2 824	2 342	1 610	2 739	3 366	4 111
1930	2 897	2 258	1 571	2 620	3 291	4 014
1931	2 972	2 134	1 631	2 529	3 101	3 793
1932	2 885	2 289	1 643	2 559	3 198	3 675
1933	2 800	2 395	1 732	2 486	3 087	3 779
1934	2 882	2 418	1 784	2 556	3 198	3 909
1935	2 966	2 480	1 669	2 583	3 320	4 045
1936	3 052	2 455	1 523	2 072	3 462	4 162
1937	2 957	2 769	1 757	1 808	3 620	4 317
1938	3 052	2 677	1 747	1 790	3 697	4 399
1939	3 052	2 638	1 749	1 915	3 891	4 624
1940	3 052	2 223	1 615	2 080	3 824	4 548
1941	3 052	1 874	1 747	2 030	3 874	4 589
1942	3 052	1 579	1 708	2 126	3 834	4 544
1943	3 052	1 327	1 806	2 188	3 832	4 542
1944	3 052	1 116	1 893	2 271	3 666	4 361
1945	3 019	938	1 804	2 102	3 188	3 806
1946	3 052	1 386	1 928	2 179	3 009	3 628
1947	3 092	1 763	2 071	2 198	3 171	3 824
1948	3 230	1 798	2 046	2 186	3 367	4 039
1949	3 404	1 869	2 057	2 155	3 620	4 319
1950	3 453	1 915	2 086	2 189	3 846	4 579
1951	3 544	2 062	2 168	2 386	3 722	4 816
1952	3 642	2 053	2 161	2 558	3 964	4 963
1953	3 747	2 309	2 298	2 528	4 090	5 186
1954	3 794	2 358	2 393	2 696	4 178	5 437
1955	3 920	2 514	2 475	2 778	4 375	5 740
1956	3 897	2 706	2 564	2 978	4 604	5 962
1957	3 914	2 859	2 659	3 046	4 737	6 181
1958	3 870	2 963	2 672	3 150	4 796	6 282
1959	4 038	3 040	2 794	3 050	4 923	6 530
1960	4 282	3 146	2 956	3 072	4 988	6 896
1961	4 508	3 393	3 119	3 436	5 169	7 203
1962	4 636	3 499	3 330	3 800	5 361	7 483
1963	4 821	3 841	3 504	4 151	5 585	7 767
1964	4 986	4 141	3 718	4 515	5 779	8 167
1965	5 051	4 509	3 992	4 762	6 135	8 441
1966	5 080	4 749	4 164	5 060	6 379	8 686
1967	5 352	4 951	4 481	5 334	6 579	8 936
1968	5 770	5 266	4 873	5 588	6 739	9 355
1969	6 089	5 766	4 987	6 032	7 154	9 825

b.   From 1921 the figures refer to the Irish Republic.

68

Table 1c. **Per Capita GDP in 4 West European Countries and Average WEC, 1970-2001**
(1990 international Geary-Khamis dollars)

	Ireland	Greece	Portugal	Spain	13 small WEC	29 WEC
1970	6 199	6 211	5 473	6 319	7 399	**10 195**
1971	6 354	6 624	5 871	6 618	7 841	**10 465**
1972	6 663	7 400	6 355	7 099	8 256	**10 860**
1973	6 867	7 655	7 063	7 661	8 627	**11 416**
1974	7 042	7 350	7 048	8 149	8 560	**11 611**
1975	7 316	7 722	6 517	8 346	8 357	**11 521**
1976	7 302	8 105	6 814	8 599	8 900	**11 983**
1977	7 795	8 255	7 166	8 833	9 415	**12 289**
1978	8 250	8 695	7 340	9 023	9 830	**12 621**
1979	8 366	8 904	7 733	9 068	10 221	**13 041**
1980	8 541	8 971	8 044	9 203	10 436	**13 197**
1981	8 716	8 896	8 114	9 186	10 582	**13 185**
1982	8 821	8 876	8 280	9 293	10 834	**13 270**
1983	8 740	8 860	8 255	9 478	11 026	**13 491**
1984	9 056	9 058	8 089	9 571	11 525	**13 794**
1985	9 306	9 304	8 306	9 722	11 858	**14 113**
1986	9 265	9 425	8 641	9 998	12 381	**14 476**
1987	9 698	9 357	9 185	10 520	12 824	**14 857**
1988	10 234	9 763	9 868	11 046	13 453	**15 406**
1989	10 880	10 086	10 372	11 582	14 080	**15 856**
1990	11 818	9 988	10 826	12 055	14 452	**15 966**
1991	11 969	10 172	11 095	12 294	14 784	**16 152**
1992	12 277	10 170	11 310	12 351	14 952	**16 256**
1993	12 538	9 952	11 136	12 183	15 424	**16 129**
1994	13 198	10 105	11 385	12 437	15 805	**16 517**
1995	14 445	10 290	11 700	12 756	16 145	**16 860**
1996	15 472	10 511	12 097	13 045	16 557	**17 097**
1997	16 978	10 870	12 557	13 562	17 192	**17 502**
1998	18 233	11 212	13 106	14 129	17 847	**17 974**
1999	19 981	11 571	13 548	14 696	18 501	**18 413**
2000	22 015	12 044	14 022	15 269	19 401	**19 002**
2001	23 201	12 511	14 229	15 659	19 859	**19 256**

HS–2: Western Offshoots: 1500–2001
(Australia, Canada, New Zealand, and the United States)

These four countries have experienced much more rapid growth since 1820 than Western Europe or the rest of the world. Between 1820 and 2001 their combined population increased 35–fold, compared with less than 3–fold in Western Europe. Their GDP increased 679–fold compared with 47–fold in Western Europe. Average per capita GDP (in terms of 1990 international dollars) rose from $1 202 to $26 943; Western Europe's from $1 204 to $19 256.

The disparity was due partly to huge differences in natural resource endowment. In 1820, land per head of population in France, Germany and the United Kingdom averaged 1.5 hectares compared to 240 hectares in the Western Offshoots. Their growth was facilitated by large–scale immigration, foreign investment and distance from foreign wars. They inherited institutional arrangements and traditions which gave them political stability, a fair degree of social mobility, relatively high levels of education, secure property rights, and a willingness to use market forces, which were more favourable to growth than was the case of the Iberian offshoots in Latin America.

Table 2-1. **Population and GDP of Australia, 1700-1870**

	Population (000)			GDP (million 1990 international $)			Per capita GDP (international $)		
	European	Aboriginal	Total	European	Aboriginal	Total	European	Aboriginal	Average
1700	0	450	450	0	180	180		400	400
1820	34	300	334	53	120	173	1 559	400	518
1830	70	260	330	176	104	280	2 514	400	848
1840	190	230	420	485	92	577	2 553	400	1 374
1850	405	200	605	1 115	80	1 195	2 951	400	1 975
1860	1 146	180	1 326	3 766	72	3 838	3 349	400	2 894
1870	1 620	155	1 775	5 748	62	5 810	3 548	400	3 273

Table 2-2. **Population and GDP of the United States, 1700-1870**

	Population (000)			GDP (million 1990 international $)			Per capita GDP (international $)		
	European and African	Indigenous	Total	European and African	Indigenous	Total	European and African	Indigenous	Average
1700	250	750	1 000	227	300	527	909	400	527
1820	9 656	325	9 981	12 418	130	12 548	1 286	400	1 257
1830	12 951	289	13 240	18 103	116	18 219	1 398	400	1 376
1840	17 187	257	17 444	27 591	103	27 694	1 605	400	1 588
1850	23 352	228	23 580	42 492	91	42 583	1 820	400	1 806
1860	31 636	203	31 839	69 265	81	69 346	2 189	400	2 178
1870	40 061	180	40 241	98 302	72	98 374	2 454	400	2 445

In the past, most measures of their performance have concentrated on the economies created by European settlement, and disregarded the fact that they displaced and destroyed indigenous economies whose output and populations contracted. I have attempted to provide a crude measure of this disruptive impact up to 1870, estimating what Noel Butlin called a "multicultural" estimate of GDP. For the indigenous economies the population figures are rough and the per capita GDP estimates are stylised. For the settler economies the estimates are at least as good as those for Western Europe.

Australia: Australia has a distinguished record of national income measurement. It was the first country with official estimates.. They were started in 1886 by Timothy Coghlan (1857–1926), government statistician for New South Wales who published estimates of the *Wealth and Progress of New South Wales* as well as a *Statistical Abstract for the Seven Colonies of Australasia* covering New Zealand and the six colonies which became the constituent states of Australia. Publication was discontinued in 1905 when he accepted a diplomatic post as agent general for New South Wales in London, and official national accounts did not reappear until 1946. Bryan Haig is the custodian of the Coghlan archive, and has written an as yet unpublished memoir on Coghlan's work "The First Official National Accounting Estimates" (see also Heinz Arndt, "A Pioneer of National Income Estimates", *Economic Journal*, December, 1949).

In 1938, Colin Clark (1905–89) and John Crawford (1910-84) published estimates of income and product for the 1920s and 30s, annual estimates of real income for 1914–39, and rough estimates of productivity for some years back to 1886 (see their *National Income of Australia*, Angus and Robertson, Sydney, 1938). Clark used this material in the first edition of *Conditions of Economic Progress*, 1940, pp. 84–5, improved on it in the 1951 edition, pp. 140–1, and modified his estimates showing faster growth of real product for 1914–38 in the 1957 edition, pp. 90–7 (see Table 2–4).

Noel Butlin (1921–91) published a continuous stream of studies on the quantitative economic history of Australia from 1946 onwards (see Graeme Snooks, "Life and Work of Noel George Butlin", *Australian Economic History Review*, September 1991). He was an admirer of Kuznets and much of his work is in the Kuznetsian tradition with meticulous indication of sources and transparent explanation of methodology. His first major book (1962) provided annual estimates of GDP, GNP, net domestic and net national product from 1861 to1938/9. It showed nominal and real value added by industry of origin at factor cost and market prices, together with very detailed estimates of capital formation and the balance of payments on current and capital account. It contained more than 200 pages describing his sources and estimating procedures, and 274 tables.

As Butlin's work covered the whole span of Australian history, I relied heavily on his estimates in Maddison (1995 and 2001). 1820 to 1828 GDP movement was derived from N.G. Butlin, "Our 200 Years", *Queensland Calendar*, 1988. 1828–60 annual GDP volume movement by eight industries of origin at 1848–50 prices from N.G. Butlin, "Contours of the Australian Economy 1788–1860", *Australian Economic History Review*, Sept. 1986, pp. 96–147. Annual GDP movement 1861–1938/9, by 13 industries of origin in 1910/11 prices from N.G. Butlin, *Australian Domestic Product, Investment and Foreign Borrowing 1861–1938/39*, Cambridge, 1962, pp. 460–l; amended as indicated in N.G. Butlin, *Investment in Australian Economic Development l861–1900*, Cambridge, 1964, p. 453, with revised deflator for 1911–1938/9 shown in M.W. Butlin, *A Preliminary Annual Database 1900/01 to 1973/74*, Discussion Paper 7701, Reserve Bank of Australia, May 1977, p.41. 1938/9–1950 real expenditure aggregates in 1966/7 prices from M.W. Butlin, p. 85. 1860–1 link derived by using the GDP deflator in W. Vamplew (ed.), *Australians: Historical Statistics*, Fairfax, Broadway, 1987, p. 219. 1950 onwards from OECD sources. Where necessary, GDP figures were adjusted to a calendar year basis. Population 1788–1949 from Butlin (1988), adjusted to a calendar year basis from 1870. Butlin's estimate of the pre–contact population is much higher than is conventional (1.1 million instead of 300 000). His analysis of the destructive impact of white settlement makes it difficult to accept the conventional estimate, but his depopulation coefficient seems exaggerated. As a compromise, I assumed a pre–contact population of 450 000, 1820–70 from L.R. Smith, *The Aboriginal Population of Australia*, ANU, Canberra, 1980, p. 210.

Recently, Bryan Haig rejected Butlin's estimates *en bloc* (see his "New Estimates of Australian GDP: 1861–1948/49", *Australian Economic History Review*, March 2001, pp. 1–34). He argues that Butlin's approach (deflation of nominal estimates of value added by price indices) is "unworkable" because of the weakness of existing price indices, and the inherent difficulty of improving them; Butlin "relied on existing series of wholesale prices, wage rates and retail price indices", and "no useful research has been undertaken by academics on Australian price indices since Butlin produced his estimates". Butlin did not take his price indices from the shelf, but constructed ten special deflators for sectors of GDP, and eight for components of capital investment. Butlin's deflators are imperfect but improvable. Australian academics have not abandoned the field (see Ian McLean and S.J. Woodland "Consumer Prices in Australia, 1850–1914" *Working Paper 92–4*, Economics Dept, University of Adelaide, 1992), and Australia seems better endowed with historical price statistics than many other countries (see Shergold's chapter in Vamplew,1987).

Haig's second fundamental objection is that Butlin's results are "unreasonable" as they show contours of development which conflict with traditional views and generated a new interpretation of Australian economic history. I see no harm in this. It is up to those who disagree with Butlin to prove him wrong.

Table 2-3. **Alternative Measures of Australian Sector Growth and Structure, 1861-1938/9**

	Confrontation of Butlin (1962) and Haig (2001) Estimates							
	Annual Growth % 1861-1911		1891 level: million 1891 pounds		Annual Growth % 1911/12-1938/9		1938/9 level: million 1938/9 pounds	
	Butlin	Haig	Butlin	Haig	Butlin	Haig	Butlin	Haig
Pastoral	4.81	4.30	29.5	28.7	1.39	0.96	74.5	63.2
Agriculture	3.39	3.81	10.5	15.3	1.13	2.38	41.7	41.2
Dairy	3.69	3.96	9.7	6.8	3.54	2.64	49.3	40.8
Mining	1.83	1.98	11.3	12.0	-2.21	-0.60	27.9	27.1
Manufacturing	6.13	3.72	21.3	29.5	2.01	2.43	157.0	198.0
Construction	3.01	2.37	28.4	15.1	0.34	2.27	56.2	65.0
Water Transport	4.56	n.a.	3.6	n.a.	-0.41	n.a.	7.9	n.a.
Public Undertakings	5.88	n.a.	6.8	n.a.	1.06	n.a.	45.5	n.a.
Public services	1.99	n.a.	8.5	n.a.	2.62	n.a.	40.7	n.a.
Finance	1.55	n.a.	6.7	n.a.	2.73	n.a.	21.1	n.a.
Distribution	4.33	n.a.	23.9	n.a.	2.40	n.a.	159.8	n.a.
Other services	3.16	n.a.	22.5	n.a.	0.89	n.a.	91.0	n.a.
Total Services	**3.63**	**3.33**	**72.0**	**52.0**	**1.77**	**2.35**	**366.0**	**291.0**
Imputed Rent	3.34	3.27	21.9	18.3	2.20	2.19	72.0	60.0
Unallocated	4.91	n.a.	1.8	0.0	2.93	n.a.	-4.1	0.0
GDP	**3.67**	**3.34**	**202.8**	**177.8**	**1.58**	**2.09**	**840.5**	**797.0**
GDP New South Wales	n.a.	4.00	n.a.	57.3				
GDP Victoria	n.a.	2.06	n.a.	53.3				

Source: Columns 1 and 5 from Butlin, pp. 160-1. Butlin shows fiscal years (beginning July 1st) from 1901/2 onwards, Haig from 1911/2 onwards. 1911 calendar year for Butlin derived by averaging his estimates for 1910/11 and 1911/12. Columns 2 and 6 from Haig, pp. 28-34. Columns 3 and 7 from Butlin, pp. 10-11. Columns 4 and 8 from Haig, pp. 28-34.

Table 2-4. **Alternative Estimates of Australian Real GDP, calendar years 1861-1900**
(million 1990 international Geary-Khamis dollars)

	Haig	Butlin		Haig	Butlin	Clark
1861	4 453	4 188	1901	17 764	16 201	
1862	4 625	4 133	1902	16 905	16 366	
1863	4 750	4 271	1903	18 436	17 661	
1864	4 867	4 739	1904	17 733	18 846	
1865	5 132	4 711	1905	19 038	19 066	
1866	5 539	5 014	1906	19 741	20 361	
1867	5 515	5 621	1907	19 936	21 187	
1868	5 929	5 896	1908	20 694	21 904	
1869	6 101	5 951	1909	21 608	23 695	
1870	5 898	6 392	1910	22 662	25 348	
1871	6 210	6 144	1911	22 967	25 541	
1872	6 484	6 805	1912	23 764	26 147	
1873	6 656	7 522	1913	24 861	27 552	
1874	7 187	7 770	1914	24 797	25 430	21 294
1875	7 398	8 624	1915	24 341	23 943	20 782
1876	7 593	8 596	1916	24 172	25 623	19 902
1877	7 796	8 954	1917	23 716	26 202	17 519
1878	7 976	9 809	1918	23 155	26 340	16 138
1879	8 249	9 946	1919	24 488	26 092	17 819
1880	8 421	10 470	1920	25 534	28 075	19 969
1881	8 929	11 241	1921	26 818	30 831	22 263
1882	9 702	10 608	1922	28 225	31 051	25 058
1883	10 694	12 178	1923	29 579	31 685	27 275
1884	11 132	12 233	1924	31 524	34 109	29 324
1885	11 296	13 032	1925	33 002	35 239	30 872
1886	11 702	13 197	1926	33 792	34 798	32 587
1887	12 265	14 603	1927	34 305	34 716	34 068
1888	12 546	14 685	1928	34 368	34 164	34 759
1889	13 702	15 953	1929	33 662	33 834	34 848
1890	13 772	15 402	1930	30 458	32 181	33 411
1891	13 890	16 586	1931	28 416	32 720	31 406
1892	13 640	14 547	1932	30 025	31 878	31 640
1893	13 663	13 748	1933	32 110	33 696	31 199
1894	13 819	14 217	1934	33 810	34 991	34 603
1895	14 015	13 418	1935	35 798	36 424	35 427
1896	14 288	14 437	1936	37 414	38 160	36 195
1897	15 147	13 638	1937	39 306	40 336	37 509
1898	15 749	15 760	1938	40 639	40 639	40 639
1899	16 592	15 760				
1900	17 186	16 697				

Source: Haig, pp. 28-30. He gives calendar year estimates for 1861-1911, fiscal years (beginning July 1st) for 1911/12 onwards. I adjusted the latter to a calendar year basis. For 1910/11, he presents no figures for the primary sector or GDP. To make the link between his two temporal segments, I used the 1910/11-1911/12 primary movement shown by Butlin. Clark (1957), pp. 90-1, real product adjusted to calendar year basis.

A more legitimate objection is that Butlin probably exaggerated the long boom from 1861 to 1891 by understating manufacturing employment and output at the beginning of the period. This is a point which Haig should have tackled more rigorously, showing his own employment estimates for Australian manufacturing and comparing them with those of Butlin (see Butlin and Dowie, "Estimates of Australian Work Force and Employment, 1861–1961", *Australian Economic History Review*, September, 1969). Instead he presents a comparison for the state of Victoria.

Haig's alternative to the Butlin approach is to use quantitative measures of output for seven sectors of GDP. This is a desirable crosscheck, but for 1861–1911 Haig does not have quantitative measures for 70 per cent of GDP, and uses employment (available in direct form only for NSW and Victoria) as a proxy. He amalgamates his sector estimates using 1891 output weights which Coghlan published in 1893. Although he makes a few comparisons between his results and those of Butlin they are limited and casual. A further problem is that Haig describes his estimating procedure parsimoniously in five pages whereas Butlin provided 200. Table 2–4 facilitates systematic confrontation of their sector growth rates and structure (Butlin's value added and Coghlan's gross output). Haig relies heavily on measures for New South Wales and Victoria to fill gaps in information for Australia as a whole, whereas Butlin covers a wider and perhaps more representative range of states. For 1861–1911, Haig's estimates imply per capita growth of 1.6 per cent a year in NSW, 0.42 in Victoria, and 0.57 per cent in Australia.

For 1911–12 to 1938–39, Haig's estimates are of better quality. He has quantity indicators for manufacturing from his "Manufacturing Output and Productivity, 1910 to 1948/9", *Australian Economic History Review*, September, 1975. For the rest of the economy he was able to adjust his employment indicators for productivity change. The weights from his "1938/9 National Income Estimates", *Australian Economic History Review*, 1967, p. 176, are also more satisfactory. I have now adopted Haig's estimates for 1911–38, but would like to see more detail of his evidence before adopting his estimates for 1861–1911.

All the above refers to the white settler economy. In the 1980s Butlin made a major innovation in proposing a "multicultural" estimate. In 1983 he published a masterpiece of demographic modelling (*Our Original Aggression*, Allen & Unwin, Sydney and London) analysing the impact of white settlement on the Aboriginal population and its economy, with detailed specification of the different vectors of mortality. This was similar in intent to studies by Borah and others on the impact of European conquest on the Americas, but Butlin was much more rigorous. His analysis of Aboriginal history was enlarged in *Economics and the Dreamtime: A Hypothetical History*, Cambridge University Press, 1993. A further posthumous work *Forming A Colonial Economy: Australia 1810–1850*, Cambridge University Press, appeared in 1994.

Canada: GDP and population of French–Canadian settlers in 1700 derived from Morris Altman, "Economic Growth in Canada, 1695–1739: Estimates and Analysis", *William and Mary Quarterly*, October 1988. 1820–50 per capita product of non–indigenous population assumed to grow at the same rate as in the United States. GDP for 1851, 1860 and 1870 from O.J. Firestone, "Canada's Changing Economy in the Second Half of the 19th Century", NBER, New York, 1957. 1870–1926 GDP from M.C. Urquhart and Associates, ed., *Gross National Product, Canada 1870–1926: The Derivation of the Estimates*, McGill Queen's University Press, Montreal, 1993, pp. 11–12 and 24–5. 1926–60 from Statistics Canada, *National Income and Expenditure Accounts*, vol. 1, *The Annual Estimates 1926–1974*, Ottawa, 1975, p. 323. 1960 onwards from OECD sources. 1820–1948 GDP raised by 1.32 per cent and population by 2.6 to include Newfoundland, acquired in 1949. Indigenous population before 1820 from same sources as for the United States. Population 1820–50 supplied by Marvin McInnis; 1850–1950 from M.C. Urquhart and K.A.H. Buckley, *Historical Statistics of Canada*, Cambridge, 1965, p. 14.

Table 2-5. **Population and GDP of Canada and New Zealand, 1700-1870**

	Population (000)			GDP (million 1990 international $)			Per capita GDP (international $)		
	European	Indigenous	Total	European	Indigenous	Total	European	Indigenous	Average
				Canada					
1700	15	185	200	12	74	86	800	400	430
1820	741	75	816	708	30	738	955	400	904
1830	1 101	68	1 169	1 142	27	1 169	1 038	400	1 000
1840	1 636	61	1 697	1 948	24	1 972	1 191	400	1 162
1850	2 430	55	2 485	3 282	22	3 304	1 351	400	1 330
1860	3 319	50	3 369	4 867	20	4 887	1 466	400	1 451
1870	3 736	45	3 781	6 389	18	6 407	1 710	400	1 695
				New Zealand					
1700	0	100	100	0	40	40		400	400
1820	0	100	100	0	40	40		400	400
1830	0	100	100	0	40	40		400	400
1840	0	70	70	0	28	28		400	400
1850	25	65	90	77	26	103	3 080	400	1 144
1860	76	56	132	270	22	292	3 553	400	2 212
1870	243	48	291	883	19	902	3 633	400	3 100

New Zealand: GNP, 1870–1939, in 1910/11 prices from K. Rankin, "New Zealand's Gross National Product: 1859–1939, *Review of Income and Wealth*, March 1992, pp. 60–1. These are proxy estimates based on regression involving assumptions about velocity of circulation, nominal money supply, a variety of price indices (wholesale, export, import, farm and non–farm) and population. 1939–50 from C. Clark, *The Conditions of Economic Progress*, third edition, Macmillan, London, 1957, pp. 171–2 (which Clark derived by deflating official estimates in current prices). 1950 onwards from OECD sources. GDP estimates are for calendar years to 1939 and fiscal years starting April 1st thereafter. For 1820–70 I assumed per capita income of Maoris to have been 400 international 1990 dollars. Per capita GDP of white settlers was assumed to have grown 0.8 per cent a year from 1850 to 1870 (the rate shown by Rankin for 1859–70). Maori population 1820–1919 and non–Maoris 1820–60 from G.R. Hawke, *The Making of New Zealand*, Cambridge University Press, 1985, pp. 10–11 and 20; 1861–1919 non–Maoris from Rankin (1992), pp. 58–9. 1920–49 population from UN, *Demographic Yearbook*, 1960, pp. 148–50.

United States: GDP Estimates

1700–1820: Robert Gallman, "The Pace and Pattern of American Economic Growth", in L. Davis and Associates (eds.), *American Economic Growth: An Economist's History of the United States*, Harper and Row, New York, 1972, estimated per capita growth in net national product of 0.42 per cent a year between 1710 and 1840 (taking the mid–point of the range he suggested for 1710). His figures refer to the neo–European economy of the white and black population. Adjusting for the faster growth of their per capita income in 1820–40 (see below), Gallman's estimate implies a per capita growth of about 0.29 per cent a year from 1700 to 1820 (from a level of $909 to $1 286). Assuming an unchanged per capita income of $400 a year in the indigenous hunter–gatherer economy, the average level for the whole population would have risen from $527 in 1700 to $1 257 in 1820.

P.C. Mancall and Weiss, "Was Econonmic Growth Likely in British North America?", *Journal of Economic History*, March 1999, made a "multicultural" estimate which shows much slower growth for the eighteenth century. I consider their growth rate to be much too slow, given the huge change in the relative size of the neo–European and indigenous populations. They show no figures for total population or GDP, so it is not possible to replicate their multicultural measure. They make no reference to the Gallman estimate I used.

1820–2001

Modern GDP estimation relies heavily on the massive contribution of Simon Kuznets. He took over the NBER research in this field around 1930, and also prepared the first official estimates, *National Income 1929–32*, which were transmitted to the Finance Committee of the US Senate by the Dept. of Commerce in January 1934. This showed the flows of different categories of income broken down by industry together with corresponding employment estimates prepared by Robert Nathan. A cost of living index was provided as a tentative deflator, together with very fully documented appendices with sources. This approach was further elaborated in S. Kuznets, *National Income and Its Composition 1919–38*, NBER, New York, 1941, which contained estimates (at current and 1929 prices) of the industrial distribution of different categories of income (wage, property, and entrepreneurial).

Kuznets also derived estimates by category of expenditure for 1919 onwards by the "commodity flow" method, i.e. he used census and other information on production, and determined what part represented the final flow to consumers and capital formation. These flows from producers were given distributive mark–ups to reflect final sales values. Rougher estimates were made for services. This work was sponsored by the Committee on Credit and Banking which was interested in commodity flows as a counterpart to its interest in flows of financial resources. The details of this approach are described in S. Kuznets, *Commodity Flow and Capital Formation*, NBER, New York, 1938. The expenditure estimates were extended back to 1869 in S. Kuznets, L. Epstein and E. Jenks, *National Product Since 1869*, NBER, New York, 1946 (but these referred to overlapping decades and were not annual). This extension back to 1869 relied very heavily on W.H. Shaw, *Value of Commodity Output Since 1869*, NBER, New York, 1947, who used the same procedure for making commodity flow estimates of values as Kuznets (1938) did. Shaw also supplied price deflators. Estimates in the same form can also be found (in an analytical context) in S. Kuznets, *Income and Wealth of the United States: Trends and Structure*, Income and Wealth Series II, Bowes and Bowes, Cambridge, 1952. This study contains an annex on the estimates for 1800 to 1870 by Martin and King. Kuznets had a poor opinion of these, and although he did not produce alternative estimates, he gave a clear indication of the direction in which they were biased, and some clues for constructing estimates with limited information.

The final version of Kuznets' massive work appeared in his *Capital in the American Economy*, NBER, Princeton, 1961. Here he published annual estimates of GNP by type of expenditure in current and in 1929 dollars (pp. 555–8) back to 1889. As the underlying census information was inadequate before 1889, he showed only 5–year moving averages back to 1871 (pp. 559–64). He had three variants of GNP with different assumptions about which products were intermediate.

The US Department of Commerce did not adopt the Kuznets' definitions of the scope of GNP. He explained his disagreement with their procedures in S. Kuznets, "Discussion of the New Department of Commerce Income Series", *Review of Economics and Statistics*, August 1948. The official side was not convinced by his arguments, see M. Gilbert, G. Jaszi, E.F. Denison and C.F. Schwartz, "Objectives of National Income Measurement: A Reply to Professor Kuznets" in the same publication.

The Kuznets estimates were published in transparent form with the full scholarly apparatus characteristic of the NBER. It was therefore possible for John Kendrick (who in any case had access to the worksheets) to convert the Kuznets annual estimates of GNP (variant III) back to 1889 (with some minor adjustment) by type of expenditure to a Dept. of Commerce basis, see J.W. Kendrick, *Productivity Trends in the United States*, NBER, Princeton, 1961, pp. 298–9. Like Kuznets, Kendrick used fixed

1929 weights for his volume estimates, but he also gave a chain weighted alternative, which for 1889–1929 shows a growth rate of 3.82 per cent a year compared with 3.68 for his fixed weight index for the private domestic economy (p. 327). For 1869–1889 Kendrick presented only decade averages, as it seemed probable that they exaggerated growth. Kendrick (1961) augmented the NBER sectoral production studies (by Barger, Fabricant and others) to show annual movements in output or value added on an annual basis back to 1869 in many cases. However, he did not construct an estimate of GDP by industry of origin. His aggregate (pp. 302–3) covers 9 production sectors in combination with total private GDP by type of expenditure. The bulk of private service activity was derived as a residual. Even then his estimates were presented only for 10 benchmark years. Thus we have the paradox that the United States is one of the few countries where the construction of historical accounts by industry of origin has been neglected, though the statistical basis for such estimates is better than elsewhere.

1820–40: For this period the evidence is still rather weak, and one must still rely on the kind of reasoning which Kuznets (1952) first applied, and which can be found in P.A. David, "The Growth of Real Product in the United States before 1840: New Evidence, Controlled Conjectures", *Journal of Economic History*, June 1967, and more recently in T. Weiss, "US Labor Force Estimates and Economic Growth, 1800–1860", in R.E. Gallman and J.J. Wallis, eds., *American Economic Growth and Standards of Living Before the Civil War*, University of Chicago Press, 1992, p. 27. I used a variant of the Kuznets–David inferential approach. I calculated agricultural productivity 1820–40, taking agricultural value added (output of crops and livestock products plus change in livestock inventories, minus intermediate products consumed) from M.W. Towne and W.D. Rasmussen, "Farm Gross Product and Gross Investment in the Nineteenth Century", in Parker, ed. (1960), p. 25, and agricultural employment from Weiss (1992), p. 51. Agricultural productivity (thus measured) grew by .62 per cent a year from 1820–40. Like Kuznets and David, I assumed that productivity growth in the rest of the economy was faster (1 per cent a year). Although service productivity growth is likely to have been modest, the assumption of faster growth in non–agriculture seems warranted as K.L. Sokoloff found manufacturing productivity to have grown by 2.2 per cent a year, see his "Productivity Growth in Manufacturing During Early Industrialisation: Evidence from the American Northeast, 1820–1860", in S.L. Engerman and R.E. Gallmann, *Long Term Factors in American Economic Growth*, Chicago, 1986, p. 695.

1840–69: derived from Robert Gallman who revised and extended the Kuznets estimates backwards (variant I) using the same commodity flow approach and techniques of presentation. He first estimated value added (in 1879 prices) for agriculture, mining, manufacturing and construction for benchmark years, see R.E. Gallman, "Commodity Output, 1839–1899", in W.N. Parker, *Trends in the American Economy in the Nineteenth Century*, NBER, Princeton, 1960, p. 43. He used these results, census, and other information to construct his estimates of GNP by type of expenditure (four–way breakdown of consumption and three–way breakdown of capital formation) in 1860 prices, see R.E. Gallman, "Gross National Product in the United States 1834–1909", in D.S. Brady, ed., *Output, Employment and Productivity in the United States after 1800*, NBER, New York, 1966, p. 26. Unfortunately he provided figures only for five benchmark years, 1839, 1844, 1849, 1854, and 1859 and for overlapping decades from 1834–43 to 1899–1908, and did not publish the full detail of his procedures.

1869–90: from N.S. Balke and R.J. Gordon, "The Estimation of Prewar Gross National Product: Methodology and New Evidence", *Journal of Political Economy*, February 1989, p. 84. They revamped the Gallman–Kendrick–Kuznets commodity flow estimates, using additional information on construction, transport and communications, to provide annual estimates of nominal GNP, real GNP and a GNP deflator. For 1869–90, their average annual estimate for real GNP growth was 4.16 per cent a year, which is lower than the unpublished Kendrick figure of 5.44 per cent, or the 5.55 per cent of Kuznets. As both Kuznets and Kendrick thought their 1869 level (as described above) was too low, the Balke–Gordon estimate seems acceptable.

1890–1929: GDP volume movement with 1929 weights from J.W. Kendrick (1961), pp. 298–9.

1929–50: GDP movement at 1987 prices as shown by the Bureau of Economic Analysis (BEA) in *National Income and Product Accounts of the United States*, vol. 1, US Dept. of Commerce, Washington, D.C., February 1993.

1950–2001: 1950–59 from "GDP and other Major NIPA Series, 1929–97", *Survey of Current Business*, August 1998; 1959–90 GDP movement and 1990 level in 1990 prices from E.P. Seskin, "Improved Estimates of the National Income and Product Accounts for 1958–98: Results of the Comprehensive Revision", *Survey of Current Business*, December 1999; 1990–8 from S.K.S. Lum, B.C. Moyer and R.E. Yuscavage, "Improved Estimates of Gross Product by Industry for 1947–98", *Survey of Current Business*, June 2000, p. 46; 1998–2001 from E.P. Seskin and S.M. McCulla, "Annual Revision of the National Income and Product Accounts", *Survey of Current Business*, August 2002, p. 11. Figures for years before 1960 are adjusted to include Alaska and Hawaii, which added 0.294 per cent to 1960 GDP (see *Survey of Current Business*, December 1980, p. 17).

Population: Indigenous population before 1820 from R. Thornton, *American Indian Holocaust and Survival: A Population History Since 1492*, University of Oklahoma, 1987 and D.H. Ubelaker, "Prehistoric New World Population Size: Historical Review and Current Appraisal of North American Estimates, *American Journal of Physical Anthropology*, 1976, pp. 661–6, as indicated in Maddison (2001), pp. 232–3. White and black population, 1630–1949 from *Historical Statistics of the United States, Colonial Times to 1970*, US Department of Commerce, 1975, pp. 8 and 1168. The figures refer to the present territory of the United States. 1820–1949 increased by 0.39 per cent to include Alaska and Hawaii, incorporated in l950. 1950–2001 from International Programs Center, US Bureau of the Census. In 1820, the territory of the United States was half of what it is today. The increase was due to the acquisition of Texas, California and other Western lands from Mexico between 1845 and 1853. The settlement of the border with Canada brought in the territory which is now Idaho, Oregon and Washington in 1846. These territories were sparsely settled and consisted very largely of the indigenous population which was not separately specified in US censuses before 1860. Before 1890 the censuses excluded those living in Indian territory or reservations. I added 325 000 for the indigenous population in 1820 and 180 000 for 1850, (see Maddison, 1995, p. 97).

Three Recent Modifications in US Official Measures of GDP

Annual Chain Indices for GDP: The official figures I use for 1950 onwards are based on a chain index as described in J.S. Landefeld and R.P. Parker, "BEA's Chain Indexes, Time Series and Measures of Long Term Growth", *Survey of Current Business*, May 1997. This is an index where the weights change every year. The annual GDP volume change is measured by a Fisher index which is the geometric mean of two indices, one of which (a Laspeyres index) uses the prices of year *t-1* as weights, and the other (a Paasche index) uses prices of year *t*. Annual changes calculated this way are multiplied together to form a time series. This procedure is a sharp break with the tradition of the Department of Commerce which for six decades used a fixed weight for the whole period it covered (though the chosen year was changed quinquennially). Before making the switch, BEA experimented with alternative weighting systems. A.H. Young, "Alternative Measures of Changes in Real Output and Prices, Quarterly Estimates for 1959–92", *Survey of Current Business*, March 1993 presented three alternative indices for 1959–92. The old fixed weight index showed a real GDP growth rate of 2.88 a year, the annual Fisher chain index 3.12 per cent and a Fisher index with weights changed every 5 years 3.16 a year. In Maddison (1995) I used the third measure because it was closer to the procedure used in other OECD countries at that time. BEA did not present these three options for earlier years as it announced. Instead it made a sudden switch to chain indexation back to 1929. The new measure shows a GDP growth of 3.5 per cent a year for 1929–50, the traditional measure 2.6 per cent. This is a much bigger difference between fixed and chain weights than Young found for 1959–92 or Kendrick for 1889–1929. Acceptance of the new measure for this period would involve a major reinterpretation of American economic history. It implies a GDP level in 1929 16 per cent lower than the old index and would lower the level for earlier years.

If used as a link, it would imply a US level of labour productivity in 1913 below that in the United Kingdom. The new BEA index also changes the picture of the war and immediate postwar recovery. It seems hazardous to use it for 1929–50 without further investigation of the reasons why the new method had such a big impact. One must also remember that no other country uses a chain index technique for such a long period in the past.

Hedonic Indices for the New Economy: A major reason why BEA switched to chain indexation was its adoption of "hedonic" price indices for computers and peripherals in 1985 and extended use of this type of measure back to 1959. By the year 2000, the components of GDP deflated by this technique represented 18 per cent of the total (see J.S. Landefeld and B.T. Grimm, "A Note on the Impact of Hedonics and Computers on Real GDP", *Survey of Current Business*, December 2000). This technique imputes quality improvements by specifying computing power in terms of several characteristics, e.g. speed, memory etc. and estimating price change by regression. The manufacturers of computers were understandably helpful in supplying detail of these improved characteristics and the application of hedonic techniques to the measuerement of computer prices was in fact pioneered by IBM. The hedonic measure implied that prices dropped 32 per cent a year from 1994 onwards. If this rate had prevailed for the 1990s, it would mean that a consumer who spent $1 000 on a computer in 1990 and again in 2000, would be getting sixteen times as much for his money in the latter year. Hedonic weights (advocated since 1961 by Zvi Griliches) are perfectly respectable, but one can be a bit sceptical about the assumption that quality change was so large and monotonically positive. The hedonic techniques used by BEA imply a direct connection between computing power (speed, memory etc.) and computer output without considering the quality of the software that converts power to output. In addition, hedonic techniques assume competitive markets where prices accurately reflect consumer utility, but recent anti–trust cases suggest that this assumption may be unrealistic. One would like to see a more rigorous and detailed examination of alternatives and a smaller dose of euphoric reassurance that the results are robust. However, adoption of annual chain weights helped moderate the accelerative impact of hedonic indices on GDP growth.

Treatment of Computer Software as Investment: A third innovation which raised the level of GDP modestly and raised the growth rate, was the decision to treat computer software as investment rather than as an intermediate product. This practice was introduced in 1999 and applied retrospectively to 1959. The average service life for such investment is assumed (rather generously) to be 3–5 years (see BEA, "Recognition of Software as Investment in the US National Accounts", *OECD Meeting of National Accounts Experts*, September 1999). The change was recommended in the 1993 revision of the *System of National Accounts* of EU, IMF, OECD and World Bank, and has been adopted by other OECD countries. Given the fact that hedonic indexation already makes generous allowance for quality change in computers which derive in large part from improved software, there is an element of double–counting in the new procedure. It is also a little odd to treat this rapidly depreciating advance in knowledge as investment, whilst ignoring the more durable impact of scientific academies. However, the hallowed status of computer technology seems to be firmly esconced in most statistical offices.

Table 2a. **Population of Western Offshoots, 1500-1899**
(000 at mid-year)

	Australia	*New Zealand*	*Canada*	*United States*	*4 Western Offshoots*
1500	450	100	250	2 000	**2 800**
1600	450	100	250	1 500	**2 300**
1700	450	100	200	1 000	**1 750**
1820	334	100	816	9 981	**11 231**
1830	330	100	1 169	13 240	**14 839**
1840	420	70	1 697	17 444	**19 631**
1850	605	90	2 485	23 580	**26 760**
1860	1 326	132	3 369	31 839	**36 666**
1870	1 775	291	3 781	40 241	**46 088**
1871	1 675	306	3 801	41 098	**46 880**
1872	1 722	320	3 870	42 136	**48 048**
1873	1 769	335	3 943	43 174	**49 221**
1874	1 822	367	4 012	44 212	**50 413**
1875	1 874	406	4 071	45 245	**51 596**
1876	1 929	434	4 128	46 287	**52 778**
1877	1 995	450	4 184	47 325	**53 954**
1878	2 062	467	4 244	48 362	**55 135**
1879	2 127	494	4 312	49 400	**56 333**
1880	2 197	520	4 384	50 458	**57 559**
1881	2 269	539	4 451	51 743	**59 002**
1882	2 348	555	4 503	53 027	**60 433**
1883	2 447	574	4 560	54 311	**61 892**
1884	2 556	598	4 617	55 595	**63 366**
1885	2 650	614	4 666	56 879	**64 809**
1886	2 741	626	4 711	58 164	**66 242**
1887	2 835	640	4 760	59 448	**67 683**
1888	2 932	649	4 813	60 732	**69 126**
1889	3 022	656	4 865	62 016	**70 559**
1890	3 107	665	4 918	63 302	**71 992**
1891	3 196	674	4 972	64 612	**73 454**
1892	3 274	686	5 022	65 922	**74 904**
1893	3 334	705	5 072	67 231	**76 342**
1894	3 395	722	5 121	68 541	**77 779**
1895	3 460	735	5 169	69 851	**79 215**
1896	3 523	748	5 218	71 161	**80 650**
1897	3 586	764	5 269	72 471	**82 090**
1898	3 642	779	5 325	73 781	**83 527**
1899	3 691	794	5 383	75 091	**84 959**

Table 2a. **Population of Western Offshoots, 1900-1955**
(000 at mid-year)

	Australia	*New Zealand*	*Canada*	*United States*	*4 Western Offshoots*
1900	3 741	807	5 457	76 391	**86 396**
1901	3 795	824	5 536	77 888	**88 043**
1902	3 850	844	5 650	79 469	**89 813**
1903	3 896	867	5 813	80 946	**91 522**
1904	3 946	893	5 994	82 485	**93 318**
1905	4 004	919	6 166	84 147	**95 236**
1906	4 062	946	6 282	85 770	**97 060**
1907	4 127	969	6 596	87 339	**99 031**
1908	4 197	996	6 813	89 055	**101 061**
1909	4 278	1 024	6 993	90 845	**103 140**
1910	4 375	1 045	7 188	92 767	**105 375**
1911	4 500	1 067	7 410	94 234	**107 211**
1912	4 661	1 092	7 602	95 703	**109 058**
1913	4 821	1 122	7 852	97 606	**111 401**
1914	4 933	1 143	8 093	99 505	**113 674**
1915	4 971	1 152	8 191	100 941	**115 255**
1916	4 955	1 155	8 214	102 364	**116 688**
1917	4 950	1 152	8 277	103 817	**118 196**
1918	5 032	1 156	8 374	104 958	**119 520**
1919	5 193	1 195	8 548	105 473	**120 409**
1920	5 358	1 241	8 798	106 881	**122 278**
1921	5 461	1 275	9 028	108 964	**124 728**
1922	5 574	1 304	9 159	110 484	**126 521**
1923	5 697	1 326	9 256	112 387	**128 666**
1924	5 819	1 350	9 394	114 558	**131 121**
1925	5 943	1 382	9 549	116 284	**133 158**
1926	6 064	1 412	9 713	117 857	**135 046**
1927	6 188	1 437	9 905	119 502	**137 032**
1928	6 304	1 454	10 107	120 971	**138 836**
1929	6 396	1 471	10 305	122 245	**140 417**
1930	6 469	1 493	10 488	123 668	**142 118**
1931	6 527	1 514	10 657	124 633	**143 331**
1932	6 579	1 527	10 794	125 436	**144 336**
1933	6 631	1 540	10 919	126 180	**145 270**
1934	6 682	1 552	11 030	126 978	**146 242**
1935	6 732	1 562	11 136	127 859	**147 289**
1936	6 783	1 573	11 243	128 681	**148 280**
1937	6 841	1 587	11 341	129 464	**149 233**
1938	6 904	1 604	11 452	130 476	**150 436**
1939	6 971	1 627	11 570	131 539	**151 707**
1940	7 042	1 636	11 688	132 637	**153 003**
1941	7 111	1 629	11 818	133 922	**154 480**
1942	7 173	1 639	11 969	135 386	**156 167**
1943	7 236	1 633	12 115	137 272	**158 256**
1944	7 309	1 654	12 268	138 937	**160 168**
1945	7 389	1 688	12 404	140 474	**161 955**
1946	7 474	1 759	12 634	141 940	**163 807**
1947	7 578	1 797	12 901	144 688	**166 964**
1948	7 715	1 833	13 180	147 203	**169 931**
1949	7 919	1 871	13 469	149 770	**173 029**
1950	8 267	1 908	14 011	152 271	**176 458**
1951	8 511	1 947	14 331	154 878	**179 667**
1952	8 691	1 995	14 786	157 553	**183 025**
1953	8 858	2 047	15 183	160 184	**186 273**
1954	9 064	2 093	15 636	163 026	**189 819**
1955	9 277	2 136	16 050	165 931	**193 395**

Table 2a. **Population of Western Offshoots, 1956-2003**
(000 at mid-year)

	Australia	*New Zealand*	*Canada*	*United States*	*4 Western Offshoots*
1956	9 501	2 178	16 445	168 903	**197 027**
1957	9 713	2 229	17 010	171 984	**200 936**
1958	9 915	2 282	17 462	174 882	**204 541**
1959	10 132	2 331	17 872	177 830	**208 165**
1960	10 361	2 372	18 267	180 671	**211 671**
1961	10 599	2 432	18 635	183 691	**215 357**
1962	10 795	2 489	18 986	186 538	**218 807**
1963	11 001	2 541	19 343	189 242	**222 128**
1964	11 218	2 592	19 711	191 889	**225 410**
1965	11 439	2 640	20 071	194 303	**228 454**
1966	11 655	2 688	20 448	196 560	**231 351**
1967	11 872	2 728	20 820	198 712	**234 132**
1968	12 102	2 759	21 143	200 706	**236 710**
1969	12 379	2 789	21 448	202 677	**239 293**
1970	12 660	2 828	21 750	205 052	**242 290**
1971	12 937	2 875	22 026	207 661	**245 500**
1972	13 177	2 929	22 285	209 896	**248 287**
1973	13 380	2 992	22 560	211 909	**250 841**
1974	13 599	3 058	22 875	213 854	**253 386**
1975	13 771	3 118	23 209	215 973	**256 071**
1976	13 916	3 154	23 518	218 035	**258 622**
1977	14 074	3 165	23 796	220 239	**261 274**
1978	14 249	3 166	24 036	222 585	**264 036**
1979	14 422	3 165	24 277	225 055	**266 918**
1980	14 616	3 170	24 593	227 726	**270 106**
1981	14 923	3 185	24 900	229 966	**272 975**
1982	15 184	3 211	25 202	232 188	**275 785**
1983	15 394	3 246	25 456	234 307	**278 403**
1984	15 579	3 279	25 702	236 348	**280 908**
1985	15 788	3 298	25 942	238 466	**283 494**
1986	16 018	3 308	26 204	240 651	**286 181**
1987	16 257	3 317	26 550	242 804	**288 928**
1988	16 520	3 331	26 895	245 021	**291 768**
1989	16 780	3 342	27 379	247 342	**294 843**
1990	17 022	3 360	27 791	250 132	**298 304**
1991	17 258	3 397	28 118	253 493	**302 265**
1992	17 482	3 438	28 524	256 894	**306 337**
1993	17 689	3 475	28 921	260 255	**310 340**
1994	17 893	3 517	29 262	263 436	**314 108**
1995	18 116	3 566	29 619	266 557	**317 858**
1996	18 348	3 621	29 983	269 667	**321 620**
1997	18 565	3 676	30 306	272 912	**325 459**
1998	18 769	3 726	30 629	276 115	**329 239**
1999	18 968	3 774	30 957	279 295	**332 994**
2000	19 165	3 820	31 278	282 339	**336 601**
2001	19 358	3 864	31 593	285 024	**339 838**
2002	19 547	3 908	31 902	287 676	**343 033**
2003	19 732	3 951	32 207	290 343	**346 233**

Table 2b. **GDP Levels in Western Offshoots, 1500-1899**
(million 1990 international Geary-Khamis dollars)

	Australia	New Zealand	Canada	United States	4 Western Offshoots
1500	180	40	100	800	**1 120**
1600	180	40	100	600	**920**
1700	180	40	86	527	**833**
1820	173	40	738	12 548	**13 499**
1830	280	40	1 169	18 219	**19 708**
1840	577	28	1 972	27 694	**30 271**
1850	1 195	103	3 304	42 583	**47 185**
1860	3 838	292	4 887	69 346	**78 363**
1870	5 810	902	6 407	98 374	**111 493**
1871	5 525	965	6 669	102 289	**115 448**
1872	6 119	1 127	6 599	106 360	**120 205**
1873	6 764	1 283	7 263	110 593	**125 903**
1874	6 987	1 411	7 437	114 994	**130 829**
1875	7 755	1 497	7 263	119 571	**136 086**
1876	7 730	1 572	6 774	124 330	**140 406**
1877	8 052	1 792	7 228	129 278	**146 350**
1878	8 820	1 994	6 948	134 423	**152 186**
1879	8 944	1 763	7 612	139 772	**158 091**
1880	9 415	1 948	7 961	145 335	**164 659**
1881	10 108	2 029	9 078	151 119	**172 334**
1882	9 539	2 023	9 497	157 133	**178 193**
1883	10 951	2 006	9 532	163 387	**185 876**
1884	11 000	2 214	10 300	169 889	**193 403**
1885	11 719	2 203	9 672	176 651	**200 244**
1886	11 867	2 255	9 776	183 681	**207 579**
1887	13 131	2 307	10 091	190 991	**216 519**
1888	13 205	2 307	10 824	198 592	**224 928**
1889	14 345	2 428	10 894	206 496	**234 163**
1890	13 850	2 497	11 697	214 714	**242 758**
1891	14 914	2 515	11 976	224 027	**253 432**
1892	13 081	2 607	11 906	245 757	**273 352**
1893	12 362	2 671	11 837	233 857	**260 726**
1894	12 784	2 584	12 395	227 131	**254 894**
1895	12 066	2 677	12 256	254 552	**281 551**
1896	12 982	2 983	11 941	249 379	**277 285**
1897	12 264	3 018	13 233	273 178	**301 693**
1898	14 172	3 104	13 757	278 869	**309 903**
1899	14 172	3 208	15 049	304 221	**336 650**

Table 2b. **GDP Levels in Western Offshoots, 1900-1955**
(million 1990 international Geary-Khamis dollars)

	Australia	*New Zealand*	*Canada*	*United States*	*4 Western Offshoots*
1900	15 014	3 469	15 887	312 499	**346 869**
1901	14 568	3 480	17 144	347 681	**382 873**
1902	14 717	3 746	18 820	351 303	**388 586**
1903	15 881	4 099	19 378	368 377	**407 735**
1904	16 947	4 081	19 658	363 720	**404 406**
1905	17 145	4 457	21 962	390 624	**434 188**
1906	18 309	4 879	24 162	435 636	**482 987**
1907	19 052	5 174	25 559	442 362	**492 147**
1908	19 697	4 816	24 336	406 146	**454 995**
1909	21 307	4 885	26 920	455 814	**508 927**
1910	22 793	5 556	29 225	460 471	**518 044**
1911	22 967	5 862	31 215	475 475	**535 519**
1912	23 764	5 689	33 275	497 722	**560 450**
1913	24 861	5 781	34 916	517 383	**582 941**
1914	24 797	5 931	32 577	477 545	**540 849**
1915	24 341	5 960	34 672	490 996	**555 969**
1916	24 172	5 914	38 163	558 774	**627 023**
1917	23 716	5 769	39 734	544 804	**614 024**
1918	23 155	5 677	37 186	593 956	**659 973**
1919	24 488	6 313	34 357	599 130	**664 288**
1920	25 534	7 001	33 973	593 438	**659 946**
1921	26 818	6 538	30 307	579 986	**643 650**
1922	28 225	6 313	34 741	612 064	**681 343**
1923	29 579	6 822	36 801	692 776	**765 978**
1924	31 524	6 943	37 360	713 989	**789 816**
1925	33 002	7 313	41 445	730 545	**812 305**
1926	33 792	6 926	43 680	778 144	**862 542**
1927	34 305	6 729	48 010	785 905	**874 948**
1928	34 368	7 475	52 269	794 700	**888 812**
1929	33 662	7 741	52 199	843 334	**936 936**
1930	30 458	7 405	50 454	768 314	**856 631**
1931	28 416	6 775	42 667	709 332	**787 191**
1932	30 025	6 608	39 630	615 686	**691 948**
1933	32 110	7 047	36 801	602 751	**678 710**
1934	33 810	7 400	40 712	649 316	**731 237**
1935	35 798	7 747	43 994	698 984	**786 523**
1936	37 414	9 186	46 368	798 322	**891 290**
1937	39 306	9 683	50 733	832 469	**932 191**
1938	40 639	10 365	52 060	799 357	**902 421**
1939	40 749	10 510	55 167	862 995	**969 421**
1940	43 422	10 308	62 744	929 737	**1 046 211**
1941	48 271	9 984	71 508	1 098 921	**1 228 684**
1942	53 837	11 082	84 182	1 318 809	**1 467 911**
1943	55 738	11 313	87 988	1 581 122	**1 736 162**
1944	53 809	11 360	91 305	1 713 572	**1 870 047**
1945	51 109	11 695	88 477	1 644 761	**1 796 042**
1946	49 291	12 597	87 569	1 305 357	**1 454 814**
1947	50 503	14 100	91 445	1 285 697	**1 441 744**
1948	53 754	12 701	93 121	1 334 331	**1 493 907**
1949	57 308	14 071	95 146	1 339 505	**1 506 030**
1950	61 274	16 136	102 164	1 455 916	**1 635 490**
1951	63 892	14 904	107 960	1 566 784	**1 753 540**
1952	64 470	15 552	115 816	1 625 245	**1 821 083**
1953	66 481	16 084	121 228	1 699 970	**1 903 763**
1954	70 614	18 298	120 390	1 688 804	**1 898 106**
1955	74 471	18 639	131 633	1 808 126	**2 032 869**

Table 2b. **GDP Levels in Western Offshoots, 1956-2001**
(million 1990 international Geary-Khamis dollars)

	Australia	*New Zealand*	*Canada*	*United States*	*4 Western Offshoots*
1956	77 034	19 605	142 282	1 843 455	**2 082 376**
1957	78 577	20 165	146 402	1 878 063	**2 123 207**
1958	82 351	20 957	149 021	1 859 088	**2 111 417**
1959	87 421	22 449	155 062	1 997 061	**2 261 993**
1960	91 085	22 449	159 880	2 046 727	**2 320 141**
1961	91 713	23 704	164 598	2 094 396	**2 374 411**
1962	97 444	24 215	176 130	2 220 732	**2 518 521**
1963	103 413	25 749	185 041	2 316 765	**2 630 968**
1964	110 488	27 004	197 098	2 450 915	**2 785 505**
1965	116 131	28 724	210 203	2 607 294	**2 962 352**
1966	119 363	30 536	223 832	2 778 086	**3 151 817**
1967	127 422	29 142	230 647	2 847 549	**3 234 760**
1968	134 913	29 095	242 703	2 983 081	**3 389 792**
1969	143 118	32 099	255 497	3 076 517	**3 507 231**
1970	152 220	31 644	262 098	3 081 900	**3 527 862**
1971	158 992	33 285	276 694	3 178 106	**3 647 077**
1972	163 453	34 711	291 314	3 346 554	**3 836 032**
1973	172 314	37 177	312 176	3 536 622	**4 058 289**
1974	176 586	39 390	324 928	3 526 724	**4 067 628**
1975	181 367	38 937	332 269	3 516 825	**4 069 398**
1976	188 678	39 887	350 467	3 701 163	**4 280 195**
1977	190 653	37 944	362 245	3 868 829	**4 459 671**
1978	196 184	38 097	376 894	4 089 548	**4 700 723**
1979	206 515	38 874	392 561	4 228 647	**4 866 597**
1980	210 642	39 141	397 814	4 230 558	**4 878 155**
1981	218 780	41 041	410 164	4 336 141	**5 006 126**
1982	218 512	41 809	397 671	4 254 870	**4 912 862**
1983	218 539	42 955	409 246	4 433 129	**5 103 869**
1984	233 618	45 072	432 711	4 755 958	**5 467 359**
1985	245 444	45 420	456 107	4 940 383	**5 687 354**
1986	250 539	46 372	468 055	5 110 480	**5 875 446**
1987	262 925	46 564	487 138	5 290 129	**6 086 756**
1988	274 737	46 435	510 815	5 512 845	**6 344 832**
1989	286 820	46 850	523 177	5 703 521	**6 560 368**
1990	291 180	46 729	524 475	5 803 200	**6 665 584**
1991	288 661	45 908	514 459	5 775 948	**6 624 976**
1992	296 225	46 304	519 148	5 952 089	**6 813 766**
1993	307 489	48 654	531 096	6 110 061	**6 997 300**
1994	322 819	51 554	556 209	6 356 710	**7 287 292**
1995	336 990	53 599	571 447	6 526 361	**7 488 397**
1996	350 470	55 368	580 590	6 759 427	**7 745 855**
1997	362 601	57 083	605 162	7 046 304	**8 071 150**
1998	382 147	56 761	630 306	7 349 878	**8 419 092**
1999	399 670	59 173	664 021	7 651 223	**8 774 087**
2000	412 813	61 156	694 308	7 941 969	**9 110 246**
2001	423 596	62 282	704 594	7 965 795	**9 156 267**

Table 2c. **Per Capita GDP in Western Offshoots, 1500-1899**
(1990 international Geary-Khamis dollars)

	Australia	New Zealand	Canada	United States	4 Western Offshoots
1500	400	400	400	400	**400**
1600	400	400	400	400	**400**
1700	400	400	430	527	**476**
1820	518	400	904	1 257	**1 202**
1830	848	400	1 000	1 376	**1 328**
1840	1 374	400	1 162	1 588	**1 542**
1850	1 975	1 144	1 330	1 806	**1 763**
1860	2 894	2 212	1 451	2 178	**2 137**
1870	3 273	3 100	1 695	2 445	**2 419**
1871	3 299	3 155	1 755	2 489	**2 463**
1872	3 553	3 523	1 705	2 524	**2 502**
1873	3 824	3 831	1 842	2 562	**2 558**
1874	3 835	3 843	1 854	2 601	**2 595**
1875	4 138	3 688	1 784	2 643	**2 638**
1876	4 007	3 623	1 641	2 686	**2 660**
1877	4 036	3 982	1 727	2 732	**2 712**
1878	4 277	4 271	1 637	2 780	**2 760**
1879	4 205	3 569	1 765	2 829	**2 806**
1880	4 285	3 747	1 816	2 880	**2 861**
1881	4 455	3 765	2 040	2 921	**2 921**
1882	4 063	3 646	2 109	2 963	**2 949**
1883	4 475	3 495	2 090	3 008	**3 003**
1884	4 304	3 703	2 231	3 056	**3 052**
1885	4 422	3 587	2 073	3 106	**3 090**
1886	4 329	3 602	2 075	3 158	**3 134**
1887	4 632	3 604	2 120	3 213	**3 199**
1888	4 504	3 554	2 249	3 270	**3 254**
1889	4 747	3 701	2 239	3 330	**3 319**
1890	4 458	3 755	2 378	3 392	**3 372**
1891	4 666	3 731	2 409	3 467	**3 450**
1892	3 995	3 801	2 371	3 728	**3 649**
1893	3 708	3 788	2 334	3 478	**3 415**
1894	3 766	3 579	2 420	3 314	**3 277**
1895	3 487	3 642	2 371	3 644	**3 554**
1896	3 685	3 988	2 288	3 504	**3 438**
1897	3 420	3 950	2 512	3 769	**3 675**
1898	3 891	3 985	2 583	3 780	**3 710**
1899	3 840	4 041	2 796	4 051	**3 963**

Table 2c. **Per Capita GDP in Western Offshoots, 1900-1955**
(1990 international Geary-Khamis dollars)

	Australia	*New Zealand*	*Canada*	*United States*	*4 Western Offshoots*
1900	4 013	4 298	2 911	4 091	**4 015**
1901	3 839	4 223	3 097	4 464	**4 349**
1902	3 823	4 438	3 331	4 421	**4 327**
1903	4 076	4 727	3 334	4 551	**4 455**
1904	4 295	4 570	3 280	4 410	**4 334**
1905	4 282	4 850	3 562	4 642	**4 559**
1906	4 507	5 158	3 846	5 079	**4 976**
1907	4 616	5 340	3 875	5 065	**4 970**
1908	4 693	4 835	3 572	4 561	**4 502**
1909	4 981	4 770	3 850	5 017	**4 934**
1910	5 210	5 316	4 066	4 964	**4 916**
1911	5 104	5 494	4 213	5 046	**4 995**
1912	5 098	5 209	4 377	5 201	**5 139**
1913	5 157	5 152	4 447	5 301	**5 233**
1914	5 027	5 189	4 025	4 799	**4 758**
1915	4 897	5 174	4 233	4 864	**4 824**
1916	4 878	5 120	4 646	5 459	**5 373**
1917	4 791	5 008	4 801	5 248	**5 195**
1918	4 602	4 911	4 441	5 659	**5 522**
1919	4 716	5 283	4 019	5 680	**5 517**
1920	4 766	5 641	3 861	5 552	**5 397**
1921	4 911	5 128	3 357	5 323	**5 160**
1922	5 064	4 841	3 793	5 540	**5 385**
1923	5 192	5 144	3 976	6 164	**5 953**
1924	5 417	5 143	3 977	6 233	**6 024**
1925	5 553	5 292	4 340	6 282	**6 100**
1926	5 573	4 905	4 497	6 602	**6 387**
1927	5 544	4 683	4 847	6 576	**6 385**
1928	5 452	5 141	5 172	6 569	**6 402**
1929	5 263	5 262	5 065	6 899	**6 673**
1930	4 708	4 960	4 811	6 213	**6 028**
1931	4 354	4 475	4 004	5 691	**5 492**
1932	4 564	4 327	3 671	4 908	**4 794**
1933	4 842	4 576	3 370	4 777	**4 672**
1934	5 060	4 768	3 691	5 114	**5 000**
1935	5 318	4 959	3 951	5 467	**5 340**
1936	5 516	5 840	4 124	6 204	**6 011**
1937	5 746	6 102	4 473	6 430	**6 247**
1938	5 886	6 462	4 546	6 126	**5 999**
1939	5 846	6 460	4 768	6 561	**6 390**
1940	6 166	6 300	5 368	7 010	**6 838**
1941	6 788	6 129	6 051	8 206	**7 954**
1942	7 505	6 762	7 033	9 741	**9 400**
1943	7 703	6 928	7 263	11 518	**10 971**
1944	7 362	6 868	7 443	12 333	**11 676**
1945	6 917	6 928	7 133	11 709	**11 090**
1946	6 595	7 161	6 931	9 197	**8 881**
1947	6 664	7 846	7 088	8 886	**8 635**
1948	6 967	6 929	7 065	9 065	**8 791**
1949	7 237	7 521	7 064	8 944	**8 704**
1950	7 412	8 456	7 291	9 561	**9 268**
1951	7 507	7 653	7 533	10 116	**9 760**
1952	7 418	7 796	7 833	10 316	**9 950**
1953	7 505	7 856	7 984	10 613	**10 220**
1954	7 791	8 743	7 699	10 359	**10 000**
1955	8 027	8 725	8 201	10 897	**10 512**

Table 2c. **Per Capita GDP in Western Offshoots, 1956-2001**
(1990 international Geary-Khamis dollars)

	Australia	*New Zealand*	*Canada*	*United States*	*4 Western Offshoots*
1956	8 108	9 000	8 652	10 914	**10 569**
1957	8 090	9 045	8 607	10 920	**10 567**
1958	8 305	9 185	8 534	10 631	**10 323**
1959	8 628	9 630	8 676	11 230	**10 866**
1960	8 791	9 465	8 753	11 328	**10 961**
1961	8 653	9 745	8 833	11 402	**11 025**
1962	9 027	9 731	9 277	11 905	**11 510**
1963	9 400	10 132	9 566	12 242	**11 844**
1964	9 849	10 418	9 999	12 773	**12 357**
1965	10 152	10 879	10 473	13 419	**12 967**
1966	10 241	11 362	10 946	14 134	**13 624**
1967	10 733	10 682	11 078	14 330	**13 816**
1968	11 148	10 545	11 479	14 863	**14 320**
1969	11 561	11 511	11 912	15 179	**14 657**
1970	12 024	11 189	12 050	15 030	**14 560**
1971	12 290	11 576	12 562	15 304	**14 856**
1972	12 404	11 850	13 072	15 944	**15 450**
1973	12 878	12 424	13 838	16 689	**16 179**
1974	12 985	12 879	14 205	16 491	**16 053**
1975	13 170	12 489	14 316	16 284	**15 892**
1976	13 559	12 648	14 902	16 975	**16 550**
1977	13 546	11 989	15 223	17 567	**17 069**
1978	13 769	12 034	15 680	18 373	**17 803**
1979	14 320	12 284	16 170	18 789	**18 233**
1980	14 412	12 347	16 176	18 577	**18 060**
1981	14 660	12 884	16 472	18 856	**18 339**
1982	14 391	13 022	15 779	18 325	**17 814**
1983	14 197	13 234	16 076	18 920	**18 333**
1984	14 995	13 746	16 836	20 123	**19 463**
1985	15 546	13 772	17 582	20 717	**20 062**
1986	15 641	14 017	17 862	21 236	**20 531**
1987	16 173	14 037	18 348	21 788	**21 067**
1988	16 630	13 939	18 993	22 499	**21 746**
1989	17 093	14 020	19 108	23 059	**22 250**
1990	17 106	13 909	18 872	23 201	**22 345**
1991	16 727	13 514	18 297	22 785	**21 918**
1992	16 945	13 470	18 201	23 169	**22 243**
1993	17 383	14 001	18 364	23 477	**22 547**
1994	18 042	14 657	19 008	24 130	**23 200**
1995	18 602	15 031	19 293	24 484	**23 559**
1996	19 101	15 290	19 364	25 066	**24 084**
1997	19 531	15 528	19 968	25 819	**24 799**
1998	20 361	15 233	20 579	26 619	**25 571**
1999	21 070	15 679	21 450	27 395	**26 349**
2000	21 540	16 010	22 198	28 129	**27 065**
2001	21 883	16 118	22 302	27 948	**26 943**

HS–3: A. Eastern Europe and Former USSR

Until 1990, there were 8 countries in this group, 5 still have the same frontiers, but 22 successor states have emerged, 2 from Czechoslovakia, 5 from Yugoslavia, and 15 from USSR. The tables show GDP, population and per capita GDP for the 8 countries, 1820–2001 within their 1989 frontiers and 1990–2001 for the 22 successor states within their new boundaries.

The former DDR (German Democratic Republic) lasted from 1946 to 1990, when it was absorbed into the Federal Republic. As the estimates for Germany in HS–1 include the area of the former DDR, it is not shown here (see Maddison, 1995, p.132 for East German population and GDP, 1936–1993).

Estimates for 1820–2001

POPULATION: 1950 onwards all countries of Eastern Europe and the former USSR from the International Programs Center of the US Bureau of the Census, October 2002 revision. For 1820–1949, I have made some revisions and filled gaps from Colin McEvedy and Richard Jones (1978), *Atlas of World Population History,* Penguin, London. They provide estimates adjusted throughout to 1978 frontiers. Sources for 1820–1949 are indicated in the country notes below.

GDP LEVELS: sources are indicated in the country notes below. For 1820–1913, there are significant gaps in the GDP estimates for Eastern European countries, which makes it difficult to get meaningful group totals and averages. I have therefore used the proxy estimates of Good and Ma (1999) to fill most of these gaps as indicated below. In all cases the GDP estimates for the communist period have been adjusted to correspond to the norms of the UN standardised system of national accounts. The problems in doing this and the relevant sources are discussed in Maddison (1995), pp. 139–43 and in Maddison "Measuring the Performance of a Communist Command Economy: An Assessment of CIA Estimates for the USSR", *Review of Income and Wealth*, September, 1998.

Albania: 1950 and 1990 GDP levels from Maddison, 1995, p. 217. 1870–1950 per capita GDP was assumed to move in the same proportion as the average for the other 6 East European countries.

Bulgaria: 1926–39 from A. Chakalov, *The National Income and Outlay of Bulgaria: 1924–1945* (in Bulgarian), Knipegraph, Sofia, 1946; 1939–65 from T.P. Alton, "Economic Structure and Growth in Eastern Europe", in *Economic Developments in Countries of Eastern Europe*, Joint Economic Committee, US Congress, 1970, p. 46. 1965–75 from T.P. Alton, "East European GNPs: Origins of Product, Final Uses, Rates of Growth and International Comparisons", in *East European Economies: Slow Growth in the 1980s*, vol. I, *Economic Performance and Policy*, Joint Economic Committee, US Congress, October 1985, pp. 109–10. 1975–90 real GNP by industry of origin from T.P. Alton and Associates, "Economic Growth in Eastern Europe", *Occasional Papers* 120 and 124, Research Project on National Income in East Central Europe, New York, 1992 and 1993. GDP movement 1990–2001 from Statistics Division, Economic Commission for Europe, Geneva. Population 1820–50 from McEvedy and Jones (1978); 1870–1940 from I. Svennilson, *Growth and Stagnation in the European Economy*, ECE, Geneva, 1954, p. 237 (adjusted to postwar frontiers); 1941–9 from UN, *Demographic Yearbook*, New York, 1960.

Czechoslovakia: 1820–1913 growth rate of per capita GDP assumed to fall midway between those for Austria proper and for rest of Cisleithania in A. Kausel, "Österreichs Volkseinkommen 1830 bis 1913", in "Geschichte und Ergebnisse der zentralen amtlichen Statistik in Österreich 1829–1979", *Beiträge zum Österreichischen Statistik*, 550, Vienna, 1979. 1913–37 GDP from F.L. Pryor, Z.P. Pryor, M. Stadnik, and G.J. Staller "Czechoslovakia: Aggregate Production in the Inter–war Period", *Review of Income and Wealth*, March 1971, p.36. 1937–65 from G. Lazarcik, "Czechoslovak Gross National Product by Sector of Origin and Final Use, 1937, and 1948–65", *Occasional Paper* 26, Research Project on National Income in East Central Europe, New York, 1969. 1965–90 as for Bulgaria. 1990–2001 for Czech republic from OECD sources; Slovakia from Statistics Division, Economic Commission for Europe. Population 1820–50 from McEvedy and Jones (1978), 1870–1910 supplied by David Good, 1913–49 as for Bulgaria.

Hungary: 1870–1900 GDP from Max–Stephan Schulze, "Patterns of Growth and Stagnation in the Late Nineteenth Century Habsburg Economy", *European Review of Economic History*, no. 4, 2000, pp. 311–340. Schulze's estimates refer to imperial Hungary, but the movement he shows is the best available proxy for development within present frontiers. 1900–38 net national product within present frontiers from A. Eckstein, "National Income and Capital Formation in Hungary, 1900–50", in S. Kuznets, ed., *Income and Wealth*, series V, Bowes and Bowes, London, 1955, p. 175; 1938–65 real GNP by industry of origin from L. Czirjak, "Hungarian GNP by Sectors of Origin of Product and End Uses, 1938 and 1946–67", *Occasional Paper* 43, Research Project on East Central Europe, New York, 1973. 1965–91 as for Bulgaria. Thereafter from OECD sources. Population 1820–70 assumed to grow at the same pace as in imperial Hungary as shown in Kausel (1985), p. 12. 1870–1949 as for Bulgaria.

Friedich von Fellner estimated the breakdown of population, income, and wealth between present–day Hungary and other successor states of imperial Hungary for 1910. Present–day Hungary had 36.7 per cent of the population (7 605 thousand out of a total 20 745) and 39.7 per cent of the national income. 21.4 per cent of income went to an area which became part of Romania, 20.2 to Yugoslavia, 16.9 to Czechoslovakia and 1.8 per cent to present–day Austria. See "Die Verteilung des Volksvermögens und Volkseinkommens der Länder der ungarischen Heiligen Krone zwischen dem heutigen Ungarn und der Successions–Staaten", *Metron*, July 1923, pp. 302–3. Per capita income was about 8 per cent higher in present–day Hungary than in the rest.

Poland: 1929–38 from K. Laski, *Akumulacja i spozycie i procesie uprzemyslowienia Polski Ludowej*, Ksiazka i Wiedza, Warsaw, 1956, pp. 86–90 as cited by N. Spulber, *The State and Economic Development in Eastern Europe*, Random House, New York, 1966, p. 59; 1937–65 from T.P. Alton (1970), p. 46, 1965–90 as for Bulgaria. 1990 onwards from OECD sources. Population 1820–70 from McEvedy and Jones (1978), thereafter as for Bulgaria.

Romania: 1926–38 from "Venitul National", in *Enciclopedia Romaniei*, Bucharest, 1940, vol. 4, pp. 941–966 as cited by N. Spulber, p. 54, *op. cit.*; 1938–50 from D. Grindea, *Venitul National in Republica Socialista Romania*, Stiintifica, Bucharest, 1967, p. 113; 1950–65 from Alton (1970), *op. cit.*, p. 46; 1965–75 from T.P. Alton (1985), *op. cit.*, pp. 109–10; 1975–90 as for Bulgaria. 1990–2001 from Statistics Division, Economic Commission for Europe, Geneva. Population 1820–1900 from McEvedy and Jones (1978), thereafter as for Bulgaria.

Yugoslavia: Movement of net domestic product adjusted to enhance international comparability 1909–12, 1920–39, and 1947–50 from I. Vinski, "National Product and Fixed Assets in the Territory of Yugoslavia 1900–59", in P. Deane, ed., *Income and Wealth*, Series IX, Bowes and Bowes, London, 1961, p. 221 1950–68 from T.P. Alton, *op. cit.* (1970). 1968–75 from World Bank, *World Tables*, various issues. 1975–90 from "Economic Growth in Eastern Europe 1975–91" in T.P. Alton and Associates, *Occasional Paper*, 120, Research Project on National Income in East Central Europe, New York, 1992. 1990–2001 GDP for Bosnia–Herczegovina, Croatia, Macedonia, Slovenia, and Serbia–Montenegro from Statistics Division, Economic Commission for Europe. Population 1820–1949 as for Bulgaria.

USSR: 1820–70 per capita GDP movement assumed to parallel the average for Eastern Europe. 1870–1913 volume movement of GDP components from R.W. Goldsmith, "The Economic Growth of Tsarist Russia 1860–1913", *Economic Development and Cultural Change*, April 1961, pp. 450, and 462–3. I used his estimates of crop and livestock output, his industrial index and estimate for handicraft activity. I assumed forestry and fishing to move parallel to agriculture; construction, transport and communication parallel to industry. I used 1913 weights for the components from M.E. Falkus, "Russia's National Income 1913: A Revaluation", *Economica*, February 1968, pp. 62 and 67. For 1913–28, I used the same technique of estimation and weights, taking net agricultural product from S.G. Wheatcroft in R.W. Davies, ed., *From Tsarism to the New Economic Policy*, Macmillan, London, 1990, p. 279, and industrial output from G.W. Nutter, *Growth of Industrial Production in the Soviet Union*, Princeton, 1962, p. 150. 1928–40 and 1945–50 gross national product at 1937 prices by industry of origin from R. Moorsteen and R.P. Powell, *The Soviet Capital Stock 1928–1962*, Irwin, Illinois, 1966, p. 361 with the 1939–40 increase reduced to offset the population increase due to territorial acquisitions at that time. 1950–90 from CIA, "Sector of Origin GNP for the Soviet Union, Factor Cost Prices", March 29, 1991, processed. This was an update of *Measures of Soviet Gross National Product in 1982 Prices*, Joint Economic Committee, US Congress, November 1990. 1990 breakdown of GDP level for the 15 successor republics derived from B.M. Bolotin, "The Former Soviet Union as Reflected in National Accounts Statistics", in S. Hirsch, ed., *Memo 3:In Search of Answers in the Post–Soviet Era*, Bureau of National Affairs, Washington DC, 1992. 1973–93 GDP level for the fifteen successor states from Maddison (2001), pp. 182, 184 and 339. Annual movement 1994–2002 from IMF, *World Economic Outlook*, September, 2002.

Population 1820–1900 from McEvedy and Jones, pp. 79 and 159–163; 1913–40 from F. Lorimer, *The Population of the Soviet Union: History and Prospects*, League of Nations, Geneva, 1946. 1946–9 movement from G.W. Nutter, *The Growth of Industrial Production in the Soviet Union*, NBER, Princeton, 1962, p. 519.

For the Tsarist period to 1928 there are alternative estimates by P.R. Gregory, *Russian National Income 1885–1913*, Cambridge University Press, 1982, pp. 56–7. He measures expenditure components (private consumption, government current spending, and investment) in current prices and deflates by price indices. The two methods concord well. The industry of origin approach yields a GDP index of 43.2 for 1890, 66.3 for 1900 and 100.0 for 1913. Gregory's two net national product alternatives average 42.9, 66.2 and 100.0 for these years.

Proxy Estimates to Fill Gaps in GDP Estimates for Eastern Europe, 1820–1913

David Good and Tongshu Ma, "The Economic Growth of Central and Eastern Europe, 1870–1989", *European Review of Economic History*, August 1999 provide proxy estimates of the level and movement of GDP per capita for the years 1870, 1890 and 1910 for Austria and 6 East European countries. For the 1920s onwards they used Maddison (1995) estimates, and my *numeraire* (1990 international Geary–Khamis dollars). These estimates are shown as relatives to the United States. Virtually identical results are given in Good and Ma (1998), "New Estimates of Income levels in Central and Eastern Europe, 1870–1910", in F. Baltzarek, F. Butschek and G. Tichy (eds.), (1998), *Von der Theorie zur Wirtschaftspolitik–ein österreichische Weg*, Lucius, Stuttgart, where they are shown as levels rather than relatives. In 1998, they showed figures for 1880 and 1900, but not the link with years after the first world war.

Their proxy estimates are derived by regression using three indicators (letters posted per capita, crude birth rate and the share of non–agricultural employment in the labour force). The relationship of GDP per capita to this cocktail of indicators is tested for 12 countries deemed to have reasonably good national income data. Although I reject the proxies as a substitute for direct estimates, they seem plausible enough to fill gaps in the database until direct estimates become available. Table 3–1 shows their proxies. Table 3–2 shows my estimates and my use of their proxies (in italics). I extrapolated the proxies to 1913, using 1900–1910 growth rates. Per capita proxies were multiplied by population to derive GDP.

It should be noted that the Good and Ma proxies refer mostly to territory within the Austro–Hungarian empire where comparison was facilitated by the existence of a currency and customs union. Their estimates are likely to be less representative for Poland, where only 15 per cent of the population lived within the borders of the Habsburg empire.

Table 3-1. **Good and Ma Proxy Measures of Per Capita GDP**

(1990 international Geary-Khamis dollars)

	1870	*1890*	*1910*	*1920*	*1929*
Austria	*1 892*	*2 289*	*3 017*	2 429	3 722
Bulgaria		*1 131*	*1 456*	589	1 181
Czechoslovakia	*1 509*	*1 912*	*2 495*	1 935	3 046
Hungary	*1 179*	*1 572*	*2 192*	1 707	2 473
Poland	946	*1 284*	*1 690*	678	2 120
Romania	931	*1 246*	*1 660*	828	1 153
Yugoslavia	864	*1 216*	*1 525*	1 056	1 368
United States	2 457	3 396	4 970	5 559	6 907

Source: Good and Ma (1999), p.111. They show their proxies as relatives to the US level in the given year. I have unscrambled them, using the Maddison (1995) estimates for the US shown above. Proxies are in italics.

Table 3-2. **Maddison Estimates of Per Capita GDP and Proxies Derived from Good and Ma**

(1990 international Geary-Khamis dollars)

	1870	*1890*	*1910*	*1920*	*1929*
Austria	1 863	2 443	3 290	2 412	3 699
Bulgaria		*1 131*	*1 456*		1 180
Czechoslovakia	1 164	1 505	1 991	1 933	3 042
Hungary	1 092	1 473	2 000	1 709	2 476
Poland	946	*1 284*	*1 690*		2 117
Romania	931	*1 246*	*1 660*		1 152
Yugoslavia	599	843	1 057	1 031	1 364

Source: For Bulgaria, Poland and Romania, I used the Good-Ma proxies without adjustment as they are benchmarked on my estimates for 1929. For Yugoslavia I made the link at 1910 and adjusted the Good-Ma proxies for the difference in level in 1910. Proxies are in italics.

Estimates for 1500–1820

Population 1500–1820 from McEvedy and Jones (1978), except for Hungary 1820, as noted above. Direct estimates of GDP movement for 1500–1820 are not available. As a proxy, I assumed slower per capita growth than in Western Europe at 0.1 per cent per annum for 1500–1820 (as I did in Maddison, 1995).

Table 3-3. **Eastern Europe and Russia (Former USSR area): Population and GDP, 1500-1820**

	1500	1600	1700	1820
		Population (000)		
Albania	200	200	300	437
Bulgaria	800	1 250	1 250	2 187
Czechoslovakia	3 000	4 500	4 500	7 657
Hungary	1 250	1 250	1 500	4 146
Poland	4 000	5 000	6 000	10 426
Romania	2 000	2 000	2 500	6 389
Yugoslavia	2 250	2 750	2 750	5 215
Total	13 500	16 950	18 800	36 457
Russia	16 950	20 700	26 550	54 765
		GDP (million 1990 international $)		
Total E. Europe	6 696	9 289	11 393	24 906
Russia	8 458	11 426	16 196	37 678
		Per Capita GDP (1990 international $)		
Average E. Europe	496	548	606	683
Russia	499	552	610	688

Source: see text.

Table 3a. **Population of Former Eastern Europe and USSR, 1820-1949**
(000 at mid-year)

	Albania	Bulgaria	Czecho-slovakia	Hungary	Poland	Romania	Yugoslavia	Total 7 EE	USSR
1820	437	2 187	7 657	4 146	10 426	6 389	5 215	36 457	54 765
1850	500	2 500	9 250	5 161	13 000	8 000	6 000	44 411	73 750
1870	603	2 586	10 155	5 917	16 865	9 179	8 252	53 557	88 672
1890	726	3 445	11 253	6 622	22 854	10 373	9 690	64 963	110 664
1900	800	4 000	12 142	7 127	24 750	11 000	11 174	70 993	124 500
1910	874	4 520	12 984	7 644	26 644	11 866	13 052	77 584	
1913	898	4 720	13 245	7 840	26 710	12 527	13 590	79 530	156 192
1920	932	5 072	12 979	7 950	23 968	12 340	12 422	75 663	154 607
1921	937	5 148	13 008	8 029	24 330	12 479	12 607	76 538	152 836
1922	942	5 255	13 159	8 103	24 935	12 666	12 796	77 856	152 403
1923	947	5 365	13 293	8 173	25 569	12 843	12 987	79 177	153 055
1924	952	5 476	13 413	8 232	25 992	13 020	13 180	80 265	155 581
1925	956	5 590	13 537	8 299	26 425	13 209	13 378	81 394	158 983
1926	962	5 705	13 644	8 383	26 815	13 399	13 578	82 486	162 621
1927	967	5 798	13 728	8 454	27 148	13 574	13 780	83 449	166 117
1928	972	5 873	13 807	8 520	27 509	13 760	13 986	84 427	169 269
1929	977	5 950	13 884	8 583	27 856	13 952	14 194	85 396	172 017
1930	982	6 027	13 964	8 649	28 204	14 141	14 407	86 374	174 212
1931	988	6 106	14 052	8 723	28 615	14 355	14 618	87 457	175 987
1932	993	6 186	14 138	8 785	29 022	14 554	14 819	88 497	176 807
1933	998	6 267	14 216	8 848	29 421	14 730	15 022	89 502	177 401
1934	1 003	6 349	14 282	8 919	29 771	14 924	15 228	90 476	178 453
1935	1 009	6 415	14 339	8 985	30 129	15 069	15 439	91 385	179 636
1936	1 014	6 469	14 387	9 046	30 471	15 256	15 651	92 294	181 502
1937	1 030	6 514	14 429	9 107	30 791	15 434	15 860	93 165	184 626
1938	1 040	6 564	14 603	9 167	31 062	15 601	16 084	94 121	188 498
1939	1 070	6 614	14 683	9 227	31 365	15 751	16 305	95 015	192 379
1940	1 088	6 666	14 713	9 287	30 021	15 907			195 970
1941	1 100	6 715	14 671	9 344		15 774			
1942	1 117	6 771	14 577	9 396		15 839			
1943	1 119	6 828	14 538	9 442		15 840			
1944	1 122	6 885	14 593	9 497		15 946			
1945	1 138	6 942	14 152	9 024		15 929			
1946	1 154	7 000	12 916	9 042	23 959	15 971			173 900
1947	1 175	7 064	12 164	9 079	23 734	15 849	15 596	84 661	174 000
1948	1 192	7 130	12 339	9 158	23 980	15 893	15 817	85 509	175 100
1949	1 209	7 195	12 339	9 250	24 410	16 084	16 040	86 527	177 500

Table 3a. **Population of Former Eastern Europe and USSR, 1950-2003**
(000 at mid-year)

	Albania	*Bulgaria*	*Czecho-slovakia*	*Hungary*	*Poland*	*Romania*	*Yugoslavia*	*Total 7 EE*	*USSR*
1950	1 227	7 251	12 389	9 338	24 824	16 311	16 298	87 637	179 571
1951	1 254	7 258	12 532	9 423	25 262	16 464	16 519	88 713	182 677
1952	1 283	7 275	12 683	9 504	25 731	16 630	16 708	89 814	185 856
1953	1 315	7 346	12 820	9 595	26 221	16 847	16 937	91 081	188 961
1954	1 353	7 423	12 952	9 706	26 715	17 040	17 151	92 341	192 171
1955	1 392	7 499	13 093	9 825	27 221	17 325	17 364	93 719	195 613
1956	1 434	7 576	13 229	9 911	27 744	17 583	17 508	94 985	199 103
1957	1 477	7 651	13 358	9 839	28 235	17 829	17 659	96 049	202 604
1958	1 521	7 728	13 474	9 882	28 693	18 056	17 796	97 149	206 201
1959	1 571	7 798	13 565	9 937	29 152	18 226	17 968	98 217	209 928
1960	1 623	7 867	13 654	9 984	29 590	18 403	18 133	99 254	213 780
1961	1 677	7 943	13 779	10 029	29 979	18 567	18 318	100 292	217 618
1962	1 728	8 013	13 858	10 063	30 330	18 681	18 500	101 172	221 227
1963	1 780	8 078	13 948	10 091	30 662	18 813	18 685	102 057	224 585
1964	1 832	8 144	14 052	10 124	30 976	18 927	18 852	102 908	227 698
1965	1 884	8 201	14 147	10 153	31 262	19 027	19 038	103 713	230 513
1966	1 933	8 258	14 224	10 185	31 532	19 141	19 221	104 494	233 139
1967	1 984	8 310	14 277	10 223	31 785	19 285	19 390	105 256	235 630
1968	2 039	8 370	14 323	10 264	32 035	19 721	19 552	106 302	237 983
1969	2 100	8 434	14 284	10 303	32 281	20 010	19 705	107 117	240 253
1970	2 157	8 490	14 319	10 337	32 526	20 253	19 840	107 921	242 478
1971	2 209	8 536	14 381	10 365	32 778	20 470	20 015	108 753	244 887
1972	2 264	8 576	14 456	10 394	33 040	20 663	20 197	109 589	247 343
1973	2 296	8 621	14 549	10 426	33 331	20 828	20 367	110 418	249 712
1974	2 348	8 679	14 658	10 471	33 643	21 029	20 550	111 377	252 111
1975	2 401	8 721	14 772	10 532	33 969	21 245	20 732	112 372	254 519
1976	2 455	8 755	14 884	10 589	34 299	21 446	20 930	113 357	256 883
1977	2 509	8 797	14 990	10 637	34 621	21 659	21 126	114 339	259 225
1978	2 563	8 803	15 089	10 673	34 929	21 832	21 309	115 199	261 525
1979	2 618	8 812	15 182	10 698	35 257	22 001	21 490	116 058	263 751
1980	2 671	8 844	15 255	10 711	35 578	22 130	21 615	116 804	265 973
1981	2 724	8 869	15 312	10 712	35 902	22 257	21 707	117 483	268 217
1982	2 780	8 892	15 352	10 706	36 227	22 357	21 860	118 173	270 533
1983	2 837	8 910	15 388	10 689	36 571	22 407	21 968	118 772	273 010
1984	2 896	8 928	15 423	10 668	36 904	22 454	22 012	119 285	275 574
1985	2 957	8 944	15 455	10 649	37 226	22 521	22 115	119 866	278 108
1986	3 015	8 959	15 481	10 631	37 504	22 600	22 213	120 402	280 646
1987	3 075	8 972	15 511	10 613	37 741	22 686	22 283	120 881	283 124
1988	3 137	8 982	15 537	10 443	37 867	22 769	22 358	121 092	285 482
1989	3 196	8 990	15 559	10 398	37 970	22 852	22 429	121 394	287 011
1990	3 258	8 894	15 572	10 372	38 119	22 866	22 488	121 569	289 045
1991	3 238	8 772	15 587	10 365	38 253	22 826	22 806	121 847	290 754
1992	3 175	8 659	15 619	10 349	38 371	22 797	22 912	121 880	292 079
1993	3 172	8 441	15 650	10 329	38 469	22 769	22 775	121 605	292 686
1994	3 198	8 360	15 676	10 313	38 551	22 739	22 543	121 379	292 755
1995	3 237	8 272	15 687	10 296	38 603	22 693	22 347	121 135	292 597
1996	3 280	8 181	15 686	10 274	38 633	22 628	22 303	120 983	292 188
1997	3 318	8 085	15 685	10 245	38 656	22 562	22 391	120 942	291 750
1998	3 367	7 985	15 684	10 211	38 664	22 509	22 506	120 924	291 373
1999	3 443	7 889	15 682	10 174	38 658	22 459	22 600	120 904	291 012
2000	3 490	7 797	15 680	10 139	38 646	22 411	22 750	120 913	290 654
2001	3 510	7 707	15 679	10 106	38 634	22 364	22 911	120 912	290 349
2002	3 545	7 621	15 679	10 075	38 625	22 318	23 001	120 864	290 154
2003	3 582	7 538	15 679	10 045	38 623	22 272	23 066	120 805	290 062

Table 3b. **GDP Levels in Former Eastern Europe and USSR, 1820-1949**[a]
(million 1990 international Geary-Khamis dollars)

	Albania	Bulgaria	Czecho-slovakia	Hungary	Poland	Romania	Yugoslavia	Total 7 EE	USSR
1820			6 501					24 906	37 678
1850			9 981					38 593	
1870	*269*	*2 172*	11 820	6 459	*15 954*	*8 546*	*4 943*	50 163	83 646
1890	*434*	*3 896*	16 936	9 751	*29 345*	*12 925*	*8 169*	81 456	
1900	*548*	*4 892*	20 994	11 990	*38 016*	*15 565*	*10 079*	102 084	154 049
1910	*682*	*6 581*	25 851	15 291	*45 028*	*19 698*	13 795	126 926	
1913	*728*	*7 240*	27 755	16 447	*46 449*	*21 810*	14 364	134 793	232 351
1920			25 091	13 585			12 810		
1921			27 117				13 129		
1922			26 395				13 522		
1923			28 588				14 234		
1924		4 976	31 558	15 740			15 264		
1925		5 156	35 277	18 914			16 025		
1926		6 671	35 138	18 125		16 850	17 154		
1927		7 274	37 775	18 914		16 850	16 884		
1928		7 160	41 106	20 576		16 850	18 381		231 886
1929	*905*	7 023	42 240	21 250	58 980	16 079	19 363	165 840	238 392
1930		7 741	40 856	20 789	56 247	17 235	18 995		252 333
1931		8 876	39 468	19 786	52 177	17 640	18 430		257 213
1932		8 933	37 886	19 260	48 107	16 657	16 712		254 424
1933		9 084	36 276	21 003	46 771	17 447	17 228		264 880
1934		8 308	34 889	21 135	47 439	17 640	17 866		290 903
1935		7 928	34 556	22 204	48 107	18 026	17 596		334 818
1936		9 659	37 387	23 684	49 504	18 218	19 878		361 306
1937		10 204	41 578	23 158	58 980	17 447	20 197		398 017
1938		10 470		24 342	67 788	19 375	21 817		405 220
1939		10 599		26 184			23 019		430 314
1940		10 319		24 391					420 091
1941		10 520		24 539					333 656
1942		10 018		25 773					333 656
1943		10 334							333 656
1944		9 551							333 656
1945		7 447							333 656
1946				15 559					332 727
1947				16 102			20 516		369 903
1948			38 108	20 148		12 975	24 492		420 555
1949			40 218	21 776			26 921		465 631

a) proxies are shown in bold italics.

Table 3b. **GDP Levels in Former Eastern Europe and USSR, 1950-2002**
(million 1990 international Geary-Khamis dollars)

	Albania	Bulgaria	Czecho-slovakia	Hungary	Poland	Romania	Yugoslavia	Total 7 EE	USSR
1950	1 229	11 971	43 368	23 158	60 742	19 279	25 277	185 023	510 243
1951	1 310	14 434	44 159	25 395	63 414	20 674	26 284	195 670	512 566
1952	1 342	13 773	45 630	26 250	64 872	22 169	24 200	198 236	545 792
1953	1 431	15 317	45 436	26 727	68 638	23 773	27 823	209 145	569 260
1954	1 516	15 030	47 295	27 664	72 526	25 493	29 362	218 886	596 910
1955	1 644	16 107	51 348	30 164	76 049	27 337	31 208	233 857	648 027
1956	1 711	16 121	54 373	28 799	79 450	28 544	30 495	239 494	710 065
1957	1 874	17 831	57 704	31 184	83 641	29 805	35 573	257 611	724 470
1958	2 018	19 382	62 117	33 273	87 711	31 121	37 014	272 635	778 840
1959	2 170	20 926	64 837	34 622	90 262	32 496	41 574	286 886	770 244
1960	2 355	22 908	69 749	36 431	95 121	33 931	44 190	304 685	843 434
1961	2 453	24 401	72 525	38 273	102 714	36 225	46 190	322 781	891 763
1962	2 612	26 405	73 496	39 868	101 317	37 497	47 057	328 253	915 928
1963	2 782	27 611	72 109	42 056	107 391	40 196	51 967	344 112	895 016
1964	2 962	29 787	75 495	44 424	112 190	42 741	56 919	364 518	1 010 727
1965	3 156	31 575	78 270	44 770	118 386	45 402	58 458	380 016	1 068 117
1966	3 360	34 067	81 657	47 319	125 857	50 588	61 605	404 452	1 119 932
1967	3 579	35 898	85 154	50 033	130 412	52 901	62 668	420 645	1 169 422
1968	3 810	36 559	89 123	50 641	138 309	54 019	63 983	436 444	1 237 966
1969	4 058	38 340	90 760	52 155	136 912	56 506	71 131	449 862	1 255 392
1970	4 321	40 523	92 592	51 974	144 018	57 779	74 489	465 695	1 351 818
1971	4 602	41 844	95 756	54 293	154 284	65 934	83 078	499 790	1 387 832
1972	4 901	43 826	99 142	55 460	165 521	70 175	85 945	524 971	1 395 732
1973	5 218	45 557	102 445	58 339	177 973	72 411	88 813	550 756	1 513 070
1974	5 357	46 986	106 165	59 852	188 421	76 479	100 269	583 528	1 556 984
1975	5 497	50 849	109 301	61 135	197 289	79 911	100 269	604 251	1 561 399
1976	5 643	52 371	111 050	61 316	202 209	83 998	103 375	619 961	1 634 589
1977	5 793	51 869	116 073	65 164	205 975	85 906	110 901	641 681	1 673 159
1978	5 945	52 989	117 489	66 743	213 446	88 702	117 014	662 328	1 715 215
1979	6 101	55 028	118 488	66 875	209 498	91 266	125 043	672 299	1 707 083
1980	6 270	53 449	121 763	67 549	204 213	91 517	131 058	675 819	1 709 174
1981	6 428	54 870	121 153	68 026	193 341	90 957	133 156	667 932	1 724 741
1982	6 596	56 644	123 512	70 477	191 579	91 035	134 359	674 202	1 767 262
1983	6 771	55 574	125 371	69 753	201 055	90 225	135 576	684 326	1 823 723
1984	6 951	57 412	128 313	71 579	208 526	93 811	138 682	705 274	1 847 190
1985	7 133	55 682	129 313	69 819	210 713	93 657	139 885	706 201	1 863 687
1986	7 321	57 154	131 700	71 217	217 394	95 257	145 690	725 733	1 940 363
1987	7 514	57 262	132 366	72 319	214 479	93 252	143 997	721 188	1 965 457
1988	7 713	56 903	135 308	73 421	219 217	93 020	141 983	727 564	2 007 280
1989	7 917	55 883	136 418	71 776	215 815	90 051	140 179	718 039	2 037 253
1990	8 125	49 779	132 560	66 990	194 920	80 277	129 953	662 604	1 987 995
1991	5 850	45 598	115 937	59 019	181 245	69 921	112 710	590 280	1 863 524
1992	5 429	42 689	113 318	57 211	185 804	63 768	91 392	559 611	1 592 084
1993	5 950	41 635	112 191	56 881	192 749	64 725	76 268	550 399	1 435 008
1994	6 444	42 384	115 603	58 557	202 815	67 249	79 190	572 242	1 231 738
1995	7 301	43 613	122 621	59 430	217 060	72 024	83 343	605 392	1 163 401
1996	7 965	39 514	128 423	60 226	230 147	74 833	87 483	628 591	1 125 992
1997	7 408	37 301	129 782	62 980	244 450	70 268	92 850	645 039	1 149 255
1998	8 000	38 793	130 452	66 039	257 765	66 895	95 527	663 471	1 124 868
1999	8 584	39 868	131 431	68 794	268 213	66 092	92 675	675 657	1 171 952
2000	9 252	41 829	135 313	72 366	278 826	67 282	96 878	701 746	1 264 526
2001	9 855	43 502	139 777	75 127	289 421	70 848	100 262	728 792	1 343 230
2002									1 405 639

Table 3c. **Per Capita GDP in Former Eastern Europe and USSR, 1820-1949**[a]
(1990 international Geary-Khamis dollars)

	Albania	Bulgaria	Czecho-slovakia	Hungary	Poland	Romania	Yugoslavia	Average 7 EE	USSR
1820			849					683	688
1850			1 079					869	
1870	*446*	*840*	1 164	1 092	*946*	*931*	*599*	937	943
1890	*598*	*1 131*	1 505	1 473	*1 284*	*1 246*	*843*	1 254	
1900	*685*	*1 223*	1 729	1 682	*1 536*	*1 415*	902	1 438	1 237
1910	*780*	*1 456*	1 991	2 000	*1 690*	*1 660*	1 057	1 636	
1913	*811*	*1 534*	2 096	2 098	*1 739*	*1 741*	1 057	1 695	1 488
1920			1 933	1 709			1 031		
1921			2 085				1 041		
1922			2 006				1 057		
1923			2 151				1 096		
1924		909	2 353	1 912			1 158		
1925		922	2 606	2 279			1 198		
1926		1 169	2 575	2 162		1 258	1 263		
1927		1 255	2 752	2 237		1 241	1 225		
1928		1 219	2 977	2 415		1 225	1 314		1 370
1929	*926*	1 180	3 042	2 476	2 117	1 152	1 364	1 942	1 386
1930		1 284	2 926	2 404	1 994	1 219	1 318		1 448
1931		1 454	2 809	2 268	1 823	1 229	1 261		1 462
1932		1 444	2 680	2 192	1 658	1 144	1 128		1 439
1933		1 450	2 552	2 374	1 590	1 184	1 147		1 493
1934		1 309	2 443	2 370	1 593	1 182	1 173		1 630
1935		1 236	2 410	2 471	1 597	1 196	1 140		1 864
1936		1 493	2 599	2 618	1 625	1 194	1 270		1 991
1937		1 567	2 882	2 543	1 915	1 130	1 273		2 156
1938		1 595		2 655	2 182	1 242	1 356		2 150
1939		1 603		2 838			1 412		2 237
1940		1 548		2 626					2 144
1941		1 567		2 626					
1942		1 479		2 743					
1943		1 513							
1944		1 387							
1945		1 073							
1946				1 721					1 913
1947				1 774			1 315		2 126
1948			3 088	2 200		816	1 548		2 402
1949			3 259	2 354			1 678		2 623

a)   proxies are shown in bold italics.

Table 3c. **Per Capita GDP in Former Eastern Europe and USSR, 1950-2002**
(1990 international Geary-Khamis dollars)

	Albania	Bulgaria	Czecho-slovakia	Hungary	Poland	Romania	Yugoslavia	Average 7 EE	USSR
1950	1 001	1 651	3 501	2 480	2 447	1 182	1 551	2 111	2 841
1951	1 045	1 989	3 524	2 695	2 510	1 256	1 591	2 206	2 806
1952	1 046	1 893	3 598	2 762	2 521	1 333	1 448	2 207	2 937
1953	1 089	2 085	3 544	2 786	2 618	1 411	1 643	2 296	3 013
1954	1 120	2 025	3 652	2 850	2 715	1 496	1 712	2 370	3 106
1955	1 181	2 148	3 922	3 070	2 794	1 578	1 797	2 495	3 313
1956	1 193	2 128	4 110	2 906	2 864	1 623	1 742	2 521	3 566
1957	1 269	2 330	4 320	3 169	2 962	1 672	2 014	2 682	3 576
1958	1 326	2 508	4 610	3 367	3 057	1 724	2 080	2 806	3 777
1959	1 381	2 684	4 780	3 484	3 096	1 783	2 314	2 921	3 669
1960	1 451	2 912	5 108	3 649	3 215	1 844	2 437	3 070	3 945
1961	1 463	3 072	5 263	3 816	3 426	1 951	2 522	3 218	4 098
1962	1 511	3 295	5 304	3 962	3 341	2 007	2 544	3 244	4 140
1963	1 563	3 418	5 170	4 168	3 502	2 137	2 781	3 372	3 985
1964	1 616	3 657	5 372	4 388	3 622	2 258	3 019	3 542	4 439
1965	1 675	3 850	5 533	4 410	3 787	2 386	3 071	3 664	4 634
1966	1 738	4 125	5 741	4 646	3 991	2 643	3 205	3 871	4 804
1967	1 804	4 320	5 964	4 894	4 103	2 743	3 232	3 996	4 963
1968	1 869	4 368	6 223	4 934	4 317	2 739	3 272	4 106	5 202
1969	1 932	4 546	6 354	5 062	4 241	2 824	3 610	4 200	5 225
1970	2 004	4 773	6 466	5 028	4 428	2 853	3 755	4 315	5 575
1971	2 084	4 902	6 658	5 238	4 707	3 221	4 151	4 596	5 667
1972	2 165	5 110	6 858	5 336	5 010	3 396	4 255	4 790	5 643
1973	2 273	5 284	7 041	5 596	5 340	3 477	4 361	4 988	6 059
1974	2 282	5 414	7 243	5 716	5 601	3 637	4 879	5 239	6 176
1975	2 289	5 831	7 399	5 805	5 808	3 761	4 836	5 377	6 135
1976	2 299	5 982	7 461	5 791	5 895	3 917	4 939	5 469	6 363
1977	2 309	5 896	7 744	6 126	5 949	3 966	5 250	5 612	6 454
1978	2 319	6 019	7 786	6 253	6 111	4 063	5 491	5 749	6 559
1979	2 331	6 245	7 804	6 251	5 942	4 148	5 819	5 793	6 472
1980	2 347	6 044	7 982	6 306	5 740	4 135	6 063	5 786	6 426
1981	2 360	6 186	7 912	6 351	5 385	4 087	6 134	5 685	6 430
1982	2 373	6 370	8 045	6 583	5 288	4 072	6 146	5 705	6 533
1983	2 387	6 237	8 147	6 525	5 498	4 027	6 172	5 762	6 680
1984	2 400	6 430	8 319	6 710	5 650	4 178	6 300	5 913	6 703
1985	2 413	6 226	8 367	6 557	5 660	4 159	6 325	5 892	6 701
1986	2 428	6 380	8 507	6 699	5 797	4 215	6 559	6 028	6 914
1987	2 443	6 382	8 534	6 814	5 683	4 110	6 462	5 966	6 942
1988	2 459	6 335	8 709	7 031	5 789	4 085	6 351	6 008	7 031
1989	2 477	6 216	8 768	6 903	5 684	3 941	6 250	5 915	7 098
1990	2 494	5 597	8 513	6 459	5 113	3 511	5 779	5 450	6 878
1991	1 806	5 198	7 438	5 694	4 738	3 063	4 942	4 844	6 409
1992	1 710	4 930	7 255	5 528	4 842	2 797	3 989	4 591	5 451
1993	1 876	4 933	7 169	5 507	5 010	2 843	3 349	4 526	4 903
1994	2 015	5 070	7 374	5 678	5 261	2 957	3 513	4 714	4 207
1995	2 256	5 272	7 817	5 772	5 623	3 174	3 729	4 998	3 976
1996	2 428	4 830	8 187	5 862	5 957	3 307	3 923	5 196	3 854
1997	2 233	4 614	8 274	6 148	6 324	3 114	4 147	5 333	3 939
1998	2 376	4 858	8 318	6 467	6 667	2 972	4 245	5 487	3 861
1999	2 493	5 054	8 381	6 762	6 938	2 943	4 101	5 588	4 027
2000	2 651	5 365	8 630	7 138	7 215	3 002	4 258	5 804	4 351
2001	2 807	5 644	8 915	7 434	7 491	3 168	4 376	6 027	4 626
2002									4 844

HS–3: B. 7 Successor States of Former Czechoslovakia and Yugoslavia

Table 3a. Population of Successor Republics of Yugoslavia and Czechoslovakia, 1950-2003
(000 at mid-year)

	Bosnia	Croatia	Macedonia	Slovenia	Serbia/ Montenegro	Former Yugoslavia	Czech Republic	Slovakia	Former Czecho-slovakia
1950	2 662	3 837	1 225	1 468	7 106	16 298	8 925	3 463	12 389
1951	2 721	3 860	1 256	1 483	7 199	16 519	9 023	3 509	12 532
1952	2 791	3 882	1 272	1 490	7 274	16 708	9 125	3 558	12 683
1953	2 863	3 906	1 299	1 498	7 370	16 937	9 221	3 599	12 820
1954	2 916	3 930	1 325	1 509	7 471	17 151	9 291	3 661	12 952
1955	2 974	3 956	1 340	1 517	7 577	17 364	9 366	3 727	13 093
1956	3 025	3 973	1 340	1 525	7 644	17 508	9 442	3 787	13 229
1957	3 076	3 991	1 345	1 533	7 714	17 659	9 514	3 844	13 358
1958	3 126	4 004	1 345	1 540	7 780	17 796	9 575	3 900	13 474
1959	3 185	4 021	1 354	1 549	7 860	17 968	9 619	3 946	13 565
1960	3 240	4 036	1 366	1 558	7 932	18 133	9 660	3 994	13 654
1961	3 299	4 055	1 382	1 572	8 010	18 318	9 587	4 192	13 779
1962	3 349	4 077	1 401	1 583	8 091	18 500	9 620	4 237	13 858
1963	3 399	4 099	1 422	1 595	8 170	18 685	9 666	4 282	13 948
1964	3 445	4 114	1 445	1 606	8 243	18 852	9 726	4 326	14 052
1965	3 493	4 133	1 470	1 620	8 322	19 038	9 777	4 370	14 147
1966	3 541	4 156	1 490	1 632	8 403	19 221	9 815	4 409	14 224
1967	3 585	4 174	1 512	1 647	8 472	19 390	9 835	4 442	14 277
1968	3 627	4 190	1 533	1 658	8 545	19 552	9 851	4 472	14 323
1969	3 669	4 201	1 554	1 667	8 615	19 705	9 807	4 478	14 284
1970	3 703	4 205	1 574	1 676	8 681	19 840	9 795	4 524	14 319
1971	3 761	4 216	1 596	1 686	8 756	20 015	9 825	4 557	14 381
1972	3 819	4 225	1 618	1 695	8 841	20 197	9 862	4 593	14 456
1973	3 872	4 235	1 639	1 703	8 918	20 367	9 912	4 637	14 549
1974	3 925	4 246	1 662	1 713	9 004	20 550	9 976	4 682	14 658
1975	3 980	4 255	1 684	1 722	9 091	20 732	10 042	4 730	14 772
1976	4 033	4 286	1 706	1 734	9 169	20 930	10 105	4 779	14 884
1977	4 086	4 319	1 728	1 747	9 246	21 126	10 162	4 828	14 990
1978	4 135	4 349	1 747	1 759	9 318	21 309	10 213	4 876	15 089
1979	4 181	4 380	1 768	1 773	9 388	21 490	10 260	4 923	15 182
1980	4 092	4 383	1 792	1 833	9 515	21 615	10 289	4 966	15 255
1981	4 136	4 391	1 808	1 839	9 533	21 707	10 298	5 014	15 312
1982	4 173	4 413	1 827	1 851	9 595	21 860	10 304	5 048	15 352
1983	4 207	4 431	1 838	1 858	9 633	21 968	10 307	5 081	15 388
1984	4 241	4 442	1 848	1 866	9 615	22 012	10 309	5 114	15 423
1985	4 275	4 458	1 859	1 873	9 650	22 115	10 310	5 145	15 455
1986	4 308	4 472	1 868	1 880	9 685	22 213	10 309	5 172	15 481
1987	4 339	4 484	1 878	1 883	9 698	22 283	10 312	5 199	15 511
1988	4 370	4 494	1 884	1 889	9 722	22 358	10 314	5 223	15 537
1989	4 398	4 501	1 891	1 892	9 746	22 429	10 314	5 245	15 559
1990	4 424	4 508	1 893	1 896	9 766	22 488	10 310	5 263	15 572
1991	4 449	4 541	1 903	1 894	10 018	22 806	10 305	5 282	15 587
1992	4 427	4 432	1 929	1 892	10 232	22 912	10 316	5 303	15 619
1993	4 152	4 421	1 962	1 896	10 345	22 775	10 327	5 324	15 650
1994	3 704	4 488	1 983	1 903	10 464	22 543	10 331	5 345	15 676
1995	3 356	4 455	1 986	1 909	10 641	22 347	10 325	5 362	15 687
1996	3 247	4 373	1 993	1 914	10 775	22 303	10 313	5 373	15 686
1997	3 335	4 320	2 002	1 918	10 817	22 391	10 301	5 384	15 685
1998	3 502	4 265	2 015	1 921	10 803	22 506	10 291	5 393	15 684
1999	3 690	4 254	2 032	1 924	10 698	22 600	10 281	5 401	15 682
2000	3 836	4 282	2 041	1 928	10 663	22 750	10 272	5 408	15 680
2001	3 922	4 334	2 046	1 930	10 678	22 911	10 264	5 415	15 679
2002	3 964	4 391	2 055	1 933	10 658	23 001	10 257	5 422	15 679
2003	3 989	4 422	2 063	1 936	10 656	23 066	10 249	5 430	15 679

Table 3b. **GDP Levels in Successor Republics of Yugoslavia and Czechoslovakia, 1990-2001**
(million 1990 international Geary-Khamis dollars)

	Bosnia	Croatia	Macedonia	Slovenia	Serbia/ Montenegro	Former Yugoslavia	Czech Republic	Slovakia	Former Czecho- slovakia
1990	16 530	33 139	7 394	21 624	51 266	129 953	91 706	40 854	132 560
1991	14 610	26 147	6 935	19 699	45 319	112 710	81 068	34 869	115 937
1992	10 535	23 088	6 478	18 616	32 675	91 392	80 662	32 656	113 318
1993	7 287	21 241	5 992	19 137	22 611	76 268	80 743	31 448	112 191
1994	7 484	22 494	5 884	20 152	23 176	79 190	82 520	33 083	115 603
1995	7 933	24 023	5 819	20 978	24 590	83 343	87 388	35 233	122 621
1996	8 400	25 441	5 889	21 712	26 041	87 483	91 146	37 277	128 423
1997	9 028	27 171	5 972	22 711	27 968	92 850	90 417	39 365	129 782
1998	9 261	27 850	6 175	23 574	28 667	95 527	89 512	40 940	130 452
1999	10 243	27 599	6 440	24 800	23 593	92 675	89 960	41 471	131 431
2000	10 704	28 400	6 730	25 941	25 103	96 878	92 929	42 384	135 313
2001	10 950	29 479	6 454	26 719	26 660	100 262	95 995	43 782	139 777

Table 3c. **Per Capita GDP in Successor Republics of Yugoslavia and Czechoslovakia, 1990-2001**
(1990 international Geary-Khamis dollars)

	Bosnia	Croatia	Macedonia	Slovenia	Serbia/ Montenegro	Former Yugoslavia	Czech Republic	Slovakia	Former Czecho- slovakia
1990	3 737	7 351	3 905	11 404	5 249	5 779	8 895	7 763	8 513
1991	3 284	5 758	3 644	10 402	4 524	4 942	7 867	6 602	7 438
1992	2 380	5 209	3 358	9 842	3 194	3 989	7 819	6 158	7 255
1993	1 755	4 805	3 055	10 094	2 186	3 349	7 819	5 907	7 169
1994	2 021	5 012	2 967	10 590	2 215	3 513	7 988	6 189	7 374
1995	2 364	5 392	2 930	10 987	2 311	3 729	8 464	6 571	7 817
1996	2 587	5 818	2 954	11 341	2 417	3 923	8 838	6 938	8 187
1997	2 707	6 290	2 983	11 842	2 586	4 147	8 777	7 312	8 274
1998	2 644	6 530	3 065	12 272	2 654	4 245	8 698	7 592	8 318
1999	2 776	6 487	3 169	12 886	2 205	4 101	8 750	7 679	8 381
2000	2 791	6 632	3 297	13 458	2 354	4 258	9 047	7 837	8 630
2001	2 792	6 802	3 154	13 843	2 497	4 376	9 352	8 085	8 915

HS–3: C. 15 SUCCESSOR STATES OF FORMER USSR

Table 3a. **Population of Successor Republics of USSR, 1950-2003**
(000 at mid-year)

	Armenia	Azerbaijan	Belarus	Estonia	Georgia	Kazakhstan	Kyrgyzstan	Latvia
1950	1 355	2 885	7 722	1 096	3 516	6 693	1 739	1 936
1951	1 379	2 983	7 742	1 112	3 579	6 936	1 767	1 951
1952	1 417	3 091	7 698	1 130	3 628	7 123	1 787	1 964
1953	1 456	3 159	7 667	1 140	3 687	7 261	1 817	1 976
1954	1 506	3 223	7 699	1 148	3 760	7 517	1 858	1 991
1955	1 565	3 314	7 781	1 154	3 827	7 977	1 901	2 002
1956	1 617	3 417	7 857	1 163	3 887	8 414	1 939	2 026
1957	1 672	3 526	7 913	1 174	3 937	8 710	1 976	2 056
1958	1 733	3 631	7 983	1 185	3 995	9 063	2 027	2 072
1959	1 796	3 741	8 075	1 197	4 071	9 500	2 096	2 089
1960	1 869	3 882	8 168	1 211	4 147	9 982	2 171	2 115
1961	1 944	4 034	8 263	1 224	4 211	10 467	2 255	2 146
1962	2 007	4 157	8 365	1 239	4 279	10 946	2 333	2 173
1963	2 066	4 283	8 439	1 255	4 344	11 312	2 413	2 199
1964	2 135	4 430	8 502	1 272	4 407	11 602	2 495	2 227
1965	2 206	4 567	8 591	1 288	4 465	11 902	2 573	2 254
1966	2 274	4 702	8 694	1 300	4 518	12 180	2 655	2 279
1967	2 338	4 827	8 787	1 312	4 565	12 452	2 737	2 301
1968	2 402	4 945	8 865	1 324	4 607	12 692	2 818	2 322
1969	2 463	5 059	8 946	1 343	4 650	12 900	2 896	2 342
1970	2 520	5 169	9 027	1 363	4 694	13 106	2 964	2 361
1971	2 582	5 284	9 101	1 381	4 742	13 325	3 029	2 382
1972	2 647	5 394	9 169	1 397	4 786	13 542	3 095	2 401
1973	2 713	5 498	9 236	1 411	4 826	13 754	3 161	2 421
1974	2 777	5 599	9 304	1 422	4 865	13 972	3 232	2 442
1975	2 834	5 696	9 360	1 432	4 898	14 157	3 301	2 462
1976	2 893	5 790	9 406	1 442	4 930	14 304	3 367	2 477
1977	2 955	5 887	9 457	1 453	4 963	14 455	3 432	2 491
1978	3 014	5 986	9 520	1 464	4 991	14 624	3 496	2 505
1979	3 067	6 082	9 582	1 472	5 019	14 804	3 559	2 514
1980	3 115	6 173	9 644	1 482	5 048	14 994	3 623	2 525
1981	3 165	6 271	9 713	1 493	5 078	15 192	3 690	2 538
1982	3 217	6 369	9 779	1 504	5 109	15 389	3 763	2 554
1983	3 267	6 470	9 845	1 515	5 141	15 582	3 842	2 572
1984	3 319	6 579	9 914	1 526	5 174	15 775	3 924	2 591
1985	3 369	6 682	9 982	1 538	5 208	15 966	4 006	2 610
1986	3 417	6 776	10 044	1 550	5 237	16 154	4 089	2 631
1987	3 463	6 874	10 097	1 562	5 260	16 349	4 176	2 654
1988	3 509	6 976	10 150	1 569	5 343	16 478	4 244	2 670
1989	3 319	7 102	10 184	1 571	5 424	16 568	4 304	2 674
1990	3 366	7 200	10 215	1 573	5 457	16 708	4 390	2 672
1991	3 413	7 308	10 245	1 568	5 478	16 855	4 468	2 663
1992	3 448	7 414	10 306	1 546	5 466	16 985	4 532	2 631
1993	3 458	7 497	10 361	1 517	5 422	17 016	4 552	2 586
1994	3 440	7 573	10 388	1 499	5 359	16 990	4 544	2 552
1995	3 414	7 630	10 404	1 484	5 287	16 943	4 535	2 523
1996	3 394	7 668	10 409	1 470	5 216	16 882	4 537	2 496
1997	3 378	7 695	10 404	1 458	5 154	16 824	4 552	2 470
1998	3 365	7 714	10 394	1 449	5 100	16 779	4 581	2 447
1999	3 354	7 729	10 382	1 440	5 055	16 749	4 626	2 426
2000	3 344	7 748	10 367	1 431	5 020	16 733	4 685	2 405
2001	3 336	7 771	10 350	1 423	4 989	16 731	4 753	2 385
2002	3 330	7 798	10 335	1 416	4 961	16 742	4 822	2 367
2003	3 326	7 831	10 322	1 409	4 934	16 764	4 893	2 349

Table 3a. **Population of Successor Republics of USSR, 1950-2003**
(000 at mid-year)

	Lithuania	Moldova	Russian Federation	Tajikistan	Turkmenistan	Ukraine	Uzbekistan	Former USSR
1950	2 553	2 336	101 937	1 530	1 204	36 775	6 293	179 571
1951	2 562	2 422	103 507	1 585	1 226	37 436	6 490	182 677
1952	2 584	2 467	105 385	1 641	1 253	38 006	6 681	185 856
1953	2 594	2 506	107 303	1 684	1 283	38 541	6 886	188 961
1954	2 597	2 566	109 209	1 730	1 313	38 994	7 061	192 171
1955	2 614	2 622	111 125	1 781	1 348	39 368	7 232	195 613
1956	2 641	2 682	112 859	1 837	1 382	39 940	7 441	199 103
1957	2 652	2 759	114 555	1 899	1 426	40 656	7 694	202 604
1958	2 672	2 838	116 259	1 954	1 478	41 359	7 952	206 201
1959	2 718	2 919	117 957	2 009	1 530	42 006	8 223	209 928
1960	2 765	2 999	119 632	2 081	1 585	42 644	8 531	213 780
1961	2 810	3 069	121 324	2 163	1 644	43 196	8 868	217 618
1962	2 850	3 136	122 878	2 253	1 705	43 697	9 210	221 227
1963	2 886	3 205	124 277	2 340	1 765	44 256	9 547	224 585
1964	2 923	3 271	125 522	2 424	1 825	44 786	9 878	227 698
1965	2 959	3 334	126 541	2 511	1 882	45 235	10 206	230 513
1966	2 997	3 394	127 415	2 593	1 936	45 674	10 530	233 139
1967	3 034	3 452	128 184	2 672	1 994	46 111	10 864	235 630
1968	3 069	3 506	128 876	2 759	2 054	46 510	11 232	237 983
1969	3 102	3 549	129 573	2 850	2 116	46 871	11 591	240 253
1970	3 138	3 595	130 245	2 939	2 181	47 236	11 940	242 478
1971	3 178	3 649	130 977	3 039	2 247	47 637	12 334	244 887
1972	3 213	3 703	131 769	3 145	2 313	48 027	12 742	247 343
1973	3 246	3 753	132 556	3 243	2 380	48 367	13 148	249 712
1974	3 276	3 801	133 379	3 345	2 451	48 677	13 569	252 111
1975	3 305	3 847	134 293	3 449	2 524	48 973	13 988	254 519
1976	3 334	3 886	135 269	3 554	2 594	49 234	14 404	256 883
1977	3 361	3 920	136 264	3 659	2 664	49 454	14 809	259 225
1978	3 387	3 947	137 246	3 761	2 734	49 643	15 207	261 525
1979	3 411	3 970	138 164	3 863	2 804	49 835	15 605	263 751
1980	3 436	3 996	139 045	3 969	2 875	50 047	16 000	265 973
1981	3 464	4 026	139 913	4 079	2 947	50 236	16 413	268 217
1982	3 494	4 055	140 841	4 194	3 018	50 397	16 850	270 533
1983	3 526	4 083	141 888	4 316	3 091	50 573	17 298	273 010
1984	3 559	4 113	142 955	4 446	3 165	50 769	17 764	275 574
1985	3 592	4 148	143 978	4 587	3 240	50 944	18 258	278 108
1986	3 625	4 183	145 013	4 738	3 324	51 095	18 769	280 646
1987	3 660	4 217	146 013	4 891	3 411	51 218	19 280	283 124
1988	3 681	4 290	146 926	5 036	3 492	51 423	19 694	285 482
1989	3 689	4 359	147 419	5 183	3 574	51 528	20 112	287 011
1990	3 702	4 398	148 082	5 332	3 668	51 658	20 624	289 045
1991	3 709	4 428	148 460	5 481	3 761	51 782	21 137	290 754
1992	3 707	4 448	148 587	5 601	3 848	51 946	21 614	292 079
1993	3 694	4 460	148 479	5 682	3 934	51 978	22 049	292 686
1994	3 682	4 463	148 300	5 771	4 019	51 712	22 462	292 755
1995	3 673	4 460	148 115	5 864	4 102	51 316	22 847	292 597
1996	3 662	4 451	147 757	5 964	4 184	50 879	23 220	292 188
1997	3 652	4 442	147 364	6 071	4 267	50 423	23 597	291 750
1998	3 642	4 436	146 964	6 186	4 350	49 989	23 977	291 373
1999	3 631	4 432	146 516	6 309	4 434	49 566	24 363	291 012
2000	3 621	4 431	146 001	6 441	4 518	49 153	24 756	290 654
2001	3 611	4 432	145 470	6 579	4 603	48 760	25 155	290 349
2002	3 601	4 435	144 979	6 720	4 689	48 396	25 563	290 154
2003	3 593	4 440	144 526	6 864	4 776	48 055	25 982	290 062

Table 3b. **GDP Levels in Successor Republics of USSR, 1973-2002**
(million 1990 international Geary-Khamis dollars)

	Armenia	Azerbaijan	Belarus	Estonia	Georgia	Kazakhstan	Kyrgyzstan	Latvia
1973	16 691	24 378	48 333	12 214	28 627	104 875	11 781	18 998
1990	20 483	33 397	73 389	16 980	41 325	122 295	15 787	26 413
1991	18 077	33 159	72 491	15 280	32 612	108 830	14 537	23 666
1992	10 534	25 673	65 534	13 118	17 961	103 024	12 533	15 426
1993	9 602	19 736	60 596	12 010	12 704	93 636	10 590	13 117
1994	10 121	15 848	55 142	11 770	11 383	81 838	8 493	13 196
1995	10 819	13 978	49 408	12 276	11 679	75 045	8 035	13 090
1996	11 457	14 160	45 079	12 755	12 905	75 421	8 597	13 522
1997	12 294	14 981	56 581	14 005	14 196	76 246	9 448	14 685
1998	13 191	16 479	61 277	14 649	14 607	74 797	9 646	15 258
1999	13 626	17 698	63 361	14 561	15 045	76 817	10 003	15 425
2000	14 443	19 663	67 036	15 595	15 331	84 345	10 544	16 295
2001	15 830	21 433	69 784	16 375	16 021	95 478	11 102	17 534
2002	17 025	23 126	72 227	17 111	16 582	103 117	11 591	18 411

Table 3c. **Per Capita GDP in Successor Republics of USSR, 1973-2002**
(1990 international Geary-Khamis dollars)

	Armenia	Azerbaijan	Belarus	Estonia	Georgia	Kazakhstan	Kyrgyzstan	Latvia
1973	6 152	4 434	5 233	8 657	5 932	7 625	3 727	7 846
1990	6 086	4 639	7 184	10 794	7 573	7 319	3 596	9 886
1991	5 297	4 537	7 076	9 744	5 954	6 457	3 253	8 888
1992	3 055	3 463	6 359	8 488	3 286	6 066	2 766	5 863
1993	2 776	2 632	5 849	7 916	2 343	5 503	2 326	5 071
1994	2 942	2 093	5 308	7 850	2 124	4 817	1 869	5 171
1995	3 169	1 832	4 749	8 274	2 209	4 429	1 772	5 189
1996	3 376	1 847	4 331	8 680	2 474	4 468	1 895	5 418
1997	3 640	1 947	5 438	9 605	2 755	4 532	2 076	5 944
1998	3 920	2 136	5 895	10 112	2 864	4 458	2 105	6 236
1999	4 062	2 290	6 103	10 112	2 976	4 586	2 162	6 359
2000	4 319	2 538	6 466	10 894	3 054	5 041	2 250	6 776
2001	4 745	2 758	6 742	11 505	3 211	5 707	2 336	7 351
2002	5 112	2 965	6 988	12 087	3 343	6 159	2 404	7 780

Table 3b. **GDP Levels in Successor Republics of USSR, 1973-2002**
(million 1990 international Geary-Khamis dollars)

	Lithuania	Moldova	Russian Federation	Tajikistan	Turkmenistan	Ukraine	Uzbekistan	Former USSR
1973	24 643	20 134	872 466	13 279	11 483	238 156	67 012	1 513 070
1990	32 010	27 112	1 151 040	15 884	13 300	311 112	87 468	1 987 995
1991	30 189	22 362	1 094 081	14 537	12 673	284 003	87 027	1 863 524
1992	23 768	15 889	935 072	9 844	10 778	255 602	77 328	1 592 084
1993	19 928	15 695	853 194	8 243	10 935	219 457	75 565	1 435 008
1994	17 975	10 845	738 013	6 479	9 043	169 201	72 391	1 231 738
1995	18 568	10 693	707 016	5 669	8 392	148 559	70 174	1 163 401
1996	19 181	10 063	682 978	5 420	7 863	133 703	72 888	1 125 992
1997	20 581	10 224	689 125	5 512	6 975	129 692	74 710	1 149 255
1998	21 631	9 559	655 357	5 804	7 463	127 228	77 922	1 124 868
1999	22 474	9 234	690 747	6 019	8 695	126 974	81 273	1 171 952
2000	23 328	9 428	752 914	6 518	10 260	134 465	84 361	1 264 526
2001	24 705	10 003	790 560	7 183	12 363	146 701	88 158	1 343 230
2002	25 791	10 483	825 345	7 686	12 863	153 743	90 538	1 405 639

Table 3c. **Per Capita GDP in Successor Republics of USSR, 1973-2002**
(1990 international Geary-Khamis dollars)

	Lithuania	Moldova	Russian Federation	Tajikistan	Turkmenistan	Ukraine	Uzbekistan	Former USSR
1973	7 593	5 365	6 582	4 095	4 826	4 924	5 097	6 059
1990	8 646	6 165	7 773	2 979	3 626	6 023	4 241	6 878
1991	8 139	5 051	7 370	2 652	3 370	5 485	4 117	6 409
1992	6 412	3 572	6 293	1 758	2 801	4 921	3 578	5 451
1993	5 395	3 519	5 746	1 451	2 780	4 222	3 427	4 903
1994	4 881	2 430	4 976	1 123	2 250	3 272	3 223	4 207
1995	5 055	2 398	4 773	967	2 046	2 895	3 071	3 976
1996	5 237	2 261	4 622	909	1 879	2 628	3 139	3 854
1997	5 636	2 302	4 676	908	1 635	2 572	3 166	3 939
1998	5 940	2 155	4 459	938	1 716	2 545	3 250	3 861
1999	6 189	2 083	4 714	954	1 961	2 562	3 336	4 027
2000	6 443	2 128	5 157	1 012	2 271	2 736	3 408	4 351
2001	6 842	2 257	5 435	1 092	2 686	3 009	3 505	4 626
2002	7 162	2 364	5 693	1 144	2 743	3 177	3 542	4 844

HS–4: Latin America

1500–1820s: Impact of Conquest and Colonisation on Output and Population

At the end of the fifteenth century, at the time of Spanish conquest, the Americas were thinly settled. The population was a third of that in Western Europe and the land area eleven times as large. The technological level was greatly inferior. There were no wheeled vehicles or draught animals, no metal tools, weapons or ploughs. There were no cattle, sheep, pigs or hens. The most densely populated areas (Mexico and Peru) had significant urban centres and a sophisticated vegetarian agriculture. Elsewhere, most of the inhabitants were hunter–gatherers.

American populations had no resistance to European (smallpox, measles, influenza and typhus) and African diseases (yellow fever and malaria). By the middle of the sixteenth century two thirds of them were wiped out. Mortality was twice that of Europe during the Black Death of the fourteenth century.

The two advanced civilisations (Aztec in Mexico and Inca in Peru) were destroyed. Their populations were reduced to anomie and serfdom. Hunter–gatherer populations elsewhere were marginalised or exterminated. The economy of these relatively empty lands was completely revamped. The Latin part of the continent was repopulated by shipment of 7.5 million African slaves and arrival of 1.5 million European settlers. By 1820, 22 per cent of the population were white, 24 per cent black or mulatto, 37 per cent indigenous and 16 per cent mestizo. European settlers had higher fertility, longer life expectation, and very much higher average incomes than African slaves and the indigenous population.

Although the initial impact of conquest was massively destructive, the long–term economic potential was greatly enhanced. Capacity to support a bigger population was augmented by the introduction of new crops and animals. The new items were wheat, rice, sugar cane, vines, cabbages, lettuce, olives, bananas, yams and coffee. The new animals for food were cattle, pigs, chickens, sheep and goats. The introduction of transport and traction animals — horses, oxen, asses and mules — along with wheeled vehicles and ploughs (which replaced digging sticks) were a major contribution to productive capacity. There was a reciprocal transfer of New World crops to Europe, Asia and Africa– maize, potatoes, sweet potatoes, manioc, chilis, tomatoes, groundnuts, haricot, lima and string beans, pineapples, cocoa and tobacco–which enhanced the rest of the world's production capacity and ability to sustain population growth.

The experience of the Americas from 1500 to 1820 was very different from other continents. The demographic catastrophe of the sixteenth century and the collapse of the indigenous economy had no parallel elsewhere. Population and output recovered somewhat in the seventeenth century, but in 1700 were still well below 1500 levels. Growth accelerated in the eighteenth century. By 1820, GDP was twice as big as in 1500, and average per capita income above the world average. The economy, technology and economic institutions had been transformed. Most of the continent was in process of attaining political independence. From 1820 to 2001, demographic expansion was the most dynamic aspect of Latin American development. Population rose 24–fold, compared to 3–fold in the former metropoles (Spain and Portugal). Per capita performance was less impressive. GDP per head rose 8–fold, compared with 15–fold in the old metropoles and 22–fold in North America.

Table 4-1. **The Economies of the Americas, Five Regions, 1500-2001**
(population in 000; per capita GDP in 1990 int. $; GDP in million 1990 int. $)

	1500	*1600*	*1700*	*1820*	*2001*
Mexico					
Population	7 500	2 500	4 500	6 587	101 879
Per Capita GDP	425	454	568	759	7 089
GDP	3 188	1 134	2 558	5 000	722 198
15 Other Spanish America (ex. Caribbean)					
Population	8 500	5 100	5 800	7 691	212 919
Per Capita GDP	412	432	498	683	5 663
GDP	3 500	2 201	2 889	5 255	1 205 630
30 Caribbean Countries					
Population	500	200	500	2 920	38 650
Per Capita GDP	400	430	650	636	4 373
GDP	200	86	325	1 857	169 032
Brazil					
Population	1 000	800	1 250	4 507	177 753
Per Capita GDP	400	428	459	646	5 570
GDP	400	342	574	2 912	990 076
United States and Canada					
Population	2 250	1 750	1 200	10 797	316 617
Per Capita GDP	400	400	511	1 231	27 384
GDP	900	700	613	13 286	8 670 389
Latin America					
Population	17 500	8 600	12 050	21 705	531 201
Per Capita GDP	416	438	527	692	5 811
GDP	7 288	3 763	6 346	15 024	3 086 936

Table 4-2. **Ethnic Composition of the Americas in 1820**
(000)

	Indigenous	Mestizo	Black and Mulatto	White	Total
Mexico	3 570	1 777	10	1 230	6 587
Brazil	500		2 500	1 507	4 507
Caribbean			2 366	554	2 920
Other	4 000	1 800	400	1 491	7 691
Total Latin America	8 070	3 577	5 276	4 776	21 705
United States	325		1 772	7 884	9 981
Canada	75			741	816
Total Americas	8 470	3 577	7 048	13 407	32 502

Source: Maddison (2001), p. 250 amended (see text for Caribbean).

Table 4-3. **Net Non-Slave Migration to the Americas, 1500-1998**
(000)

	1500-1820	1820-1998
Brazil	500	4 500
Spanish America	475	6 500
Caribbean	450	2 000
Canada	30	6 395
United States	718	53 150
Total Americas	2 173	72 545

Table 4-4. **Arrivals of African Slaves in the Americas, 1500-1870**
(000)

	1500-1810	1811-1870	1500-1870
Brazil	2 501	1 145	3 647
Spanish America	947	606	1 552
Non-Spanish Caribbean	3 698	96	3 793
United States	348	51	399
Total Americas	7 494	1 898	9 391

Source: P.D. Curtin (1969), *The Atlantic Slave Trade*, University of Wisconsin, Madison, p. 268.

The striking differences between the growth trajectories of Latin and North America were due in significant degree to differences in the type of colonialism and their enduring impact on institutions and social structure.

Spain concentrated its colonial activity in Mexico and Peru, which were the most densely populated at the time of conquest. The Aztec and Inca elites and their priesthood were exterminated. Old gods, calendars, records, relics, property rights and indigenous institutions disappeared. Churches and convents were built on the ruins of Aztec and Inca temples. The main agents of social control were the religious orders. Land was allocated to a privileged elite of Spaniards, giving them control of a traumatised Indian population, which was compelled to supply labour to mines and agriculture. There were rigid social distinctions between the ruling elite and the indigenous population which had no legal rights, access to education or land. The main aim of this tribute imperialism was to transfer a fiscal surplus (in precious metals) to finance government aspirations in Europe. Spain was well prepared to exercise this type of hegemony. It had several centuries of experience in reconquest of territory from the Moors. It had the military know–how and organisation for conquest, and a church experienced in evangelising, converting and indoctrinating a conquered population. Islam and Judaism were proscribed in Spain, just as the Aztec and Inca religions were extirpated in Mexico and Peru. The church was firmly under national control; the king being free to appoint bishops under a sixteenth century treaty with the Papacy. Centuries of militant struggle had concentrated power and legitimacy on the monarchy as the ultimate arbiter, against which rebellion even in very distant colonies was seldom imagined before the last quarter of the eighteenth century.

By 1825, the American empire had collapsed and more than 14 million people were no longer Spanish. In 1790, it had covered 16 million square km. Cuba and Puerto Rico were all that was left– with an area of 12 thousand square km, and a population less than 700 000. In South America, nine new nations had emerged with a total area of 8.8 million square km. Mexico had an area of 4.4 million square km. Five countries in Central America had formed a temporary union. Independence was achieved by armed struggle, and the process of state–formation was not smooth. The new states inherited the deep inequalities of the colonial period. In Mexico there were five decades of political anarchy after independence, half the land area was lost to the United States, and per capita income was a good deal lower in 1870 than in 1820. This was not untypical of what happened elsewhere.

Portugal had much more pragmatic objectives in Brazil, developing an export agriculture based on sugar plantations, with much looser imperial control. As indigenous labour was scarce, its labour force was composed largely of African slaves. Between 1500 and 1870, 3.6 million were shipped to Brazil. At the end of the colonial period, half the population were slaves. They were worked to death after a few years of service, and fed on a crude diet of beans and jerked beef. A privileged fraction of the white population enjoyed high incomes but the rest of the population (indigenous, free blacks, mulattos, and large numbers of whites) were poor. Land–ownership was concentrated on slave owners. A very unequal distribution of property buttressed a highly unequal distribution of income. Independence came very smoothly by Latin American standards. In 1808, the Portuguese Queen and the Regent fled to Rio to escape the French invasion of the motherland. They brought 10 000 of the mainland establishment with them. After the Napoleonic wars, Brazil became independent with an Emperor who was the son of the Portuguese monarch. Brazil abolished slavery and became a republic in 1889.

The Netherlands, the United Kingdom and France copied the Portuguese model in Caribbean islands they seized from Spain in the seventeenth century. These colonies were highly specialised in sugar production, importing most of their food. By 1820, they had imported 3.7 million African slaves. Output rose tenfold between the 1660s and the 1780. A large part of the profits were siphoned off to absentee owners who preferred the healthier climate of the metropoles. The loss of privileged export markets in North America after 1776, interruptions to trade during the Napoleonic wars, and the successful slave revolt in Haiti persuaded the planting lobby that their days were numbered and that it was in their interest to settle for compensation. The prohibition of the slave trade and subsequent abolition of slavery raised costs and weakened the competitive position of most Caribbean producers (in spite of the introduction of 700 000 indentured Asian workers between 1838 and 1913). In 1787 the Caribbean accounted for 90 per cent of world sugar exports; in 1913 about a sixth. Except for Cuba and Puerto Rico, the Caribbean became an economic backwater. Real GDP per head fell by a quarter in Jamaica between 1832 and 1870, exports fell from 41 to 15 per cent of GDP. In 1930, the per capita GDP level was about the same as in 1832. For the British and French islands, this experience was probably fairly typical.

Sources for 1500–1820

Population: The size of the indigenous population at the time of the Spanish conquest was a matter of considerable controversy, and there were two extreme schools of thought. Borah and Cook (1963) estimated 25 million for central Mexico on the basis of ambiguous pictographs describing the incidence of Aztec fiscal levies. They assumed a 95 per cent depopulation ratio for the indigenous population for 1519–1605, and backcast Spanish estimates for 1605 by a multiplier of 25. Rosenblat (1945) made a careful survey of literary evidence, and estimated the pre–conquest population to have been 4.5 million with a drop of less than 15 per cent in the sixteenth century. There are two reasons for scepticism about the Borah estimates for Mexico and Latin America as a whole: a) they assume very much higher disease mortality than European experience with the Black Death; b) they assume that population did not recover its alleged pre–conquest levels until the twentieth century. On the other hand, Rosenblat's depopulation ratio is clearly too low. There is a discussion of the subsequent literature and rationale for the estimates I adopted in Maddison (2001), pp. 232–236.

GDP: I made a multicultural estimate, with a stylised per capita GDP for the indigenous population ($400 international 1990 dollars for the hunter–gatherers and $425 for Mexico and Peru, which had developed agriculture and urbanisation). For the non–indigenous population, I assumed the 1820 level of per capita GDP was valid for the whole period 1500–1820. The income level for each group was assumed to be stable, but the average for the two combined was lower in earlier years when the non–indigenous proportion was smaller — see Maddison (2001), p. 250. For the Caribbean, the estimates for 1600–1820 were based largely on evidence about sugar production, inferences on per capita GDP levels at the end of the period from G. Eisner (1961), *Jamaica, 1830–1930: A Study in Economic Growth*, Manchester University Press, and the work of David Eltis and others on earlier development, see Eltis, "The Total Product of Barbados, 1664–1701", *Journal of Economic History*, (June 1995) and, "The Slave Economies of the Caribbean, Performance, Evolution and Significance", in F.W. Knight (1997), *General History of the Caribbean*, vol. III, UNESCO, London.

Sources for 1820–2001
Core Countries (Argentina, Brazil, Chile, Colombia, Mexico, Peru, Uruguay and Venezuela)

Population: 1820–1949 generally as in Maddison (1995), p. 99. Uruguay from Luis Bertola and Associates, *PBI de Uruguay 1870–1936*, Montevideo, 1998, and supplementary information supplied by Luis Bertola. Venezuela from Asdrubal Baptista, *Bases de la Economia Venezolana 1830–1989*, CCD, Caracas, 1991. 1950 onwards, all countries from US Bureau of the Census (http://www.census.gov./ ipc), October 2002.

GDP: movement 1820–1949 generally from Maddison (1995), p.143; 1901–12 Colombia and Peru interpolated with average per capita movement in Brazil and Chile. 1911–12 and 1914–20 movement in Mexico from A.A. Hofman, *The Economic Development of Latin America in the Twentieth Century*, Elgar, Cheltenham, 2000, pp. 163–4. Uruguay 1820 1949 from Bertola, *op. cit.* For Brazil and Mexico, 1820–1949, see Maddison 2001, p. 191. Updating 1998–2001 from IMF, *World Economic Outlook*. 1990 benchmark GDP levels in 1990 international dollars from Maddison (2001), p. 199.

15 Other Countries

Population: Gaps in Maddison (2001) were filled as follows: 1820 from *Cambridge History of Latin America,* vol. III, pp. 238–9, 245 and 258 for Haiti and Dominican republic; p.478 for Costa Rica, El Salvador, Guatemala, Honduras and Nicaragua; p. 508 for Ecuador; p.564 for Bolivia; pp. 668 and 673 for Paraguay. Cuba and Puerto Rico from Shepherd and Beckles, eds, (2000) *Caribbean Slavery in the Atlantic World,* Wiener, Princeton, pp. 274 and 285 respectively. Jamaica, Trinidad and Tobago from Higman (1984), *Slave Populations of the British Caribbean,* 1807–1834, Johns Hopkins University Press, Baltimore, p. 417. 1850 generally from Sanchez–Albornoz in *Cambridge History of Latin America,* vol. IV, 1986, p. 122; Jamaica from Eisner (1961), p. 153; Trinidad and Tobago from Mitchell (1983), p. 50. 1870 and 1913 generally from Maddison (2001). Annual figures for 1871–1912 for thirteen countries are interpolations of estimates for benchmark years in Sanchez Albornoz (1986). Jamaica from Eisner (1961), p. 134; 1870–1950 movement in Trinidad and Tobago assumed to be proportionately the same as in Jamaica.

Annual estimates 1920–49 from Bulmer–Thomas (1987) *The Political Economy of Central America since 1920,* C.U.P, p. 310 for Costa Rica, El Salvador, Guatemala, Honduras and Nicaragua; other countries generally from UN, *Demographic Yearbook 1960,* p. 132–8 (with some interpolation for Haiti); Cuba 1900–28 derived from C. Brundenius (1984), *Revolutionary Cuba: The Challenge of Economic Growth with Equity,* Westview Press, Boulder and London p. 140, 1929–49 from CEPAL (ECLAC), Statistics Division, (1962) *Cuadros del producto interno bruto a precios del mercado en dollares de 1950,* Santiago (mimeo). 1950–2001 as for the 8 core countries.

GDP: I added estimates for Jamaica 1820–1930 from Eisner (1961), p. 119, linked to 1938–50 from Findlay and Wellisz (1999) *The Political Economy of Poverty, Equity and Growth: Five Small Open Economies,* OUP, New York, p. 149. Jamaica is the only Caribbean economy for which GDP estimates are available for this period. Eisner's estimates imply a 24 per cent fall in per capita GDP between 1820 and 1870 as Jamaica's sugar economy decayed. I assumed that the 1820–70 per capita GDP movement in this group paralleled that in Jamaica. For the benchmark years 1870, 1913 and 1950, average per capita GDP movement in these economies was assumed parallel to the average for the 8 core countries. Annual GDP movement, 1920–50, for Costa Rica, El Salvador, Guatemala, Honduras and Nicaragua from Bulmer–Thomas (1987), p. 308, Bolivia (1945–9), Ecuador (1939), Haiti (1945–9), Panama (1945–9), and Paraguay (1939–49) from ECLAC (1978), *Series Historicas del Crecimiento de America Latina,* Santiago, pp. 14–15. 1950–98 from Maddison (2001) Appendix C, updated to 2001 from IMF *World Economic Outlook,* 2/2002. Derivation of 1990 benchmark levels from Maddison (2001), p. 199.

Estimates for Cuba are revised. 1929–59 from ECLAC (1962), *Cuadros del producto interno bruto.* At that time Cuban national accounts were compiled according to UN standardised (SNA) procedures. After the revolution, Cuba adopted the Soviet material product system (MPS), which exaggerated growth. 1959–65 from OECD Development Centre, *Latest Information on National Accounts of Developing Countries,* various issues. 1965–82 from J.F. Perez Lopez (1987), *Measuring Cuban Economic Performance,* University of Texas Press, Austin, p. 111 who recalculated Cuban GDP according to SNA concepts. The Cuban Statistical Office published estimates of GDP by industry of origin for 1975–2000 (see Oficina Nacional de Estadisticas, *Cuba: Indicadores Seleccionados, 1950–2000,* Havana, 2001, pp. 15–16. Where these estimates overlap with those of Perez Lopez (for 1975–82) they show a growth rate twice as fast. I used these official estimates for 1982–90, but scaled down the year–to–year growth by a coefficient of the differential between them and those of Perez Lopez for the overlap years. 1990–1998 from ECLAC, *Economic Survey of Latin America and the Caribbean: Current Conditions and Outlook* (2001); 1998–2001 ECLAC, *Preliminary Overview of the Economies of Latin America and the Caribbean,* Santiago (2002). These ECLAC figures are based on official Cuban sources which now seem more acceptable as the estimating procedure has been revised to conform with the UN standardised system (see *Anuario Estadistico de Cuba 2001,* Oficina Nacional de Estadisticas, Havana, 2002).

24 Small Caribbean Countries

Estimates for this group are substantially revised for 1820–1913.

Population: 1820–70 from S.L. Engerman and B.W. Higman (1997), "The demographic situation of the Caribbean slave societies in the eighteenth and nineteenth centuries", in F.W. Knight (ed.), *General History of the Caribbean*, vol. III, UNESCO, London pp. 50–7 and Higman (1984); 1913 from League of Nations, (1928), *International Statistical Yearbook 1927*, Geneva, pp. 16–17; 1920–49 from UN, *Demographic Yearbook 1960*, pp. 132–6. 1950 onwards from US Bureau of the Census estimates, October 2002.

GDP: 1820 average per capita GDP level assumed equal to that of the 15 country group; 1870–1950 per capita GDP movement assumed to parallel that in the 8 core countries. GDP 1950–90 from Maddison (2001), updated and revised as shown in Table 4–5.

Table 4-5. **GDP and Population in 24 Small Caribbean Countries, 1950-2001**

	GDP in million 1990 international $				*Population (000)*			
	1950	*1973*	*1990*	*2001*	*1950*	*1973*	*1990*	*2001*
Bahamas	756	3 159	3 946	4 700	70	182	257	293
Barbados	448	1 595	2 138	2 419	211	244	263	275
Belize	110	341	735	1083	66	130	191	253
Dominica	82	182	279	352	51	74	73	71
Grenada	71	180	310	459	76	97	92	89
Guyana	462	1 309	1 159	2 080	428	755	742	698
St. Lucia	61	199	449	532	79	109	140	158
St. Vincent	79	175	392	545	66	90	107	116
Suriname	315	1 046	1 094	1 099	208	384	395	432
Total A (9 countries)	2 384	8 186	10 502	13 269	1 255	2 065	2 260	2 385
Antigua & Barbuda	82	328	413	535	46	68	63	67
Bermuda	65	238	310		39	53	58	63
Guadeloupe	359	1 568	1 801		208	329	378	431
Guyana (Fr.)	138	238	516		26	53	116	178
Martinique	293	1 568	1 857		217	332	374	418
Neth. Antilles	393	1 097	980	1 057	110	165	189	212
St. Kitts Nevis	61	215	233	402	44	45	41	39
Total B (7 countries)	1 391	5 252	6 110	8 315	690	1 045	1 219	1 408
Total C (8 countries)	298	926	1 441	1 809	117	197	250	298
24 countries	4 073	14 364	18 053	23 393	2 062	3 308	3 727	4 091

Source: 1950–98 GDP from Maddison (2001), p. 192, updated to 2001 from IMF, *World Economic Outlook*, September, 2002. For countries for which estimates were not available, aggregate GDP movement assumed to be proportionate to that for the group A average. Population from Maddison (2001), updated from 1950 onwards from the International Programs Center, US Bureau of the Census, October 2002. The 8 countries in the third group are Anguilla, Aruba, Cayman Islands, Montserrat, St. Pierre and Miquelon, Turks and Caicos Islands, Virgin Islands, and British Virgin Islands.

Table 4a. **Population of 8 Latin American Countries, 1820-1913**
(000s at mid-year)

	Argentina	Brazil	Chile	Colombia	Mexico	Peru	Uruguay	Venezuela	Total
1820	534	4 507	885	1 206	6 587	1 317	55	718	15 809
1850	1 100	7 234	1 443	2 065	7 662	2 001	132	1 324	22 961
1870	1 796	9 797	1 943	2 392	9 219	2 606	343	1 653	29 749
1871		9 980			9 331		354	1 675	
1872		10 167			9 444		364	1 699	
1873		10 358			9 558		376	1 725	
1874		10 552			9 674		387	1 753	
1875		10 749			9 791		399	1 784	
1876		10 951			9 910		411	1 816	
1877		11 156			10 030		424	1 849	
1878		11 365			10 151		437	1 883	
1879		11 578			10 274		450	1 917	
1880		11 794			10 399		464	1 952	
1881		12 015			10 524		482	1 986	
1882		12 240			10 652		502	2 019	
1883		12 470			10 781		522	2 052	
1884		12 703			10 912		543	2 083	
1885		12 941			11 044		564	2 113	
1886		13 183			11 178		587	2 129	
1887		13 430			11 313		610	2 147	
1888		13 682			11 450		635	2 173	
1889		13 938			11 589		660	2 198	
1890	3 376	14 199	2 651	3 369	11 729	3 346	686	2 224	41 580
1891		14 539			11 904		706	2 255	
1892		14 886			12 083		727	2 285	
1893		15 242			12 263		748	2 314	
1894		15 607			12 447		770	2 346	
1895		15 980			12 663		792	2 375	
1896		16 362			12 822		815	2 408	
1897		16 753			13 014		839	2 442	
1898		17 154			13 209		864	2 475	
1899		17 564			13 406		889	2 509	
1900	4 693	17 984	2 974	3 998	13 607	3 791	915	2 542	50 504
1901	4 873	18 392	3 011	4 079	13 755	3 831	930	2 576	51 447
1902	5 060	18 782	3 048	4 162	13 904	3 871	945	2 609	52 381
1903	5 254	19 180	3 086	4 247	14 055	3 911	961	2 643	53 337
1904	5 455	19 587	3 124	4 334	14 208	3 952	977	2 690	54 327
1905	5 664	20 003	3 163	4 422	14 363	3 993	993	2 706	55 307
1906	5 881	20 427	3 202	4 512	14 519	4 035	1 009	2 720	56 305
1907	6 107	20 860	3 242	4 604	14 676	4 077	1 026	2 741	57 333
1908	6 341	21 303	3 282	4 697	14 836	4 119	1 043	2 761	58 382
1909	6 584	21 754	3 323	4 793	14 997	4 162	1 062	2 780	59 455
1910	6 836	22 216	3 364	4 890	15 000	4 206	1 081	2 805	60 398
1911	7 098	22 687	3 406	4 990	14 990	4 250	1 112	2 834	61 367
1912	7 370	23 168	3 448	5 091	14 980	4 294	1 144	2 856	62 351
1913	7 653	23 660	3 491	5 195	14 970	4 339	1 177	2 874	63 359

Table 4a. **Population of 8 Latin American Countries, 1914-1949**
(000s at mid-year)

	Argentina	Brazil	Chile	Colombia	Mexico	Peru	Uruguay	Venezuela	Total
1914	7 885	24 161	3 537	5 330	14 960	4 384	1 223	2 899	64 379
1915	8 072	24 674	3 584	5 468	14 950	4 430	1 246	2 918	65 342
1916	8 226	25 197	3 631	5 609	14 940	4 477	1 269	2 929	66 278
1917	8 374	25 732	3 679	5 754	14 930	4 523	1 292	2 944	67 228
1918	8 518	26 277	3 728	5 903	14 920	4 571	1 316	2 958	68 191
1919	8 672	26 835	3 777	6 056	14 910	4 619	1 341	2 973	69 183
1920	8 861	27 404	3 827	6 213	14 900	4 667	1 371	2 992	70 235
1921	9 092	27 969	3 877	6 374	14 895	4 730	1 402	3 008	71 347
1922	9 368	28 542	3 928	6 539	15 129	4 793	1 433	3 025	72 757
1923	9 707	29 126	3 980	6 709	15 367	4 859	1 465	3 049	74 262
1924	10 054	29 723	4 033	6 882	15 609	4 927	1 498	3 077	75 803
1925	10 358	30 332	4 086	7 061	15 854	4 996	1 534	3 114	77 335
1926	10 652	30 953	4 140	7 243	16 103	5 067	1 571	3 152	78 881
1927	10 965	31 587	4 195	7 431	16 356	5 141	1 608	3 185	80 468
1928	11 282	32 234	4 250	7 624	16 613	5 216	1 646	3 221	82 086
1929	11 592	32 894	4 306	7 821	16 875	5 294	1 685	3 259	83 726
1930	11 896	33 568	4 370	7 914	17 175	5 374	1 713	3 300	85 310
1931	12 167	34 256	4 434	8 009	17 480	5 456	1 741	3 336	86 879
1932	12 402	34 957	4 500	8 104	17 790	5 540	1 770	3 368	88 431
1933	12 623	35 673	4 567	8 201	18 115	5 626	1 799	3 401	90 005
1934	12 834	36 404	4 634	8 299	18 445	5 715	1 829	3 431	91 591
1935	13 044	37 150	4 703	8 398	18 781	5 806	1 859	3 465	93 206
1936	13 260	37 911	4 773	8 498	19 040	5 899	1 889	3 510	94 780
1937	13 490	38 687	4 843	8 599	19 370	5 995	1 921	3 565	96 470
1938	13 724	39 480	4 915	8 702	19 705	6 093	1 952	3 623	98 194
1939	13 984	40 289	5 003	8 935	20 047	6 194	1 944	3 699	100 095
1940	14 169	41 114	5 093	9 174	20 393	6 298	1 965	3 784	101 990
1941	14 402	42 069	5 184	9 419	20 955	6 415	1 987	3 858	104 289
1942	14 638	43 069	5 277	9 671	21 532	6 537	2 010	3 934	106 668
1943	14 877	44 093	5 371	9 930	22 125	6 661	2 032	4 020	109 109
1944	15 130	45 141	5 467	10 196	22 734	6 787	2 055	4 114	111 624
1945	15 390	46 215	5 565	10 469	23 724	6 919	2 081	4 223	114 586
1946	15 654	47 313	5 665	10 749	24 413	7 053	2 107	4 347	117 301
1947	15 942	48 438	5 767	11 036	25 122	7 192	2 134	4 486	120 117
1948	16 307	49 590	5 870	11 332	25 852	7 335	2 160	4 656	123 102
1949	16 737	50 769	5 975	11 635	26 603	7 480	2 188	4 843	126 230

Table 4a. **Population of 8 Latin American Countries, 1950-2003**
(000s at mid-year)

	Argentina	Brazil	Chile	Colombia	Mexico	Peru	Uruguay	Venezuela	Total
1950	17 150	53 443	6 091	11 592	28 485	7 633	2 194	5 009	131 597
1951	17 517	54 996	6 252	11 965	29 296	7 826	2 223	5 217	135 292
1952	17 877	56 603	6 378	12 351	30 144	8 026	2 253	5 440	139 070
1953	18 231	58 266	6 493	12 750	31 031	8 232	2 284	5 674	142 961
1954	18 581	59 989	6 612	13 162	31 959	8 447	2 317	5 919	146 985
1955	18 928	61 774	6 743	13 588	32 930	8 672	2 353	6 170	151 158
1956	19 272	63 632	6 889	14 029	33 946	8 905	2 389	6 431	155 493
1957	19 611	65 551	7 048	14 486	35 016	9 146	2 425	6 703	159 985
1958	19 947	67 533	7 220	14 958	36 142	9 397	2 460	6 982	164 639
1959	20 281	69 580	7 400	15 447	37 328	9 658	2 495	7 268	169 457
1960	20 616	71 695	7 585	15 953	38 579	9 931	2 531	7 556	174 446
1961	20 951	73 833	7 773	16 476	39 836	10 218	2 564	7 848	179 498
1962	21 284	76 039	7 961	17 010	41 121	10 517	2 598	8 143	184 674
1963	21 616	78 317	8 147	17 546	42 434	10 826	2 632	8 444	189 963
1964	21 949	80 667	8 330	18 090	43 775	11 144	2 664	8 752	195 370
1965	22 283	83 093	8 510	18 646	45 142	11 467	2 693	9 068	200 903
1966	22 612	85 557	8 686	19 202	46 538	11 796	2 721	9 387	206 499
1967	22 934	88 050	8 859	19 764	47 996	12 132	2 749	9 710	212 193
1968	23 261	90 569	9 030	20 322	49 519	12 476	2 777	10 041	217 994
1969	23 600	93 114	9 199	20 869	51 111	12 829	2 802	10 389	223 913
1970	23 962	95 684	9 369	21 430	52 775	13 193	2 824	10 758	229 994
1971	24 364	98 245	9 540	21 993	54 434	13 568	2 826	11 152	236 122
1972	24 780	100 840	9 718	22 543	56 040	13 955	2 830	11 516	242 220
1973	25 210	103 469	9 897	23 069	57 643	14 350	2 834	11 893	248 365
1974	25 646	106 131	10 077	23 593	59 240	14 753	2 838	12 281	254 559
1975	26 082	108 824	10 252	24 114	60 828	15 161	2 842	12 675	260 777
1976	26 531	111 545	10 432	24 620	62 404	15 573	2 857	13 082	267 046
1977	26 984	114 314	10 600	25 094	63 981	15 990	2 874	13 504	273 340
1978	27 440	117 147	10 760	25 543	65 554	16 414	2 889	13 931	279 678
1979	27 902	120 040	10 923	26 031	67 123	16 849	2 905	14 355	286 128
1980	28 370	122 958	11 094	26 583	68 686	17 295	2 920	14 768	292 673
1981	28 863	125 930	11 282	27 159	70 321	17 755	2 936	15 166	299 412
1982	29 341	128 963	11 487	27 765	71 910	18 234	2 954	15 621	306 275
1983	29 802	131 892	11 687	28 389	73 435	18 706	2 973	16 084	312 968
1984	30 236	134 626	11 879	29 028	74 945	19 171	2 990	16 545	319 420
1985	30 675	137 303	12 067	29 678	76 475	19 624	3 008	16 998	325 828
1986	31 146	140 112	12 260	30 327	78 035	20 073	3 027	17 450	332 430
1987	31 621	142 938	12 463	30 964	79 623	20 531	3 045	17 910	339 095
1988	32 091	145 782	12 678	31 589	81 231	21 000	3 064	18 379	345 813
1989	32 559	148 567	12 901	32 217	82 840	21 487	3 084	18 851	352 505
1990	33 022	151 084	13 128	32 859	84 446	21 989	3 106	19 325	358 959
1991	33 492	153 512	13 353	33 519	86 055	22 501	3 128	19 801	365 358
1992	33 959	155 976	13 573	34 203	87 667	23 015	3 149	20 266	371 808
1993	34 412	158 471	13 788	34 897	89 280	23 531	3 171	20 704	378 255
1994	34 864	160 994	14 000	35 589	90 888	24 047	3 193	21 135	384 711
1995	35 311	163 543	14 205	36 281	92 488	24 556	3 215	21 556	391 155
1996	35 754	166 074	14 404	36 971	94 080	25 058	3 237	21 969	397 547
1997	36 203	168 547	14 599	37 658	95 667	25 556	3 260	22 374	403 865
1998	36 644	170 956	14 789	38 340	97 245	26 049	3 284	22 773	410 079
1999	37 074	173 294	14 974	39 016	98 807	26 535	3 309	23 162	416 170
2000	37 498	175 553	15 154	39 686	100 350	27 013	3 334	23 543	422 131
2001	37 917	177 753	15 328	40 349	101 879	27 484	3 360	23 917	427 987
2002	38 331	179 914	15 499	41 008	103 400	27 950	3 387	24 288	433 777
2003	38 741	182 033	15 665	41 662	104 908	28 410	3 413	24 655	439 487

Table 4a. **Population of 15 Latin American Countries, 1820-1949**
(000s at mid-year)

	Bolivia	Costa Rica	Cuba	Dominican Republic	Ecuador	El Salvador	Guatemala	Haiti
1820	1 100	63	605	89	500	248	595	723
1850	1 374	101	1 186	146	816	366	850	938
1870	1 495	137	1 331	242	1 013	492	1 080	1 150
1900	1 696	297	1 658	515	1 400	766	1 300	1 560
1901	1 710	310	1 716	530	1 420	782	1 313	1 583
1902	1 723	320	1 775	546	1 441	799	1 327	1 607
1903	1 737	320	1 837	562	1 462	816	1 341	1 631
1904	1 751	330	1 879	578	1 483	834	1 355	1 655
1905	1 765	340	1 927	595	1 505	851	1 369	1 680
1906	1 779	340	1 979	613	1 527	869	1 383	1 705
1907	1 793	350	2 034	631	1 549	888	1 397	1 730
1908	1 808	350	2 092	649	1 571	907	1 412	1 756
1909	1 822	360	2 154	668	1 594	926	1 426	1 782
1910	1 837	363	2 219	688	1 617	946	1 441	1 809
1911	1 851	366	2 287	708	1 641	966	1 456	1 836
1912	1 866	369	2 358	729	1 665	987	1 470	1 863
1913	1 881	372	2 431	750	1 689	1 008	1 486	1 891
1914	1 915	390	2 507	767	1 703	1 030	1 501	1 923
1915	1 951	390	2 585	785	1 717	1 052	1 517	1 955
1916	1 986	400	2 664	803	1 731	1 074	1 533	1 988
1917	2 023	400	2 746	821	1 746	1 098	1 549	2 021
1918	2 060	410	2 828	840	1 760	1 121	1 565	2 055
1919	2 098	420	2 912	859	1 774	1 145	1 581	2 089
1920	2 136	420	2 997	879	1 790	1 170	1 597	2 124
1921	2 161	430	3 083	912	1 805	1 190	1 614	2 152
1922	2 186	430	3 170	946	1 820	1 220	1 631	2 181
1923	2 212	440	3 257	981	1 835	1 240	1 648	2 209
1924	2 237	450	3 345	1 017	1 850	1 270	1 665	2 239
1925	2 263	460	3 432	1 054	1 865	1 300	1 682	2 268
1926	2 289	470	3 519	1 092	1 881	1 330	1 699	2 298
1927	2 316	470	3 606	1 131	1 896	1 350	1 717	2 328
1928	2 343	480	3 693	1 172	1 912	1 390	1 735	2 359
1929	2 370	490	3 742	1 213	1 928	1 410	1 753	2 390
1930	2 397	500	3 837	1 256	1 944	1 440	1 771	2 422
1931	2 425	510	3 910	1 300	1 995	1 460	1 810	2 453
1932	2 453	520	3 984	1 345	2 050	1 470	1 860	2 485
1933	2 482	530	4 060	1 391	2 095	1 490	1 910	2 517
1934	2 511	540	4 137	1 438	2 140	1 510	1 940	2 549
1935	2 540	550	4 221	1 484	2 196	1 530	1 980	2 582
1936	2 569	560	4 289	1 520	2 249	1 550	2 020	2 615
1937	2 599	580	4 357	1 558	2 298	1 570	2 070	2 648
1938	2 629	590	4 428	1 596	2 355	1 590	2 110	2 682
1939	2 659	610	4 497	1 634	2 412	1 610	2 150	2 716
1940	2 690	620	4 566	1 674	2 466	1 630	2 200	2 751
1941	2 721	630	4 635	1 715	2 541	1 650	2 250	2 786
1942	2 753	650	4 704	1 757	2 575	1 680	2 300	2 820
1943	2 785	660	4 779	1 800	2 641	1 690	2 340	2 856
1944	2 817	680	4 849	1 844	2 712	1 720	2 390	2 892
1945	2 850	700	4 932	1 889	2 781	1 740	2 440	2 928
1946	2 883	710	5 039	1 935	2 853	1 760	2 500	2 961
1947	2 916	730	5 152	1 982	2 936	1 780	2 570	2 994
1948	2 950	750	5 268	2 031	3 017	1 810	2 640	3 028
1949	2 984	770	5 386	2 080	3 104	1 840	2 720	3 062

Table 4a. **Population of 15 Latin American Countries, 1820-1949**
(000s at mid-year)

	Honduras	Jamaica	Nicaragua	Panama	Paraguay	Puerto Rico	Trinidad and Tobago	Total
1820	135	401	186	–	143	248	60	5 096
1850	350	399	300	135	350	495	80	7 886
1870	404	499	337	176	384	645	124	9 509
1900	500	720	478	263	440	959	268	12 820
1901	511	728	485	269	450	974	274	13 055
1902	522	737	492	275	461	990	279	13 294
1903	533	745	499	281	472	1 006	285	13 527
1904	545	754	507	287	483	1 022	291	13 754
1905	556	763	514	293	494	1 039	298	13 989
1906	568	772	522	299	505	1 056	304	14 221
1907	581	781	529	306	517	1 073	310	14 469
1908	593	790	537	312	529	1 090	317	14 713
1909	606	799	545	319	542	1 108	324	14 975
1910	619	808	553	326	554	1 126	331	15 237
1911	632	818	561	333	567	1 144	338	15 504
1912	646	827	570	341	580	1 162	345	15 778
1913	660	837	578	348	594	1 181	352	16 058
1914	668	840	580	365	608	1 199	357	16 353
1915	677	842	595	383	622	1 217	362	16 650
1916	685	845	604	402	637	1 235	367	16 954
1917	694	847	613	422	652	1 254	373	17 259
1918	702	850	622	442	667	1 273	378	17 573
1919	711	852	631	464	683	1 292	383	17 894
1920	720	855	640	487	699	1 312	389	18 215
1921	740	860	640	489	715	1 336	367	18 494
1922	770	879	650	491	732	1 359	371	18 836
1923	800	891	650	493	749	1 383	376	19 164
1924	820	900	660	495	767	1 407	379	19 501
1925	850	910	660	497	785	1 431	382	19 839
1926	880	930	670	499	803	1 455	385	20 200
1927	890	946	670	502	822	1 478	388	20 510
1928	910	966	670	504	841	1 502	392	20 869
1929	930	985	680	506	860	1 526	398	21 181
1930	950	1 009	680	515	880	1 552	405	21 558
1931	970	1 039	690	527	901	1 584	412	21 986
1932	990	1 061	690	543	922	1 615	417	22 405
1933	1 010	1 082	700	559	944	1 647	422	22 839
1934	1 020	1 098	710	576	966	1 679	428	23 242
1935	1 040	1 113	730	592	988	1 710	435	23 691
1936	1 060	1 130	750	608	1 012	1 743	442	24 117
1937	1 080	1 142	770	623	1 036	1 777	450	24 558
1938	1 100	1 163	780	640	1 061	1 810	458	24 992
1939	1 120	1 191	810	656	1 086	1 844	466	25 461
1940	1 150	1 212	830	697	1 111	1 880	476	25 953
1941	1 170	1 230	840	720	1 137	1 935	492	26 452
1942	1 200	1 254	860	773	1 164	1 987	510	26 987
1943	1 210	1 249	880	795	1 191	2 033	525	27 434
1944	1 240	1 259	900	784	1 219	2 062	536	27 904
1945	1 260	1 266	920	791	1 247	2 099	547	28 390
1946	1 290	1 298	950	788	1 275	2 141	561	28 944
1947	1 320	1 327	980	804	1 305	2 162	583	29 541
1948	1 350	1 350	1 000	822	1 335	2 187	600	30 138
1949	1 390	1 374	1 030	838	1 366	2 197	616	30 757

Table 4a. **Population of 15 Latin American Countries, Annual Estimates, 1950-2003**
(000s at mid-year)

	Bolivia	Costa Rica	Cuba	Dominican Republic	Ecuador	El Salvador	Guatemala	Haiti
1950	2 766	867	5 785	2 353	3 370	1 940	2 969	3 097
1951	2 824	895	5 892	2 419	3 458	1 990	3 056	3 148
1952	2 883	926	6 008	2 491	3 549	2 043	3 146	3 201
1953	2 945	959	6 129	2 569	3 643	2 099	3 239	3 257
1954	3 009	994	6 254	2 651	3 740	2 159	3 335	3 316
1955	3 074	1 032	6 381	2 737	3 842	2 221	3 434	3 376
1956	3 142	1 072	6 513	2 828	3 949	2 287	3 536	3 441
1957	3 212	1 112	6 641	2 923	4 058	2 356	3 641	3 508
1958	3 284	1 154	6 763	3 023	4 172	2 428	3 749	3 577
1959	3 358	1 200	6 901	3 126	4 291	2 503	3 861	3 648
1960	3 434	1 248	7 027	3 231	4 416	2 582	3 976	3 723
1961	3 513	1 297	7 134	3 341	4 546	2 665	4 091	3 800
1962	3 594	1 345	7 254	3 453	4 682	2 748	4 209	3 880
1963	3 678	1 393	7 415	3 569	4 822	2 836	4 330	3 964
1964	3 764	1 440	7 612	3 687	4 968	2 924	4 454	4 050
1965	3 853	1 488	7 810	3 806	5 118	3 018	4 582	4 137
1966	3 945	1 538	7 985	3 926	5 273	3 128	4 713	4 227
1967	4 041	1 589	8 139	4 049	5 432	3 233	4 849	4 318
1968	4 139	1 638	8 284	4 173	5 597	3 347	4 989	4 412
1969	4 241	1 687	8 421	4 298	5 766	3 469	5 135	4 507
1970	4 346	1 736	8 543	4 423	5 939	3 604	5 289	4 605
1971	4 455	1 786	8 670	4 547	6 117	3 710	5 454	4 653
1972	4 566	1 835	8 831	4 671	6 299	3 791	5 625	4 701
1973	4 680	1 886	9 001	4 796	6 485	3 878	5 803	4 748
1974	4 796	1 937	9 153	4 922	6 676	3 972	5 988	4 795
1975	4 914	1 992	9 290	5 048	6 872	4 071	6 180	4 839
1976	4 956	2 049	9 421	5 176	7 073	4 175	6 378	4 882
1977	5 080	2 108	9 538	5 303	7 279	4 283	6 583	4 925
1978	5 205	2 192	9 634	5 431	7 489	4 396	6 795	4 970
1979	5 327	2 260	9 710	5 562	7 704	4 508	7 012	5 017
1980	5 441	2 299	9 653	5 697	7 920	4 566	7 235	5 056
1981	5 545	2 357	9 712	5 832	8 141	4 515	7 489	5 091
1982	5 642	2 424	9 789	5 968	8 366	4 475	7 714	5 149
1983	5 737	2 494	9 886	6 105	8 593	4 521	7 904	5 248
1984	5 834	2 568	9 982	6 241	8 826	4 588	8 124	5 355
1985	5 935	2 644	10 079	6 378	9 062	4 664	8 358	5 469
1986	6 041	2 723	10 162	6 516	9 301	4 751	8 601	5 588
1987	6 156	2 800	10 240	6 655	9 545	4 842	8 856	5 710
1988	6 283	2 875	10 334	6 796	9 794	4 930	9 118	5 833
1989	6 423	2 951	10 439	6 937	10 048	5 016	9 384	5 955
1990	6 574	3 027	10 545	7 076	10 317	5 100	9 654	6 075
1991	6 731	3 101	10 643	7 213	10 566	5 186	9 931	6 174
1992	6 893	3 173	10 724	7 347	10 819	5 275	10 216	6 272
1993	7 055	3 244	10 789	7 472	11 077	5 370	10 510	6 388
1994	7 217	3 315	10 846	7 595	11 337	5 467	10 814	6 500
1995	7 377	3 384	10 900	7 722	11 599	5 568	11 127	6 614
1996	7 536	3 452	10 952	7 851	11 862	5 674	11 449	6 727
1997	7 693	3 518	11 003	7 979	12 126	5 783	11 781	6 837
1998	7 849	3 583	11 051	8 105	12 391	5 895	12 121	6 952
1999	8 002	3 647	11 098	8 230	12 656	6 008	12 467	7 066
2000	8 153	3 711	11 142	8 354	12 920	6 123	12 820	7 177
2001	8 300	3 773	11 184	8 475	13 184	6 238	13 179	7 288
2002	8 445	3 835	11 224	8 596	13 447	6 354	13 542	7 405
2003	8 586	3 896	11 263	8 716	13 710	6 470	13 909	7 528

Table 4a. **Population of 15 Latin American Countries, 1950-2003**
(000s at mid-year)

	Honduras	Jamaica	Nicaragua	Panama	Paraguay	Puerto Rico	Trinidad and Tobago	Total
1950	1 431	1 385	1 098	893	1 476	2 218	632	32 279
1951	1 474	1 406	1 131	916	1 515	2 235	649	33 008
1952	1 517	1 426	1 166	940	1 556	2 227	663	33 743
1953	1 562	1 446	1 202	962	1 597	2 204	678	34 492
1954	1 611	1 468	1 239	985	1 640	2 214	698	35 311
1955	1 662	1 489	1 277	1 011	1 683	2 250	721	36 192
1956	1 715	1 510	1 317	1 037	1 727	2 249	743	37 064
1957	1 770	1 535	1 359	1 064	1 771	2 260	765	37 974
1958	1 829	1 566	1 402	1 085	1 816	2 299	789	38 935
1959	1 889	1 599	1 446	1 115	1 862	2 322	817	39 939
1960	1 952	1 632	1 493	1 148	1 910	2 358	841	40 969
1961	2 017	1 648	1 541	1 181	1 959	2 403	861	41 997
1962	2 082	1 665	1 591	1 216	2 010	2 448	887	43 064
1963	2 151	1 698	1 642	1 251	2 062	2 497	904	44 213
1964	2 224	1 739	1 695	1 288	2 115	2 552	924	45 437
1965	2 299	1 777	1 750	1 326	2 170	2 597	939	46 671
1966	2 375	1 820	1 807	1 365	2 228	2 627	953	47 912
1967	2 453	1 861	1 865	1 405	2 288	2 649	960	49 132
1968	2 534	1 893	1 926	1 447	2 349	2 674	963	50 365
1969	2 618	1 920	1 988	1 489	2 412	2 722	963	51 636
1970	2 683	1 944	2 053	1 531	2 477	2 722	955	52 849
1971	2 767	1 967	2 120	1 573	2 545	2 766	962	54 091
1972	2 864	1 998	2 183	1 616	2 614	2 847	975	55 416
1973	2 964	2 036	2 247	1 659	2 692	2 863	985	56 725
1974	3 066	2 071	2 320	1 706	2 773	2 887	995	58 057
1975	3 152	2 105	2 394	1 748	2 850	2 935	1 007	59 399
1976	3 240	2 133	2 473	1 790	2 919	3 026	1 021	60 711
1977	3 331	2 157	2 554	1 840	2 984	3 081	1 039	62 085
1978	3 431	2 179	2 608	1 873	3 051	3 118	1 056	63 430
1979	3 528	2 207	2 688	1 915	3 119	3 168	1 073	64 799
1980	3 635	2 229	2 804	1 956	3 193	3 210	1 091	65 986
1981	3 756	2 258	2 900	1 996	3 276	3 239	1 102	67 210
1982	3 861	2 298	2 978	2 036	3 366	3 279	1 116	68 463
1983	3 963	2 323	3 047	2 077	3 463	3 316	1 133	69 811
1984	4 072	2 347	3 119	2 120	3 564	3 350	1 150	71 239
1985	4 186	2 371	3 188	2 164	3 668	3 382	1 166	72 713
1986	4 301	2 394	3 258	2 208	3 776	3 413	1 180	74 216
1987	4 417	2 413	3 334	2 252	3 887	3 444	1 191	75 743
1988	4 505	2 428	3 415	2 297	4 000	3 475	1 198	77 282
1989	4 634	2 444	3 502	2 342	4 117	3 506	1 200	78 898
1990	4 757	2 463	3 643	2 388	4 236	3 537	1 198	80 591
1991	4 878	2 485	3 817	2 434	4 359	3 562	1 193	82 272
1992	5 009	2 505	3 947	2 480	4 484	3 585	1 184	83 915
1993	5 148	2 525	4 055	2 524	4 612	3 615	1 175	85 560
1994	5 293	2 547	4 164	2 568	4 744	3 649	1 167	87 222
1995	5 443	2 569	4 274	2 615	4 878	3 683	1 160	88 912
1996	5 594	2 589	4 384	2 663	5 015	3 725	1 151	90 623
1997	5 747	2 608	4 493	2 705	5 154	3 759	1 141	92 328
1998	5 902	2 624	4 600	2 745	5 296	3 781	1 136	94 032
1999	6 044	2 639	4 706	2 792	5 440	3 800	1 131	95 727
2000	6 201	2 653	4 813	2 836	5 586	3 816	1 125	97 428
2001	6 358	2 666	4 918	2 879	5 734	3 840	1 118	99 135
2002	6 514	2 680	5 024	2 920	5 884	3 863	1 112	100 846
2003	6 670	2 696	5 129	2 961	6 037	3 886	1 104	102 561

Table 4a. **Population of 47 Latin American Countries, 1820-1949**
(000s at mid-year)

	Total 8 core countries	Total 15 countries	Total 24 small Caribbean countries	Total 47 countries
1820	15 809	5 096	800	21 705
1850	22 961	7 886	946	31 793
1870	29 749	9 509	1 141	40 399
1890	41 580	10 859	1 383	53 822
1900	50 504	12 820	1 440	64 764
1901	51 447	13 055	1 446	65 948
1902	52 381	13 294	1 452	67 127
1903	53 337	13 527	1 458	68 322
1904	54 327	13 754	1 464	69 545
1905	55 307	13 989	1 470	70 766
1906	56 305	14 221	1 475	72 001
1907	57 333	14 469	1 481	73 283
1908	58 382	14 713	1 488	74 583
1909	59 455	14 975	1 494	75 924
1910	60 398	15 237	1 500	77 135
1911	61 367	15 504	1 506	78 377
1912	62 351	15 778	1 512	79 641
1913	63 359	16 058	1 518	80 935
1914	64 379	16 353	1 531	82 263
1915	65 342	16 650	1 543	83 535
1916	66 278	16 954	1 556	84 788
1917	67 228	17 259	1 569	86 056
1918	68 191	17 573	1 582	87 346
1919	69 183	17 894	1 596	88 673
1920	70 235	18 215	1 609	90 059
1921	71 347	18 494	1 622	91 463
1922	72 757	18 836	1 635	93 228
1923	74 262	19 164	1 649	95 075
1924	75 803	19 501	1 663	96 967
1925	77 335	19 839	1 677	98 851
1926	78 881	20 200	1 690	100 771
1927	80 468	20 510	1 705	102 683
1928	82 086	20 869	1 719	104 674
1929	83 726	21 181	1 733	106 640
1930	85 310	21 558	1 747	108 615
1931	86 879	21 986	1 762	110 627
1932	88 431	22 405	1 777	112 613
1933	90 005	22 839	1 791	114 635
1934	91 591	23 242	1 806	116 639
1935	93 206	23 691	1 821	118 718
1936	94 780	24 117	1 836	120 733
1937	96 470	24 558	1 852	122 880
1938	98 194	24 992	1 867	125 053
1939	100 095	25 461	1 883	127 439
1940	101 990	25 953	1 898	129 841
1941	104 289	26 452	1 914	132 655
1942	106 668	26 987	1 930	135 585
1943	109 109	27 434	1 946	138 489
1944	111 624	27 904	1 962	141 490
1945	114 586	28 390	1 978	144 954
1946	117 301	28 944	1 995	148 240
1947	120 117	29 541	2 011	151 669
1948	123 102	30 138	2 028	155 268
1949	126 230	30 757	2 045	159 032

Table 4a. **Population of 47 Latin American Countries, 1950-2003**
(000s at mid-year)

	Total 8 core countries	Total 15 countries	Total 24 small Caribbean countries	Total 47 countries
1950	131 597	32 279	2 062	165 938
1951	135 292	33 008	2 111	170 411
1952	139 070	33 743	2 161	174 975
1953	142 961	34 492	2 211	179 664
1954	146 985	35 311	2 267	184 563
1955	151 158	36 192	2 323	189 673
1956	155 493	37 064	2 378	194 935
1957	159 985	37 974	2 435	200 395
1958	164 639	38 935	2 494	206 069
1959	169 457	39 939	2 555	211 951
1960	174 446	40 969	2 614	218 029
1961	179 498	41 997	2 662	224 157
1962	184 674	43 064	2 711	230 450
1963	189 963	44 213	2 781	236 957
1964	195 370	45 437	2 841	243 648
1965	200 903	46 671	2 900	250 474
1966	206 499	47 912	2 959	257 370
1967	212 193	49 132	3 014	264 339
1968	217 994	50 365	3 071	271 430
1969	223 913	51 636	3 121	278 670
1970	229 994	52 849	3 164	286 007
1971	236 122	54 091	3 215	293 427
1972	242 220	55 416	3 264	300 900
1973	248 365	56 725	3 308	308 399
1974	254 559	58 057	3 341	315 957
1975	260 777	59 399	3 348	323 524
1976	267 046	60 711	3 351	331 109
1977	273 340	62 085	3 366	338 791
1978	279 678	63 430	3 385	346 493
1979	286 128	64 799	3 399	354 326
1980	292 673	65 986	3 410	362 069
1981	299 412	67 210	3 435	370 057
1982	306 275	68 463	3 466	378 204
1983	312 968	69 811	3 499	386 279
1984	319 420	71 239	3 534	394 193
1985	325 828	72 713	3 569	402 110
1986	332 430	74 216	3 602	410 248
1987	339 095	75 743	3 632	418 470
1988	345 813	77 282	3 663	426 758
1989	352 505	78 898	3 694	435 097
1990	358 959	80 591	3 727	443 276
1991	365 358	82 272	3 757	451 387
1992	371 808	83 915	3 790	459 512
1993	378 255	85 560	3 824	467 639
1994	384 711	87 222	3 857	475 790
1995	391 155	88 912	3 890	483 957
1996	397 547	90 623	3 923	492 093
1997	403 865	92 328	3 956	500 150
1998	410 079	94 032	3 983	508 094
1999	416 170	95 727	4 019	515 916
2000	422 129	97 428	4 055	523 612
2001	427 987	99 135	4 091	531 213
2002	433 777	100 846	4 128	538 751
2003	439 487	102 561	4 164	546 212

GDP LEVELS IN LATIN AMERICA

Table 4b. **GDP Levels in 8 Latin American Countries, 1820-1913**
(million 1990 international Geary-Khamis dollars)

	Argentina	Brazil	Chile	Colombia	Mexico	Peru	Uruguay	Venezuela	Total
1820		2 912			5 000				11 275
1850		4 959							
1870	2 354	6 985			6 214		748	941	22 273
1871		7 154					771		
1872		7 327					958		
1873		7 504					978		
1874		7 686					896		
1875		7 872					775		
1876		8 062					865		
1877		8 257					900		
1878		8 457					982		
1879		8 662					877		
1880		8 871					966		
1881		9 086					931		
1882		9 306					1 044		
1883		9 531					1 251		
1884		9 761					1 262		
1885		9 998					1 449		
1886		10 240					1 531		
1887		10 487					1 383		
1888		10 741					1 726		
1889		11 001					1 594		
1890	7 265	11 267			11 860		1 473		
1891		11 232					1 617		
1892		10 865					1 668		
1893		9 474					1 823		
1894		9 695					2 046		
1895		12 519			14 337		2 034		
1896		11 616					2 155		
1897		11 712					2 092		
1898		12 300					1 944		
1899		12 347					2 010		
1900	12 932	12 201	5 798	3 891	18 585	3 096	2 030	2 087	60 619
1901	14 036	13 425	5 992	4 169	20 167	3 287	2 077	2 053	65 206
1902	13 746	13 425	6 196	4 245	18 741	3 310	2 431	2 233	64 327
1903	15 722	13 693	6 400	4 374	20 840	3 379	2 513	2 414	69 334
1904	17 407	13 961	6 622	4 503	21 203	3 446	2 579	2 357	72 078
1905	19 703	14 365	6 844	4 656	23 407	3 530	2 318	2 329	77 152
1906	20 691	15 735	7 076	4 977	23 147	3 732	2 556	2 173	80 087
1907	21 127	15 754	7 317	5 069	24 495	3 767	2 829	2 173	82 530
1908	23 190	15 639	7 557	5 148	24 469	3 789	3 101	2 322	85 216
1909	24 353	16 886	7 687	5 421	25 195	3 950	3 140	2 405	89 036
1910	26 125	17 078	8 317	5 682	25 403	4 101	3 390	2 484	92 580
1911	26 590	18 959	8 243	5 993	25 584	4 284	3 288	2 655	95 596
1912	28 770	18 747	9 160	6 292	25 740	4 453	4 013	2 747	99 922
1913	29 060	19 188	9 261	6 420	25 921	4 500	3 896	3 172	101 419

Table 4b. GDP Levels in 8 Latin American Countries, 1914-1949
(million 1990 international Geary-Khamis dollars)

	Argentina	Brazil	Chile	Colombia	Mexico	Peru	Uruguay	Venezuela	Total
1914	26 038	18 844	8 632	6 199	26 095	4 063	3 246	2 773	95 890
1915	26 183	19 688	8 020	6 173	26 270	4 315	3 078	2 858	96 586
1916	25 428	20 263	9 511	6 854	26 446	5 620	3 183	2 697	100 002
1917	23 364	21 664	10 280	7 434	26 624	5 418	3 511	3 147	101 442
1918	27 665	21 223	10 299	7 391	26 803	5 274	3 721	3 128	105 504
1919	28 683	24 024	8 141	7 588	26 983	6 088	4 204	2 922	108 632
1920	30 775	26 393	9 298	7 797	27 164	6 209	3 666	3 509	114 811
1921	31 559	26 944	8 002	7 999	27 346	4 378	3 857	3 651	113 737
1922	34 059	28 801	8 558	8 206	27 994	4 959	4 411	3 753	120 740
1923	37 837	30 454	10 651	8 420	28 953	6 403	4 644	4 330	131 691
1924	40 772	30 434	11 614	8 637	28 487	6 493	5 089	5 016	136 541
1925	40 597	30 556	11 753	8 860	30 250	5 782	4 890	6 481	139 169
1926	42 544	31 210	11 456	9 707	32 064	6 443	5 338	7 839	146 603
1927	45 567	33 476	10 984	10 581	30 664	7 249	6 106	8 794	153 420
1928	48 414	37 333	13 327	11 357	30 846	7 757	6 429	9 847	165 312
1929	50 623	37 415	14 624	11 768	29 653	8 572	6 483	11 167	170 305
1930	48 531	35 187	13 735	11 666	27 787	7 613	7 368	11 367	163 253
1931	45 160	34 401	10 345	11 595	28 720	6 700	6 094	9 187	152 202
1932	43 678	35 599	10 234	12 243	24 417	6 362	5 657	8 800	146 991
1933	45 712	38 374	12 114	12 930	27 191	8 572	4 948	9 628	159 469
1934	49 344	41 585	13 790	12 661	29 031	10 016	5 891	10 275	172 594
1935	51 524	42 722	14 050	14 080	31 183	10 291	6 238	11 021	181 108
1936	51 873	46 824	14 587	14 824	33 671	10 750	6 534	12 106	191 168
1937	55 650	48 355	15 698	15 055	34 786	10 984	6 651	13 889	201 068
1938	55 883	50 376	15 430	16 038	35 356	10 705	7 176	15 015	205 978
1939	58 004	50 876	15 902	17 020	37 248	11 668	7 177	15 926	213 820
1940	58 963	51 381	16 596	17 386	37 767	11 483	7 193	15 307	216 077
1941	61 986	54 981	16 615	17 681	40 851	12 815	7 317	15 056	227 302
1942	62 712	52 944	17 532	17 713	43 754	11 483	6 709	13 166	226 013
1943	62 218	60 317	18 263	17 790	45 387	10 943	6 768	14 371	236 058
1944	69 280	62 562	18 523	18 991	49 094	12 455	7 613	17 727	256 245
1945	67 042	64 236	20 199	19 883	50 623	13 872	7 832	21 547	265 235
1946	73 029	71 013	21 449	21 681	53 967	14 430	8 603	25 855	290 028
1947	81 136	73 523	20 014	22 535	55 807	14 858	9 203	30 925	308 001
1948	85 641	79 157	22 339	23 235	58 114	15 357	9 515	34 427	327 784
1949	84 478	84 239	22 200	24 519	61 303	16 446	9 854	36 534	339 572

Table 4b. **GDP Levels in 8 Latin American Countries, 1950-2001**
(million 1990 international Geary-Khamis dollars)

	Argentina	Brazil	Chile	Colombia	Mexico	Peru	Uruguay	Venezuela	Total
1950	85 524	89 342	23 274	24 955	67 368	17 270	10 224	37 377	355 334
1951	88 866	93 608	24 274	25 726	72 578	18 669	11 015	39 979	374 715
1952	84 333	99 181	25 663	27 350	75 481	19 848	11 167	43 472	386 495
1953	88 866	103 957	27 006	29 026	75 688	20 901	11 736	45 147	402 327
1954	92 528	110 836	27 117	31 042	83 258	22 246	12 488	49 820	429 335
1955	99 125	118 960	27 080	32 242	90 307	23 317	12 593	53 991	457 615
1956	101 856	120 674	27 238	33 539	96 502	24 316	12 807	58 677	475 609
1957	107 087	130 717	30 090	34 766	103 812	25 936	12 932	67 414	512 754
1958	113 655	142 577	30 915	35 639	109 333	25 805	13 292	68 540	539 756
1959	106 303	154 538	30 748	38 207	112 599	26 737	12 125	72 658	553 915
1960	114 614	167 397	32 767	39 831	121 723	30 017	12 554	72 889	591 792
1961	122 809	179 951	34 341	41 847	126 365	32 226	12 912	70 643	621 094
1962	120 833	190 932	35 971	44 120	132 039	34 922	12 624	73 762	645 203
1963	117 927	192 912	38 240	45 571	141 839	36 217	12 686	77 134	662 526
1964	130 074	199 423	39 092	48 389	157 312	38 580	12 940	83 688	709 498
1965	141 960	203 444	39 407	50 136	167 116	40 501	13 088	89 240	744 892
1966	142 919	216 181	43 797	52 806	177 427	43 921	13 536	90 842	781 429
1967	146 755	224 877	45 223	55 028	188 258	45 581	12 975	96 334	815 031
1968	153 002	244 921	46 844	58 398	201 669	45 734	13 181	102 916	866 665
1969	166 080	266 292	48 585	62 116	213 924	47 448	13 984	106 612	925 041
1970	174 972	292 480	49 586	66 308	227 970	50 229	14 638	114 807	990 990
1971	183 458	322 159	54 022	70 250	237 480	52 331	14 498	116 494	1 050 692
1972	189 183	356 880	53 373	75 637	257 636	53 838	13 992	117 982	1 118 521
1973	200 720	401 643	50 401	80 728	279 302	56 713	14 098	126 364	1 209 969
1974	213 739	433 322	50 891	85 370	296 370	61 969	14 541	129 038	1 285 240
1975	211 850	455 918	44 316	87 347	312 998	64 075	15 406	132 728	1 324 638
1976	211 327	498 823	45 881	91 488	326 267	65 334	16 026	142 978	1 398 124
1977	224 084	522 154	50 401	95 283	337 499	65 600	16 205	151 927	1 463 153
1978	214 233	548 342	54 540	103 366	365 340	65 784	17 058	155 528	1 524 191
1979	229 547	587 289	59 060	108 906	398 788	69 609	18 110	156 752	1 628 061
1980	232 802	639 093	63 654	113 375	431 983	72 723	19 205	149 735	1 722 570
1981	219 434	611 007	67 192	115 789	469 972	76 035	19 575	149 253	1 728 257
1982	212 518	614 538	57 634	116 938	466 649	76 147	17 724	146 150	1 708 298
1983	220 016	593 575	57 245	118 806	446 602	66 567	16 688	140 665	1 660 164
1984	224 491	625 438	60 875	123 037	462 678	69 650	16 505	142 664	1 725 338
1985	209 641	675 090	62 366	127 076	475 505	71 247	16 746	144 843	1 782 514
1986	224 985	729 252	65 895	134 844	457 655	77 857	18 231	152 244	1 860 963
1987	230 797	753 685	69 674	142 086	466 148	84 237	19 676	157 698	1 924 001
1988	226 438	751 910	74 814	147 896	471 953	77 285	19 676	166 879	1 936 851
1989	212 373	776 547	82 269	152 686	491 767	68 399	19 930	152 577	1 956 548
1990	212 518	743 765	84 038	159 042	516 692	64 979	20 105	160 648	1 961 787
1991	233 770	751 203	90 173	161 587	538 508	66 603	20 687	177 516	2 040 047
1992	254 575	748 949	100 092	167 889	558 049	66 004	22 218	189 942	2 107 718
1993	269 341	782 652	106 698	175 444	568 934	69 766	22 907	189 182	2 184 924
1994	291 696	831 176	112 139	186 496	594 054	79 254	24 166	182 183	2 301 164
1995	282 653	866 086	122 344	196 567	557 419	86 070	23 683	192 931	2 327 753
1996	295 090	891 202	130 786	200 695	586 144	88 050	24 867	192 160	2 408 994
1997	318 698	925 068	139 941	203 706	625 759	95 622	26 112	204 843	2 539 749
1998	334 314	926 918	144 279	205 132	655 910	95 718	27 313	204 433	2 594 017
1999	322 947	934 333	142 836	196 722	679 523	96 579	26 548	191 963	2 591 451
2000	320 364	975 444	149 121	202 230	724 371	99 573	26 203	198 105	2 695 411
2001	308 510	990 076	153 296	205 263	722 198	99 773	25 391	203 454	2 707 961

Table 4b. **GDP Levels in 15 Latin American Countries, 1820-1949**
(million 1990 international Geary-Khamis dollars)

	Bolivia	Costa Rica	Cuba	Dominican Republic	Ecuador	El Salvador	Guatemala	Haiti
1820								
1850								
1870								
1913								
1914								
1915								
1916								
1917								
1918								
1919								
1920		682				1 091	2 032	
1921		668				1 094	2 231	
1922		727				1 159	2 106	
1923		672				1 208	2 316	
1924		769				1 292	2 504	
1925		766				1 203	2 456	
1926		847				1 422	2 480	
1927		769				1 250	2 643	
1928		809				1 466	2 702	
1929		775	6 132			1 468	3 016	
1930		813	5 776			1 505	3 145	
1931		803	4 853			1 349	2 933	
1932		739	3 894			1 210	2 567	
1933		880	4 213			1 374	2 593	
1934		776	4 948			1 419	2 933	
1935		840	5 788			1 562	3 390	
1936		896	6 747			1 527	4 657	
1937		1 045	7 753			1 672	4 567	
1938		1 107	6 012			1 554	4 693	
1939		1 139	6 345	3 137	1 667	5 282	
1940		1 093	5 516	3 344	1 811	6 033	
1941		1 224	7 410	3 361	1 772	6 356	
1942		1 097	6 214	3 502	1 925	6 439	
1943		1 095	6 889	3 946	2 087	4 293	
1944		992	7 907	3 998	1 980	4 162	
1945	4 816	1 130	8 759	4 014	1 898	4 226	3 059
1946	4 902	1 249	9 541	4 492	1 928	5 006	3 085
1947	4 987	1 486	10 925	4 991	2 425	5 076	3 137
1948	5 095	1 571	9 706	5 673	3 090	5 248	3 168
1949	5 202	1 635	10 547	5 776	2 806	5 741	3 202

Table 4b. **GDP Levels in 15 Latin American Countries, 1820-1949**
(million 1990 international Geary-Khamis dollars)

	Honduras	Jamaica	Nicaragua	Panama	Paraguay	Puerto Rico	Trinidad and Tobago	Total
1820		281						3 240
1850		217						
1870		267						4 620
1913		509						16 670
1914								
1915								
1916								
1917								
1918								
1919								
1920	917		809					
1921	927		840					
1922	1 008		769					
1923	1 002		823					
1924	936		872					
1925	1 130		963					
1926	1 140		837					
1927	1 252		841					
1928	1 408		1 065					
1929	1 394		1 190					
1930	1 485		962					
1931	1 517		900					
1932	1 359		810					
1933	1 275		1 019					
1934	1 235		925					
1935	1 180		940					
1936	1 201		748					
1937	1 148		811					
1938	1 215	1 131	839					
1939	1 249		1 042		2 057			
1940	1 334		1 139		1 947			
1941	1 331		1 246		1 979			
1942	1 217	1 217	1 200		2 095			
1943	1 219	1 436	1 316		2 139			
1944	1 247		1 303		2 185			
1945	1 536		1 309	1 671	2 108			
1946	1 653	2 141	1 422	1 698	2 314			
1947	1 760	2 007	1 426	1 769	2 012			
1948	1 797		1 550	1 664	2 035			
1949	1 822		1 522	1 702	2 377			

Table 4b. **GDP Levels in 15 Latin American Countries, 1950-2001**
(million 1990 international Geary-Khamis dollars)

	Bolivia	Costa Rica	Cuba	Dominican Republic	Ecuador	El Salvador	Guatemala	Haiti
1950	5 309	1 702	11 837	2 416	6 278	2 888	6 190	3 254
1951	5 683	1 747	12 818	2 701	6 346	2 945	6 277	3 302
1952	5 855	1 958	13 257	2 921	7 129	3 166	6 408	3 489
1953	5 301	2 256	11 647	2 884	7 279	3 392	6 643	3 378
1954	5 412	2 275	12 238	3 049	7 867	3 431	6 767	3 654
1955	5 698	2 538	12 794	3 237	8 074	3 608	6 934	3 507
1956	5 360	2 466	13 967	3 562	8 373	3 891	7 565	3 814
1957	5 183	2 676	15 980	3 787	8 751	4 098	7 992	3 587
1958	5 306	3 007	15 980	3 989	9 007	4 187	8 365	3 871
1959	5 289	3 118	14 263	4 012	9 490	4 375	8 778	3 688
1960	5 516	3 389	14 419	4 209	10 106	4 553	8 992	3 926
1961	5 631	3 530	14 625	4 114	10 360	4 713	9 378	3 767
1962	5 945	3 746	14 845	4 815	10 911	5 276	9 709	4 128
1963	6 327	4 067	15 064	5 129	11 189	5 504	10 635	3 860
1964	6 632	4 265	15 296	5 472	11 977	6 017	11 128	3 772
1965	6 958	4 651	15 529	4 791	13 131	6 340	11 613	3 813
1966	7 461	5 013	16 380	5 434	13 475	6 794	12 255	3 790
1967	7 928	5 320	18 294	5 617	14 188	7 164	12 757	3 713
1968	8 604	5 730	17 230	5 628	14 973	7 396	13 877	3 860
1969	8 989	6 111	17 018	6 244	15 792	7 653	14 532	3 986
1970	9 459	6 515	16 380	6 906	16 899	7 881	15 364	4 174
1971	9 820	6 945	17 656	7 637	17 872	8 245	16 221	4 445
1972	10 321	7 556	18 507	8 581	18 972	8 712	17 412	4 603
1973	11 030	8 145	20 209	9 617	21 337	9 084	18 593	4 810
1974	11 598	8 583	21 272	10 171	22 585	9 675	19 779	5 114
1975	12 364	8 755	22 336	10 659	23 772	10 193	20 164	4 995
1976	13 118	9 231	22 974	11 377	26 075	10 572	21 654	5 422
1977	13 670	10 055	24 038	11 930	27 731	11 189	23 344	5 448
1978	14 128	10 677	25 527	12 207	29 664	11 935	24 511	5 710
1979	14 125	11 207	26 165	12 733	31 274	11 744	25 667	6 127
1980	13 995	11 290	25 527	13 511	32 706	10 748	26 632	6 591
1981	14 124	11 035	27 654	14 069	34 041	9 869	26 804	6 410
1982	13 508	10 266	28 292	14 324	34 421	9 324	25 858	6 191
1983	12 905	10 551	29 104	14 959	33 702	9 386	25 193	6 238
1984	13 034	11 379	30 146	14 999	35 081	9 595	25 321	6 256
1985	12 943	11 475	30 694	14 620	36 570	9 819	25 167	6 269
1986	12 530	12 107	30 714	15 057	37 648	9 926	25 199	6 261
1987	12 858	12 683	30 468	16 189	35 288	10 193	26 094	6 214
1988	13 348	13 114	31 022	16 300	39 060	10 384	27 110	6 263
1989	13 735	13 867	31 128	18 377	39 123	10 491	28 179	6 329
1990	14 446	14 370	31 087	17 503	40 267	10 805	29 050	6 323
1991	15 226	14 686	27 481	17 643	42 280	11 108	30 125	6 329
1992	15 485	15 729	23 689	18 772	43 549	11 918	31 601	5 456
1993	16 135	16 641	19 898	19 148	44 507	12 681	32 865	5 336
1994	16 910	17 357	20 296	19 971	46 465	13 442	34 212	4 893
1995	17 705	17 739	20 986	20 870	47 859	14 275	35 923	5 138
1996	18 484	17 899	22 812	22 373	48 816	14 532	37 000	5 349
1997	19 408	18 901	23 565	24 230	50 476	15 157	38 518	5 493
1998	20 417	20 489	23 871	25 998	50 678	15 732	40 482	5 614
1999	20 499	22 415	25 494	28 078	46 978	16 268	42 020	5 765
2000	20 991	22 908	26 896	30 600	40 059	16 626	43 533	5 817
2001	21 243	23 114	27 703	30 943	50 750	16 925	44 317	5 718

Table 4b. **GDP Levels in 15 Latin American Countries, 1950-2001**
(million 1990 international Geary-Khamis dollars)

	Honduras	Jamaica	Nicaragua	Panama	Paraguay	Puerto Rico	Trinidad and Tobago	Total
1950	1 880	1 837	1 774	1 710	2 338	4 755	2 322	56 490
1951	1 982	1 985	1 894	1 695	2 383	4 929	2 526	59 213
1952	2 058	2 145	2 215	1 787	2 343	5 214	2 612	62 557
1953	2 220	2 446	2 268	1 895	2 410	5 445	2 682	62 146
1954	2 094	2 727	2 480	1 963	2 452	5 669	2 730	64 808
1955	2 149	3 008	2 646	2 077	2 564	5 961	3 111	67 906
1956	2 322	3 307	2 645	2 185	2 672	6 388	3 756	72 273
1957	2 429	3 789	2 868	2 414	2 795	6 708	4 088	77 145
1958	2 506	3 849	2 877	2 432	2 952	6 901	4 423	79 652
1959	2 569	4 064	2 920	2 589	2 944	7 521	4 692	80 312
1960	2 728	4 330	2 960	2 744	2 970	8 066	5 258	84 166
1961	2 798	4 453	3 182	3 040	3 111	8 835	5 488	87 025
1962	2 959	4 533	3 529	3 295	3 330	9 500	5 781	92 302
1963	3 069	4 681	3 912	3 606	3 421	10 488	6 076	97 028
1964	3 229	5 050	4 370	3 761	3 569	11 232	6 283	102 053
1965	3 509	5 456	4 786	4 091	3 773	12 254	6 603	107 298
1966	3 713	5 695	4 944	4 395	3 815	13 119	6 891	113 174
1967	3 922	5 915	5 288	4 762	4 058	13 944	7 035	119 905
1968	4 154	6 218	5 360	5 109	4 202	14 606	7 400	124 347
1969	4 187	6 681	5 716	5 507	4 365	15 899	7 604	130 284
1970	4 296	7 481	5 771	5 839	4 636	17 280	7 873	136 754
1971	4 462	7 481	6 055	6 312	4 839	18 375	7 954	144 319
1972	4 635	7 706	6 248	6 645	5 088	19 732	8 414	153 132
1973	4 866	8 411	6 566	7 052	5 487	20 908	8 553	164 668
1974	4 826	8 095	7 505	7 221	5 945	20 919	9 011	172 299
1975	4 949	8 093	7 493	7 338	6 328	20 388	9 181	177 008
1976	5 467	7 603	7 880	7 458	6 758	21 464	10 059	187 112
1977	6 047	7 443	8 556	7 546	7 478	22 867	10 698	198 040
1978	6 662	7 496	7 884	8 285	8 297	24 379	11 947	209 309
1979	6 976	7 363	5 785	8 651	9 215	25 868	12 500	215 400
1980	7 014	6 957	6 043	9 961	10 549	26 263	13 501	221 288
1981	7 196	7 142	6 367	10 367	11 458	26 544	14 096	227 176
1982	7 078	7 237	6 312	10 939	11 058	25 734	13 271	223 813
1983	7 030	7 405	6 609	11 013	10 724	25 855	12 231	222 905
1984	7 312	7 343	6 474	10 963	11 061	27 747	12 967	229 678
1985	7 640	7 003	6 204	11 480	11 501	28 319	12 436	232 140
1986	7 710	7 119	6 077	11 857	11 486	30 630	12 028	236 349
1987	8 167	7 668	6 035	12 150	11 988	32 136	11 473	239 604
1988	8 571	7 889	5 367	10 256	12 764	34 228	11 027	246 703
1989	8 894	8 428	5 296	10 215	13 509	35 919	10 937	254 427
1990	8 898	8 890	5 297	10 688	13 923	37 277	11 110	259 934
1991	9 138	8 917	5 281	11 650	14 271	38 136	11 499	263 770
1992	9 668	9 140	5 323	12 605	14 514	39 877	11 372	268 698
1993	10 355	9 304	5 302	13 273	15 094	41 729	11 236	273 504
1994	10 158	9 481	5 514	13 685	15 547	43 475	11 708	283 114
1995	10 534	9 642	5 762	13 945	16 247	45 453	12 188	294 266
1996	10 913	9 497	6 033	14 280	16 458	46 953	12 651	304 050
1997	11 459	9 355	6 340	14 908	16 886	48 549	13 043	316 288
1998	11 791	9 317	6 600	15 504	16 819	50 103	13 669	327 084
1999	11 567	9 308	7 889	16 000	16 903	52 207	14 598	335 989
2000	12 134	9 411	7 500	16 400	16 835	53 826	15 299	338 835
2001	12 449	9 693	7 725	16 450	16 970	55 494	15 988	355 482

Table 4b. **GDP Levels in 47 Latin American Countries, 1820-1949**
(million 1990 international Geary-Khamis dollars)

	Total 8 core countries	Total 15 countries	Total 24 small Caribbean countries	Total 47 countries
1820	11 275	3 240	509	15 024
1850				
1870	22 273	4 620	626	27 519
1900	60 619	9 974	1 217	71 810
1901	65 206			
1902	64 327			
1903	69 334			
1904	72 078			
1905	77 152			
1906	80 087			
1907	82 530			
1908	85 216			
1909	89 036			
1910	92 580			
1911	95 596			
1912	99 922			
1913	101 419	16 670	1 782	119 871
1914	95 890			
1915	96 586			
1916	100 002			
1917	101 442			
1918	105 504			
1919	108 632			
1920	114 811			
1921	113 737			
1922	120 740			
1923	131 691			
1924	136 541			
1925	139 169			
1926	146 603			
1927	153 420			
1928	165 312			
1929	170 305			
1930	163 253			
1931	152 202			
1932	146 991			
1933	159 469			
1934	172 594			
1935	181 108			
1936	191 168			
1937	201 068			
1938	205 978			
1939	213 820			
1940	216 077			
1941	227 302			
1942	226 013			
1943	236 058			
1944	256 245			
1945	265 235			
1946	290 028			
1947	308 001			
1948	327 784			
1949	339 572			

Table 4b. **GDP Levels in 47 Latin American Countries, 1950-2001**
(million 1990 international Geary-Khamis dollars)

	Total 8 *core countries*	*Total 15* *countries*	*Total 24 small* *Caribbean countries*	*Total 47* *countries*
1950	355 334	56 490	4 083	415 907
1951	374 715	59 213	4 313	438 241
1952	386 495	62 557	4 556	453 608
1953	402 327	62 146	4 813	469 286
1954	429 335	64 808	5 083	499 226
1955	457 615	67 906	5 370	530 891
1956	475 609	72 273	5 671	553 553
1957	512 754	77 145	5 991	595 890
1958	539 756	79 652	6 328	625 736
1959	553 915	80 312	6 685	640 912
1960	591 792	84 166	7 060	683 018
1961	621 094	87 025	7 458	715 577
1962	645 203	92 302	7 878	745 383
1963	662 526	97 028	8 321	767 875
1964	709 498	102 053	8 790	820 341
1965	744 892	107 298	9 285	861 475
1966	781 429	113 174	9 808	904 411
1967	815 031	119 905	10 359	945 295
1968	866 665	124 347	10 942	1 001 954
1969	925 041	130 284	11 558	1 066 883
1970	990 990	136 754	12 210	1 139 954
1971	1 050 692	144 319	12 897	1 207 908
1972	1 118 521	153 132	13 544	1 285 197
1973	1 209 969	164 668	14 392	1 389 029
1974	1 285 240	172 299	14 585	1 472 124
1975	1 324 638	177 008	14 783	1 516 429
1976	1 398 124	187 112	14 983	1 600 219
1977	1 463 153	198 040	15 187	1 676 380
1978	1 524 191	209 309	15 392	1 748 892
1979	1 628 061	215 400	15 601	1 859 062
1980	1 722 570	221 288	15 812	1 959 670
1981	1 728 257	227 176	16 026	1 971 459
1982	1 708 298	223 813	16 243	1 948 354
1983	1 660 164	222 905	16 462	1 899 531
1984	1 725 338	229 678	16 686	1 971 702
1985	1 782 514	232 140	16 912	2 031 566
1986	1 860 963	236 349	17 142	2 114 454
1987	1 924 001	239 604	17 374	2 180 979
1988	1 936 851	246 703	17 611	2 201 165
1989	1 956 548	254 427	17 851	2 228 826
1990	1 961 787	259 934	18 094	2 239 815
1991	2 040 047	263 770	18 545	2 322 362
1992	2 107 718	268 698	19 007	2 395 423
1993	2 184 924	273 504	19 481	2 477 909
1994	2 301 164	283 114	19 966	2 604 244
1995	2 327 753	294 266	20 464	2 642 483
1996	2 408 994	304 050	20 975	2 734 019
1997	2 539 749	316 288	21 497	2 877 534
1998	2 594 017	327 084	22 033	2 943 134
1999	2 591 451	335 989	22 634	2 950 074
2000	2 695 411	338 835	22 846	3 057 092
2001	2 707 961	355 482	23 563	3 087 006

PER CAPITA GDP IN LATIN AMERICA

Table 4c. **Per Capita GDP in 8 Latin American Countries, 1820-1913**
(1990 international Geary-Khamis dollars)

	Argentina	Brazil	Chile	Colombia	Mexico	Peru	Uruguay	Venezuela	Average
1820		646			759				713
1850		686							
1870	1 311	713			674		2 181	569	749
1871		717					2 178		
1872		721					2 632		
1873		724					2 601		
1874		728					2 315		
1875		732					1 942		
1876		736					2 105		
1877		740					2 123		
1878		744					2 247		
1879		748					1 949		
1880		752					2 082		
1881		756					1 932		
1882		760					2 080		
1883		764					2 397		
1884		768					2 324		
1885		773					2 569		
1886		777					2 608		
1887		781					2 267		
1888		785					2 718		
1889		789					2 415		
1890	2 152	794			1 011		2 147		
1891		773					2 290		
1892		730					2 294		
1893		622					2 437		
1894		621					2 657		
1895		783			1 132		2 568		
1896		710					2 644		
1897		699					2 493		
1898		717					2 250		
1899		703					2 261		
1900	2 756	678	1 949	973	1 366	817	2 219	821	1 200
1901	2 880	730	1 990	1 022	1 466	858	2 233	797	1 267
1902	2 717	715	2 033	1 020	1 348	855	2 572	856	1 228
1903	2 992	714	2 074	1 030	1 483	864	2 615	913	1 300
1904	3 191	713	2 120	1 039	1 492	872	2 640	876	1 327
1905	3 479	718	2 164	1 053	1 630	884	2 334	861	1 395
1906	3 518	770	2 210	1 103	1 594	925	2 533	799	1 422
1907	3 459	755	2 257	1 101	1 669	924	2 757	793	1 439
1908	3 657	734	2 303	1 096	1 649	920	2 973	841	1 460
1909	3 699	776	2 313	1 131	1 680	949	2 957	865	1 498
1910	3 822	769	2 472	1 162	1 694	975	3 136	886	1 533
1911	3 746	836	2 420	1 201	1 707	1 008	2 957	937	1 558
1912	3 904	809	2 656	1 236	1 718	1 037	3 508	962	1 603
1913	3 797	811	2 653	1 236	1 732	1 037	3 310	1 104	1 601

Table 4c. **Per Capita GDP in 8 Latin American Countries, 1914-1949**
(1990 international Geary-Khamis dollars)

	Argentina	Brazil	Chile	Colombia	Mexico	Peru	Uruguay	Venezuela	Average
1914	3 302	780	2 440	1 163	1 744	927	2 654	956	1 489
1915	3 244	798	2 238	1 129	1 757	974	2 470	980	1 478
1916	3 091	804	2 620	1 222	1 770	1 255	2 508	921	1 509
1917	2 790	842	2 794	1 292	1 783	1 198	2 717	1 069	1 509
1918	3 248	808	2 763	1 252	1 796	1 154	2 828	1 057	1 547
1919	3 307	895	2 155	1 253	1 810	1 318	3 135	983	1 570
1920	3 473	963	2 430	1 255	1 823	1 331	2 674	1 173	1 635
1921	3 471	859	2 064	1 255	1 836	926	2 751	1 214	1 594
1922	3 636	1 009	2 179	1 255	1 850	1 035	3 078	1 241	1 659
1923	3 898	1 046	2 676	1 255	1 884	1 318	3 170	1 420	1 773
1924	4 055	1 024	2 880	1 255	1 825	1 318	3 397	1 630	1 801
1925	3 919	1 007	2 876	1 255	1 908	1 157	3 188	2 081	1 800
1926	3 994	1 008	2 767	1 340	1 991	1 272	3 398	2 487	1 859
1927	4 156	1 060	2 618	1 424	1 875	1 410	3 797	2 761	1 907
1928	4 291	1 158	3 136	1 490	1 857	1 487	3 906	3 057	2 014
1929	4 367	1 137	3 396	1 505	1 757	1 619	3 847	3 426	2 034
1930	4 080	1 048	3 143	1 474	1 618	1 417	4 301	3 444	1 914
1931	3 712	1 004	2 333	1 448	1 643	1 228	3 500	2 754	1 752
1932	3 522	1 018	2 274	1 511	1 373	1 148	3 196	2 613	1 662
1933	3 621	1 076	2 652	1 577	1 501	1 524	2 750	2 831	1 772
1934	3 845	1 142	2 976	1 526	1 574	1 753	3 221	2 995	1 884
1935	3 950	1 150	2 987	1 677	1 660	1 772	3 356	3 181	1 943
1936	3 912	1 235	3 056	1 744	1 768	1 822	3 459	3 449	2 017
1937	4 125	1 250	3 241	1 751	1 796	1 832	3 462	3 896	2 084
1938	4 072	1 276	3 139	1 843	1 794	1 757	3 676	4 144	2 098
1939	4 148	1 263	3 178	1 905	1 858	1 884	3 692	4 305	2 136
1940	4 161	1 250	3 259	1 895	1 852	1 823	3 661	4 045	2 119
1941	4 304	1 307	3 205	1 877	1 949	1 998	3 682	3 903	2 180
1942	4 284	1 229	3 322	1 832	2 032	1 757	3 338	3 347	2 119
1943	4 182	1 368	3 400	1 792	2 051	1 643	3 331	3 575	2 164
1944	4 579	1 386	3 388	1 863	2 159	1 835	3 705	4 309	2 296
1945	4 356	1 390	3 630	1 899	2 134	2 005	3 764	5 102	2 315
1946	4 665	1 501	3 786	2 017	2 211	2 046	4 083	5 948	2 473
1947	5 089	1 518	3 470	2 042	2 221	2 066	4 313	6 894	2 564
1948	5 252	1 596	3 806	2 050	2 248	2 094	4 405	7 394	2 663
1949	5 047	1 659	3 715	2 107	2 304	2 199	4 504	7 544	2 690

Table 4c. **Per Capita GDP in 8 Latin American Countries, 1950-2001**
(1990 international Geary-Khamis dollars)

	Argentina	Brazil	Chile	Colombia	Mexico	Peru	Uruguay	Venezuela	Average
1950	4 987	1 672	3 821	2 153	2 365	2 263	4 659	7 462	2 700
1951	5 073	1 702	3 883	2 150	2 477	2 385	4 955	7 663	2 770
1952	4 717	1 752	4 024	2 214	2 504	2 473	4 957	7 992	2 779
1953	4 874	1 784	4 159	2 277	2 439	2 539	5 139	7 956	2 814
1954	4 980	1 848	4 101	2 358	2 605	2 634	5 391	8 417	2 921
1955	5 237	1 926	4 016	2 373	2 742	2 689	5 352	8 750	3 027
1956	5 285	1 896	3 954	2 391	2 843	2 731	5 360	9 124	3 059
1957	5 461	1 994	4 269	2 400	2 965	2 836	5 333	10 058	3 205
1958	5 698	2 111	4 282	2 383	3 025	2 746	5 402	9 816	3 278
1959	5 241	2 221	4 155	2 473	3 016	2 768	4 860	9 997	3 269
1960	5 559	2 335	4 320	2 497	3 155	3 023	4 960	9 646	3 392
1961	5 862	2 437	4 418	2 540	3 172	3 154	5 036	9 002	3 460
1962	5 677	2 511	4 518	2 594	3 211	3 321	4 858	9 058	3 494
1963	5 455	2 463	4 694	2 597	3 343	3 345	4 820	9 134	3 488
1964	5 926	2 472	4 693	2 675	3 594	3 462	4 858	9 562	3 632
1965	6 371	2 448	4 631	2 689	3 702	3 532	4 860	9 841	3 708
1966	6 321	2 527	5 042	2 750	3 813	3 723	4 974	9 677	3 784
1967	6 399	2 554	5 105	2 784	3 922	3 757	4 721	9 922	3 841
1968	6 578	2 704	5 188	2 874	4 073	3 666	4 747	10 249	3 976
1969	7 037	2 860	5 281	2 976	4 185	3 698	4 991	10 262	4 131
1970	7 302	3 057	5 293	3 094	4 320	3 807	5 184	10 672	4 309
1971	7 530	3 279	5 663	3 194	4 363	3 857	5 130	10 446	4 450
1972	7 635	3 539	5 492	3 355	4 597	3 858	4 945	10 245	4 618
1973	7 962	3 882	5 093	3 499	4 845	3 952	4 974	10 625	4 872
1974	8 334	4 083	5 050	3 618	5 003	4 200	5 123	10 507	5 049
1975	8 122	4 190	4 323	3 622	5 146	4 226	5 421	10 472	5 080
1976	7 965	4 472	4 398	3 716	5 228	4 195	5 608	10 929	5 236
1977	8 304	4 568	4 755	3 797	5 275	4 103	5 639	11 251	5 353
1978	7 807	4 681	5 069	4 047	5 573	4 008	5 903	11 164	5 450
1979	8 227	4 892	5 407	4 184	5 941	4 131	6 234	10 920	5 690
1980	8 206	5 198	5 738	4 265	6 289	4 205	6 577	10 139	5 886
1981	7 603	4 852	5 956	4 263	6 683	4 283	6 668	9 841	5 772
1982	7 243	4 765	5 017	4 212	6 489	4 176	6 000	9 356	5 578
1983	7 383	4 500	4 898	4 185	6 082	3 559	5 614	8 745	5 305
1984	7 425	4 646	5 125	4 239	6 174	3 633	5 520	8 623	5 401
1985	6 834	4 917	5 168	4 282	6 218	3 631	5 567	8 521	5 471
1986	7 224	5 205	5 375	4 446	5 865	3 879	6 023	8 725	5 598
1987	7 299	5 273	5 590	4 589	5 854	4 103	6 461	8 805	5 674
1988	7 056	5 158	5 901	4 682	5 810	3 680	6 422	9 080	5 601
1989	6 523	5 227	6 377	4 739	5 936	3 183	6 462	8 094	5 550
1990	6 436	4 923	6 402	4 840	6 119	2 955	6 474	8 313	5 465
1991	6 980	4 893	6 753	4 821	6 258	2 960	6 614	8 965	5 584
1992	7 497	4 802	7 374	4 909	6 366	2 868	7 055	9 373	5 669
1993	7 827	4 939	7 738	5 028	6 372	2 965	7 224	9 137	5 776
1994	8 367	5 163	8 010	5 240	6 536	3 296	7 567	8 620	5 982
1995	8 005	5 296	8 612	5 418	6 027	3 505	7 365	8 950	5 951
1996	8 253	5 366	9 080	5 428	6 230	3 514	7 681	8 747	6 060
1997	8 803	5 488	9 586	5 409	6 541	3 742	8 009	9 155	6 289
1998	9 123	5 422	9 756	5 350	6 745	3 675	8 317	8 977	6 326
1999	8 711	5 392	9 539	5 042	6 877	3 640	8 024	8 288	6 227
2000	8 544	5 556	9 841	5 096	7 218	3 686	7 859	8 415	6 385
2001	8 137	5 570	10 001	5 087	7 089	3 630	7 557	8 507	6 327

Table 4b. **Per Capita GDP in 15 Latin American Countries, 1820-1949**
(1990 international Geary-Khamis dollars)

	Bolivia	Costa Rica	Cuba	Dominican Republic	Ecuador	El Salvador	Guatemala	Haiti
1820								
1850								
1870								
1913								
1914								
1915								
1916								
1917								
1918								
1919								
1920		1 624				932	1 272	
1921		1 553				919	1 382	
1922		1 691				950	1 291	
1923		1 527				974	1 405	
1924		1 709				1 017	1 504	
1925		1 665				925	1 460	
1926		1 802				1 069	1 460	
1927		1 636				926	1 539	
1928		1 685				1 055	1 557	
1929		1 582	1 639			1 041	1 720	
1930		1 626	1 505			1 045	1 776	
1931		1 575	1 241			924	1 620	
1932		1 421	977			823	1 380	
1933		1 660	1 038			922	1 358	
1934		1 437	1 982			940	1 512	
1935		1 527	1 371			1 021	1 712	
1936		1 600	1 573			985	2 305	
1937		1 802	1 779			1 065	2 206	
1938		1 876	1 358			977	2 224	
1939		1 867	1 411		1 301	1 035	2 457	
1940		1 763	1 208		1 356	1 111	2 742	
1941		1 943	1 599		1 323	1 074	2 825	
1942		1 688	1 321		1 360	1 146	2 800	
1943		1 659	1 442		1 494	1 235	1 835	
1944		1 459	1 631		1 474	1 151	1 741	
1945	1 690	1 614	1 776		1 443	1 091	1 732	1 045
1946	1 700	1 759	1 893		1 574	1 095	2 002	1 042
1947	1 710	2 036	2 121		1 700	1 362	1 975	1 048
1948	1 727	2 095	1 842		1 880	1 707	1 988	1 046
1949	1 743	2 123	1 958		1 861	1 525	2 111	1 046

Table 4b. **Per Capita GDP in 15 Latin American Countries, 1820-1949**
(1990 international Geary-Khamis dollars)

	Honduras	Jamaica	Nicaragua	Panama	Paraguay	Puerto Rico	Trinidad and Tobago	Total
1820		700						636
1850		522						
1870		535						486
1913		620						1 038
1914								
1915								
1916								
1917								
1918								
1919								
1920	1 274		1 264					
1921	1 253		1 313					
1922	1 309		1 183					
1923	1 253		1 266					
1924	1 141		1 321					
1925	1 329		1 459					
1926	1 295		1 249					
1927	1 407		1 255					
1928	1 547		1 590					
1929	1 499		1 750					
1930	1 563		1 415					
1931	1 564		1 304					
1932	1 373		1 174					
1933	1 262		1 456					
1934	1 211		1 303					
1935	1 135		1 288					
1936	1 133		997					
1937	1 063		1 053					
1938	1 105	972	1 076					
1939	1 115		1 286		1 894			
1940	1 160		1 372		1 752			
1941	1 138		1 483		1 741			
1942	1 014	970	1 395		1 800			
1943	1 007	1 150	1 495		1 796			
1944	1 006		1 448		1 792			
1945	1 219		1 423	2 113	1 690			
1946	1 281	1 649	1 497	2 155	1 815			
1947	1 333	1 512	1 455	2 200	1 542			
1948	1 331		1 550	2 024	1 524			
1949	1 311		1 478	2 031	1 740			

Table 4b. Per Capita GDP in 15 Latin American Countries, 1950-2001
(1990 international Geary-Khamis dollars)

	Bolivia	Costa Rica	Cuba	Dominican Republic	Ecuador	El Salvador	Guatemala	Haiti
1950	1 919	1 963	2 046	1 027	1 863	1 489	2 085	1 051
1951	2 013	1 951	2 176	1 117	1 835	1 480	2 054	1 049
1952	2 031	2 114	2 207	1 172	2 009	1 550	2 037	1 090
1953	1 800	2 353	1 900	1 123	1 998	1 616	2 051	1 037
1954	1 799	2 289	1 957	1 150	2 103	1 589	2 029	1 102
1955	1 853	2 460	2 005	1 183	2 101	1 624	2 019	1 039
1956	1 706	2 301	2 145	1 260	2 121	1 701	2 140	1 108
1957	1 614	2 406	2 406	1 296	2 156	1 740	2 195	1 023
1958	1 616	2 605	2 363	1 320	2 159	1 725	2 231	1 082
1959	1 575	2 598	2 067	1 284	2 211	1 748	2 273	1 011
1960	1 606	2 715	2 052	1 302	2 289	1 764	2 262	1 055
1961	1 603	2 723	2 050	1 232	2 279	1 769	2 292	991
1962	1 654	2 785	2 046	1 394	2 331	1 920	2 307	1 064
1963	1 720	2 919	2 032	1 437	2 320	1 941	2 456	974
1964	1 762	2 961	2 009	1 484	2 411	2 058	2 498	931
1965	1 806	3 127	1 988	1 259	2 566	2 101	2 534	922
1966	1 891	3 258	2 051	1 384	2 556	2 172	2 600	897
1967	1 962	3 349	2 248	1 387	2 612	2 216	2 631	860
1968	2 079	3 497	2 080	1 349	2 675	2 210	2 782	875
1969	2 120	3 622	2 021	1 453	2 739	2 206	2 830	884
1970	2 176	3 754	1 917	1 561	2 845	2 187	2 905	906
1971	2 204	3 889	2 037	1 680	2 922	2 222	2 974	955
1972	2 260	4 118	2 096	1 837	3 012	2 298	3 096	979
1973	2 357	4 319	2 245	2 005	3 290	2 342	3 204	1 013
1974	2 418	4 430	2 324	2 067	3 383	2 436	3 303	1 066
1975	2 516	4 396	2 404	2 111	3 459	2 504	3 263	1 032
1976	2 647	4 506	2 439	2 198	3 687	2 532	3 395	1 111
1977	2 691	4 769	2 520	2 250	3 810	2 613	3 546	1 106
1978	2 715	4 870	2 650	2 248	3 961	2 715	3 607	1 149
1979	2 652	4 959	2 695	2 289	4 060	2 605	3 661	1 221
1980	2 572	4 911	2 644	2 372	4 129	2 354	3 681	1 304
1981	2 547	4 681	2 847	2 413	4 181	2 186	3 579	1 259
1982	2 394	4 235	2 890	2 400	4 114	2 084	3 352	1 202
1983	2 249	4 230	2 944	2 450	3 922	2 076	3 187	1 189
1984	2 234	4 432	3 020	2 403	3 975	2 091	3 117	1 168
1985	2 181	4 340	3 045	2 292	4 036	2 105	3 011	1 146
1986	2 074	4 446	3 022	2 311	4 048	2 089	2 930	1 120
1987	2 089	4 530	2 975	2 432	3 697	2 105	2 947	1 088
1988	2 124	4 561	3 002	2 399	3 988	2 106	2 973	1 074
1989	2 138	4 698	2 982	2 649	3 894	2 092	3 003	1 063
1990	2 197	4 747	2 948	2 474	3 903	2 119	3 009	1 041
1991	2 262	4 736	2 582	2 446	4 002	2 142	3 034	1 025
1992	2 246	4 957	2 209	2 555	4 025	2 259	3 093	870
1993	2 287	5 129	1 844	2 563	4 018	2 362	3 127	835
1994	2 343	5 237	1 871	2 629	4 099	2 459	3 164	753
1995	2 400	5 242	1 925	2 703	4 126	2 564	3 229	777
1996	2 453	5 186	2 083	2 850	4 115	2 561	3 232	795
1997	2 523	5 372	2 142	3 037	4 163	2 621	3 269	803
1998	2 601	5 718	2 160	3 208	4 090	2 669	3 340	808
1999	2 562	6 146	2 297	3 412	3 712	2 708	3 370	816
2000	2 575	6 174	2 414	3 663	3 101	2 716	3 396	810
2001	2 559	6 126	2 477	3 651	3 849	2 713	3 363	785

Table 4b. **Per Capita GDP in 15 Latin American Countries,1950-2001**
(1990 international Geary-Khamis dollars)

	Honduras	Jamaica	Nicaragua	Panama	Paraguay	Puerto Rico	Trinidad and Tobago	Total
1950	1 313	1 327	1 616	1 916	1 584	2 144	3 674	1 750
1951	1 344	1 412	1 674	1 851	1 573	2 205	3 894	1 794
1952	1 356	1 504	1 900	1 901	1 506	2 341	3 941	1 854
1953	1 421	1 691	1 888	1 969	1 509	2 471	3 954	1 802
1954	1 300	1 858	2 002	1 993	1 495	2 561	3 914	1 835
1955	1 293	2 020	2 072	2 055	1 523	2 649	4 316	1 876
1956	1 354	2 190	2 008	2 108	1 547	2 840	5 059	1 950
1957	1 372	2 468	2 111	2 270	1 578	2 968	5 344	2 032
1958	1 370	2 458	2 052	2 241	1 625	3 002	5 609	2 046
1959	1 360	2 541	2 019	2 322	1 581	3 239	5 743	2 011
1960	1 398	2 654	1 983	2 391	1 555	3 421	6 251	2 054
1961	1 387	2 702	2 065	2 574	1 588	3 677	6 371	2 072
1962	1 421	2 722	2 219	2 710	1 657	3 881	6 514	2 143
1963	1 427	2 757	2 382	2 882	1 659	4 201	6 718	2 195
1964	1 452	2 904	2 578	2 920	1 687	4 401	6 801	2 246
1965	1 526	3 070	2 734	3 085	1 739	4 719	7 030	2 299
1966	1 563	3 129	2 736	3 219	1 712	4 993	7 234	2 362
1967	1 599	3 178	2 835	3 388	1 774	5 264	7 327	2 440
1968	1 639	3 284	2 783	3 531	1 789	5 463	7 684	2 469
1969	1 599	3 480	2 875	3 699	1 810	5 840	7 897	2 523
1970	1 601	3 849	2 812	3 814	1 872	6 349	8 244	2 588
1971	1 613	3 803	2 856	4 012	1 902	6 642	8 272	2 668
1972	1 618	3 858	2 862	4 111	1 946	6 930	8 628	2 763
1973	1 642	4 130	2 921	4 250	2 038	7 302	8 685	2 903
1974	1 574	3 908	3 236	4 232	2 144	7 247	9 053	2 968
1975	1 570	3 845	3 129	4 198	2 220	6 946	9 118	2 980
1976	1 687	3 564	3 187	4 167	2 315	7 093	9 847	3 082
1977	1 815	3 451	3 350	4 102	2 506	7 422	10 296	3 190
1978	1 942	3 439	3 023	4 424	2 719	7 819	11 319	3 300
1979	1 977	3 336	2 152	4 518	2 954	8 164	11 649	3 324
1980	1 930	3 121	2 155	5 091	3 304	8 183	12 380	3 354
1981	1 916	3 162	2 195	5 194	3 498	8 195	12 794	3 380
1982	1 833	3 150	2 119	5 372	3 285	7 848	11 888	3 269
1983	1 774	3 188	2 169	5 301	3 097	7 797	10 794	3 193
1984	1 795	3 128	2 076	5 172	3 104	8 283	11 273	3 224
1985	1 825	2 953	1 946	5 306	3 135	8 373	10 664	3 193
1986	1 793	2 973	1 865	5 370	3 042	8 974	10 192	3 185
1987	1 849	3 178	1 810	5 394	3 085	9 330	9 631	3 163
1988	1 903	3 249	1 571	4 465	3 191	9 850	9 202	3 192
1989	1 919	3 449	1 512	4 361	3 282	10 246	9 112	3 225
1990	1 871	3 609	1 454	4 476	3 287	10 539	9 271	3 225
1991	1 873	3 588	1 384	4 786	3 274	10 706	9 641	3 206
1992	1 930	3 648	1 348	5 083	3 237	11 123	9 603	3 202
1993	2 011	3 684	1 308	5 259	3 273	11 542	9 560	3 197
1994	1 919	3 722	1 324	5 329	3 277	11 913	10 032	3 246
1995	1 935	3 753	1 348	5 333	3 331	12 341	10 503	3 310
1996	1 951	3 668	1 376	5 363	3 282	12 606	10 989	3 355
1997	1 994	3 588	1 411	5 512	3 276	12 914	11 426	3 426
1998	1 998	3 550	1 435	5 647	3 176	13 251	12 036	3 478
1999	1 914	3 526	1 676	5 731	3 107	13 738	12 908	3 510
2000	1 957	3 548	1 558	5 782	3 014	14 106	13 598	3 478
2001	1 958	3 636	1 571	5 715	2 959	14 452	14 295	3 586

Table 4c. **Per Capita GDP in 47 Latin American Countries, 1820-1949**
(1990 international Geary-Khamis dollars)

	Average 8 core countries	Average 15 countries	Average 24 small Caribbean countries	Average 47 countries
1820	713	636	636	692
1850				
1870	749	486	549	681
1900	1 200	778	880	1 110
1901	1 267			
1902	1 228			
1903	1 300			
1904	1 327			
1905	1 395			
1906	1 422			
1907	1 439			
1908	1 460			
1909	1 498			
1910	1 533			
1911	1 558			
1912	1 603			
1913	1 601	1 038	1 174	1 481
1914	1 489			
1915	1 478			
1916	1 509			
1917	1 509			
1918	1 547			
1919	1 570			
1920	1 635			
1921	1 594			
1922	1 659			
1923	1 773			
1924	1 801			
1925	1 800			
1926	1 859			
1927	1 907			
1928	2 014			
1929	2 034			
1930	1 914			
1931	1 752			
1932	1 662			
1933	1 772			
1934	1 884			
1935	1 943			
1936	2 017			
1937	2 084			
1938	2 098			
1939	2 136			
1940	2 119			
1941	2 180			
1942	2 119			
1943	2 164			
1944	2 296			
1945	2 315			
1946	2 473			
1947	2 564			
1948	2 663			
1949	2 690			

Table 4c. **Per Capita GDP in 47 Latin American Countries, 1950-2001**
(1990 international Geary-Khamis dollars)

	Average 8 core countries	*Average 15 countries*	*Average 24 small Caribbean countries*	*Average 47 countries*
1950	2 700	1 750	1 980	2 506
1951	2 770	1 794	2 043	2 572
1952	2 779	1 854	2 109	2 592
1953	2 814	1 802	2 177	2 612
1954	2 921	1 835	2 242	2 705
1955	3 027	1 876	2 311	2 799
1956	3 059	1 950	2 385	2 840
1957	3 205	2 032	2 460	2 974
1958	3 278	2 046	2 537	3 037
1959	3 269	2 011	2 616	3 024
1960	3 392	2 054	2 701	3 133
1961	3 460	2 072	2 801	3 192
1962	3 494	2 143	2 905	3 234
1963	3 488	2 195	2 992	3 241
1964	3 632	2 246	3 094	3 367
1965	3 708	2 299	3 201	3 439
1966	3 784	2 362	3 315	3 514
1967	3 841	2 440	3 437	3 576
1968	3 976	2 469	3 563	3 691
1969	4 131	2 523	3 703	3 828
1970	4 309	2 588	3 859	3 986
1971	4 450	2 668	4 012	4 117
1972	4 618	2 763	4 150	4 271
1973	4 872	2 903	4 350	4 504
1974	5 049	2 968	4 366	4 659
1975	5 080	2 980	4 415	4 687
1976	5 236	3 082	4 471	4 833
1977	5 353	3 190	4 512	4 948
1978	5 450	3 300	4 547	5 047
1979	5 690	3 324	4 589	5 247
1980	5 886	3 354	4 636	5 412
1981	5 772	3 380	4 665	5 327
1982	5 578	3 269	4 686	5 152
1983	5 305	3 193	4 704	4 918
1984	5 401	3 224	4 721	5 002
1985	5 471	3 193	4 738	5 052
1986	5 598	3 185	4 759	5 154
1987	5 674	3 163	4 784	5 212
1988	5 601	3 192	4 808	5 158
1989	5 550	3 225	4 833	5 123
1990	5 465	3 225	4 855	5 053
1991	5 584	3 206	4 937	5 145
1992	5 669	3 202	5 016	5 213
1993	5 776	3 197	5 095	5 299
1994	5 982	3 246	5 177	5 474
1995	5 951	3 310	5 261	5 460
1996	6 060	3 355	5 347	5 556
1997	6 289	3 426	5 434	5 753
1998	6 326	3 478	5 532	5 793
1999	6 223	3 510	5 632	5 718
2000	6 378	3 478	5 634	5 838
2001	6 314	3 586	5 759	5 811

HS–5: Asia

Estimates for Asia are shown in three groups. The first consists of 16 East Asian countries which produced 88 per cent of Asian GDP and had 89 per cent of Asian population in 2001. For these countries the GDP estimates are well documented and of reasonable quality for 1950 onwards and scholars have been active in developing historical accounts for earlier years. There have been major problems for China where official estimates of GDP exaggerate growth and understate its level. Maddison (1998), *Chinese Economic Performance in the Long Run*, OECD, Paris, provides a detailed examination of these problems and makes adjustments to provide a close approximation to Western SNA accounting practice. Chinese official statisticians adopted SNA norms several years ago. Misstatement is not deliberate, but is a transitional problem in moving away from a detailed reporting practice inherited from the long period in which the norms of the Soviet material product system (MPS) prevailed.

The second group consists of 26 East Asian countries, which produced 1.6 per cent of Asian GDP and had 4.3 per cent of Asian population in 2001.

The third group consists of 15 West Asian countries, which produced about 10 per cent of Asian GDP and had 6.5 per cent of Asian population in 2001. The biggest countries in this group, in terms of GDP are Turkey, Iran, and Saudi Arabia.

Eight independent Asian countries emerged from the collapse of the former Soviet Union in 1991, and a third of the GDP of the Russian Federation is generated in Asia. It is not possible to construct satisfactory GDP estimates for this area before 1973, because the problem of disaggregating the former USSR is compounded by the difficulty of converting from an MPS to an SNA basis. Estimates for 1973–2001 are shown in HS–3. Inclusion of the 8 new states would have added 1.9 per cent to our Asian GDP for 2001.

16 East Asian Countries

Population: 1820–1949 as in Maddison (2001) and Maddison (1995), except as specified below. 1950 onwards revised and updated from International Programs Center, US Bureau of the Census (October 2002), except for China, India and Indonesia where estimates were derived from sources specified below.

GDP: 1820–1993 movement from Maddison (2001) revised and updated to 2001 from IMF, *World Economic Outlook,* April 2002, except as specified below. Benchmark 1990 levels in international Geary–Khamis dollars were derived as shown in Maddison (2001), pp. 174, 219–20.

China: Population and GDP 1820–1998 from Maddison (1998), pp. 155–9, 167–170. 1933 GDP level from Maddison (1998), p. 158, and annual volume movement 1929–38 from Maddison (1995), p. 158. Updating to 2001 from *China Statistical Yearbook,* Beijing, (2001) with adjustment of growth rate to conform to SNA measurement procedure as indicated in Maddison (2001), p. 202, and described in detail in Maddison (1998). Unfortunately the IMF and many journalists continue to cite the official growth rates or levels without caveat or correction. One also finds frequent references to

Japan being the world's second biggest economy. My estimates show a GDP growth rate for China about threequarters the official estimate and a GDP level about 70 per cent higher than in Japan (when converted by purchasing power parity rather than exchange rates). See Xu Xianchun, Ye Yanfei and Derek Blades (2000), *National Accounts for China: Sources and Methods,* OECD, Paris and Maddison (1998).

India: 1900–1990 real GDP and population from Siva Sivasubramonian, *The National Income of India in the Twentieth Century,* Oxford University Press, Delhi, 2000, updated from his posthumous work, *The Sources of Economic Growth in India,* 1950 to 1999, OUP, Delhi, forthcoming. GDP movement 1820–1900 from Maddison 2001, pp. 202–3, annual movement 1884–99 from Alan Heston, in Kumar and Desai, eds., *Cambridge Economic History of India,* vol. 2, 1983, pp. 397–8. The present estimates refer to undivided India until 1946, and to the Indian Union since 1947. The GDP and population estimates are centred on October 1st (the middle of the fiscal year). The following table shows the population breakdown for India, Bangladesh and Pakistan for 1820–1946. Population figures for 1932–46 were misplaced in Maddison (2001), p. 203 and have been corrected. Per capita GDP in 1946 in undivided India was 622 in 1990 Geary–Khamis dollars, 624 in the Indian Union, 566 in Bangladesh, and 672 in Pakistan.

Table 5-1. **Population of Undivided India, Bangladesh and Pakistan, 1820-1946**

(000s)

	Undivided India	Indian Union	Bangladesh	Pakistan
1820	209 000	175 349	20 000	13 651
1870	253 000	212 189	24 721	16 090
1913	303 700	251 906	31 786	20 008
1929	333 100	275 861	34 427	22 812
1941	391 700	321 565	41 966	28 169
1946	415 200	340 857	41 660	32 683

Source: Maddison (1995), pp. 109, 114-5, and 232. Population of Bangladesh and Pakistan for benchmark year 1941 from M.W.M Yeatts, *Census of India 1941, vol. 1, Part I. Tables, Delhi, 1943,* pp. 62-3. Bangladesh assumed to move (with intercensal interpolation) as in prepartition Bengal (plus native states and agencies); Pakistan as in the prepartition total for Punjab (province, states, etc.), Sind and North West Frontier Province. Rough estimates 1946 for areas of Bangladesh and Pakistan when they were "wings" of undivided Pakistan from *20 Years of Pakistan in Statistics 1947-1967,* Karachi, 1968. Figures are for 1st October, the midpoint of the fiscal year.

Indonesia: Population and GDP 1820–70 from Maddison (1989) "Dutch Income in and from Indonesia, 1700–1938", *Modern Asian Studies,* pp. 645–70; 1870–1993 supplied by Pierre van der Eng (see Maddison, 2001, p. 204). Estimates include East Timor.

Japan: GDP 1820–1990 from Maddison (2001), pp. 204–7, revised and updated 1990–2001 from OECD, *Quarterly National Accounts,* vol. 2002/2.

Malaysia: The estimates refer to modern Malaysia (old federated and unfederated Malay states, Sabah and Sarawak) excluding Brunei and Singapore. Population 1820–1913 supplied by Don Hoerr, 1913–49 by Pierre van der Eng. Annual GDP estimates 1911–90 supplied by Pierre van der Eng. They are an extension of the estimates by industry of origin for West Malaysia of V.V. Bhanoji Rao, *National Accounts of West Malaysia, 1947–1971,* Heinemann, Kuala Lumpur, 1976, adjusted to include Sabah and Sarawak. New estimates for West Malaysia, by type of expenditure, are under preparation by a research team at the Asia–Europe Institute, University of Malaya. The preliminary results for 1900–1939 were presented by HRH Raja Nazrin at the International Economic History Congress in Buenos Aires, July 2002.

Philippines: GDP movement 1902–50 from unpublished estimates of Richard Hooley. They are a substantially revised version of R.W. Hooley, "Long term Growth of the Philippine Economy 1902–1961", *The Philippine Economic Journal* (1968). GDP movement 1950–90 from the National Statistical Coordination Board, Manila, updated from Asian Development Bank (ADB) *Key Indicators*, see Maddison (2001), p. 205.

South Korea: Population movement, 1820–1910, for the whole of Korea from T.H. Kwon and Y.–H. Shin, "On Population Estimates of the Yi Dynasty, 1392–1910", *Tong–a Munhwa*, 14, 1977, p. 328 linked to 1910–44 level estimates of S.–C. Suh, *Growth and Structural Change in the Korean Economy, 1910–1940*, Harvard, 1978, p. 41. Suh, p. 132 gives a breakdown of population in the North and South for 1925–44; in 1925, South Korea had 68.375 per cent of total population. I assumed this ratio applied for 1820–1924. 1944–49 from *UN Demographic Yearbook 1960*, p. 142. GDP movement 1911–53 from Maddison (1995), pp. 146, 158–9, 1953–70 from *National Income in Korea 1975*, Bank of Korea, pp. 142–3, 1970–90 from OECD *National Accounts 1960–97*, vol.1, Paris, 1999. 1990–2001 from OECD *Quarterly National Accounts*, vol. 2002/2.

Table 5-2. **Population of Korea, North and South, 1820-1950**
(000s)

	Korea	*South*	*North*
1820	13 740	9 395	4 345
1870	14 264	9 753	4 511
1910	14 766	10 096	4 670
1913	15 486	10 589	4 897
1925	19 020	13 005	6 014
1930	20 438	13 900	6 537
1935	22 280	15 020	7 187
1940	23 547	15 627	7 920
1944	25 133	16 574	8 558
1950	30 317	20 846	9 471

Source: 1910-44 total from Suh (1978), p. 41, linked to 1820-1910 population movement from Kwon and Shin (1977), p. 328. The latter estimates are an upward adjustment of the old household registers. Suh used the population censuses which began in 1925, as the basis of his estimates. For the overlap year, 1910, Kwon and Shin show a higher level than Suh. I assume that their upward adjustment was too big, but this should not affect their 1820-1910 growth rate.

Sri Lanka: New annual estimates of population, 1820–1949, and GDP, 1820–1990, were supplied by Pierre van der Eng. His GDP estimates are by industry of origin for 11 major sectors, with considerable commodity detail for agriculture. He draws to some extent on the statistical appendix in D.R. Snodgrass, *Ceylon: An Export Economy in Transition*, Irwin, Illinois, 1966, and on N.K. Sarkar, *The Demography of Ceylon*, Colombo, 1957, but there is substantial new research, significant revision, and a much more complete annual coverage.

Thailand: GDP movement 1870–1951 from Maddison (2001), pp. 208 and 298, with slight revision.

Taiwan: GDP movement 1912–90 from expenditure estimates of Toshiyuki Mizoguchi, *Long Term Economic Statistics of Taiwan 1905–1990*, Institute of Economic Research, Hitotsubashi University, 1999, pp. 22–4.; the 1939–45 gap in these estimates was filled by Hsing's figures as cited by S.P.S. Ho, *Economic Development of Taiwan, 1860–1970*, Yale, 1978, pp. 298–9; 1945–9 interpolated assuming equal percentage growth each year. GDP movement from 1990 onwards from ADB, *Key Indicators*.

Bangladesh, Burma, Hong Kong, Nepal, Pakistan, and Singapore: as indicated in Maddison (2001).

Conjectures to Fill Gaps in the Estimates: There are no gaps for population for benchmark years 1820, 1870 and 1913, but several countries for which GDP estimates are not available. As the objective is to provide a picture for the world as a whole, it was necessary to fill gaps in the dataset by conjectures (see Table 5–3).

Table 5-3. **16 East Asian Countries: GDP Conjectures and Estimates, 1820-1913**

	GDP (million international $)			GDP Per Capita (1990 int. $)			Population (000)		
	1820	*1870*	*1913*	*1820*	*1870*	*1913*	*1820*	*1870*	*1913*
Burma	*1 767*	*2 139*		*504*	*504*		3 506	4 245	
HongKong	*12*	*84*	*623*	*615*	*682*	*1 279*	20	123	487
Malaysia	*173*	*530*		*603*	*663*		287	800	
Nepal	*1 541*	*1 865*	*3 039*	*397*	*397*	*539*	3 881	4 698	5 639
Philippines	*1 532*	*3 929*		*704*	*776*		2 176	5 063	
Singapore	*18*	*57*		*615*	*682*		30	84	
South Korea	*5 637*	*5 891*		*600*	*604*		9 395	9 753	
Taiwan	*998*	*1 290*		*499*	*550*		2 000	2 345	
Thailand	*3 014*			*646*			4 665		
Total Conjectures	*14 693*	*15 785*	*3 661*	*567*	*582*	*598*	25 960	27 111	6 126
East Asia Sample	**372 323**	**375 428**	**608 413**	**581**	**550**	**680**	**640 140**	**682 920**	**895 121**
16 East Asia Total	**387 016**	**391 213**	**612 074**	**581**	**551**	**679**	**666 100**	**710 031**	**901 247**

For 1913, there were two gaps. I assumed the 1913–50 per capita GDP movement in Hong Kong was parallel to that in Singapore; in Nepal parallel to India.

For 1870, there were eight gaps. For Hong Kong and Singapore I assumed 1870–1913 per capita GDP movement was proportionately the same as in Japan. For the other six countries (Burma, South Korea, Malaysia, Nepal, Philippines and Taiwan), per capita GDP was assumed to move parallel to the average 1870–1913 for Indonesia, Sri Lanka and Thailand.

For 1820, there were nine gaps. Per capita GDP in Korea was taken to be the same as in China. Per capita GDP in Burma and Nepal was assumed to have been stagnant between 1820 and 1870 as it was in India. Average per capita GDP movement for the other six countries was assumed to be parallel to that in Japan.

For 1820, the proxy estimates represented 3.8 per cent of the total GDP of the 16 countries, 4 per cent in 1870, and 0.6 per cent in 1913. In the basic tables the proxy entries are shown in italics.

Other East Asian Countries

GDP for 1950 onwards from Maddison (2001) updated from IMF, *World Economic Outlook,* 1/ 2002 wherever possible. Revisions and updating for 6 of the small countries (Bhutan, Brunei, Fiji, Macao, Maldives and Papua New Guinea) are shown in Table 5–4, with consolidated figures for the other 14 (American Samoa, French Polynesia, Guam, Kiribati, Marshall Islands, Micronesia, New Caledonia, Northern Mariana Islands, Palau, Solomon Islands, Tonga, Vanuatu, Wallis and Futuna, and Western Samoa). Population from US Bureau of the Census (October 2002).

Table 5-4. **Population and GDP in 20 Small East Asian Countries, 1950–2001**

	Population (000 at mid-year)				GDP (million 1990 international dollars)			
	1950	*1973*	*1990*	*2001*	*1950*	*1973*	*1990*	*2001*
Bhutan	734	1 111	1 598	2 049	369	645	1 407	2 511
Brunei	45	145	258	344	224	1 156	1 663	2 030
Macao	205	259	352	454	127	735	3 078	4 935
Maldives	79	126	216	311	43	107	497	993
Total 4 Countries	1 063	1 641	2 424	3 158	763	2 641	6 645	10 469
Fiji	287	556	738	844	851	2 348	3 440	4 961
Papua New Guinea	1 412	2 477	3 825	5 049	1 356	4 847	5 865	8 893
14 Other Pacific Islands	649	1 210	1 782	2 014	875	2 296	3 496	4 729
16 Pacific Islands Total	2 279	4 104	6 164	7 924	3 082	9 491	12 711	18 582
20 Small Countries	3 342	5 748	8 588	11 082	3 845	11 952	19 356	29 051

Table 5-5. **26 East Asian Countries: Conjectures and Estimates for GDP, 1820-1913**

	Population (000)			GDP (million international $)			Per Capita GDP (1990 int. $)		
	1820	*1870*	*1913*	*1820*	*1870*	*1913*	*1820*	*1870*	*1913*
Afghanistan	3 280	4 207	5 730						
Cambodia	2 090	2 340	3 070						
Laos	470	755	1 387						
Mongolia	619	668	725						
20 Small Countries	1 798	1 903	2 237						
Total	8 257	9 873	13 149	*4 591*	*5 282*	*9 796*	*556*	*535*	*745*
North Korea	4 345	4 511	4 670	*2 607*	*2 725*	*3 829*	*600*	*604*	*820*
Vietnam	6 551	10 528	19 339	*3 453*	*5 321*	*14 062*	*527*	*505*	*727*
North Korea + Vietnam	10 896	15 039	24 009	*6 060*	*8 046*	*17 891*	*556*	*535*	*745*
Grand Total	19 153	24 912	37 158	*10 651*	*13 328*	*27 687*	*556*	*535*	*745*

For 1820–1913, provisional estimates of Vietnamese GDP volume movement were supplied by Jean–Pascal Bassino; North Korea was assumed to have the same per capita GDP as South Korea. For other countries no GDP estimates were available. I assumed the average per capita GDP, 1820–1913, for the whole group was the same as the average for North Korea and Vietnam (see Table 5–5). Population levels from McEvedy and Jones (1978), except for Vietnam, where I used Maks Banens' provisional estimate for 1913, with 1820–1913 population movement from McEvedy and Jones. See Table 5–5.

West Asian Countries

GDP for 1950 onwards from Maddison (2001) updated for 1993–2002 for 11 countries from ESCWA, *National Accounts Bulletin,* No. 21, Beirut, (November, 2002), Iran and Israel from IMF, *World Economic Outlook,* 2/2002, Turkey 1991–2000 from OECD *National Accounts, 1989–2000,* thereafter from IMF. No estimates were available for the West Bank and Gaza where the assumed volume increase 1998/9 was the same as 1997–8, with no change between 1999–2000, and 20 per cent falls in 2001 and 2002. Population 1950 onwards from US Bureau of the Census (October 2002).

Before the First World War, most of this area was part the Ottoman Empire. It accounted for 28 million of the 1913 population. The other 11 million lived in Iran. The 1820, 1870 and 1913 population figures shown in Table 5–6 are from Colin McEvedy and Richard Jones, *Atlas of World Population History*, Penguin (1978), pp. 133–154.

Sevket Pamuk has recently made tentative estimates of per capita GDP for several countries which permit estimates for the region much better than those in Maddison (2001), pp. 210–215. See Pamuk, "Economic Growth in Southeastern Europe and the Middle East since 1820", European Historical Economics Society Conference, Oxford, September 2001. They were derived from a variety of evidence in Ottoman archives and other research material on the region. He linked them to the Maddison (2001) estimates for later years and used the same numeraire, i.e. 1990 international Geary–Khamis dollars.

Table 5–6 contains estimates for three groups of countries in the region. For the countries in Arabia no GDP estimates are available before the second world war. They have now been transformed by the discovery and development of oil resources, but production did not start until the inter–war period. However, in the nineteenth century there was significant income from trade in the Persian Gulf, Southern Arabia and the Red Sea coast. Oman controlled large trading territories on the East African littoral. Yemen was a major exporter of coffee. For this group, I assumed a modest increase in per capita income from $550 to $600 between 1820 and 1913, as world trade expanded.

Table 5-6. **West Asian Population, GDP and Per Capita GDP, 1820-1913**

	Population (000)			GDP (million international $)			Per Capita GDP (1990 int. $)		
	1820	1870	1913	1820	1870	1913	1820	1870	1913
Gulf Coast (a)	200	200	254						
Oman	318	367	444						
Saudi Arabia	2 091	2 338	2 676						
Yemen	2 593	2 840	3 284						
Total Arabia (a)	5 202	5 745	6 658	2 861	3 303	3 995	550	575	600
Iraq	1 093	1 580	2 613	643	1 136	2 613	588	719	1 000
Jordan	217	266	348	128	191	348	588	719	1 000
Palestine-Israel	332	429	700	204	322	875	613	750	1 250
Syria	1 337	1 582	1 994	880	1 335	2 692	658	844	1 350
Lebanon	332	476	649	218	402	876	658	844	1 350
Total 5 countries	3 311	4 333	6 304	2 073	3 386	7 404	626	781	1 174
Iran	6 560	8 415	10 994	3 857	6 050	10 994	588	719	1 000
Turkey	10 074	11 793	15 000	6 478	9 729	18 195	643	825	1 213
Grand Total	25 147	30 286	38 956	15 269	22 468	40 588	607	742	1 042

a)   Includes Bahrain, Kuwait, Qatar and UAE.
Source: Population from McEvedy and Jones (1978) pp. 133-154. Turkish GDP as shown below, otherwise derived from Sevket Pamuk (2001).

The second group consists of five more prosperous countries (Iraq, Jordan, Palestine, Syria and Lebanon) with an ancient history as sophisticated traders with East Asia, Africa and Europe. Pamuk provides per capita estimates for Syria, which I assumed valid for Lebanon as well. His estimate for Jordan was taken to be valid for Iraq and Iran. I used his estimate for Palestine.

For Turkey see Table 5–7. The GDP benchmark for 1990 is from Maddison (2001), p. 219. GDP volume movement for 1948 onwards from OECD *National Accounts,* various issues, 1923–48 from T. Bulutay, Y.S. Tezel and N. Yilderim, *Turkiye Milli Geliri* 1923–48, Ankara, 1974, with 1913 per capita GDP assumed to be the same as in 1929. I linked the 1913 level to the per capita volume movement for 1820–1913 shown in Pamuk (2001). His major source was V. Eldem, *Osmanli Imparatorlugunun Iktisadi sartlari Hakkinda Bir Tetkik* (A Study of Economic Conditions in the Ottoman Empire), Is Bank, Istanbul, (1970). Population is from McEvedy and Jones (1978).

Table 5-7. **Turkish Population, GDP and Per Capita GDP, 1820-1950**

	Population (000s)	*GDP (million 1990 int. $)*	*Per Capita GDP (1990 int. $)*
1820	10 074	6 478	643
1870	11 793	9 729	825
1913	15 000	18 195	1 213
1923	13 877	9 882	712
1924	13 968	11 819	846
1925	14 059	13 159	936
1926	14 151	15 275	1 079
1927	14 250	13 886	974
1928	14 476	15 388	1 063
1929	14 705	17 842	1 213
1930	14 928	18 649	1 249
1931	15 174	19 763	1 302
1932	15 414	18 568	1 205
1933	15 658	21 007	1 342
1934	15 906	21 491	1 351
1935	16 158	21 927	1 357
1936	16 434	26 093	1 588
1937	16 725	26 965	1 612
1938	17 016	29 338	1 724
1939	17 517	31 776	1 814
1940	17 821	29 855	1 675
1941	18 011	27 158	1 508
1942	18 203	28 337	1 557
1943	18 396	25 721	1 398
1944	18 592	24 623	1 324
1945	18 790	21 297	1 133
1946	19 235	27 514	1 430
1947	19 690	29 064	1 476
1948	20 156	33 003	1 637
1949	20 634	31 340	1 519
1950	21 122	34 279	1 623

Summary Totals for Asia, 1820–1913

Table 5–8 shows the regional components and the totals for the 57 Asian countries, 1820–1913. Estimates for 1700 and earlier years in Maddison (2001) are unchanged (see tables in HS–8).

Table 5-8. **Total Asian Population, GDP and Per Capita GDP, 1820-1913**

	Population (000s)			GDP (million 1990 int. $)			Per Capita GDP (1990 int. $)		
	1820	1870	1913	1820	1870	1913	1820	1870	1913
16 East Asia	666 100	710 031	901 247	387 016	391 213	612 074	581	551	679
26 East Asia	19 153	24 912	37 158	10 651	13 328	27 687	556	535	745
15 West Asia	25 147	30 286	38 956	15 269	22 468	40 588	607	742	1 042
57 Asia	710 400	765 229	977 361	412 936	427 009	680 349	581	558	696

POPULATION, GDP LEVELS AND PER CAPITA GDP IN ASIA

Table 5a. **Population of 16 East Asian Countries, 1820-1913**
(000 at mid-year)

	China	India	Indonesia	Japan	Philippines	South Korea	Thailand	Taiwan
1820	381 000	209 000	17 927	31 000	2 176	9 395	4 665	2 000
1850	412 000	235 800	22 977	32 000	3 612	9 545	5 230	2 200
1870	358 000	253 000	28 922	34 437	5 063	9 753	5 775	2 345
1871	358 988	253 417	29 463	34 648				
1872	359 978	253 834	30 060	34 859				
1873	360 971	254 253	30 555	35 070				
1874	361 967	254 672	30 962	35 235				
1875	362 966	255 091	31 197	35 436				
1876	363 967	255 512	31 394	35 713				
1877	364 971	255 933	31 740	36 018				
1878	365 978	256 354	32 035	36 315				
1879	366 988	256 777	32 293	36 557				
1880	368 000	257 200	32 876	36 807				
1881	369 183	259 359	33 213	37 112				
1882	370 369	261 536	33 394	37 414				
1883	371 560	263 732	33 816	37 766				
1884	372 754	265 946	34 162	38 138				
1885	373 952	268 179	34 790	38 427				
1886	375 154	270 430	35 402	38 622				
1887	376 359	272 700	35 898	38 866				
1888	377 569	274 990	36 345	39 251				
1889	378 783	277 298	36 662	39 688				
1890	380 000	279 626	37 579	40 077	6 476	9 848	6 670	2 500
1891	381 979	280 110	37 792	40 380				
1892	383 969	280 594	38 288	40 684				
1893	385 969	281 079	38 263	41 001				
1894	387 979	281 565	38 782	41 350				
1895	390 000	282 052	39 476	41 775				
1896	391 980	282 540	39 936	42 196				
1897	393 970	283 029	40 620	42 643				
1898	395 970	283 518	41 316	43 145				
1899	397 980	284 009	42 025	43 626				
1900	400 000	284 500	42 746	44 103	7 324	9 896	7 320	2 864
1901	402 243	286 200	43 275	44 662	7 465		7 413	2 903
1902	404 498	288 000	43 810	45 255	7 609		7 507	2 942
1903	406 766	289 700	44 352	45 841	7 755		7 602	2 982
1904	409 047	291 500	44 901	46 378	7 904		7 699	3 022
1905	411 340	293 300	45 457	46 829	8 056		7 797	3 085
1906	413 646	295 100	45 993	47 227	8 211		7 896	3 140
1907	415 965	296 900	46 535	47 691	8 369		7 996	3 172
1908	418 297	298 700	47 085	48 260	8 530		8 098	3 200
1909	420 642	300 500	47 642	48 869	8 694		8 201	3 232
1910	423 000	302 100	48 206	49 518	8 861	10 096	8 305	3 275
1911	427 662	303 100	48 778	50 215	9 032	10 258	8 431	3 334
1912	432 375	303 400	49 358	50 941	9 206	10 422	8 559	3 402
1913	437 140	303 700	49 934	51 672	9 384	10 589	8 689	3 469

Table 5a. **Population of 16 East Asian Countries, 1820-1913**
(000 at mid-year)

	Bangladesh	Burma	Hong Kong	Malaysia	Nepal	Pakistan	Singapore	Sri Lanka	16 country Total
1820		3 506	20	287	3 881		30	1 213	666 100
1850		3 932	33	530	4 352		56	2 217	734 484
1870	4 245		123	800	4 698		84	2 786	710 031
1871								2 820	
1872								2 842	
1873								2 863	
1874								2 885	
1875								2 908	
1876								2 930	
1877								2 952	
1878								2 975	
1879								2 998	
1880								3 021	
1881								3 044	
1882								3 073	
1883								3 107	
1884								3 144	
1885								3 170	
1886								3 194	
1887								3 221	
1888								3 261	
1889								3 311	
1890		7 489	214	1 585	5 192		157	3 343	780 756
1891								3 404	
1892								3 470	
1893								3 524	
1894								3 584	
1895								3 626	
1896								3 693	
1897								3 752	
1898								3 820	
1899								3 874	
1900		10 174	306	2 232	5 283		215	3 912	804 251
1901		10 490		2 288				4 031	
1902		10 642		2 345				4 071	
1903		10 796		2 404				4 156	
1904		10 953		2 467				4 233	
1905		11 112		2 532				4 383	
1906		11 273		2 601				4 458	
1907		11 437		2 672				4 467	
1908		11 603		2 745				4 520	
1909		11 771		2 821				4 585	
1910		11 942		2 893				4 668	
1911		12 115		2 967				4 757	
1912		12 220		3 025				4 784	
1913		12 326	487	3 084	5 639		323	4 811	901 247

Table 5a. **Population of 16 East Asian Countries, 1914-1949**
(000 at mid-year)

	China	India	Indonesia	Japan	Philippines	South Korea	Thailand	Taiwan
1914	441 958	304 000	50 517	52 396	9 565	10 764	8 822	3 528
1915	446 829	304 200	51 108	53 124	9 749	10 911	8 957	3 562
1916	451 753	304 500	51 705	53 815	9 937	11 086	9 094	3 583
1917	456 732	304 800	52 083	54 437	10 128	11 263	9 232	3 621
1918	461 766	305 100	52 334	54 886	10 323	11 443	9 418	3 658
1919	466 855	305 300	53 027	55 253	10 522	11 627	9 608	3 692
1920	472 000	305 600	53 723	55 818	10 725	11 804	9 802	3 736
1921	473 673	307 300	54 367	56 490	10 932	12 040	10 000	3 797
1922	475 352	310 400	55 020	57 209	11 143	12 281	10 202	3 870
1923	477 037	313 600	55 683	57 937	11 358	12 526	10 435	3 940
1924	478 728	316 700	56 354	58 686	11 577	12 777	10 673	4 009
1925	480 425	319 900	57 036	59 522	11 800	13 005	10 916	4 095
1926	482 128	323 200	57 727	60 490	12 026	13 179	11 165	4 195
1927	483 837	326 400	58 429	61 430	12 305	13 356	11 419	4 289
1928	485 552	329 700	59 140	62 361	12 543	13 535	11 734	4 388
1929	487 273	333 100	59 863	63 244	12 890	13 716	12 058	4 493
1930	489 000	336 400	60 596	64 203	13 194	13 900	12 392	4 614
1931	492 640	341 000	61 496	65 205	13 507	14 117	12 735	4 742
1932	496 307	345 800	62 400	66 189	13 829	14 338	13 087	4 867
1933	500 000	350 700	63 314	67 182	14 158	14 562	13 399	4 995
1934	502 639	355 600	64 246	68 090	14 497	14 789	13 718	5 128
1935	505 292	360 600	65 192	69 238	14 843	15 020	14 045	5 255
1936	507 959	365 700	66 154	70 171	15 199	15 139	14 379	5 384
1937	510 640	370 900	67 136	71 278	15 563	15 260	14 721	5 530
1938	513 336	376 100	68 131	71 879	15 934	15 381	14 980	5 678
1939	516 046	381 400	69 145	72 364	16 275	15 504	15 244	5 821
1940	518 770	386 800	70 175	72 967	16 585	15 627	15 513	5 987
1941	521 508	391 700	71 316	74 005	16 902	15 859	15 787	6 163
1942	524 261	396 300	72 475	75 029	17 169	16 094	16 060	6 339
1943	527 028	400 900	73 314	76 005	17 552	16 332	16 462	6 507
1944	529 810	405 600	73 565	77 178	17 887	16 574	16 868	6 520
1945	532 607	410 400	73 332	76 224	18 228	17 917	17 284	6 533
1946	535 418	415 200	74 132	77 199	18 775	19 369	17 710	6 546
1947	538 244	346 000	75 146	78 119	19 338	19 886	18 148	6 346
1948	541 085	350 000	76 289	80 155	19 918	20 027	18 569	6 697
1949	543 941	355 000	77 654	81 971	20 516	20 208	19 000	7 280

Table 5a. **Population of 16 East Asian Countries, 1914-1949**
(000 at mid-year)

	Bangladesh	Burma	Hong Kong	Malaysia	Nepal	Pakistan	Singapore	Sri Lanka	16 country Total
1914		12 433	507	3 144			331	4 838	
1915		12 541	528	3 207			341	4 905	
1916		12 650	550	3 271			351	4 971	
1917		12 760	573	3 337			360	5 040	
1918		12 871	597	3 404			370	5 109	
1919		12 893	622	3 473			380	5 179	
1920		13 096	648	3 545			391	5 250	
1921		13 212	625	3 618			418	5 304	
1922		13 351	638	3 698			436	5 367	
1923		13 491	668	3 779			458	5 426	
1924		13 633	696	3 863			469	5 452	
1925		13 776	725	3 949			492	5 505	
1926		13 921	710	4 038			511	5 545	
1927		14 067	725	4 128			532	5 591	
1928		14 215	753	4 221			553	5 730	
1929		14 364	785	4 316			575	5 669	
1930		14 515	821	4 413			596	5 707	
1931		14 667	840	4 513			563	5 748	
1932		14 870	901	4 604			580	5 788	
1933		15 075	923	4 697			515	5 825	
1934		15 283	944	4 793			525	5 872	
1935		15 494	966	4 890			572	5 897	
1936		15 708	988	4 993			603	5 943	
1937		15 925	1 282	5 099			651	5 989	
1938		16 145	1 479	5 207			710	6 045	
1939		16 368	1 750	5 317			728	6 095	
1940		16 594	1 786	5 434			751	6 134	
1941		16 824	1 639	5 554			769	6 169	
1942		16 727		5 592				6 191	
1943		16 908		5 630				6 296	
1944		17 090		5 668				6 442	
1945		17 272		5 707				6 650	
1946		17 454	1 550	5 746				6 854	
1947		17 636	1 750	5 786			938	7 037	
1948		17 818	1 800	5 922			961	7 244	
1949		18 000	1 857	6 061			979	7 455	

Table 5a. **Population of 16 East Asian Countries, 1950-2003**
(000 at mid-year)

	China	India	Indonesia	Japan	Philippines	South Korea	Thailand	Taiwan
1950	546 815	359 000	79 043	83 805	21 131	20 846	20 042	7 981
1951	557 480	365 000	80 525	85 164	21 775	20 876	20 653	8 251
1952	568 910	372 000	82 052	86 459	22 439	20 948	21 289	8 550
1953	581 390	379 000	83 611	87 655	23 122	21 060	21 964	8 850
1954	595 310	386 000	85 196	88 754	23 827	21 259	22 685	9 160
1955	608 655	393 000	86 807	89 815	24 553	21 552	23 451	9 486
1956	621 465	401 000	88 456	90 766	25 301	22 031	24 244	9 825
1957	637 408	409 000	90 124	91 563	26 072	22 612	25 042	10 164
1958	653 235	418 000	91 821	92 389	26 867	23 254	25 845	10 500
1959	666 005	426 000	93 565	93 297	27 685	23 981	26 667	10 853
1960	667 070	434 000	95 254	94 092	28 529	24 784	27 513	11 209
1961	660 330	444 000	97 085	94 943	29 410	25 614	28 376	11 563
1962	665 770	454 000	99 028	95 832	30 325	26 420	29 263	11 919
1963	682 335	464 000	101 009	96 812	31 273	27 211	30 174	12 277
1964	698 355	474 000	103 031	97 826	32 254	27 984	31 107	12 631
1965	715 185	485 000	105 093	98 883	33 268	28 705	32 062	12 978
1966	735 400	495 000	107 197	99 790	34 304	29 436	33 036	13 321
1967	754 550	506 000	109 343	100 825	35 357	30 131	34 024	13 649
1968	774 510	518 000	111 532	101 961	36 424	30 838	35 028	13 962
1969	796 025	529 000	113 765	103 172	37 507	31 544	36 050	14 282
1970	818 315	541 000	116 044	104 345	38 604	32 241	37 091	14 598
1971	841 105	554 000	118 368	105 697	39 718	32 883	38 202	14 918
1972	862 030	567 000	121 282	107 188	40 850	33 505	39 276	15 226
1973	881 940	580 000	124 271	108 707	41 998	34 073	40 302	15 526
1974	900 350	593 000	127 338	110 162	43 162	34 692	41 306	15 824
1975	916 395	607 000	130 485	111 573	44 337	35 281	42 272	16 122
1976	930 685	620 000	133 713	112 775	45 574	35 860	43 221	16 450
1977	943 455	634 000	137 026	113 872	46 851	36 436	44 148	16 785
1978	956 165	648 000	140 425	114 913	48 172	37 019	45 057	17 112
1979	969 005	664 000	143 912	115 890	49 537	37 534	46 004	17 450
1980	981 235	679 000	147 490	116 807	50 940	38 124	47 026	17 848
1981	993 861	692 000	150 657	117 648	52 195	38 723	47 941	18 177
1982	1 000 281	708 000	153 894	118 455	53 457	39 326	48 837	18 501
1983	1 023 288	723 000	157 204	119 270	54 698	39 910	49 709	18 803
1984	1 036 825	739 000	160 588	120 035	55 964	40 406	50 553	19 083
1985	1 051 040	755 000	164 047	120 754	57 288	40 806	51 367	19 337
1986	1 066 790	771 000	166 976	121 492	58 649	41 214	52 160	19 556
1987	1 084 035	788 000	169 959	122 091	60 018	41 622	52 946	19 758
1988	1 101 630	805 000	172 999	122 613	61 385	42 031	53 725	19 976
1989	1 118 650	822 000	176 094	123 108	62 814	42 449	54 493	20 208
1990	1 135 185	839 000	179 248	123 537	64 318	42 869	55 250	20 279
1991	1 150 780	856 000	182 223	123 946	65 789	43 313	55 982	20 493
1992	1 164 970	872 000	185 259	124 329	67 186	43 795	56 718	20 687
1993	1 178 440	891 000	188 359	124 668	68 611	44 279	57 449	20 883
1994	1 191 835	908 000	191 524	125 014	70 112	44 758	58 173	21 088
1995	1 204 855	927 000	194 755	125 341	71 717	45 236	58 894	21 283
1996	1 217 550	943 000	198 025	125 645	73 386	45 695	59 608	21 449
1997	1 230 075	959 000	201 350	125 956	75 013	46 131	60 311	21 629
1998	1 242 700	975 000	204 390	126 246	76 576	46 535	61 003	21 823
1999	1 252 704	991 691	207 429	126 494	78 134	46 903	61 684	21 993
2000	1 264 093	1 007 702	210 875	126 700	79 740	47 261	62 352	22 151
2001	1 275 392	1 023 590	214 303	126 892	81 370	47 619	63 007	22 304
2002				127 066	82 995	47 963	63 645	22 454
2003				127 214	84 620	48 289	64 265	22 603

Table 5a. **Population of 16 East Asian Countries, 1950-2003**
(000 at mid-year)

	Bangladesh	Burma	Hong Kong	Malaysia	Nepal	Pakistan	Singapore	Sri Lanka	16 country Total
1950	45 646	19 488	2 237	6 434	8 990	39 448	1 022	7 533	1 269 461
1951	46 152	19 788	2 015	6 582	9 086	40 382	1 068	7 752	1 292 551
1952	46 887	20 093	2 126	6 748	9 183	41 347	1 127	7 982	1 318 140
1953	47 660	20 403	2 242	6 929	9 280	42 342	1 192	8 221	1 344 923
1954	48 603	20 721	2 365	7 118	9 379	43 372	1 248	8 457	1 373 454
1955	49 602	21 049	2 490	7 312	9 479	44 434	1 306	8 679	1 401 669
1956	50 478	21 385	2 615	7 520	9 580	45 536	1 372	8 898	1 430 473
1957	51 365	21 732	2 736	7 739	9 682	46 680	1 446	9 129	1 462 494
1958	52 399	22 088	2 854	7 966	9 789	47 869	1 519	9 362	1 495 757
1959	53 485	22 456	2 967	8 196	9 906	49 104	1 587	9 610	1 525 365
1960	54 622	22 836	3 075	8 428	10 035	50 387	1 646	9 879	1 543 360
1961	55 741	23 229	3 168	8 663	10 176	51 719	1 702	10 152	1 555 872
1962	56 839	23 634	3 305	8 906	10 332	53 101	1 750	10 422	1 580 848
1963	58 226	24 053	3 421	9 148	10 500	54 524	1 795	10 687	1 617 447
1964	59 403	24 486	3 505	9 397	10 677	55 988	1 842	10 942	1 653 429
1965	60 332	24 933	3 598	9 648	10 862	57 495	1 887	11 202	1 691 130
1966	61 548	25 394	3 630	9 900	11 057	59 046	1 934	11 470	1 731 464
1967	62 822	25 870	3 723	10 155	11 262	60 642	1 978	11 737	1 772 067
1968	64 133	26 362	3 803	10 409	11 473	62 282	2 012	12 010	1 814 741
1969	65 483	26 867	3 864	10 662	11 692	63 970	2 043	12 275	1 858 201
1970	67 403	27 386	3 959	10 910	11 919	65 706	2 075	12 532	1 904 127
1971	69 227	27 919	4 045	11 171	12 155	67 491	2 113	12 776	1 951 789
1972	70 759	28 466	4 116	11 441	12 413	69 326	2 152	13 017	1 998 048
1973	72 471	29 227	4 213	11 712	12 685	71 121	2 193	13 246	2 043 683
1974	74 679	29 799	4 320	11 986	12 973	72 912	2 230	13 450	2 088 182
1975	76 253	30 357	4 396	12 267	13 278	74 712	2 263	13 660	2 130 651
1976	77 928	30 929	4 518	12 554	13 599	76 456	2 293	13 887	2 170 444
1977	80 428	31 514	4 584	12 845	13 933	78 153	2 325	14 117	2 210 473
1978	82 936	32 024	4 668	13 139	14 280	80 051	2 354	14 371	2 250 684
1979	85 492	32 611	4 930	13 444	14 641	82 374	2 384	14 649	2 293 856
1980	88 077	33 283	5 063	13 764	15 016	85 219	2 414	14 900	2 336 207
1981	90 666	33 884	5 183	14 097	15 403	88 417	2 533	15 152	2 376 537
1982	93 074	34 490	5 265	14 442	15 796	91 257	2 647	15 410	2 413 132
1983	95 384	35 103	5 345	14 793	16 200	93 720	2 681	15 618	2 464 726
1984	97 612	35 699	5 398	15 157	16 613	96 284	2 732	15 810	2 507 760
1985	99 753	36 257	5 456	15 545	17 038	99 053	2 736	16 021	2 551 498
1986	101 769	36 783	5 525	15 941	17 472	101 955	2 733	16 256	2 596 270
1987	103 764	37 277	5 585	16 332	17 917	104 893	2 775	16 495	2 643 467
1988	105 771	37 735	5 628	16 729	18 374	107 863	2 846	16 735	2 691 040
1989	107 807	38 152	5 661	17 118	18 843	110 883	2 931	16 971	2 738 182
1990	109 897	38 526	5 688	17 504	19 325	113 975	3 016	17 193	2 784 811
1991	111 936	38 855	5 752	17 906	19 819	117 001	3 097	17 391	2 830 283
1992	113 705	39 073	5 834	18 320	20 326	118 975	3 179	17 587	2 871 942
1993	115 448	39 336	5 944	18 748	20 846	121 009	3 268	17 826	2 916 114
1994	117 280	39 750	6 083	19 180	21 373	123 858	3 367	18 075	2 959 469
1995	119 186	40 166	6 247	19 611	21 907	126 630	3 481	18 304	3 004 613
1996	121 189	40 539	6 420	20 045	22 450	129 538	3 610	18 510	3 046 659
1997	123 315	40 876	6 607	20 476	23 001	132 485	3 741	18 699	3 088 664
1998	125 573	41 193	6 813	20 912	23 560	135 471	3 871	18 885	3 130 552
1999	127 943	41 491	6 992	21 354	24 127	138 496	4 008	19 065	3 175 945
2000	130 407	41 772	7 116	21 793	24 702	141 554	4 152	19 239	3 211 608
2001	132 975	42 035	7 211	22 229	25 284	144 617	4 300	19 409	3 252 537
2002	135 657	42 282	7 303	22 662	25 874	147 663	4 453	19 577	
2003	138 448	42 511	7 394	23 093	26 470	150 695	4 609	19 742	

Table 5a. **Population of 15 West Asian Countries, 1950-2003**
(000 at mid-year)

	Bahrain	Iran	Iraq	Israel	Jordan	Kuwait	Lebanon	Oman	Qatar
1950	115	16 357	5 163	1 286	561	145	1 364	489	25
1951	118	16 809	5 300	1 490	584	152	1 401	498	27
1952	120	17 272	5 442	1 621	608	160	1 440	508	29
1953	123	17 742	5 589	1 667	633	168	1 479	517	31
1954	127	18 226	5 743	1 712	659	177	1 519	528	33
1955	130	18 729	5 903	1 772	687	187	1 561	539	35
1956	134	19 249	6 073	1 850	716	197	1 604	550	37
1957	139	19 792	6 249	1 944	747	213	1 647	562	39
1958	144	20 362	6 433	2 025	779	235	1 692	573	41
1959	150	20 958	6 625	2 082	813	262	1 739	586	43
1960	157	21 577	6 822	2 141	849	292	1 786	599	45
1961	164	22 214	7 026	2 217	887	325	1 836	614	49
1962	172	22 874	7 240	2 311	934	358	1 887	628	53
1963	179	23 554	7 468	2 407	975	394	1 940	645	58
1964	186	24 264	7 711	2 498	1 017	433	1 996	662	64
1965	191	25 000	7 971	2 578	1 061	476	2 058	679	70
1966	197	25 764	8 240	2 641	1 107	523	2 122	697	77
1967	202	26 538	8 519	2 694	1 255	575	2 187	715	85
1968	208	27 321	8 808	2 747	1 383	632	2 254	735	94
1969	214	28 119	9 106	2 817	1 454	690	2 320	756	103
1970	220	28 933	9 414	2 903	1 503	748	2 383	779	113
1971	225	29 763	9 732	2 997	1 556	793	2 529	803	122
1972	231	30 614	10 062	3 096	1 614	842	2 680	829	132
1973	239	31 491	10 402	3 197	1 674	894	2 825	857	142
1974	248	32 412	10 754	3 286	1 738	948	2 988	884	153
1975	259	33 379	11 118	3 354	1 803	1 007	3 098	913	165
1976	274	34 381	11 494	3 424	1 870	1 072	3 119	956	177
1977	297	35 473	11 883	3 496	1 938	1 140	3 116	1 005	189
1978	323	36 634	12 317	3 570	2 007	1 214	3 109	1 059	202
1979	336	37 963	12 768	3 653	2 077	1 292	3 099	1 116	216
1980	348	39 548	13 233	3 737	2 163	1 370	3 086	1 175	231
1981	363	41 270	13 703	3 801	2 254	1 432	3 081	1 238	242
1982	378	43 016	14 173	3 858	2 347	1 497	3 087	1 301	252
1983	393	44 764	14 652	3 927	2 440	1 566	3 090	1 363	284
1984	408	46 542	15 161	4 005	2 533	1 637	3 090	1 424	315
1985	424	48 344	15 694	4 075	2 628	1 733	3 088	1 482	345
1986	440	50 162	16 247	4 137	2 724	1 811	3 087	1 538	375
1987	455	51 983	16 543	4 203	2 820	1 891	3 089	1 594	402
1988	469	53 650	17 038	4 272	2 917	1 973	3 096	1 652	430
1989	485	55 355	17 568	4 344	3 019	2 057	3 107	1 712	457
1990	500	57 551	18 135	4 512	3 262	2 142	3 147	1 773	481
1991	515	59 590	17 472	4 756	3 631	954	3 193	1 843	505
1992	529	60 800	17 862	4 937	3 867	1 418	3 220	1 915	529
1993	544	61 001	18 405	5 062	3 984	1 484	3 252	1 989	557
1994	558	61 133	18 970	5 185	4 082	1 551	3 291	2 059	585
1995	573	61 925	19 557	5 305	4 202	1 621	3 335	2 131	613
1996	586	62 768	20 162	5 420	4 364	1 693	3 382	2 206	641
1997	599	63 655	20 776	5 531	4 526	1 765	3 430	2 284	667
1998	611	64 487	21 398	5 639	4 686	1 836	3 479	2 364	694
1999	623	65 240	22 031	5 743	4 843	1 905	3 529	2 447	719
2000	634	66 006	22 676	5 842	4 999	1 974	3 578	2 533	744
2001	645	66 791	23 332	5 938	5 153	2 042	3 628	2 622	769
2002	656	67 538	24 002	6 030	5 307	2 112	3 678	2 713	793
2003	667	68 279	24 683	6 117	5 460	2 183	3 728	2 807	817

Table 5a. **Population of 15 West Asian Countries, 1950-2003**
(000 at mid-year)

	Saudi Arabia	Syria	Turkey	UAE	Yemen	West Bank and Gaza	Total
1950	3 860	3 495	21 122	72	4 777	1 017	59 847
1951	3 932	3 577	21 669	73	4 869	1 022	61 522
1952	4 006	3 662	22 236	75	4 964	1 031	63 172
1953	4 082	3 750	22 831	77	5 061	1 040	64 792
1954	4 160	3 842	23 464	80	5 162	1 049	66 482
1955	4 243	3 938	24 145	83	5 265	1 054	68 271
1956	4 329	4 041	24 877	86	5 380	1 061	70 184
1957	4 420	4 150	25 671	89	5 498	1 070	72 230
1958	4 514	4 268	26 506	93	5 619	1 078	74 361
1959	4 614	4 395	27 356	98	5 744	1 101	76 563
1960	4 718	4 533	28 217	103	5 872	1 113	78 825
1961	4 828	4 681	29 030	109	5 994	1 110	81 083
1962	4 943	4 835	29 789	116	6 120	1 133	83 392
1963	5 065	4 993	30 509	124	6 248	1 156	85 716
1964	5 192	5 157	31 227	133	6 378	1 182	88 101
1965	5 327	5 326	31 951	144	6 510	1 211	90 554
1966	5 469	5 500	32 678	157	6 625	1 236	93 033
1967	5 618	5 681	33 411	172	6 741	1 143	95 535
1968	5 775	5 867	34 165	191	6 859	1 000	98 038
1969	5 939	6 059	34 952	218	6 978	1 006	100 731
1970	6 109	6 258	35 758	249	7 098	1 032	103 500
1971	6 287	6 479	36 580	288	7 251	1 060	106 467
1972	6 473	6 701	37 493	336	7 407	1 090	109 598
1973	6 667	6 931	38 503	391	7 580	1 124	112 918
1974	6 868	7 169	39 513	453	7 755	1 167	116 336
1975	7 199	7 416	40 530	523	7 934	1 201	119 899
1976	7 608	7 670	41 485	598	8 171	1 228	123 525
1977	8 108	7 933	42 404	684	8 404	1 261	127 330
1978	8 680	8 203	43 317	779	8 641	1 296	131 349
1979	9 307	8 484	44 223	884	8 883	1 330	135 631
1980	9 949	8 774	45 121	1 000	9 133	1 360	140 226
1981	10 565	9 073	46 222	1 100	9 390	1 389	145 126
1982	11 179	9 410	47 329	1 204	9 658	1 426	150 116
1983	11 822	9 757	48 440	1 316	9 936	1 475	155 225
1984	12 502	10 114	49 554	1 438	10 229	1 525	160 477
1985	13 208	10 481	50 669	1 570	10 540	1 576	165 856
1986	13 858	10 857	51 780	1 714	10 870	1 630	171 230
1987	14 461	11 243	52 881	1 778	11 219	1 691	176 255
1988	15 055	11 632	53 966	1 839	11 591	1 758	181 339
1989	15 631	12 018	55 031	1 897	11 986	1 821	186 488
1990	15 847	12 436	56 085	1 951	12 416	1 897	192 136
1991	16 075	12 849	57 135	2 002	12 882	1 997	195 399
1992	16 692	13 219	58 179	2 049	13 368	2 105	200 689
1993	17 324	13 579	59 213	2 093	13 886	2 216	204 589
1994	17 970	13 939	60 221	2 136	14 395	2 346	208 421
1995	18 632	14 310	61 189	2 176	14 859	2 502	212 929
1996	19 290	14 691	62 128	2 216	15 327	2 666	217 539
1997	19 946	15 081	63 048	2 254	15 826	2 826	222 216
1998	20 620	15 481	63 946	2 293	16 352	2 932	226 816
1999	21 311	15 889	64 820	2 331	16 905	3 041	231 376
2000	22 024	16 306	65 667	2 369	17 479	3 152	235 983
2001	22 757	16 729	66 494	2 407	18 078	3 269	240 655
2002	23 513	17 156	67 309	2 446	18 701	3 390	245 344
2003	24 294	17 586	68 109	2 485	19 350	3 512	250 077

Table 5a. **Population of 26 East Asian Countries, 1950-2003**
(000 at mid-year)

	Afghanistan	Cambodia	Laos	Mongolia	North Korea	Vietnam	20 small countries	26 country Total
1950	8 150	4 163	1 886	779	9 471	25 348	3 342	53 139
1951	8 284	4 266	1 921	789	9 162	25 794	3 401	53 617
1952	8 425	4 371	1 957	801	8 865	26 247	3 461	54 127
1953	8 573	4 478	1 995	814	8 580	26 724	3 530	54 695
1954	8 728	4 589	2 035	828	8 572	27 210	3 599	55 561
1955	8 891	4 702	2 077	844	8 839	27 738	3 675	56 766
1956	9 062	4 827	2 121	862	9 116	28 327	3 755	58 070
1957	9 241	4 956	2 166	882	9 411	28 999	3 833	59 488
1958	9 429	5 088	2 213	904	9 727	29 775	3 922	61 059
1959	9 625	5 224	2 261	929	10 054	30 683	4 013	62 788
1960	9 829	5 364	2 309	955	10 392	31 656	4 106	64 612
1961	10 043	5 511	2 359	982	10 651	32 701	4 205	66 453
1962	10 267	5 761	2 409	1 010	10 917	33 796	4 315	68 476
1963	10 501	5 914	2 460	1 031	11 210	34 932	4 434	70 482
1964	10 744	6 071	2 512	1 061	11 528	36 099	4 547	72 562
1965	10 998	6 232	2 565	1 090	11 869	37 258	4 670	74 683
1966	11 262	6 396	2 619	1 119	12 232	38 378	4 799	76 807
1967	11 538	6 565	2 674	1 150	12 617	39 464	4 923	78 930
1968	11 825	6 738	2 730	1 181	13 024	40 512	5 055	81 065
1969	12 123	6 917	2 787	1 214	13 455	41 542	5 186	83 223
1970	12 431	6 984	2 845	1 248	13 912	42 577	5 332	85 327
1971	12 749	7 011	2 904	1 283	14 365	43 614	5 483	87 410
1972	13 079	7 110	2 964	1 321	14 781	44 655	5 617	89 528
1973	13 421	7 205	3 027	1 360	15 161	45 736	5 748	91 658
1974	13 772	7 294	3 092	1 403	15 501	46 902	5 866	93 831
1975	14 132	7 188	3 161	1 446	15 801	48 075	5 999	95 802
1976	14 501	6 915	3 176	1 487	16 069	49 273	6 131	97 553
1977	14 880	6 679	3 208	1 528	16 325	50 534	6 270	99 425
1978	15 269	6 472	3 248	1 572	16 580	51 663	6 417	101 220
1979	15 556	6 436	3 268	1 617	16 840	52 668	6 571	102 956
1980	14 985	6 586	3 293	1 662	17 114	53 661	6 733	104 034
1981	14 087	6 801	3 337	1 709	17 384	54 792	6 893	105 002
1982	13 645	7 064	3 411	1 756	17 648	55 972	7 060	106 556
1983	13 709	7 347	3 495	1 805	17 918	57 204	7 240	108 718
1984	13 826	7 535	3 577	1 856	18 196	58 466	7 425	110 880
1985	13 898	7 695	3 657	1 908	18 481	59 730	7 608	112 977
1986	13 936	7 965	3 762	1 961	18 772	61 006	7 796	115 199
1987	14 071	8 277	3 869	2 015	19 068	62 320	7 986	117 606
1988	14 326	8 599	3 980	2 071	19 371	63 630	8 177	120 153
1989	14 635	8 930	4 094	2 159	19 688	65 206	8 378	123 090
1990	14 750	9 271	4 210	2 216	20 019	66 637	8 588	125 692
1991	14 939	9 622	4 331	2 268	20 361	68 008	8 798	128 326
1992	16 589	10 068	4 454	2 313	20 711	69 321	9 014	132 470
1993	18 840	10 569	4 581	2 349	21 064	70 633	9 233	137 270
1994	20 319	10 950	4 712	2 383	21 340	71 935	9 453	141 091
1995	21 489	11 240	4 846	2 421	21 562	73 172	9 676	144 406
1996	22 429	11 510	4 971	2 459	21 649	74 341	9 901	147 260
1997	23 234	11 754	5 099	2 495	21 585	75 448	10 131	149 745
1998	24 065	11 982	5 229	2 531	21 455	76 487	10 365	152 113
1999	24 961	12 208	5 362	2 566	21 445	77 497	10 602	154 640
2000	25 889	12 433	5 498	2 601	21 648	78 518	10 841	157 426
2001	26 813	12 660	5 636	2 637	21 940	79 544	11 082	160 312
2002	27 756	12 890	5 778	2 674	22 215	80 577	11 326	163 217
2003	28 717	13 125	5 922	2 712	22 466	81 625	11 571	166 138

Table 5a. **Population of 57 Asian Countries, 1820-2001**
(000 at mid-year)

	16 East Asia	*26 East Asia*	*15 West Asia*	*Total 57 Asia*
1820	666 100	19 153	25 147	710 400
1870	710 031	24 912	30 286	765 229
1900	804 251	32 972	36 101	873 324
1913	901 247	37 158	38 956	977 361
1950	1 269 461	53 139	59 847	1 382 447
1951	1 292 551	53 617	61 522	1 407 689
1952	1 318 140	54 127	63 172	1 435 439
1953	1 344 923	54 695	64 792	1 464 409
1954	1 373 454	55 561	66 482	1 495 497
1955	1 401 669	56 766	68 271	1 526 707
1956	1 430 473	58 070	70 184	1 558 727
1957	1 462 494	59 488	72 230	1 594 212
1958	1 495 757	61 059	74 361	1 631 177
1959	1 525 365	62 788	76 563	1 664 717
1960	1 543 360	64 612	78 825	1 686 796
1961	1 555 872	66 453	81 083	1 703 409
1962	1 580 848	68 476	83 392	1 732 716
1963	1 617 447	70 482	85 716	1 773 645
1964	1 653 429	72 562	88 101	1 814 092
1965	1 691 130	74 683	90 554	1 856 366
1966	1 731 464	76 807	93 033	1 901 303
1967	1 772 067	78 930	95 535	1 946 533
1968	1 814 741	81 065	98 038	1 993 844
1969	1 858 201	83 223	100 731	2 042 155
1970	1 904 127	85 327	103 500	2 092 954
1971	1 951 789	87 410	106 467	2 145 665
1972	1 998 048	89 528	109 598	2 197 174
1973	2 043 683	91 658	112 918	2 248 260
1974	2 088 182	93 831	116 336	2 298 349
1975	2 130 651	95 802	119 899	2 346 352
1976	2 170 444	97 553	123 525	2 391 522
1977	2 210 473	99 425	127 330	2 437 228
1978	2 250 684	101 220	131 349	2 483 253
1979	2 293 856	102 956	135 631	2 532 444
1980	2 336 207	104 034	140 226	2 580 468
1981	2 376 537	105 002	145 126	2 626 665
1982	2 413 132	106 556	150 116	2 669 803
1983	2 464 726	108 718	155 225	2 728 669
1984	2 507 760	110 880	160 477	2 779 117
1985	2 551 498	112 977	165 856	2 830 331
1986	2 596 270	115 199	171 230	2 882 699
1987	2 643 467	117 606	176 255	2 937 328
1988	2 691 040	120 153	181 339	2 992 532
1989	2 738 182	123 090	186 488	3 047 760
1990	2 784 811	125 692	192 136	3 102 638
1991	2 830 283	128 326	195 399	3 154 008
1992	2 871 942	132 470	200 689	3 205 102
1993	2 916 114	137 270	204 589	3 257 972
1994	2 959 469	141 091	208 421	3 308 981
1995	3 004 613	144 406	212 929	3 361 948
1996	3 046 659	147 260	217 539	3 411 457
1997	3 088 664	149 745	222 216	3 460 624
1998	3 130 552	152 113	226 816	3 509 481
1999	3 175 945	154 640	231 376	3 561 961
2000	3 211 608	157 426	235 983	3 605 017
2001	3 252 537	160 312	240 655	3 653 504

Table 5b. **GDP Levels in 16 East Asian Countries, 1820-1913**
(million 1990 international Geary-Khamis dollars)

	China	India	Indonesia	Japan	Philippines	South Korea	Thailand	Taiwan
1820	228 600	111 417	10 970	20 739	*1 532*	*5 637*	*3 014*	*998*
1850	247 200							
1870	189 740	134 882	18 929	25 393	*3 929*	*5 891*	4 112	*1 290*
1871			19 021	25 709				
1872			19 158	26 005				
1873			19 660	26 338				
1874			20 162	26 644				
1875			20 481	28 698				
1876			21 028	28 019				
1877			21 302	28 910				
1878			21 028	28 825				
1879			21 439	30 540				
1880			21 758	31 779				
1881			23 218	30 777				
1882			22 443	31 584				
1883			22 214	31 618				
1884		146 409	24 495	31 872				
1885		151 985	24 815	33 052				
1886		148 134	24 678	35 395				
1887		155 899	24 951	36 982				
1888		158 358	25 179	35 310				
1889		155 063	25 316	37 016				
1890	205 304	163 341	24 815	40 556			5 229	
1891		148 317	25 362	38 621				
1892		160 224	26 411	41 200				
1893		164 280	27 187	41 344				
1894		166 799	27 643	46 288				
1895		162 696	28 281	46 933				
1896		150 699	28 099	44 353				
1897		178 236	28 509	45 285				
1898		178 599	28 874	53 883				
1899		164 690	30 608	49 870				
1900	218 074	170 466	31 748	52 020				
1901		173 957	31 352	53 883				
1902		188 504	30 904	51 089	5 320			
1903		191 141	32 637	54 671	6 450			
1904		192 060	33 314	55 101	5 979			
1905		188 587	33 823	54 170	5 979			
1906		193 979	34 869	61 263	6 322			
1907		182 234	35 698	63 198	6 648			
1908		184 844	35 800	63 628	6 834			
1909		210 241	37 659	63 556	6 944			
1910		210 439	40 180	64 559	7 984			
1911		209 354	42 442	68 070	8 539	7 966		
1912		208 946	42 818	70 507	8 969	8 148		2 456
1913	241 344	204 242	45 152	71 653	9 877	8 678	7 304	2 591

Table 5b. GDP Levels in 16 East Asian Countries, 1820-1913
(million 1990 international Geary-Khamis dollars)

	Bangladesh	Burma	Hong Kong	Malaysia	Nepal	Pakistan	Singapore	Sri Lanka	16 country Total
1820		1 767	12	173	1 541		18	597	387 016
1850								1 250	
1870		2 139	84	530	1 865		57	2 372	391 213
1871								2 332	
1872								2 230	
1873								2 257	
1874								2 235	
1875								2 270	
1876								2 311	
1877								2 341	
1878								2 135	
1879								2 307	
1880								2 509	
1881								2 699	
1882								2 874	
1883								2 925	
1884								2 844	
1885								2 670	
1886								2 588	
1887								3 044	
1888								3 004	
1889								2 985	
1890								3 494	
1891								3 529	
1892								3 651	
1893								3 709	
1894								3 739	
1895								3 934	
1896								4 018	
1897								4 221	
1898								4 461	
1899								4 779	
1900								5 048	500 686
1901		7 332						4 804	
1902								4 785	
1903								5 093	
1904								5 144	
1905								5 167	
1906		6 385						5 307	
1907								5 509	
1908								5 520	
1909								5 286	
1910								5 639	
1911		7 348		2 376				5 519	
1912				2 486				5 533	
1913	8 445		623	2 776	3 039		413	5 938	612 075

Table 5b. **GDP Levels in 16 East Asian Countries, 1914-1949**
(million 1990 international Geary-Khamis dollars)

	China	India	Indonesia	Japan	Philippines	South Korea	Thailand	Taiwan
1914		215 400	45 076	69 503	9 713	9 276		2 634
1915		210 110	45 647	75 952	9 017	10 535		2 725
1916		216 245	46 350	87 703	10 332	10 743		3 449
1917		212 341	46 513	90 641	11 924	11 498		3 826
1918		185 202	47 597	91 573	13 649	12 435		3 384
1919		210 730	51 402	100 959	13 400	12 201		3 624
1920		194 051	50 779	94 654	13 826	11 914		3 581
1921		208 785	51 212	105 043		12 654		3 316
1922		217 594	52 033	104 757		12 496		3 793
1923		210 511	52 858	104 828		12 904		4 046
1924		220 763	55 683	107 766		13 095		4 110
1925		223 375	57 610	112 209	16 361	13 216		4 502
1926		230 410	60 781	113 212	17 170	13 685		4 314
1927		230 426	64 989	114 860	17 732	14 500		4 337
1928		232 745	68 099	124 246	18 483	14 171		5 315
1929	273 991	242 409	70 015	128 116	19 363	13 902	9 568	5 149
1930	277 467	244 097	70 525	118 801	19 478	14 179		5 073
1931	280 292	242 489	65 218	119 804	19 481	13 980		5 055
1932	289 200	245 209	64 461	129 835	21 154	14 570		5 747
1933	289 200	245 433	64 035	142 589	20 628	16 670		5 288
1934	263 996	247 712	64 400	142 876	21 567	16 488		5 677
1935	285 300	245 361	66 674	146 817	18 730	18 648		6 807
1936	303 324	254 896	71 517	157 493	21 373	19 915		6 639
1937	295 937	250 768	78 485	165 017	23 335	22 614		6 986
1938	288 549	251 375	80 044	176 051	24 252	22 440	12 380	7 395
1939		256 924	80 861	203 781	26 130	20 115		8 094
1940		265 455	86 682	209 728	26 326	22 536		8 064
1941		270 531	89 316	212 594		22 848		8 871
1942		269 278		211 448		22 718		9 524
1943		279 898		214 457		23 048		6 492
1944		276 954		205 214		22 050		4 459
1945		272 503		102 607		11 029		4 849
1946		258 164		111 492	12 131	11 984		5 274
1947		213 680		120 377	16 922	12 886		5 736
1948		215 927		138 290	19 772	13 867		6 238
1949		221 631	61 872	147 534	21 022	14 917		6 784

Table 5b. **GDP Levels in 16 East Asian Countries, 1914-1949**
(million 1990 international Geary-Khamis dollars)

	Bangladesh	Burma	Hong Kong	Malaysia	Nepal	Pakistan	Singapore	Sri Lanka	16 country Total
1914				2 893				5 853	
1915				3 007				5 574	
1916		10 405		3 258				5 829	
1917				3 449				6 137	
1918				3 300				5 658	
1919				4 020				6 041	
1920				3 936				5 733	
1921		9 392		3 889				5 617	
1922				4 259				5 831	
1923				4 194				5 782	
1924				4 095				6 148	
1925				4 743				6 534	
1926		11 326		5 316				7 022	
1927				5 165				7 053	
1928				5 865				7 202	
1929				7 261				7 571	
1930				7 219				7 220	
1931		13 235		6 988				6 914	
1932				6 431				6 604	
1933				6 762				6 699	
1934				7 380				7 397	
1935				6 672				6 982	
1936		13 167		7 380				6 981	
1937				6 672				7 466	
1938		11 942		7 089				7 407	
1939				8 557				7 230	
1940				6 945				7 673	
1941				6 878				7 875	
1942				9 354				8 189	
1943								8 085	
1944								7 437	
1945								7 420	
1946								7 199	
1947				6 186				7 554	
1948	25 197			7 017		23 477		8 397	
1949	23 266			9 277		23 764		8 939	

Table 5b. **GDP Levels in 16 East Asian Countries, 1950-2001**
(million 1990 international Geary-Khamis dollars)

	China	India	Indonesia	Japan	Philippines	South Korea	Thailand	Taiwan
1950	239 903	222 222	66 358	160 966	22 616	16 045	16 375	7 378
1951	267 228	227 362	71 304	181 025	25 054	14 810	17 532	8 179
1952	305 742	234 148	74 679	202 005	26 609	15 772	18 503	9 093
1953	321 919	248 963	78 394	216 889	28 988	20 345	20 542	10 092
1954	332 326	259 262	83 283	229 151	31 168	21 539	20 381	10 927
1955	350 115	265 527	85 571	248 855	33 331	22 708	22 162	11 853
1956	384 842	280 978	86 700	267 567	35 670	22 815	22 540	12 481
1957	406 222	277 924	92 631	287 130	37 599	24 575	22 792	13 360
1958	452 654	299 137	89 293	303 857	38 900	25 863	23 616	14 510
1959	464 006	305 499	93 129	331 570	41 548	26 865	26 457	15 871
1960	448 727	326 910	97 082	375 090	42 114	27 398	29 665	16 725
1961	368 021	336 744	103 446	420 246	44 480	28 782	31 210	17 931
1962	368 032	344 204	103 332	457 742	46 603	29 654	33 636	19 453
1963	403 732	361 442	99 371	496 514	49 893	32 268	36 360	22 150
1964	452 558	389 262	103 043	554 449	51 613	35 054	38 841	24 971
1965	505 099	373 814	104 070	586 744	54 331	37 166	41 933	26 688
1966	553 676	377 207	104 089	649 189	56 736	41 641	46 654	29 378
1967	536 987	408 349	101 739	721 132	59 756	44 670	50 552	32 688
1968	525 204	418 907	111 662	813 984	62 712	50 371	54 695	35 447
1969	574 669	446 872	125 408	915 556	65 632	58 007	58 980	38 651
1970	640 949	469 584	138 612	1 013 602	68 102	62 988	62 842	43 509
1971	671 780	474 338	146 200	1 061 230	71 799	82 932	65 886	49 591
1972	691 449	472 766	162 748	1 150 516	75 710	85 811	68 666	57 358
1973	740 048	494 832	186 900	1 242 932	82 464	96 794	75 511	63 519
1974	752 734	500 146	196 374	1 227 706	85 398	104 605	78 894	62 384
1975	800 876	544 683	196 374	1 265 661	90 150	111 548	82 799	63 818
1976	793 092	551 402	213 675	1 315 966	98 090	124 664	90 391	75 108
1977	844 157	593 834	230 338	1 373 741	103 585	137 531	99 304	84 267
1978	935 884	625 695	240 853	1 446 165	108 942	150 442	109 112	94 833
1979	1 007 734	594 510	253 961	1 525 477	115 086	161 172	114 828	101 759
1980	1 046 781	637 202	275 805	1 568 457	121 012	156 846	120 116	104 753
1981	1 096 587	675 882	294 768	1 618 185	125 154	166 581	127 211	113 222
1982	1 192 494	697 705	283 922	1 667 653	129 648	179 220	134 020	119 254
1983	1 294 304	753 942	295 296	1 706 380	132 115	199 828	141 504	132 294
1984	1 447 661	783 042	315 677	1 773 223	122 440	217 167	149 644	148 650
1985	1 599 201	814 344	323 451	1 851 315	113 493	231 386	156 598	156 878
1986	1 703 671	848 990	342 452	1 904 918	117 371	258 122	165 264	177 721
1987	1 849 563	886 154	359 323	1 984 142	122 432	287 854	180 996	190 493
1988	2 000 236	978 822	379 917	2 107 060	130 699	320 301	205 047	192 229
1989	2 044 100	1 043 912	414 090	2 208 858	138 809	340 751	230 043	195 311
1990	2 109 400	1 098 100	450 901	2 321 153	143 025	373 150	255 732	200 477
1991	2 232 306	1 112 340	473 680	2 393 300	142 191	407 899	277 618	215 622
1992	2 444 569	1 169 301	524 482	2 415 691	142 668	429 817	300 059	230 203
1993	2 683 336	1 238 272	560 544	2 425 642	145 704	453 340	325 215	244 747
1994	2 950 104	1 328 047	602 585	2 450 521	152 115	490 762	354 484	262 124
1995	3 196 343	1 425 623	651 997	2 487 838	159 264	534 599	387 097	278 900
1996	3 433 255	1 537 439	704 156	2 574 912	168 507	570 952	409 936	295 913
1997	3 657 242	1 610 621	735 844	2 619 694	177 264	599 285	404 197	315 739
1998	3 873 352	1 716 369	639 448	2 592 327	176 200	559 190	361 756	330 263
1999	4 082 513	1 825 709	644 564	2 609 742	182 191	620 135	377 673	348 097
2000	4 329 913	1 924 297	675 503	2 669 450	190 207	677 871	395 046	368 635
2001	4 569 790	2 003 193	697 794	2 624 523	196 294	698 721	402 157	361 631

Table 5b. **GDP Levels in 16 East Asian Countries, 1950-2001**
(million 1990 international Geary-Khamis dollars)

	Bangladesh	Burma	Hong Kong	Malaysia	Nepal	Pakistan	Singapore	Sri Lanka	16 country Total
1950	24 628	7 711	4 962	10 032	4 462	25 366	2 268	9 438	840 730
1951	24 974	8 834	4 626	9 478	4 591	24 534	2 406	10 025	901 962
1952	25 706	9 028	5 054	9 930	4 748	24 625	2 569	10 485	978 696
1953	26 072	9 265	5 515	9 977	5 038	26 983	2 758	10 688	1 042 428
1954	26 581	8 690	6 021	10 607	5 145	27 603	2 896	10 979	1 086 559
1955	25 177	9 822	6 564	10 677	5 248	28 238	3 078	11 621	1 140 547
1956	27 821	10 472	7 136	11 320	5 484	29 069	3 200	11 698	1 219 793
1957	27 231	11 089	7 729	11 257	5 484	30 339	3 352	11 869	1 270 583
1958	26 702	10 785	8 345	11 256	5 792	30 762	3 485	12 214	1 357 171
1959	28 126	12 457	8 981	12 026	5 957	31 095	3 470	12 385	1 419 442
1960	29 733	12 871	9 637	12 899	6 091	32 621	3 803	12 841	1 484 207
1961	31 421	13 183	10 276	13 794	6 238	34 602	4 123	13 104	1 477 601
1962	31 258	14 332	12 072	14 578	6 385	37 111	4 411	13 575	1 536 378
1963	34 573	14 737	13 968	15 271	6 537	39 439	4 848	13 856	1 644 959
1964	34 939	14 999	15 165	16 235	6 689	42 417	4 680	14 515	1 799 430
1965	36 647	15 379	17 360	17 405	6 849	44 307	5 033	14 971	1 887 796
1966	37 115	14 737	17 659	18 278	7 331	47 919	5 593	14 804	2 022 006
1967	36 302	15 151	17 959	18 587	7 216	49 718	6 255	16 157	2 123 218
1968	39 678	16 148	18 557	20 217	7 265	53 195	7 123	17 362	2 252 527
1969	40 227	16 815	20 652	21 382	7 590	56 642	8 098	18 053	2 473 234
1970	42 403	17 575	22 548	22 684	7 787	62 522	9 209	18 912	2 703 828
1971	40 552	18 149	24 144	24 359	7 693	62 824	10 362	18 752	2 830 591
1972	35 732	18 284	26 639	26 195	7 934	63 323	11 752	19 147	2 974 030
1973	35 997	18 352	29 931	29 982	7 894	67 828	13 108	19 922	3 206 014
1974	40 817	19 323	30 629	32 222	8 393	70 141	13 994	20 570	3 244 330
1975	40 308	20 125	30 729	32 489	8 518	73 043	14 549	21 047	3 396 717
1976	42 098	21 350	35 718	36 536	8 893	76 898	15 588	21 669	3 521 138
1977	42 525	22 625	39 908	39 513	9 161	79 951	16 797	23 082	3 740 319
1978	45 657	24 086	43 300	42 970	9 563	86 406	18 245	24 523	4 006 676
1979	47 846	25 222	48 289	46 469	9 790	89 580	19 932	26 125	4 187 780
1980	48 239	27 381	53 177	50 333	9 563	98 907	21 865	27 550	4 367 987
1981	49 877	28 930	58 066	53 901	9 563	106 753	23 960	29 302	4 577 942
1982	50 487	30 499	59 662	57 102	10 749	114 852	25 601	30 788	4 783 656
1983	52 961	31 827	63 055	60 588	10 433	122 649	27 695	32 366	5 057 237
1984	55 833	33 397	69 340	65 290	11 441	127 518	30 006	33 951	5 384 280
1985	57 519	34 349	69 639	64 617	12 146	138 632	29 451	35 381	5 688 400
1986	60 011	33 986	77 122	65 434	12 664	147 421	29 975	37 163	5 982 285
1987	62 521	32 624	87 099	68 898	13 164	155 994	32 817	37 529	6 351 603
1988	64 329	28 921	94 083	74 982	14 199	166 031	36 491	38 520	6 831 867
1989	65 948	29 989	96 478	81 996	14 525	174 001	39 857	39 543	7 158 211
1990	70 320	30 834	99 770	89 823	15 609	182 014	43 330	42 089	7 525 727
1991	72 629	30 633	104 858	97 545	16 603	192 138	45 832	44 118	7 859 312
1992	76 245	33 593	111 343	105 151	17 285	206 957	49 399	46 050	8 302 813
1993	79 722	35 622	118 227	113 927	17 950	211 653	55 622	49 235	8 758 758
1994	83 309	38 044	124 611	124 408	19 425	220 966	61 963	51 992	9 315 460
1995	87 308	40 783	129 471	136 600	20 099	231 793	66 920	54 852	9 889 487
1996	91 674	43 394	135 297	150 260	21 170	238 515	72 073	56 936	10 504 389
1997	96 532	45 867	142 062	161 229	22 025	242 808	78 271	60 580	10 969 260
1998	102 324	48 527	134 533	149 298	22 435	250 335	78 193	63 427	11 097 977
1999	107 850	53 817	138 569	158 406	23 175	260 599	83 588	66 155	11 582 783
2000	113 890	56 508	152 980	171 553	24 681	271 805	92 198	70 124	12 184 661
2001	119 242	59 220	153 286	172 411	25 989	281 590	90 354	69 142	12 525 337

Table 5b. **GDP Levels in 15 West Asian Countries, 1950-2002**
(million 1990 international Geary-Khamis dollars)

	Bahrain	Iran	Iraq	Israel	Jordan	Kuwait	Lebanon	Oman	Qatar
1950	242	28 128	7 041	3 623	933	4 181	3 313	304	763
1951	257	28 128	7 661	4 707	990	4 532	2 972	324	827
1952	273	28 128	8 470	4 910	1 049	4 804	3 157	344	876
1953	290	28 156	11 899	4 852	1 112	5 280	3 634	366	963
1954	309	28 156	14 145	5 776	1 178	5 882	4 171	389	1 073
1955	328	28 156	13 568	6 558	1 116	6 020	4 506	413	1 099
1956	349	30 659	14 511	7 142	1 532	6 464	4 399	439	1 180
1957	371	34 939	14 370	7 761	1 571	6 693	4 476	467	1 223
1958	394	39 013	16 039	8 319	1 729	7 024	3 840	496	1 282
1959	419	42 360	16 715	9 370	1 858	7 747	4 164	528	1 415
1960	445	46 467	18 658	9 986	1 977	8 420	4 274	560	1 496
1961	474	50 405	20 806	11 077	2 381	8 495	4 555	567	1 497
1962	504	51 389	21 841	12 171	2 446	9 474	4 731	681	1 555
1963	536	57 043	21 447	13 461	2 582	9 984	4 771	711	1 657
1964	571	61 178	24 024	14 780	3 032	10 962	5 059	712	1 712
1965	607	68 688	26 206	16 171	3 379	11 205	5 569	715	1 837
1966	646	75 579	27 593	16 349	3 474	12 584	5 950	752	2 493
1967	688	84 102	26 953	16 758	3 839	12 885	5 668	1 250	3 014
1968	732	96 759	31 740	19 320	3 696	14 089	6 381	2 274	3 474
1969	779	109 304	32 818	21 755	4 031	14 474	6 520	2 858	3 706
1970	832	120 865	32 691	23 520	3 600	22 944	6 950	2 957	3 756
1971	898	135 829	34 712	26 107	3 682	24 537	7 590	2 983	4 665
1972	969	157 909	33 430	29 342	3 800	25 503	8 514	3 262	5 263
1973	1 046	171 466	39 042	30 839	3 999	23 847	8 915	2 809	6 228
1974	1 136	186 655	41 133	32 941	4 355	20 799	10 465	3 132	5 661
1975	1 015	195 684	47 977	34 038	4 657	18 287	10 724	3 897	5 823
1976	1 180	229 241	57 735	34 480	5 789	19 466	10 989	4 397	6 263
1977	1 322	226 315	59 320	34 480	6 166	18 722	11 260	4 410	5 586
1978	1 424	199 481	70 127	36 144	7 462	20 072	11 539	4 326	6 114
1979	1 419	182 267	86 258	38 416	8 142	22 827	10 873	4 511	6 364
1980	1 525	156 643	84 392	41 053	9 689	18 178	10 879	4 784	6 816
1981	1 568	151 918	69 078	43 173	10 147	14 737	10 366	5 599	5 834
1982	1 669	175 826	68 501	43 948	10 897	13 006	9 680	6 245	4 731
1983	1 785	199 031	62 544	45 496	11 115	14 039	9 584	7 288	4 246
1984	1 860	202 379	62 699	45 905	12 071	14 775	9 786	8 507	4 143
1985	1 854	207 245	61 714	47 489	12 493	14 148	10 028	9 697	3 699
1986	1 897	187 780	61 073	49 760	13 626	15 352	9 581	9 906	3 130
1987	1 935	184 939	62 812	53 344	13 997	14 733	6 705	10 699	3 192
1988	2 003	174 532	49 540	54 417	13 853	15 247	6 099	11 018	3 240
1989	2 053	181 227	45 160	54 895	12 387	16 389	6 106	11 481	3 275
1990	2 054	199 819	44 583	58 511	12 371	13 111	6 099	11 487	3 276
1991	2 148	220 999	16 540	61 848	12 656	7 735	8 429	12 176	3 263
1992	2 316	234 472	21 370	66 051	14 807	13 723	8 808	13 211	3 566
1993	2 508	239 395	21 370	68 298	15 666	18 416	9 425	14 017	3 552
1994	2 502	244 901	20 306	74 172	16 445	19 970	10 179	14 556	3 635
1995	2 600	252 983	18 475	79 215	17 495	20 186	10 841	15 259	3 742
1996	2 707	267 403	20 799	82 938	17 861	19 518	11 274	15 700	3 922
1997	2 791	280 773	19 996	85 675	18 409	19 708	11 725	16 671	4 865
1998	2 924	285 827	22 993	88 246	18 950	19 354	12 077	17 121	5 275
1999	3 050	296 117	24 948	87 903	19 530	19 173	12 198	16 954	5 443
2000	3 212	312 995	27 692	94 408	20 288	20 151	12 198	17 462	5 987
2001	3 341	328 019	30 185	93 558	20 896	20 654	12 442	18 161	6 359
2002	3 454	347 044	32 297	92 155	21 732	21 068	12 753	18 796	6 740

Table 5b. **GDP Levels in 15 West Asian Countries, 1950-2002**
(million 1990 international Geary-Khamis dollars)

	Saudi Arabia	Syria	Turkey	UAE	Yemen	West Bank and Gaza	Total
1950	8 610	8 418	34 279	1 130	4 353	965	106 283
1951	9 334	8 098	38 667	1 225	4 468	1 009	113 196
1952	9 893	10 202	43 295	1 298	4 584	1 055	122 340
1953	10 875	11 566	48 128	1 427	4 708	1 104	134 360
1954	12 115	13 266	46 757	1 590	4 831	1 157	140 794
1955	12 399	11 970	50 528	1 628	4 959	1 206	144 454
1956	13 312	14 175	52 173	1 749	5 091	1 260	154 435
1957	13 785	15 051	56 321	1 812	5 228	1 321	165 389
1958	14 465	12 972	58 892	1 902	5 367	1 380	173 113
1959	15 955	13 460	61 600	2 097	5 510	1 462	184 660
1960	17 548	13 704	63 417	2 312	5 660	1 534	196 458
1961	19 632	14 832	64 480	2 526	5 810	1 588	209 125
1962	21 974	18 351	68 422	2 809	5 970	1 683	223 998
1963	23 885	18 342	74 866	3 097	6 148	1 783	240 313
1964	25 986	18 755	77 951	3 414	6 307	1 891	256 333
1965	29 137	18 704	80 008	3 762	6 486	2 010	274 485
1966	33 374	17 265	89 366	4 147	6 674	2 130	298 375
1967	36 310	18 696	93 377	4 570	6 868	2 045	317 024
1968	39 547	19 394	99 650	5 037	7 052	1 859	351 005
1969	42 578	23 031	104 929	5 554	7 260	1 931	381 528
1970	46 573	22 155	110 071	6 123	8 731	2 044	413 812
1971	53 289	24 352	120 046	7 147	10 253	2 169	458 258
1972	61 469	30 447	127 931	8 343	11 070	2 306	509 558
1973	73 601	27 846	133 858	9 739	12 431	2 455	548 120
1974	84 700	34 563	144 829	12 894	13 152	2 632	599 047
1975	84 924	41 306	157 855	13 307	14 152	2 797	636 442
1976	92 251	45 834	171 601	15 308	16 363	2 958	713 856
1977	106 191	45 254	179 005	17 978	18 167	3 137	737 313
1978	112 511	49 202	184 113	17 557	19 711	3 332	743 114
1979	120 028	50 986	182 536	21 926	20 805	3 531	760 889
1980	132 160	57 097	181 165	27 717	20 918	3 732	756 749
1981	142 630	62 527	189 014	28 492	22 191	3 940	761 214
1982	144 989	63 857	198 495	26 145	22 563	4 176	794 728
1983	129 404	64 766	205 811	24 833	23 856	4 465	808 263
1984	129 258	62 131	217 637	25 893	24 778	4 769	826 592
1985	120 605	65 928	228 744	25 287	24 578	5 094	838 601
1986	113 260	62 670	244 752	19 919	25 115	5 446	823 267
1987	118 495	63 865	266 108	20 631	26 135	5 834	853 424
1988	122 284	72 342	276 460	20 580	27 249	6 265	855 130
1989	126 701	65 860	279 614	22 766	28 203	6 706	862 823
1990	144 438	70 894	305 395	25 496	28 212	7 222	932 968
1991	156 571	75 927	308 227	25 547	28 297	7 853	948 217
1992	160 955	81 318	326 672	26 237	29 683	8 555	1 011 745
1993	159 989	89 938	352 945	26 001	30 544	9 308	1 061 372
1994	160 811	96 821	333 688	28 228	31 205	10 189	1 067 608
1995	161 564	102 698	357 688	30 459	34 594	11 234	1 119 033
1996	163 815	109 904	382 743	32 356	36 631	12 381	1 179 952
1997	167 106	112 640	411 555	34 517	39 592	13 573	1 239 596
1998	169 987	121 201	424 282	35 916	41 532	14 807	1 280 492
1999	168 674	119 012	404 302	37 296	43 067	*16 153*	1 273 820
2000	176 233	121 988	433 220	39 233	45 229	*16 153*	1 346 449
2001	182 402	126 258	401 162	39 626	46 889	*12 922*	1 342 874
2002	186 961	130 046	416 807	40 577	48 862	*10 338*	1 389 630

Table 5b. **GDP Levels in 26 East Asian Countries, 1950-2001**
(million 1990 international Geary-Khamis dollars)

	Afghanistan	Cambodia	Laos	Mongolia	North Korea	Vietnam	20 small countries	26 country Total
1950	5 255	2 155	1 156	339	7 293	16 681	3 845	36 724
1951	5 408	2 228	1 192	353	6 496	17 445	3 987	37 109
1952	5 591	2 368	1 229	370	6 675	18 209	4 225	38 667
1953	5 933	2 392	1 267	387	8 288	19 034	4 316	41 617
1954	6 059	2 670	1 306	406	8 683	19 920	4 471	43 515
1955	6 180	2 614	1 347	426	9 316	20 806	4 636	45 325
1956	6 458	2 963	1 388	448	9 444	21 631	4 820	47 152
1957	6 458	3 163	1 431	473	10 230	22 486	5 012	49 253
1958	6 821	3 322	1 476	499	10 816	23 372	5 200	51 506
1959	7 016	3 646	1 521	528	11 260	24 289	5 403	53 663
1960	7 268	3 863	1 568	559	11 483	25 297	5 640	55 678
1961	7 331	3 827	1 617	592	11 972	26 554	5 938	57 831
1962	7 457	4 139	1 667	627	12 249	29 917	6 130	62 186
1963	7 594	4 451	1 718	660	13 295	30 821	6 496	65 035
1964	7 741	4 331	1 772	699	14 445	32 322	6 794	68 104
1965	7 914	4 538	1 826	740	15 370	32 666	7 172	70 226
1966	7 993	4 744	1 883	782	17 308	32 975	7 561	73 246
1967	8 214	4 988	1 941	828	18 711	28 829	7 854	71 365
1968	8 508	5 214	2 001	876	21 268	28 329	8 347	74 543
1969	8 645	5 292	2 063	927	24 743	30 702	8 750	81 122
1970	8 819	4 785	2 127	982	27 184	31 295	9 581	84 773
1971	8 398	4 546	2 193	1 041	36 229	32 889	10 376	95 672
1972	8 240	4 301	2 261	1 103	37 854	35 815	10 939	100 513
1973	9 181	5 858	2 331	1 170	43 072	38 238	11 952	111 802
1974	9 680	5 007	2 403	1 243	44 038	36 744	12 594	111 709
1975	10 184	4 342	2 477	1 319	44 891	34 130	12 765	110 108
1976	10 694	4 650	2 554	1 396	45 652	39 879	13 181	118 006
1977	9 959	5 016	2 633	1 479	46 379	41 343	13 403	120 212
1978	10 752	5 484	2 714	1 567	47 104	41 622	14 102	123 345
1979	10 715	5 593	2 798	1 661	47 842	41 873	15 175	125 657
1980	10 427	5 705	2 885	1 758	48 621	40 671	14 880	124 947
1981	10 547	5 774	2 974	1 905	49 388	42 103	14 965	127 656
1982	10 726	6 218	3 066	2 064	50 138	45 526	15 226	132 964
1983	11 157	6 660	3 161	2 184	50 905	48 042	15 662	137 771
1984	11 336	7 106	3 258	2 314	51 695	52 355	15 899	143 963
1985	11 299	7 554	3 359	2 446	52 505	55 481	16 565	149 209
1986	12 161	7 998	3 463	2 675	53 331	57 056	17 368	154 052
1987	10 064	7 839	3 570	2 768	54 172	59 127	17 984	155 524
1988	9 228	8 035	3 681	2 909	55 033	62 685	18 633	160 204
1989	9 284	8 233	3 795	3 031	55 934	65 615	19 306	165 198
1990	8 861	8 235	3 912	2 954	56 874	68 959	19 356	169 151
1991	8 932	8 860	4 031	2 681	57 846	72 963	20 212	175 525
1992	9 021	9 482	4 245	2 426	53 391	79 312	21 107	178 984
1993	8 741	9 870	4 674	2 354	53 552	85 718	22 041	186 950
1994	8 479	10 258	4 964	2 408	39 468	93 292	23 016	181 885
1995	10 700	10 940	5 230	2 560	32 758	102 192	24 034	188 414
1996	11 342	11 543	5 355	2 620	27 091	111 736	25 098	194 785
1997	12 023	11 846	5 636	2 726	25 249	120 845	26 208	204 533
1998	12 744	11 998	5 806	2 821	25 130	127 851	26 662	213 012
1999	13 508	12 826	6 096	2 821	25 310	133 221	28 797	222 579
2000	13 508	13 518	6 450	2 821	25 310	140 548	28 820	230 975
2001	12 157	14 235	6 785	2 821	25 310	147 154	29 051	237 513

Table 5b. **GDP Levels in 57 Asian Countries, 1820-2001**
(million 1990 international Geary-Khamis dollars)

	16 East Asia	*26 East Asia*	*15 West Asia*	*Total 57 Asia*
1820	387 016	10 651	15 269	412 936
1870	391 213	13 328	22 468	427 009
1900	500 686	22 224	33 935	556 845
1913	612 074	27 687	40 588	680 349
1950	840 730	36 724	106 283	983 737
1951	901 962	37 109	113 196	1 052 267
1952	978 696	38 667	122 340	1 139 703
1953	1 042 428	41 617	134 360	1 218 405
1954	1 086 559	43 515	140 794	1 270 868
1955	1 140 547	45 325	144 454	1 330 326
1956	1 219 793	47 152	154 435	1 421 380
1957	1 270 583	49 253	165 389	1 485 225
1958	1 357 171	51 506	173 113	1 581 790
1959	1 419 442	53 663	184 660	1 657 765
1960	1 484 207	55 678	196 458	1 736 343
1961	1 477 601	57 831	209 125	1 744 557
1962	1 536 378	62 186	223 998	1 822 562
1963	1 644 959	65 035	240 313	1 950 307
1964	1 799 430	68 104	256 333	2 123 867
1965	1 887 796	70 226	274 485	2 232 507
1966	2 022 006	73 246	298 375	2 393 627
1967	2 123 218	71 365	317 024	2 511 607
1968	2 252 527	74 543	351 005	2 678 075
1969	2 473 234	81 122	381 528	2 935 884
1970	2 703 828	84 773	413 812	3 202 413
1971	2 830 591	95 672	458 258	3 384 521
1972	2 974 030	100 513	509 558	3 584 101
1973	3 206 014	111 802	548 120	3 865 936
1974	3 244 330	111 709	599 047	3 955 086
1975	3 396 717	110 108	636 442	4 143 267
1976	3 521 138	118 006	713 856	4 353 000
1977	3 740 319	120 212	737 313	4 597 844
1978	4 006 676	123 345	743 114	4 873 135
1979	4 187 780	125 657	760 889	5 074 326
1980	4 367 987	124 947	756 749	5 249 683
1981	4 577 942	127 656	761 214	5 466 812
1982	4 783 656	132 964	794 728	5 711 348
1983	5 057 237	137 771	808 263	6 003 271
1984	5 384 280	143 963	826 592	6 354 835
1985	5 688 400	149 209	838 601	6 676 210
1986	5 982 285	154 052	823 267	6 959 604
1987	6 351 603	155 524	853 424	7 360 551
1988	6 831 867	160 204	855 130	7 847 201
1989	7 158 211	165 198	862 823	8 186 232
1990	7 525 727	169 151	932 968	8 627 846
1991	7 859 312	175 525	948 217	8 983 054
1992	8 302 813	178 984	1 011 745	9 493 542
1993	8 758 758	186 950	1 061 372	10 007 080
1994	9 315 460	181 885	1 067 608	10 564 953
1995	9 889 487	188 414	1 119 033	11 196 934
1996	10 504 389	194 785	1 179 952	11 879 126
1997	10 969 260	204 533	1 239 596	12 413 389
1998	11 097 977	213 012	1 280 492	12 591 481
1999	11 582 783	222 579	1 273 820	13 079 182
2000	12 184 661	230 975	1 346 449	13 762 085
2001	12 525 337	237 513	1 342 874	14 105 724

Table 5c. **Per Capita GDP in 16 East Asian Countries, 1820-1913**
(1990 international Geary-Khamis dollars)

	China	India	Indonesia	Japan	Philippines	South Korea	Thailand	Taiwan
1820	600	533	612	669	*704*	*600*	*646*	*499*
1850	600							
1870	530	533	654	737	*776*	*604*	712	*550*
1871			646	742				
1872			637	746				
1873			643	751				
1874			651	756				
1875			657	810				
1876			670	785				
1877			671	803				
1878			656	794				
1879			664	835				
1880			662	863				
1881			699	829				
1882			672	844				
1883			657	837				
1884		551	717	836				
1885		567	713	860				
1886		548	697	916				
1887		572	695	952				
1888		576	693	900				
1889		559	691	933				
1890	540	584	660	1 012			784	
1891		529	671	956				
1892		571	690	1 013				
1893		584	711	1 008				
1894		592	713	1 119				
1895		577	716	1 123				
1896		533	704	1 051				
1897		630	702	1 062				
1898		630	699	1 249				
1899		580	728	1 143				
1900	545	599	743	1 180				
1901		608	724	1 206				
1902		655	705	1 129	699			
1903		660	736	1 193	832			
1904		659	742	1 188	756			
1905		643	744	1 157	742			
1906		657	758	1 297	770			
1907		614	767	1 325	794			
1908		619	760	1 318	801			
1909		700	790	1 301	799			
1910		697	834	1 304	901			
1911		691	870	1 356	945	777		
1912		689	867	1 384	974	782		722
1913	552	673	904	1 387	1 053	820	841	747

Table 5c. **Per Capita GDP in 16 East Asian Countries, 1820-1913**
(1990 international Geary-Khamis dollars)

	Bangladesh	Burma	Hong Kong	Malaysia	Nepal	Pakistan	Singapore	Sri Lanka	16 country average
1820		504	615	603	397		615	492	581
1850								564	
1870		504	683	663	397		682	851	551
1871								827	
1872								785	
1873								788	
1874								775	
1875								781	
1876								789	
1877								793	
1878								718	
1879								770	
1880								831	
1881								887	
1882								935	
1883								941	
1884								905	
1885								842	
1886								810	
1887								945	
1888								921	
1889								902	
1890								1 045	
1891								1 037	
1892								1 052	
1893								1 052	
1894								1 043	
1895								1 085	
1896								1 088	
1897								1 125	
1898								1 168	
1899								1 234	
1900								1 290	623
1901								1 192	
1902								1 175	
1903								1 225	
1904								1 215	
1905								1 179	
1906								1 190	
1907								1 233	
1908								1 221	
1909								1 153	
1910								1 208	
1911				801				1 160	
1912				822				1 157	
1913	685		1 279	900	539		1 279	1 234	679

Table 5c. **Per Capita GDP in 16 East Asian Countries, 1914-1949**
(1990 international Geary-Khamis dollars)

	China	India	Indonesia	Japan	Philippines	South Korea	Thailand	Taiwan
1914		709	892	1 327	1 015	862		747
1915		691	893	1 430	925	966		765
1916		710	896	1 630	1 040	969		963
1917		697	893	1 665	1 177	1 021		1 057
1918		607	909	1 668	1 322	1 087		925
1919		690	969	1 827	1 274	1 049		982
1920		635	945	1 696	1 289	1 009		959
1921		679	942	1 860		1 051		873
1922		701	946	1 831		1 018		980
1923		671	949	1 809		1 030		1 027
1924		697	988	1 836		1 025		1 025
1925		698	1 010	1 885	1 387	1 016		1 099
1926		713	1 053	1 872	1 428	1 038		1 028
1927		706	1 112	1 870	1 441	1 086		1 011
1928		706	1 151	1 992	1 474	1 047		1 211
1929	562	728	1 170	2 026	1 502	1 014	793	1 146
1930	567	726	1 164	1 850	1 476	1 020		1 099
1931	569	711	1 061	1 837	1 442	990		1 066
1932	583	709	1 033	1 962	1 530	1 016		1 181
1933	578	700	1 011	2 122	1 457	1 145		1 059
1934	525	697	1 002	2 098	1 488	1 115		1 107
1935	565	680	1 023	2 120	1 262	1 242		1 295
1936	597	697	1 081	2 244	1 406	1 315		1 233
1937	580	676	1 169	2 315	1 499	1 482		1 263
1938	562	668	1 175	2 449	1 522	1 459	826	1 302
1939		674	1 169	2 816	1 606	1 297		1 390
1940		686	1 235	2 874	1 587	1 442		1 347
1941		691	1 252	2 873		1 441		1 439
1942		679		2 818		1 412		1 502
1943		698		2 822		1 411		998
1944		683		2 659		1 330		684
1945		664		1 346		616		742
1946		622		1 444	646	619		806
1947		618		1 541	875	648		904
1948		617		1 725	993	692		931
1949		624	797	1 800	1 025	738		932

Table 5c. **Per Capita GDP in 16 East Asian Countries, 1914-1949**
(1990 international Geary-Khamis dollars)

	Bangladesh	Burma	Hong Kong	Malaysia	Nepal	Pakistan	Singapore	Sri Lanka	16 country average
1914				920				1 210	
1915				938				1 136	
1916		823		996				1 173	
1917				1 034				1 218	
1918				969				1 107	
1919				1 158				1 166	
1920				1 110				1 092	
1921		711		1 075				1 059	
1922				1 152				1 086	
1923				1 110				1 066	
1924				1 060				1 128	
1925				1 201				1 187	
1926		814		1 316				1 266	
1927				1 251				1 261	
1928				1 389				1 257	
1929				1 682				1 336	
1930				1 636				1 265	
1931		902		1 548				1 203	
1932				1 397				1 141	
1933				1 440				1 150	
1934				1 540				1 260	
1935				1 364				1 184	
1936		838		1 478				1 175	
1937				1 308				1 247	
1938		740		1 361				1 225	
1939				1 609				1 186	
1940				1 278				1 251	
1941				1 238				1 277	
1942				1 673				1 323	
1943								1 284	
1944								1 154	
1945								1 116	
1946								1 050	
1947				1 069				1 073	
1948				1 185				1 159	
1949				1 531				1 199	

Table 5c. **Per Capita GDP in 16 East Asian Countries, 1950-2001**
(1990 international Geary-Khamis dollars)

	China	India	Indonesia	Japan	Philippines	South Korea	Thailand	Taiwan
1950	439	619	840	1 921	1 070	770	817	924
1951	479	623	885	2 126	1 151	709	849	991
1952	537	629	910	2 336	1 186	753	869	1 063
1953	554	657	938	2 474	1 254	966	935	1 140
1954	558	672	978	2 582	1 308	1 013	898	1 193
1955	575	676	986	2 771	1 358	1 054	945	1 250
1956	619	701	980	2 948	1 410	1 036	930	1 270
1957	637	680	1 028	3 136	1 442	1 087	910	1 314
1958	693	716	972	3 289	1 448	1 112	914	1 382
1959	697	717	995	3 554	1 501	1 120	992	1 462
1960	673	753	1 019	3 986	1 476	1 105	1 078	1 492
1961	557	758	1 066	4 426	1 512	1 124	1 100	1 551
1962	553	758	1 043	4 777	1 537	1 122	1 149	1 632
1963	592	779	984	5 129	1 595	1 186	1 205	1 804
1964	648	821	1 000	5 668	1 600	1 253	1 249	1 977
1965	706	771	990	5 934	1 633	1 295	1 308	2 056
1966	753	762	971	6 506	1 654	1 415	1 412	2 205
1967	712	807	930	7 152	1 690	1 483	1 486	2 395
1968	678	809	1 001	7 983	1 722	1 633	1 561	2 539
1969	722	845	1 102	8 874	1 750	1 839	1 636	2 706
1970	783	868	1 194	9 714	1 764	1 954	1 694	2 980
1971	799	856	1 235	10 040	1 808	2 522	1 725	3 324
1972	802	834	1 342	10 734	1 853	2 561	1 748	3 767
1973	839	853	1 504	11 434	1 964	2 841	1 874	4 091
1974	836	843	1 542	11 145	1 979	3 015	1 910	3 942
1975	874	897	1 505	11 344	2 033	3 162	1 959	3 958
1976	852	889	1 598	11 669	2 152	3 476	2 091	4 566
1977	895	937	1 681	12 064	2 211	3 775	2 249	5 020
1978	979	966	1 715	12 585	2 262	4 064	2 422	5 542
1979	1 040	895	1 765	13 163	2 323	4 294	2 496	5 831
1980	1 067	938	1 870	13 428	2 376	4 114	2 554	5 869
1981	1 103	977	1 957	13 754	2 398	4 302	2 653	6 229
1982	1 192	985	1 845	14 078	2 425	4 557	2 744	6 446
1983	1 265	1 043	1 878	14 307	2 415	5 007	2 847	7 036
1984	1 396	1 060	1 966	14 773	2 188	5 375	2 960	7 790
1985	1 522	1 079	1 972	15 331	1 981	5 670	3 049	8 113
1986	1 597	1 101	2 051	15 679	2 001	6 263	3 168	9 088
1987	1 706	1 125	2 114	16 251	2 040	6 916	3 418	9 641
1988	1 816	1 216	2 196	17 185	2 129	7 621	3 817	9 623
1989	1 827	1 270	2 352	17 942	2 210	8 027	4 222	9 665
1990	1 858	1 309	2 516	18 789	2 224	8 704	4 629	9 886
1991	1 940	1 299	2 599	19 309	2 161	9 417	4 959	10 522
1992	2 098	1 341	2 831	19 430	2 123	9 814	5 290	11 128
1993	2 277	1 390	2 976	19 457	2 124	10 238	5 661	11 720
1994	2 475	1 463	3 146	19 602	2 170	10 965	6 094	12 430
1995	2 653	1 538	3 348	19 849	2 221	11 818	6 573	13 104
1996	2 820	1 630	3 556	20 494	2 296	12 495	6 877	13 796
1997	2 973	1 679	3 655	20 798	2 363	12 991	6 702	14 598
1998	3 117	1 760	3 129	20 534	2 301	12 016	5 930	15 134
1999	3 259	1 841	3 107	20 631	2 332	13 222	6 123	15 827
2000	3 425	1 910	3 203	21 069	2 385	14 343	6 336	16 642
2001	3 583	1 957	3 256	20 683	2 412	14 673	6 383	16 214

Table 5c. **Per Capita GDP in 16 East Asian Countries, 1950-2001**
(1990 international Geary-Khamis dollars)

	Bangladesh	Burma	Hong Kong	Malaysia	Nepal	Pakistan	Singapore	Sri Lanka	16 country average
1950	540	396	2 218	1 559	496	643	2 219	1 253	662
1951	541	446	2 295	1 440	505	608	2 253	1 293	698
1952	548	449	2 377	1 471	517	596	2 280	1 314	742
1953	547	454	2 460	1 440	543	637	2 314	1 300	775
1954	547	419	2 546	1 490	549	636	2 320	1 298	791
1955	508	467	2 636	1 460	554	635	2 358	1 339	814
1956	551	490	2 729	1 505	572	638	2 333	1 315	853
1957	530	510	2 825	1 455	566	650	2 318	1 300	869
1958	510	488	2 924	1 413	592	643	2 295	1 305	907
1959	526	555	3 027	1 467	601	633	2 186	1 289	931
1960	544	564	3 134	1 530	607	647	2 310	1 300	962
1961	564	568	3 244	1 592	613	669	2 422	1 291	950
1962	550	606	3 652	1 637	618	699	2 520	1 303	972
1963	594	613	4 083	1 669	623	723	2 701	1 297	1 017
1964	588	613	4 327	1 728	626	758	2 541	1 326	1 088
1965	607	617	4 825	1 804	631	771	2 667	1 336	1 116
1966	603	580	4 865	1 846	663	812	2 891	1 291	1 168
1967	578	586	4 824	1 830	641	820	3 163	1 377	1 198
1968	619	613	4 880	1 942	633	854	3 540	1 446	1 241
1969	614	626	5 345	2 005	649	885	3 965	1 471	1 331
1970	629	642	5 695	2 079	653	952	4 439	1 509	1 420
1971	586	650	5 968	2 180	633	931	4 904	1 468	1 450
1972	505	642	6 473	2 289	639	913	5 460	1 471	1 488
1973	497	628	7 105	2 560	622	954	5 977	1 504	1 569
1974	547	648	7 091	2 688	647	962	6 276	1 529	1 554
1975	529	663	6 991	2 648	642	978	6 430	1 541	1 594
1976	540	690	7 906	2 910	654	1 006	6 797	1 560	1 622
1977	529	718	8 707	3 076	657	1 023	7 224	1 635	1 692
1978	551	752	9 277	3 271	670	1 079	7 752	1 706	1 780
1979	560	773	9 796	3 457	669	1 087	8 362	1 783	1 826
1980	548	823	10 503	3 657	637	1 161	9 058	1 849	1 870
1981	550	854	11 202	3 824	621	1 207	9 460	1 934	1 926
1982	542	884	11 333	3 954	680	1 259	9 674	1 998	1 982
1983	555	907	11 797	4 096	644	1 309	10 330	2 072	2 052
1984	572	936	12 846	4 307	689	1 324	10 982	2 147	2 147
1985	577	947	12 763	4 157	713	1 400	10 764	2 208	2 229
1986	590	924	13 960	4 105	725	1 446	10 966	2 286	2 304
1987	603	875	15 597	4 219	735	1 487	11 827	2 275	2 403
1988	608	766	16 716	4 482	773	1 539	12 821	2 302	2 539
1989	612	786	17 043	4 790	771	1 569	13 599	2 330	2 614
1990	640	800	17 541	5 132	808	1 597	14 365	2 448	2 702
1991	649	788	18 230	5 447	838	1 642	14 801	2 537	2 777
1992	671	860	19 084	5 740	850	1 740	15 537	2 618	2 891
1993	691	906	19 889	6 077	861	1 749	17 018	2 762	3 004
1994	710	957	20 486	6 486	909	1 784	18 404	2 876	3 148
1995	733	1 015	20 726	6 965	917	1 830	19 225	2 997	3 291
1996	756	1 070	21 075	7 496	943	1 841	19 963	3 076	3 448
1997	783	1 122	21 503	7 874	958	1 833	20 921	3 240	3 551
1998	815	1 178	19 748	7 139	952	1 848	20 198	3 359	3 545
1999	843	1 297	19 819	7 418	961	1 882	20 854	3 470	3 647
2000	873	1 353	21 499	7 872	999	1 920	22 207	3 645	3 794
2001	897	1 409	21 259	7 756	1 028	1 947	21 011	3 562	3 851

Table 5c. **Per Capita GDP in 15 West Asian Countries, 1950-2002**
(1990 international Geary-Khamis dollars)

	Bahrain	*Iran*	*Iraq*	*Israel*	*Jordan*	*Kuwait*	*Lebanon*	*Oman*	*Qatar*
1950	2 104	1 720	1 364	2 817	1 663	28 878	2 429	623	30 387
1951	2 185	1 673	1 445	3 159	1 695	29 777	2 121	650	30 550
1952	2 267	1 629	1 557	3 029	1 726	30 023	2 193	677	30 161
1953	2 351	1 587	2 129	2 910	1 757	31 361	2 457	707	31 002
1954	2 436	1 545	2 463	3 374	1 787	33 200	2 745	736	32 418
1955	2 518	1 503	2 298	3 701	1 625	32 257	2 886	766	31 277
1956	2 599	1 593	2 389	3 860	2 139	32 876	2 744	799	31 933
1957	2 674	1 765	2 300	3 992	2 104	31 447	2 717	831	31 547
1958	2 739	1 916	2 493	4 109	2 220	29 907	2 269	866	31 620
1959	2 796	2 021	2 523	4 501	2 287	29 568	2 395	900	33 161
1960	2 843	2 154	2 735	4 663	2 330	28 813	2 393	935	33 104
1961	2 882	2 269	2 961	4 996	2 685	26 112	2 482	923	30 737
1962	2 931	2 247	3 017	5 267	2 620	26 443	2 507	1 084	29 362
1963	2 994	2 422	2 872	5 593	2 649	25 331	2 459	1 103	28 505
1964	3 073	2 521	3 115	5 916	2 981	25 303	2 534	1 075	26 799
1965	3 173	2 748	3 288	6 272	3 183	23 533	2 706	1 053	26 132
1966	3 283	2 934	3 349	6 190	3 137	24 050	2 804	1 080	32 239
1967	3 402	3 169	3 164	6 222	3 059	22 409	2 592	1 749	35 393
1968	3 520	3 542	3 604	7 033	2 674	22 300	2 831	3 094	36 982
1969	3 646	3 887	3 604	7 723	2 773	20 963	2 810	3 782	35 884
1970	3 788	4 177	3 473	8 101	2 395	30 695	2 917	3 799	33 160
1971	3 983	4 564	3 567	8 711	2 366	30 930	3 001	3 716	38 182
1972	4 198	5 158	3 323	9 478	2 355	30 291	3 177	3 934	39 933
1973	4 376	5 445	3 753	9 645	2 388	26 689	3 155	3 279	43 806
1974	4 574	5 759	3 825	10 025	2 506	21 934	3 503	3 541	36 914
1975	3 922	5 862	4 315	10 148	2 583	18 162	3 461	4 267	35 198
1976	4 313	6 668	5 023	10 071	3 096	18 166	3 524	4 597	35 424
1977	4 444	6 380	4 992	9 863	3 182	16 417	3 614	4 390	29 562
1978	4 415	5 445	5 693	10 125	3 718	16 539	3 711	4 086	30 278
1979	4 222	4 801	6 756	10 515	3 919	17 675	3 508	4 044	29 491
1980	4 388	3 961	6 377	10 984	4 480	13 271	3 526	4 072	29 552
1981	4 313	3 681	5 041	11 357	4 502	10 290	3 364	4 523	24 061
1982	4 414	4 087	4 833	11 390	4 643	8 685	3 136	4 800	18 750
1983	4 542	4 446	4 269	11 586	4 556	8 966	3 102	5 346	14 955
1984	4 557	4 348	4 136	11 461	4 767	9 024	3 167	5 976	13 163
1985	4 374	4 287	3 932	11 654	4 754	8 165	3 247	6 545	10 718
1986	4 316	3 743	3 759	12 028	5 002	8 475	3 104	6 442	8 345
1987	4 257	3 558	3 797	12 691	4 963	7 789	2 170	6 712	7 938
1988	4 267	3 253	2 908	12 739	4 750	7 727	1 970	6 670	7 540
1989	4 235	3 274	2 571	12 637	4 103	7 968	1 965	6 708	7 173
1990	4 104	3 472	2 458	12 968	3 792	6 121	1 938	6 479	6 804
1991	4 170	3 709	947	13 003	3 486	8 108	2 640	6 606	6 467
1992	4 374	3 856	1 196	13 380	3 829	9 677	2 735	6 898	6 737
1993	4 611	3 924	1 161	13 492	3 932	12 412	2 898	7 048	6 377
1994	4 481	4 006	1 070	14 305	4 029	12 872	3 093	7 071	6 210
1995	4 540	4 085	945	14 932	4 164	12 454	3 251	7 161	6 103
1996	4 619	4 260	1 032	15 302	4 093	11 529	3 333	7 117	6 123
1997	4 663	4 411	962	15 489	4 067	11 164	3 418	7 300	7 290
1998	4 787	4 432	1 075	15 649	4 044	10 542	3 471	7 242	7 605
1999	4 899	4 539	1 132	15 307	4 033	10 063	3 457	6 928	7 567
2000	5 065	4 742	1 221	16 159	4 059	10 210	3 409	6 893	8 042
2001	5 177	4 911	1 294	15 756	4 055	10 115	3 430	6 926	8 268
2002	5 262	5 138	1 346	15 284	4 095	9 977	3 468	6 927	8 496

Table 5c. **Per Capita GDP in 15 West Asian Countries, 1950-2002**
(1990 international Geary-Khamis dollars)

	Saudi Arabia	Syria	Turkey	UAE	Yemen	West Bank and Gaza	15 country Average
1950	2 231	2 409	1 623	15 798	911	949	1 776
1951	2 374	2 264	1 784	16 709	918	987	1 840
1952	2 470	2 786	1 947	17 246	924	1 024	1 937
1953	2 664	3 084	2 108	18 418	930	1 061	2 074
1954	2 912	3 453	1 993	19 884	936	1 103	2 118
1955	2 922	3 039	2 093	19 683	942	1 144	2 116
1956	3 075	3 508	2 097	20 377	946	1 187	2 200
1957	3 119	3 627	2 194	20 282	951	1 234	2 290
1958	3 204	3 039	2 222	20 372	955	1 280	2 328
1959	3 458	3 062	2 252	21 426	959	1 328	2 412
1960	3 719	3 023	2 247	22 433	964	1 378	2 492
1961	4 066	3 168	2 221	23 180	969	1 431	2 579
1962	4 445	3 796	2 297	24 250	975	1 485	2 686
1963	4 715	3 673	2 454	25 025	984	1 542	2 804
1964	5 005	3 637	2 496	25 676	989	1 600	2 910
1965	5 469	3 512	2 504	26 164	996	1 660	3 031
1966	6 102	3 139	2 735	26 483	1 007	1 724	3 207
1967	6 463	3 291	2 795	26 610	1 019	1 790	3 318
1968	6 848	3 306	2 917	26 374	1 028	1 858	3 580
1969	7 170	3 801	3 002	25 495	1 040	1 919	3 788
1970	7 624	3 540	3 078	24 552	1 230	1 980	3 998
1971	8 475	3 759	3 282	24 806	1 414	2 046	4 304
1972	9 497	4 544	3 412	24 806	1 495	2 116	4 649
1973	11 040	4 017	3 477	24 887	1 640	2 184	4 854
1974	12 333	4 821	3 665	28 449	1 696	2 256	5 149
1975	11 797	5 570	3 895	25 465	1 784	2 329	5 308
1976	12 126	5 976	4 136	25 598	2 003	2 408	5 779
1977	13 097	5 705	4 221	26 296	2 162	2 488	5 791
1978	12 963	5 998	4 250	22 545	2 281	2 571	5 658
1979	12 897	6 010	4 128	24 802	2 342	2 656	5 610
1980	13 284	6 508	4 015	27 709	2 290	2 744	5 397
1981	13 500	6 891	4 089	25 894	2 363	2 837	5 245
1982	12 969	6 786	4 194	21 721	2 336	2 929	5 294
1983	10 946	6 638	4 249	18 870	2 401	3 028	5 207
1984	10 339	6 143	4 392	18 007	2 422	3 128	5 151
1985	9 131	6 290	4 514	16 104	2 332	3 231	5 056
1986	8 173	5 772	4 727	11 624	2 311	3 340	4 808
1987	8 194	5 681	5 032	11 601	2 329	3 450	4 842
1988	8 122	6 219	5 123	11 189	2 351	3 564	4 716
1989	8 106	5 480	5 081	12 003	2 353	3 683	4 627
1990	9 115	5 701	5 445	13 070	2 272	3 806	4 856
1991	9 740	5 909	5 395	12 764	2 197	3 932	4 853
1992	9 643	6 152	5 615	12 806	2 220	4 065	5 041
1993	9 235	6 623	5 961	12 420	2 200	4 200	5 188
1994	8 949	6 946	5 541	13 216	2 168	4 344	5 122
1995	8 671	7 177	5 846	13 995	2 328	4 490	5 255
1996	8 492	7 481	6 161	14 604	2 390	4 644	5 424
1997	8 378	7 469	6 528	15 312	2 502	4 803	5 578
1998	8 244	7 829	6 635	15 666	2 540	5 050	5 646
1999	7 915	7 490	6 237	16 001	2 548	5 312	5 505
2000	8 002	7 481	6 597	16 560	2 588	5 124	5 706
2001	8 015	7 547	6 033	16 460	2 594	3 953	5 580
2002	7 951	7 580	6 192	16 589	2 613	3 050	5 664

Table 5c. **Per Capita GDP in 57 Asian Countries, 1820-2001**
(1990 international Geary-Khamis dollars)

	16 East Asia	*26 East Asia*	*15 West Asia*	*Average 57 Asia*
1820	581	556	607	581
1870	551	535	742	558
1910	623	674	940	638
1913	679	745	1 042	696
1950	662	691	1 854	712
1951	698	692	1 926	748
1952	742	714	2 030	794
1953	775	761	2 175	832
1954	791	783	2 214	850
1955	814	798	2 217	871
1956	853	812	2 302	912
1957	869	828	2 398	932
1958	907	844	2 437	970
1959	931	855	2 521	996
1960	962	862	2 602	1 029
1961	950	870	2 688	1 024
1962	972	908	2 799	1 052
1963	1 017	923	2 923	1 100
1964	1 088	939	3 033	1 171
1965	1 116	940	3 153	1 203
1966	1 168	954	3 339	1 259
1967	1 198	904	3 453	1 290
1968	1 241	920	3 720	1 343
1969	1 331	975	3 932	1 438
1970	1 420	994	4 146	1 530
1971	1 450	1 095	4 421	1 577
1972	1 488	1 123	4 781	1 631
1973	1 569	1 220	4 972	1 720
1974	1 554	1 191	5 241	1 721
1975	1 594	1 149	5 381	1 766
1976	1 622	1 210	5 880	1 820
1977	1 692	1 209	5 882	1 887
1978	1 780	1 219	5 732	1 962
1979	1 826	1 220	5 689	2 004
1980	1 870	1 201	5 453	2 034
1981	1 926	1 216	5 310	2 081
1982	1 982	1 248	5 344	2 139
1983	2 052	1 267	5 276	2 200
1984	2 147	1 298	5 235	2 287
1985	2 229	1 321	5 132	2 359
1986	2 304	1 337	4 884	2 414
1987	2 403	1 322	4 936	2 506
1988	2 539	1 333	4 782	2 622
1989	2 614	1 342	4 680	2 686
1990	2 702	1 346	4 911	2 781
1991	2 777	1 368	4 903	2 848
1992	2 891	1 351	5 084	2 962
1993	3 004	1 362	5 211	3 072
1994	3 148	1 289	5 066	3 193
1995	3 291	1 305	5 148	3 330
1996	3 448	1 323	5 273	3 482
1997	3 551	1 366	5 398	3 587
1998	3 545	1 400	5 407	3 588
1999	3 647	1 439	5 417	3 672
2000	3 794	1 467	5 426	3 817
2001	3 851	1 482	5 435	3 861

HS–6: AFRICA

Contours of African Development

As the long–term economic development of Africa is difficult to quantify with any precision, it is useful to consider the broad contours and salient features I had in mind when making conjectures about the development of per capita income.

There is a marked difference between the historical experience of the lands North of the Sahara and the rest of the continent. For most of the past two millennia, there were higher levels of income and urbanisation, more sophisticated economic and political institutions in the North than in the South. North African history is reasonably well documented because there are substantial written records. Knowledge of the South is based on archaeological or linguistic evidence until the ninth century when written evidence of northern visitors becomes available.

Over the long run, population growth was much more dynamic South of the Sahara. Two thousand years ago, about half lived in the north; by 1820, four–fifths in the south. Between the first century AD and 1820, the population of the North had increased by a third (with many intervening setbacks). In the South it increased nearly eightfold (see Table 6–1). In terms of extensive growth (i.e. capacity to accommodate population increase), the south clearly had the edge. In terms of per capita real income, it seems likely that the average Northern level was lower in 1820 than in the first century. South of the Sahara, it is probable that it increased modestly (see Table 6–2).

The greater demographic dynamism of the south is surprising, because of its substantial losses from the slave trade. There seem to be three reasons for this: a) in Egypt and the Maghreb, plague seems to have been endemic from the sixth to the early nineteenth century. It does not seem to have crossed the Sahara; b) before the eighth century, there was virtually no contact between North and South. Possibilities for trade across the Sahara were revolutionised by the introduction of camels between the fifth and eighth centuries. They could carry about a third of a ton of freight, go without food for several days, and without water for up to 15 days. The growth in trade benefitted both parties. The partial Islamisation of black Africa increased the sophistication and organisational ability of the ruling elites in the Sahel and savannah lands of West Africa south of the Sahara; c) probably the most important was the spread of improved agricultural technology and new crops. Two thousand years ago, much of black Africa was inhabited by hunter–gatherers using stone–age technology. By 1820, they had been pushed aside and were a fraction of the population. The proportion of agriculturalists and pastoralists with iron–age tools and weapons increased dramatically. Land productivity was also helped by the introduction and gradual diffusion of maize, cassava and sweet potatoes from the Americas from 1500 onwards.

Egypt

In the first century AD, all of North Africa was under Roman rule. The Mediterranean was a Roman lake with magnificent ports in Italy and Alexandria and substantial flows of trade between Africa, Europe and the Middle East. Egypt was the most prosperous area, with a relatively large urban population, a sedentary agriculture, a substantially monetised economy, a significant industrial and

Table 6-1. **African Population, 1-2001 AD**
(000)

	1	1000	1500	1600	1700	1820	2001
Egypt	4 000	5 000	4 000	5 000	4 500	4 194	71 902
Morocco	1 000	2 000	1 500	2 250	1 750	2 689	30 645
Algeria	2 000	2 000	1 500	2 250	1 750	2 689	31 736
Tunisia	800	1 000	800	1 000	800	875	9 705
Libya	400	500	500	500	500	538	5 241
Total North Africa	**8 200**	**10 500**	**8 300**	**11 000**	**9 300**	**10 985**	**149 229**
Sahel	1 000	2 000	3 000	3 500	4 000	4 887	32 885
Other West Africa	3 000	7 000	11 000	14 000	18 000	20 777	218 393
Total West Africa	**4 000**	**9 000**	**14 000**	**17 500**	**22 000**	**25 664**	**251 278**
Ethiopia and Eritrea	500	1 000	2 000	2 250	2 500	3 154	68 208
Sudan	2 000	3 000	4 000	4 200	4 400	5 156	36 080
Somalia	200	400	800	800	950	1 000	7 489
Other East Africa	300	3 000	6 000	7 000	8 000	10 389	103 338
Total East Africa	**3 000**	**7 400**	**12 800**	**14 250**	**15 850**	**19 699**	**215 115**
Angola, Zaire, Equatoria	**1 000**	**4 000**	**8 000**	**8 500**	**9 000**	**10 757**	**87 235**
Malawi, Zambia, Zimbabwe	75	500	1 000	1 100	1 200	1 345	33 452
Mozambique	50	300	1 000	1 250	1 500	2 096	17 142
South Africa, Swaziland and Lesotho	100	300	600	700	1 000	1 550	45 562
Namibia and Botswana	75	100	200	200	200	219	3 444
Madagascar	0	200	700	800	1 000	1 683	15 983
Indian Ocean	0	0	10	20	30	238	2 648
Southern Africa	**300**	**1 400**	**3 510**	**4 070**	**4 930**	**7 131**	**118 231**
Total Africa	**16 500**	**32 300**	**46 610**	**55 320**	**61 080**	**74 236**	**821 088**

Source: 1-1820 from McEvedy and Jones (1978), 2001 from US Bureau of Census. **Sahel** includes Chad, Mauritania, Mali, Niger. **Other West Africa** includes Senegal, Gambia, Guinea Bissau, Guinea, Sierra Leone, Liberia, Burkina Faso, Côte d'Ivoire, Ghana, Togo, Benin, Nigeria, Cape Verde, W. Sahara. **Equatoria** includes Cameroon, Central African Rep., Congo, Equatorial Guinea, Gabon, São Tomé & Principe. **Indian Ocean** includes Comoros, Mauritius, Mayotte, Reunion, Seychelles. **Other East Africa** includes Burundi, Djibouti, Kenya, Rwanda, Tanzania, Uganda.

commercial sector, and a very long history as an organised state. Its natural waterways lowered the cost of transporting freight and passengers through its most densely populated area. As the prevailing winds blew from the North, one could sail upstream and float downstream. Agricultural productivity was high because of the abundant and reliable flow of Nile water and the annual renewal of topsoil in the form of silt.

Egypt produced a surplus that the Pharoahs and the Ptolemies used to support a brilliant civilisation. From the first to the tenth century, it was siphoned off; first to Rome, then to Constantinople. After the Muslim conquest, it was redirected by the authorities in Damascus then Baghdad. Under the Fatimid, Ayyubid and Mamluk regimes, tribute ceased, but in 1516 Egypt became a provincial backwater under a Turkish viceroy, paying tribute to the Ottoman sultan. Foreign rule generally impeded trade through the Red Sea to the Indian Ocean which had flourished in the first and second centuries, and was restored from the tenth to the fifteenth century. Virtually all trade with Europe disappeared from the fourth until the twelfth century. The entrepot trade, manufactured exports and population of Alexandria withered away.

Table 6-2. **Tentative Conjectures for African Per Capita GDP and GDP, 1-1820 AD**

	1	1000	1500	1600	1700	1820
	(per cent of African Population)					
Egypt	24.2	15.5	8.6	9.0	7.4	5.7
Morocco	6.1	6.2	3.2	4.1	2.9	3.6
Other North Africa	19.4	10.8	6.0	6.8	5.0	5.5
Total North Africa	**49.7**	**32.5**	**17.8**	**19.9**	**15.3**	**14.8**
Sahel and West Africa	24.2	27.9	30.0	31.6	36.0	34.6
Rest of Africa	24.1	39.6	52.2	48.5	48.7	50.6
Total	100.0	100.0	100.0	100.0	100.0	100.0
	(Conjectured per capita GDP in 1990 international $)					
Egypt	500	500	475	475	475	475
Morocco	400	430	430	430	430	430
Other North Africa	430	430	430	430	430	430
Average North Africa	**460**	**463**	**452**	**451**	**452**	**447**
Sahel and West Africa	400	415	415	415	415	415
Rest of Africa	400	400	400	415	415	415
Average Africa	430	425	414	422	421	420
	(Estimated GDP in million 1990 international $)					
Egypt	2 000	2 500	1 900	2 375	2 138	1 992
Morocco	400	860	645	968	753	1 156
Other North Africa	1 376	1 505	1 204	1 613	1 312	1 764
Total North Africa	**3 776**	**4 865**	**3 749**	**4 956**	**4 203**	**4 912**
Sahel and West Africa	1 600	3 735	5 810	7 263	9 130	10 650
Rest of Africa	1 720	5 120	9 724	11 130	12 359	15 599
Total Africa	7 096	13 720	19 283	23 349	25 692	31 161

Source: The stylised conjectures are for per capita income in each of the five regions at different points of time; GDP is derivative (i.e. per capita conjectures are multiplied by population estimates in Table 6-1). The rationale for the conjectures is derived from the analysis of main currents in African history in the following text. In the first century AD, North Africa belonged to the Roman Empire. Egypt was the richest part of the Roman world because of the special character of its agriculture, which had yielded a large surplus for governance and monuments in Pharaonic times, and was generally siphoned off as tribute by Roman and Arab rulers. Libya and most of the Maghreb (except Morocco) had a prosperous and urbanised coastal fringe in Roman times, with Berber tribes between them and the Sahara. There was no contact then with black Africa which I assume had an average income only slightly above subsistence ($400 in my *numeraire*). After the Arab conquest of North Africa in the seventh century, camel transport permitted trade across the Sahara, permitting a rise in per capita income in Morocco, the Sahel and West Africa. I assume that the gradual transition within Black Africa from a hunter-gatherer to an agricultural mode of production permitted greatly increased density of settlement with higher per capita labour inputs, but had little impact on per capita income.

By 1820, the Egyptian population was below its level in the eleventh century and the same is likely to have been true for per capita income. In the same period, Western Europe trebled its per capita income and increased its population more than fivefold.

The Maghreb

In West Africa, Roman ships did not venture beyond Cape Bojador (just south of the Canary Islands), because the prevailing winds made it impossible for them to make the return journey. Overland trade between the western provinces of Africa and the lands to the south was negligible. Roman settlement was essentially coastal except in Tunisia where large irrigated estates were worked mainly by tenant farmers. Exports from these provinces were heavily concentrated on grain shipped to Italy from Carthage and olive oil from Tripolitania. Roman economic activity in Morocco was vestigial.

When the Arabs conquered the Maghreb they severed the Mediterranean trading links which had previously existed and explored new opportunities across the desert. They established camel caravan routes from Tunisia and Libya deep into the Sahara to places where it was possible to trade horses for black slaves. Bigger profits could be derived from the gold trade with ancient Ghana (about 800 kilometres north–west of modern Ghana, between the Senegal and Niger rivers, just inside the southern boundary of modern Mauretania), which had a lengthy history as state before the Arabs established contact in the early eighth century. The most direct route was through Morocco, the area which received the greatest stimulus from the new contacts with black Africa. Muslim merchants on these new routes were active in making converts to Islam. Early in the eleventh century, ancient Ghana was the first of the black African states to convert to Islam.

Gold production increased steadily in West Africa from the eighth century onwards. Until the twelfth century most of the output circulated within the Muslim world, but from then onwards there was increasing demand from Europe, mainly from Genoa, Venice, Pisa, Florence and Marseilles. European traders conducted their operations in Muslim ports on the Mediterranean coast. They had only minimal contact with African gold producing areas until the second half of the fifteenth century when Portugal gained access to the West African coast.

From the eighth to the twelfth century, the main market for Muslim traders was Awdaghast in Ghana. The goldfield was at Bambuk, somewhat further south, but its exact whereabouts was kept secret. Most exports were in the form of gold dust which was melted and moulded into ingots. In the fourteenth century, pressure of demand was such that production was started further south at the Akan mines (in present–day Ghana). In the fifteenth and sixteenth centuries the main trading centre for gold was Timbuktu in the empire of Songhay. Mining wealth was the main reason why ancient Ghana, Mali and Songhay were able to emerge as powerful states. Income from gold produced an economic surplus which allowed the rulers to maintain the attributes of power. It made it possible for them to import horses and weapons and maintain cavalry forces.

The main barter transactions between the Maghreb and black Africa were exchange of salt for gold. In the Sahel region, salt was very scarce, but was a necessity for people doing heavy work. Some of the salt came from maritime sources on the Atlantic coast. But it was much easier to transport rock salt. From the eleventh to the sixteenth century, the main source was in the Sahara at Taghaza, where it was mined by slave labour, cut into large blocks, and transported south by camel. Salt was not the only trade item in this north–south trade. There was also a lively exchange between trading centres within the Sahel and West Africa, particularly in kola nuts — the African equivalent of coffee or tobacco. Further east, Kanem was the main centre of the slave trade. At a later stage there was a diversity of gold routes to Morocco, Algeria, Tunisia and Egypt and from Mediterranean ports to European customers. In the eleventh and twelfth centuries, Muslim countries were the only ones to mint gold coins. Marseilles first issued them in 1227, Florence in 1252, and Venice in 1284.

Black Africa

In spite of the advance beyond hunter–gatherer techniques, the agriculture of black Africa contrasted sharply with that of Egypt. There was an abundance of land in relation to population, but soils were poor, and were not regenerated by manure, crop rotation, natural or human provision of irrigation. As a consequence, there was an extensive, shifting cultivation, with land being left fallow for a decade or more after the first crops. Nomadic pastoralists were generally transhumant over wide areas for the same reason — poor soils. The main agricultural implements were digging sticks, iron hoes for tillage, axes and machetes for clearing trees and bush. There were no ploughs (except in Ethiopia) and virtually no use of traction animals in agriculture. There were no wheeled vehicles, no water mills, windmills or other instruments of water management.

There were no individual property rights in land. Tribes, kin–groups or other communities had customary rights to farm or graze in the areas where they lived, but collective property rights and boundaries were vague. Chiefs and rulers did not collect rents, land taxes, or feudal levies. Their main instrument of exploitation was slavery. Slaves were generally acquired by raids on neighbouring groups. Hence there was a substantial beggar–your–neighbour element in inter–group relations.

It is not clear how widespread slavery was before contact with Muslim Africa, but the contact certainly reinforced the institution because it made it possible to derive a substantial income from export of slaves across the Sahara. The traffic was organised by Muslim traders from the North. The flow from north to south was negligible. Slaves usually walked through the desert with a caravan of camels carrying food, water, slave drivers and other passengers.

Transport facilities in black Africa were poor. Camels thrived in the dry heat of the desert but could not function further south. Muslim Africa had ships which could navigate and trade in the Mediterranean, and in Egypt there was substantial and relatively safe travel on the sailing boats of the Nile. In the Sahel and West Africa, there were partially navigable rivers, particularly the Niger, the Senegal and Gambia, but river traffic moved in rather primitive paddle–boats made of hollowed–out tree trunks and the frequency of cataracts meant that merchandise frequently had to be trans–shipped by head porterage. Horses were very expensive and had a short life expectation, because of the climate and the fact that they were highly sensitive to tsetse flies. They were used almost exclusively for military and prestige purposes by the ruling groups and their lightly armed cavalry (horses and riders wore padded armour as a defence against arrows).

A striking feature of black Africa before contact with the Islamic world, was universal illiteracy and absence of written languages (except in Ethiopia). This made it difficult to transmit knowledge across generations and between African societies. Contact with Islam brought obvious advantages. The Arabs who came as traders had a written language, and an evangelising bent. They included sophisticated members of the Muslim intelligentsia (*ulama*), who were able to promote knowledge of property institutions, law, and techniques of governance as well cutting business deals. Before the Moroccan conquest of Songhay in 1591, Muslim visitors were generally peaceful and posed no threat to African chiefs and rulers. They saw clear advantages in Islamisation which helped them build bigger empires and acquire stronger instruments of coercion. They were able to exchange gold and slaves for horses and weapons (steel sword blades and tips for spears, and, at a later stage, guns and gunpowder). Black African traders also saw the advantages of conversion. As converts (*dyulas*) they became members of an œcumene with free access to markets well beyond their previous horizons. Thus there was a gradual spread of hybrid Islam in black Africa from the eleventh century onwards. Conversion had its main effect on the ruling groups whose insignia and sanctions of power were a mix of Islam and tradition, whilst most of their subjects continued to be animists.

Analysts of state formation in black Africa make a distinction between complex and acephalous groups (see Goody, 1971). There were a great variety of polities within black Africa. The differentiation grew wider as a result of the varying degree of contact with Islam. Slave traders were generally the most Islamised. Slaves tended to be taken from the acephalous, stateless, and least Islamised groups. There were two reasons for this. The Muslim states tended to have the most powerful armed forces, and they generally avoided enslaving Muslims.

The European Encounter with Africa

Between the eleventh and the fourteenth centuries, European contact with Africa took place in the Mediterranean. European merchants were able to buy Asian spices in Alexandria and African gold on the Tunisian coast until the Ottomans captured Egypt and most of North Africa early in the sixteenth century.

Table 6-3. **World Gold Output by Major Region, 1493-1925**
(million fine ounces)

	1493-1600	1601-1700	1701-1800	1801-50	1851-1900	1901-25
Africa	8.153	6.430	5.466	2.025	23.810	200.210
Americas	8.976	19.043	52.014	22.623	140.047	152.463
Europe	4.758	3.215	3.480	6.034	17.379	8.296
Asia			0.085	6.855	49.150	51.900
Australasia					104.859	62.658
Other	1.080	0.161	0.161	0.498	0.986	
World	22.968	28.849	61.206	38.036	336.231	477.527

Note: There are 32 150 fine ounces in a metric ton.
Source: R.H. Rigway, *Summarised Data of Gold Production*, US Dept of Commerce, 1929, p. 6.

Table 6-4. **Akan (Ghanaian) Gold Production and Exports, 1400-1900**
(million fine ounces)

	1400-1500	1501-1600	1601-1700	1701-1800	1801-1900
Production	1.350	2.700	4.200	3.100	2.650
Exports to Maghreb	0.750	1.450	1.000	0.800	0.250
Exports to Europe	0.550	1.150	3.000	2.000	2.650

Note: There are 32 150 fine ounces in a metric ton.
Source: T.F. Garrard, *Akan Weights and the Gold Trade*, Longman, London, 1980, pp. 163-6.

Table 6-5. **Slave Exports from Black Africa, 650-1900, by Destination**
(000)

	650-1500	1500-1800	1800-1900	650-1900
Americas	81	7 766	3 314	11 159
Trans-Sahara	4 270	1 950	1 200	7 420
Asia	2 200	1 000	934	4 134
Total	**6 551**	**10 716**	**5 448**	**22 713**

Source: P.E. Lovejoy (2000), *Transformations in Slavery*, CUP, pp. 19, 26, 47, 142 and 147. His figures for the Americas are bigger than those of Curtin (see Table 4-4). Curtin's total for 1500-1870 is 9.4 million compared to more than 11 here. Part of the difference is that Curtin shows arrivals whereas Lovejoy does not allow for deaths in transit. The difference is also due to Lovejoy's use of the Du Bois archive in Harvard. So far, this appears to be available only as a CDROM, without the meticulously documented description of the source material which Curtin provided.

Portugal attacked Morocco in 1415 with intent to conquer and get access to African gold. It captured Ceuta, and, by 1521, established several bases on its Atlantic coast, but Moroccan forces recaptured these in 1541 and in 1578 annihilated a Portuguese invasion force. However, Portuguese innovations in the design of ships and navigational instruments made it possible to circumnavigate Africa and trade directly with India and other Asian destinations from 1497 onwards.

They created a trading base at Arquim on the Mauretanian coast in 1445, where they exchanged cloth, horses, trinkets and salt for gold. In 1482, a strongly fortified base was created at Elmina, on the coast of present day Ghana, which gave better access to the Ashanti gold mines. They succeeded in diverting a substantial part of West African gold exports from the Maghreb (see Table 6–4), and got smaller amounts in East Africa from Mutapa in Northern Zimbabwe. The Portuguese discovered quickly that the disease environment in sub–Saharan Africa was very hostile to European settlement. It was, in fact, the reverse of the situation in the Americas. Europeans had very high mortality from African diseases, but Africans were not particularly susceptible to European diseases.

Portugal created an island settlement at São Tomé (in the Bight of Guinea), where sugar production was developed with slave labour. Portuguese also acted as intermediaries in the slave trade, buying and selling between African coastal markets. With the discovery of the Americas, it became more profitable and healthier for Europeans to expand sugar production in Brazil than in Africa. Portugal became the major slave–trader across the Atlantic.

Although the Portuguese pioneered the export of African slaves for plantation agriculture in the Americas, they did not invent African slavery. Between 650 and 1500, 6.5 million slaves had been shipped from black Africa across the Sahara; to Arabia, the Persian Gulf, and India (see Table 6–5). However the Atlantic trade led to a massive increase in enslavement.

In the course of the seventeenth century, Portuguese slaving activity in Africa met fierce competition from the Dutch, British and French. The British exported more than 2.5 million slaves; most of them from Sierra Leone and the Guinea coast. The French took 1.2 million from the Senegal–Gambia region and the Dutch about half a million, mainly from the Gold Coast. The Portuguese were driven out of these regions and concentrated on shipments from Angola to Brazil and Spanish America. Their total shipments from 1500 to 1870 were about 4.5 million.

In the majority of cases, African traders controlled the slaves until the moment of sale. They brought them to the coast or the riverbanks where they were sold to European traders. Within Africa, slaves were acquired in several ways. Some were the offspring of slaves. A large proportion were captured in wars or were supplied as tribute by subject or dependent tribes. Criminals of various kinds were a steady source. There was large–scale raiding of poorly armed tribes without strong central authorities, and kidnapping of individual victims.

The flow across the Atlantic rose from an average of 9 000 a year in 1662–80 to a peak of 76 000 in 1760–89. Lovejoy shows the average price per slave in constant (1601) prices for 1663–1775. In 1663–82, the average price was £2.9 and £15.4 in 1733–75. African income from slavery therefore appears to have risen more than 40–fold from the end of the seventeenth to the end of the eighteenth century. At their peak, in the late eighteenth century, H.S. Klein (1999), *The Atlantic Slave Trade*, CUP, p. 125, suggests that it probably represented less than 5 per cent of West African income.

The demographic losses were concentrated on tribes and people who were least able to protect themselves. Population growth in black Africa was certainly reduced by slave exports. Between 1500 and 1820 it grew about 0.16 per cent a year compared with 0.26 in Western Europe and 0.29 in Asia. The disruption caused by slavery reduced income in the areas from which slaves were seized. The trade goods which slave exporters received in exchange raised consumption but had little impact on production potential. In the eighteenth century, they included Indian textiles made specially for the West African market, tobacco and alcohol, jewellery, bar iron, weapons, gunpowder and cowrie shells from the Maldives.

Slavery within black Africa rose substantially after the abolition movement reduced the Atlantic flow and the price of slaves dropped. The momentum of enslavement continued, and a much larger proportion of the captives were absorbed within Africa. Lovejoy (2000), pp. 191–210 estimates that, at the end of the nineteenth century, 30–50 per cent of the population of the western, central and Nilotic Sudan were slaves. In the 1850s half the people in the caliphate of Sokoto in northern Nigeria were slaves. In Zanzibar, the slave population rose from 15 000 in 1818 to 100 000 in the 1860s. There was a large increase of slave employment in peasant and plantation agriculture producing palm oil products, peanuts, cloves and cotton for export. In the Belgian Congo, Southeast and South Africa there was a rapid expansion of mining activity at the end of the century, with a servile labour force, whose *de facto* situation was equivalent to slavery.

An important result of Portuguese contact with black Africa was the introduction of crops from the Americas. The most important for the food supply and capacity to expand population were roots and tubers. Cassava (manioc) was brought from Brazil to the Congo, the Niger delta and the Bight of Benin early in the sixteenth century. It had high yields, was rich in starch, calcium, iron and vitamin C. It was a perennial plant, tolerant of a wide variety of soils, invulnerable to locusts, drought resistant and easy to cultivate. It could be left in reserve, unharvested, for long periods in good condition after ripening. Cassava flour could be made into cakes for long distance travel and was a staple food for slaves in transit across the Atlantic. Maize was an American crop which the Portuguese introduced on the west and east African coasts. By the seventeenth century it was present in Senegal, the Congo basin, South Africa and Zanzibar. Sweet potatoes were another significant addition to Africa's food supply.

Over the centuries these crops were widely diffused. In the mid–1960s, threequarters (43 million tons) of African output of roots and tubers came from cassava and sweet potatoes (see FAO, *Production Yearbook*, 1966). Maize (15 million tons) represented a third of black Africa's cereal output, the traditional millet and sorghum 47 per cent, rice 12 per cent and other cereals 8 per cent. Other significant American plants which were important in the long term were beans, peanuts, tobacco and cocoa. Bananas and plantains were Asian crops widely diffused in East Africa before the Portuguese arrived; coffee, tea, rubber and cloves were later introductions from Asia.

European countries did nothing to transmit technical knowledge to Africa, nor did they attempt to promote education, printing, development of alphabets etc. China had printing in the ninth century, Western Europe from 1453, Mexico in 1539, Peru 1584, and the north American colonies from the beginning of the seventeenth century. The first printing press in Africa was established in Cairo in 1822.

In 1820, there were only 50 thousand people of European descent in Africa (half of them at the Cape), compared to 13.4 million in the Americas. Africa had diseases which caused very high rates of mortality to Europeans, though Africans were not particularly susceptible to European diseases. Africans had much better weapons to defend themselves than the indigenous population of the Americas. The situation changed in the nineteenth century. Due to improvements in European weaponry, transport (steamboats and railways) and medicine (quinine), the number of European origin in Africa rose to 2.5 million in 1913.

We should note some African institutions which hindered development, but were not due to European influence. One of these, on which Ibn Khaldun commented at length, was the fragility of the states which emerged in the Muslim world (a point which applies *a fortiori* to black Africa). He demonstrated the persistence of tribal affiliations and lineages, and the continuence of nomadic traditions destructive of attempts to develop sedentary agriculture and urban civilisation. He stressed the cyclical rise and fall of Muslim regimes and saw no measure of progress from the seventh to the fourteenth century in which he lived.

African societies failed to secure property rights. The power elite were autocratic and predatory, which inhibited accumulation of capital and willingness to take business risks. This was very obvious in the Mamluk regime in Egypt. There were few countervailing forces in African societies. Goitein's (1967–93) detailed scrutiny of the Cairo Geniza archive led him to be very upbeat about the emergence of a commercial business class in Fatimid Egypt, but freedom of enterprise was snuffed out in later dynasties. The most striking example of deficient property rights was slavery itself, which was closely linked with the polgygamous family structure and limitation on the rights of women. These two institutions were probably the major impediment to physical and human capital formation.

Evidence and Conjectures on the Pace of Development, 1820–1950

Six Country Sample: Maddison (2001) contained pre–1950 estimates for Egypt, Ghana, Morocco and South Africa. I have added Algeria and Tunisia, and extended the estimates for Egypt and Ghana. Sources for the sample countries were as follows:

Egypt: Population to 1870 from McEvedy and Jones (1978); 1886–1945 from D.C. Mead (1967), *Growth and Structural Change in the Egyptian Economy,* Irwin, Illinois, pp. 295 and 302. GDP 1945–50 from Mead, p.286; 1913–45 from B. Hansen and G.A. Marzouk (1965) *Development and Economic Policy in the UAR* (Egypt), North Holland, Amsterdam, p. 3 for 1913–39, p. 318 for 1939–45; 1886/7–1912 movement of per capita GDP from B. Hansen (1979), "Income and Consumption in Egypt, 1886/1887 to 1937", *International Journal of Middle Eastern Studies,* no. 10, p. 29. 1929–39 GDP movement from B. Hansen (1991), *The Political Economy of Poverty, Equity and Growth: Egypt and Turkey,* OUP, New York, p. 6. Per capita estimate for 1870 derived by logarithmic interpolation between the 1886/7 estimate and my conjecture for 1820.

The last column of Table 6–6 compares my results with the proxy estimates of Tarik Yousef (2002), "Egypt's Growth Performance under Economic Liberalism: A Reassessment with New GDP Estimates, 1886–1945", *Review of Income and Wealth,* 48/4 December, pp. 561–79. He derives nominal GDP by a regression procedure using the money supply and assumed velocity of its circulation. He deflates it with a price index and divides by population. I show his per capita GDP movement linked to my estimate of the 1945 level. Yousef cites a miscellany of sources (including those I have used) to show that the broad contours of his proxy estimates are congruent with direct estimates for the first half of the twentieth century. However, there is a big discrepancy between his 1886–1913 per capita movement and mine. His 1886/7 level seems implausibly low, given the substantial expansion in agricultural output, exports and infrastructure investment between 1820 and the 1880s (which he acknowledges at the beginning of his article).

Table 6-6. **Egyptian Population, GDP and Per Capita GDP, 1820-2001**

	Population (000)	GDP (million 1990 int. $)	Per capita GDP (1990 int. $)	Yousef Proxy per capita GDP (1990 int. $)
1820	4 194	1 992	475	
1870	7 049	4 573	649	
1886/7	7 572	5 443	719	452
1913	12 144	10 950	902	825
1929	14 602	12 744	873	828
1939	16 588	14 790	892	812
1945	18 460	14 790	801	801
1950	21 198	19 288	910	
2001	71 902	215 109	2 992	

Algeria, Morocco and Tunisia: GDP from Samir Amin (1966), *l'Économie du Maghreb,* Editions de Minuit, Paris, pp. 104–5. For Algeria, Amin's estimates cover benchmark years between 1880 and 1955. I linked his GDP volume movement to my estimate of the 1955 level in 1990 international dollars; 1870 per capita GDP derived by logarithmic interpolation between his 1880 estimate and my conjecture for 1820, 1913 by interpolation between his figures for 1910 and 1920. I followed a similar procedure for Tunisia and Morocco, where his measures covered 1910–55 and 1920–55 respectively. Algerian population 1820–1930, Tunisian 1820–1913 and Moroccan 1820–1870 from McEvedy and Jones (1978), p. 223.

Table 6.7. **Algerian Population, GDP and Per Capita GDP, 1820-2001**

	Population (000)	GDP (million 1990 int. $)	Per Capita GDP (1990 int. $)
1820	2 689	1 157	430
1870	3 776	2 700	715
1880	4 183	3 312	792
1910	5 378	6 040	1 123
1913	5 497	6 395	1 163
1920	5 785	7 307	1 263
1930	6 507	8 963	1 377
1950	8 893	12 136	1 365
1955	9 842	14 224	1 445
2001	31 736	89 286	2 813

Ghana: R. Szereszewski (1965), *Structural Changes in the Economy of Ghana,* Weidenfeld and Nicolson, London, pp. 74, 92–3, 126, and 149 presents detailed estimates of GDP and population for 1891–1911, and 1960. Table 6–8 links his GDP movement to the 1960 level in 1990 international dollars. 1913 GDP is an extrapolation of his 1901–11 sector growth rates; the 1870 per capita level an interpolation between 1891 and my conjecture for 1820. Population 1820-1870 derived from McEvedy and Jones (1978), p. 245.

Table 6-8. **Ghanaian Population, GDP and Per Capita GDP, 1820-2001**

	Population (000)	GDP (million 1990 int. $)	Per Capita GDP (1990 int. $)
1820	1 374	570	415
1870	1 500	693	462
1891	1 650	798	484
1901	1 800	960	533
1911	2 000	1 393	697
1913	2 043	1 595	781
1950	5 297	5 943	1 122
1960	6 958	9 591	1 378
2001	19 843	26 012	1 311

Szereszewski distinguished between the traditional and modern sectors. He assumed the traditional sector expanded in line with population from 1891–1911 and rose about half in per capita terms from 1911 to 1960. The new components rose nearly 8 per cent a year in the two decades he scrutinised in detail. Cocoa exports rose from 80 lbs. in 1891 to 89 million in 1911, when 600 thousand acres and 185 thousand man–years were absorbed in its production. To a large degree the cocoa boom was sustained by more intensive use of land and previously underemployed rural labour.

The second dynamic element was gold. It had been exported for centuries, and in the 1870s there was a beginning of modern operations. The discovery of huge reserves in South Africa in 1886 sparked an analogous euphoria and investment boom in Ghana. By 1901, 42 companies were operating, and by 1911, a railway connection had been built from the coast to Kumasi through the gold mining areas. There were also improvements in transport facilities from Accra to its cocoa– growing hinterland, investment in modern port facilities in Secondi and Accra, and development of internal river transport by steam launches. The export ratio rose from 8 to 19 per cent of GDP between 1891 and 1911. The main benefits of growth were felt by the locals. In 1911 there were 2 245 Europeans (about 0.1 per cent of the population). In Algeria at that time there were three–quarters of a million European settlers (about 14 per cent of the total).

South Africa: GDP movement 1912–20 from Bureau of Census and Statistics, *Union Statistics for Fifty Years,* Pretoria, 1960; 1920–50 from L.J. Fourie, "Contribution of Factors of Production and Productivity to South African Economic Growth" IARIW, processed, 1971. 1870 per capita GDP level was derived by interpolation of the direct estimate for 1913 and my conjecture for 1820. Although direct GDP estimates are not available, it seems clear that South Africa was the most dynamic of the sample countries from 1820 to 1913. The chief beneficiaries were white settlers. In 1820 they were 30 000 (2 per cent of the population) displacing relatively weak and thinly settled indigenous herdsmen and hunters (Khoisan) in the Cape settlement which was then mainly a staging post for trade with Asia. By 1870 there were quarter of a million whites who had fanned out East and North into Natal, the Orange Free State and Transvaal, taken the best land and water supplies from Xhosa, Zulu and other indigenous groups and exploited various forms of semi–servile labour. In the next twenty years the discovery of diamonds and gold created a boom in investment and immigration. By 1913, there were 1.3 million whites (22 per cent of the population), with an elaborate system of social segregation to buttress their privileged position. Table 6–9 on the expansion of the rail network per head of population provides a clue to the comparative dynamics of African development.

Table 6-9. **Length of Railway Line in Service, 1870-1913**
(kilometres per million population)

	1870	1913
Algeria	70	632
Egypt	168	359
Ghana	0	165
Morocco	0	84
Tunisia	0	1 105
South Africa	0	2 300
Argentina	408	4 374
Australia	861	6 944
India	38	184
United Kingdom	685	715
United States	2 117	9 989

Source: *International Historical Statistics: Africa and Asia,* Macmillan, London, 1982 and Maddison, 1995, p. 64.

The top panel of Table 6–10 shows population in the 6 sample countries 1820–2001, the total for the non–sample countries and for Africa as a whole. The pace of population growth, 1820–1950, was about twice as fast in the sample as in the other countries, 1.19 per cent a year compared with 0.77 per cent. Average per capita income in the sample countries in 1950 was more than twice the level in the rest of Africa, as can be seen from the bottom panel, and in 2001, it was more than three times as high.

Table 6-10. **African GDP and Population Movement, 1820-2001**[a]

Population (000)

	1820	*1870*	*1913*	*1950*	*2001*
Algeria	2 689	3 776	5 497	8 893	31 736
Egypt	4 194	7 049	12 144	21 198	71 902
Ghana	1 374	1 500	2 043	5 297	19 843
Morocco	2 689	3 776	5 111	9 343	30 645
Tunisia	875	1 176	1 870	3 517	9 705
South Africa	1 550	2 547	6 153	13 596	42 573
6 country total	13 371	19 824	32 818	61 844	206 404
51 other countries	60 865	70 642	91 879	165 489	614 684
African Total	74 236	90 466	124 697	227 333	821 088

GDP (million 1990 international Geary-Khamis $)

	1820	*1870*	*1913*	*1950*	*2001*
Algeria	*1 157*	*2 700*	6 395	12 136	89 286
Egypt	*1 992*	*4 573*	10 950	19 288	215 109
Ghana	*570*	*693*	1 595	5 943	26 012
Morocco	*1 156*	*2 126*	3 630	13 598	82 255
Tunisia	*376*	*744*	1 651	3 920	45 714
South Africa	*643*	*2 185*	9 857	34 465	179 162
6 country total	*5 894*	*13 021*	*34 078*	89 350	637 538
51 other countries	*25 267*	*32 213*	*45 408*	113 781	585 038
African Total	*31 161*	*45 234*	79 486	203 131	1 222 577

Per Capita GDP (1990 international Geary-Khamis $)

	1820	*1870*	*1913*	*1950*	*2001*
Algeria	*430*	*715*	1 163	1 365	2 813
Egypt	*475*	*649*	902	910	2 992
Ghana	*415*	*462*	781	1 122	1 311
Morocco	*430*	*563*	710	1 455	2 782
Tunisia	*430*	*633*	883	1 115	4 710
South Africa	*415*	*858*	1 602	2 535	4 208
6 country average	*441*	*657*	1 038	1 445	3 089
51 other countries	*415*	*456*	*494*	688	952
African Average	*420*	*500*	*637*	894	1 489

a)   Conjectures are in italics.

Per capita income was assumed to increase at the same pace in the non–sample as the average for the sample countries between 1913 and 1950. Non–sample per capita GDP in 1870 is an interpolation between the conjecture for 1820 and that for 1913.

Updates for 1950–2001

Annual estimates for 1950–2001 are an update and revision of those for 1950–1998 in Maddison (2001), pp. 310–327; with detail for another nine countries. Population 1950–2001 is from International Programs Center, US Bureau of the Census, October 2002 (USBC at www.census.gov). GDP volume movement 1950–2001 revised and updated for 1993 onwards from IMF, *World Economic Outlook*, September, 2000.

I amalgamated Eritrea and Ethiopia. Eritrea became part of a federation with Ethiopia in 1952. Ten years later it was annexed as a province. It seceded in 1991, and independence was approved in a 1993 referendum. There was a border war 1998–2000. Eritrean population was 6.5 per cent of the total for the two countries in 1950, 6.2 per cent in 2001.

1990 benchmark GDP levels in million 1990 international Geary–Khamis dollars were derived from Penn World Tables version 5.6 in Maddison (2001). Here (see Table 6–11), I have used the new PWT 6.1 (October 2002) and raised the 1990 GDP level for Burkina Faso (from $5 482 to $6 748 million), Burundi (from $3 520 to $3 879), Egypt (from $112 873 to $143 000), Ethiopia and Eritrea (from $18 964 to $29 593), Lesotho (from $1 828 to $2 033), and Zaire from ($17 304 to $19 922).

Table 6-11. **Alternative Estimates of African 1990 GDP Levels by ICP and PWT**
(million international Geary-Khamis dollars)

	PWT 5.5	*PWT 5.6*	*PWT 6.1*	*ICP 5*
Benin	5 248	5 347	4 333	6 629
Botswana	5 479	4 178	6 382	5 662
Cameroon	17 115	14 393	21 881	41 534
Congo	5 972	5 394	3 578	5 358
Côte d'Ivoire	14 568	16 330	20 009	18 528
Egypt	105 684	112 873	143 000	194 267
Ethiopia	17 891	18 964	26 496	18 622
Gabon	3 639	4 500	7 736	n.a.
Guinea	3 087	3 304	13 351	n.a.
Kenya	26 028	26 093	24 354	31 855
Madagascar	9 093	9 210	8 949	8 531
Malawi	4 840	5 146	4 719	6 173
Mali	5 059	6 040	5 878	5 314
Mauritius	7 211	7 652	8 646	7 671
Morocco	60 193	64 082	72 464	83 696
Nigeria	96 521	107 459	94 572	139 453
Rwanda	5 360	6 125	6 050	5 040
Senegal	9 351	10 032	10 298	12 139
Sierra Leone	4 041	4 325	4 571	3 021
Swaziland	1 580	2 154	n.a.	2 181
Tanzania	14 676	13 852	11 043	13 199
Tunisia	26 421	27 387	35 131	35 312
Zambia	6 935	6 432	7 879	10 684
Zimbabwe	14 913	13 766	24 712	20 391

Source: This table compares three sets of PWT estimates with ICP5 results (which are available for only 22 African countries). Col. 1 from annex to R.S. Summers and A. Heston, "The Penn World Table (Mark 5): An Expanded Set of International Comparisons, 1950–1988", *Quarterly Journal of Economics*, May 1991. Col. 2 from their January 1995 diskette. Col. 3 from Alan Heston, Robert Summers and Bettina Aten, PWT Version 6.1, Center for International Comparisons at the University of Pennsylvania (CICUP), October 2002 (http://pwt.econ.upenn.edu). In some cases PWT 5.6 referred to a year before 1990, and in Maddison (2001) I updated using the volume movement of GDP, and the change in the US GDP deflator between that year and 1990. I also made proxy estimates for Libya, Equatorial Guinea, Mayotte, St. Helena, São Tomé & Principe, and W. Sahara. Although some PWT 6.1 estimates are lower than those of 5.6, the overall result for the 45 countries now available is to raise African GDP by 28 percent. Italics indicate countries where the GDP level has been raised. Other striking cases are a 63 percent rise for South Africa and a 47 percent rise for Algeria. As some of the changes are very large, I prefer to wait until a further PWT round is available before adopting the new African estimates *en bloc*. I have adopted 6.1 estimates for Burkina Faso, Burundi, Egypt, Ethiopia and Eritrea, Lesotho and Zaire, as PWT 5.6 estimates seemed implausibly low. ICP 5 from UN/Eurostat, *World Comparisons of Real GDP and Purchasing Power 1985*, New York, 1994, p. 5. adjusted to a 1990 basis.

Table 6a. **Population of 57 African Countries, 1950-2003**
(000 at mid-year)

	Algeria	Angola	Benin	Botswana	Burkina Faso	Burundi	Cameroon	Cape Verde
1950	8 893	4 118	1 673	430	4 376	2 363	4 888	146
1951	9 073	4 173	1 705	436	4 423	2 403	4 947	151
1952	9 280	4 232	1 738	442	4 470	2 445	5 009	155
1953	9 532	4 294	1 773	448	4 518	2 487	5 074	160
1954	9 611	4 358	1 809	455	4 566	2 531	5 141	164
1955	9 842	4 423	1 846	461	4 614	2 575	5 211	169
1956	10 057	4 491	1 885	468	4 664	2 619	5 284	174
1957	10 271	4 561	1 925	475	4 713	2 665	5 360	180
1958	10 485	4 636	1 967	482	4 764	2 712	5 439	185
1959	10 696	4 715	2 010	489	4 814	2 760	5 522	191
1960	10 909	4 797	2 055	497	4 866	2 812	5 609	197
1961	11 122	4 752	2 102	505	4 920	2 890	5 699	203
1962	11 001	4 826	2 152	513	4 978	2 957	5 794	210
1963	11 273	4 920	2 203	521	5 041	3 003	5 892	217
1964	11 613	5 026	2 256	530	5 109	3 083	5 996	224
1965	11 963	5 135	2 311	538	5 182	3 164	6 104	232
1966	12 339	5 201	2 368	546	5 261	3 247	6 217	239
1967	12 760	5 247	2 427	554	5 344	3 323	6 336	247
1968	13 146	5 350	2 489	562	5 434	3 393	6 460	254
1969	13 528	5 472	2 553	572	5 529	3 451	6 590	262
1970	13 932	5 606	2 620	584	5 626	3 513	6 727	269
1971	14 335	5 751	2 689	600	5 726	3 587	6 870	273
1972	14 761	5 891	2 761	620	5 833	3 520	7 021	275
1973	15 198	6 021	2 836	645	5 947	3 529	7 179	277
1974	15 653	5 978	2 914	675	6 069	3 583	7 346	279
1975	16 140	5 879	2 996	709	6 199	3 664	7 522	280
1976	16 635	5 938	3 080	748	6 336	3 736	7 721	283
1977	17 153	6 161	3 168	789	6 478	3 821	7 960	286
1978	17 703	6 279	3 260	832	6 626	3 915	8 207	289
1979	18 266	6 450	3 355	874	6 780	4 013	8 451	292
1980	18 862	6 736	3 444	914	6 942	4 138	8 748	296
1981	19 484	6 877	3 540	950	7 111	4 214	9 024	300
1982	20 132	7 020	3 641	986	7 288	4 344	9 251	305
1983	20 803	7 143	3 748	1 023	7 474	4 531	9 522	309
1984	21 488	7 256	3 861	1 063	7 670	4 668	9 816	314
1985	22 182	7 399	3 980	1 103	7 876	4 809	10 130	319
1986	22 844	7 544	4 104	1 145	8 072	4 952	10 457	325
1987	23 485	7 669	4 234	1 189	8 275	5 110	10 779	331
1988	24 102	7 805	4 371	1 232	8 517	5 284	11 096	337
1989	24 722	7 919	4 513	1 273	8 799	5 459	11 390	343
1990	25 341	8 049	4 662	1 312	9 090	5 285	11 685	349
1991	25 958	8 237	4 817	1 349	9 390	5 393	12 006	356
1992	26 570	8 472	4 976	1 384	9 701	5 478	12 323	362
1993	27 176	8 689	5 140	1 418	10 005	5 590	12 635	368
1994	27 775	8 894	5 309	1 451	10 302	5 761	12 942	373
1995	28 364	9 218	5 484	1 481	10 608	5 392	13 245	379
1996	28 946	9 443	5 664	1 509	10 922	5 366	13 547	384
1997	29 521	9 560	5 848	1 533	11 242	5 405	13 853	388
1998	30 088	9 736	6 037	1 554	11 564	5 487	14 162	393
1999	30 646	9 922	6 230	1 569	11 889	5 603	14 475	397
2000	31 194	10 132	6 428	1 578	12 217	5 714	14 792	401
2001	31 736	10 342	6 630	1 581	12 549	5 838	15 110	405
2002	32 278	10 554	6 835	1 579	12 887	5 965	15 428	409
2003	32 819	10 766	7 041	1 573	13 228	6 096	15 746	412

Table 6a. **Population of 57 African Countries, 1950-2003**
(000 at mid-year)

	Central African Rep.	Chad	Comoros	Congo	Côte d'Ivoire	Djibouti	Egypt	Eritrea and Ethiopia	Gabon
1950	1 260	2 608	148	768	2 860	60	21 198	21 577	416
1951	1 275	2 644	151	781	2 918	62	21 704	21 939	418
1952	1 292	2 682	154	794	2 977	63	22 223	22 314	421
1953	1 309	2 722	157	809	3 037	65	22 755	22 703	423
1954	1 328	2 763	160	824	3 099	66	23 299	23 107	426
1955	1 348	2 805	164	840	3 164	68	23 856	23 526	429
1956	1 370	2 849	167	856	3 231	70	24 426	23 961	432
1957	1 392	2 895	171	874	3 300	72	25 010	24 412	435
1958	1 416	2 942	175	892	3 374	74	25 608	24 880	438
1959	1 441	2 991	179	911	3 463	76	26 220	25 364	442
1960	1 467	3 042	183	931	3 576	78	26 847	25 864	446
1961	1 495	3 095	187	952	3 700	84	27 523	26 380	450
1962	1 523	3 150	192	974	3 832	90	28 173	26 913	456
1963	1 553	3 208	196	996	3 985	96	28 821	27 464	461
1964	1 585	3 271	201	1 020	4 148	103	29 533	28 034	468
1965	1 628	3 345	206	1 044	4 327	111	30 265	28 621	474
1966	1 683	3 420	212	1 070	4 527	119	30 986	29 228	482
1967	1 729	3 496	217	1 097	4 745	128	31 681	29 839	489
1968	1 756	3 573	223	1 124	4 984	137	32 338	30 480	497
1969	1 785	3 650	230	1 153	5 235	147	32 966	31 154	504
1970	1 827	3 731	236	1 183	5 504	158	33 574	31 826	515
1971	1 869	3 814	243	1 214	5 786	169	34 184	32 519	526
1972	1 910	3 899	250	1 246	6 072	179	34 807	33 257	538
1973	1 945	3 989	257	1 279	6 352	189	35 480	34 028	561
1974	1 983	4 082	265	1 314	6 622	198	36 216	34 838	597
1975	2 031	4 180	273	1 360	6 889	208	36 952	35 673	648
1976	2 071	4 282	281	1 409	7 151	217	37 737	36 588	688
1977	2 111	4 389	305	1 461	7 419	229	38 784	37 443	706
1978	2 153	4 499	314	1 515	7 692	248	40 020	38 084	726
1979	2 197	4 544	324	1 571	7 973	263	41 258	38 568	722
1980	2 244	4 542	334	1 629	8 261	279	42 634	38 967	714
1981	2 291	4 648	341	1 691	8 558	294	44 196	39 555	731
1982	2 338	4 877	349	1 755	8 866	306	45 682	40 463	754
1983	2 385	5 074	357	1 822	9 185	316	47 093	41 565	779
1984	2 451	5 125	366	1 901	9 517	289	48 550	42 815	805
1985	2 516	5 170	375	1 955	9 864	297	50 052	43 448	833
1986	2 556	5 316	385	2 010	10 221	304	51 593	44 434	859
1987	2 600	5 502	395	2 067	10 585	311	52 799	45 816	881
1988	2 654	5 678	406	2 123	10 956	327	54 024	47 439	900
1989	2 728	5 834	417	2 181	11 361	350	55 263	49 174	919
1990	2 803	6 030	429	2 240	11 901	366	56 694	50 902	938
1991	2 882	6 242	441	2 298	12 421	375	58 139	53 199	961
1992	2 964	6 443	454	2 356	12 775	384	59 402	55 240	987
1993	3 053	6 675	468	2 415	13 185	393	60 677	56 537	1 014
1994	3 139	6 912	482	2 474	13 669	403	61 983	57 967	1 041
1995	3 204	7 138	497	2 532	14 115	409	63 322	59 511	1 070
1996	3 262	7 374	512	2 590	14 503	414	64 705	61 042	1 099
1997	3 322	7 619	528	2 647	14 830	418	66 134	62 536	1 129
1998	3 383	7 875	544	2 703	15 119	422	67 602	64 004	1 160
1999	3 442	8 144	561	2 757	15 475	427	69 067	65 502	1 191
2000	3 501	8 419	578	2 809	15 866	431	70 492	66 895	1 223
2001	3 562	8 693	596	2 860	16 234	438	71 902	68 208	1 255
2002	3 623	8 971	614	2 908	16 598	447	73 313	69 560	1 288
2003	3 684	9 253	633	2 954	16 962	457	74 719	70 920	1 322

Table 6a. **Population of 57 African Countries, 1950-2003**
(000 at mid-year)

	Gambia	Ghana	Guinea	Guinea Bissau	Kenya	Lesotho	Liberia	Madagascar
1950	271	5 297	2 586	573	6 121	726	824	4 620
1951	278	5 437	2 625	577	6 289	737	843	4 690
1952	284	5 581	2 664	581	6 464	749	863	4 763
1953	291	5 731	2 705	584	6 646	761	884	4 839
1954	299	5 887	2 745	588	6 836	773	906	4 919
1955	306	6 049	2 787	592	7 034	786	928	5 003
1956	315	6 217	2 831	596	7 240	800	952	5 090
1957	323	6 391	2 877	601	7 455	813	976	5 182
1958	332	6 573	2 925	606	7 679	828	1 001	5 277
1959	342	6 761	2 975	611	7 913	843	1 028	5 378
1960	352	6 958	3 028	617	8 157	859	1 055	5 482
1961	363	7 154	3 083	622	8 412	875	1 083	5 590
1962	374	7 355	3 140	628	8 679	893	1 113	5 703
1963	386	7 564	3 199	634	8 957	912	1 144	5 821
1964	399	7 782	3 259	610	9 248	932	1 175	5 944
1965	412	8 010	3 321	604	9 549	952	1 209	6 070
1966	426	8 245	3 385	598	9 864	974	1 243	6 200
1967	440	8 490	3 451	601	10 192	996	1 279	6 335
1968	454	8 744	3 519	611	10 532	1 019	1 317	6 473
1969	469	9 009	3 589	616	10 888	1 043	1 356	6 616
1970	485	8 789	3 661	620	11 272	1 067	1 397	6 766
1971	501	9 066	3 735	623	11 685	1 092	1 439	6 920
1972	517	9 354	3 811	625	12 126	1 117	1 483	7 082
1973	534	9 650	3 890	633	12 594	1 142	1 528	7 250
1974	552	9 905	3 970	640	13 090	1 169	1 575	7 424
1975	570	10 119	4 053	681	13 615	1 195	1 624	7 604
1976	589	10 333	4 139	733	14 171	1 223	1 675	7 805
1977	608	10 538	4 227	745	14 762	1 252	1 727	8 007
1978	628	10 721	4 318	758	15 386	1 281	1 780	8 217
1979	649	10 878	4 411	771	16 045	1 312	1 835	8 442
1980	671	11 016	4 508	789	16 698	1 344	1 892	8 677
1981	693	11 177	4 607	807	17 369	1 377	1 951	8 920
1982	716	11 401	4 710	826	18 059	1 412	2 011	9 171
1983	739	12 157	4 816	846	18 769	1 447	2 074	9 432
1984	767	12 829	5 046	865	19 499	1 484	2 138	9 702
1985	796	13 228	5 327	886	20 247	1 521	2 205	9 981
1986	827	13 778	5 504	906	21 006	1 559	2 274	10 270
1987	858	14 170	5 650	928	21 761	1 596	2 345	10 569
1988	891	14 569	5 800	950	22 504	1 631	2 418	10 877
1989	926	14 977	5 955	973	23 229	1 664	2 493	11 194
1990	962	15 400	6 280	996	23 934	1 693	2 189	11 522
1991	999	15 837	6 727	1 020	24 670	1 718	1 892	11 860
1992	1 036	16 278	6 988	1 051	25 524	1 740	1 985	12 210
1993	1 075	16 784	7 194	1 084	26 269	1 760	2 063	12 573
1994	1 115	17 272	7 429	1 116	26 852	1 778	2 057	12 950
1995	1 156	17 668	7 682	1 142	27 463	1 794	1 980	13 340
1996	1 197	18 046	7 949	1 165	28 074	1 807	2 025	13 746
1997	1 238	18 419	8 048	1 193	28 681	1 820	2 296	14 165
1998	1 281	18 795	8 176	1 221	29 266	1 830	2 655	14 598
1999	1 324	19 159	8 434	1 250	29 811	1 840	2 974	15 045
2000	1 367	19 509	8 642	1 278	30 310	1 847	3 149	15 506
2001	1 411	19 843	8 717	1 306	30 777	1 853	3 206	15 983
2002	1 456	20 163	8 816	1 333	31 223	1 858	3 262	16 473
2003	1 501	20 468	9 030	1 361	31 639	1 862	3 317	16 980

Table 6a. **Population of 57 African Countries, 1950-2003**
(000 at mid-year)

	Malawi	Mali	Mauritania	Mauritius	Morocco	Mozambique	Namibia	Niger	Nigeria
1950	2 817	3 688	1 006	481	9 343	6 250	464	2 482	31 797
1951	2 866	3 761	1 014	499	9 634	6 346	475	2 538	32 449
1952	2 918	3 835	1 023	517	9 939	6 446	486	2 597	33 119
1953	2 972	3 911	1 032	536	10 206	6 552	497	2 659	33 809
1954	3 029	3 988	1 042	554	10 487	6 664	509	2 723	34 632
1955	3 088	4 067	1 053	572	10 782	6 782	522	2 790	35 464
1956	3 152	4 148	1 065	592	11 089	6 906	535	2 859	36 311
1957	3 221	4 230	1 077	610	11 406	7 038	548	2 931	37 178
1958	3 295	4 314	1 090	628	11 735	7 177	562	3 007	38 068
1959	3 370	4 399	1 103	645	12 074	7 321	576	3 085	38 981
1960	3 450	4 486	1 117	663	12 423	7 472	591	3 168	39 920
1961	3 532	4 576	1 132	681	12 736	7 628	606	3 253	40 884
1962	3 629	4 668	1 147	701	13 057	7 789	621	3 343	41 876
1963	3 726	4 763	1 162	715	13 385	7 957	637	3 437	42 897
1964	3 816	4 862	1 178	736	13 722	8 127	654	3 533	43 946
1965	3 914	4 963	1 195	756	14 066	8 301	671	3 633	45 025
1966	4 023	5 068	1 212	774	14 415	8 486	689	3 735	46 143
1967	4 147	5 177	1 231	789	14 770	8 681	707	3 842	47 305
1968	4 264	5 289	1 249	804	15 137	8 884	725	3 951	48 515
1969	4 379	5 405	1 269	816	15 517	9 093	745	4 064	49 776
1970	4 489	5 525	1 289	830	15 909	9 304	765	4 182	51 113
1971	4 606	5 649	1 311	841	16 313	9 539	786	4 303	52 495
1972	4 731	5 777	1 333	851	16 661	9 810	808	4 429	53 914
1973	4 865	5 909	1 356	861	16 998	10 088	831	4 559	55 415
1974	5 031	6 046	1 380	873	17 335	10 370	854	4 695	57 084
1975	5 268	6 188	1 404	885	17 687	10 433	879	4 836	58 916
1976	5 473	6 334	1 430	898	18 043	10 770	905	4 984	60 819
1977	5 637	6 422	1 457	913	18 397	11 128	923	5 139	62 822
1978	5 792	6 517	1 485	929	18 758	11 466	935	5 294	64 953
1979	5 956	6 620	1 516	947	19 126	11 828	955	5 459	67 224
1980	6 129	6 731	1 550	964	19 487	12 103	975	5 629	69 629
1981	6 311	6 849	1 585	979	19 846	12 364	988	5 806	72 092
1982	6 503	6 975	1 622	992	20 199	12 588	1 011	5 988	74 538
1983	6 703	7 110	1 662	1 002	20 740	12 775	1 045	6 189	75 901
1984	6 909	7 255	1 703	1 012	21 296	12 926	1 080	6 389	77 544
1985	7 124	7 408	1 747	1 022	21 857	13 065	1 116	6 589	79 884
1986	7 391	7 569	1 793	1 032	22 422	13 143	1 154	6 802	81 971
1987	7 817	7 738	1 841	1 043	22 987	12 889	1 196	7 016	84 505
1988	8 327	7 884	1 892	1 052	23 555	12 517	1 256	7 237	87 115
1989	8 800	8 050	1 937	1 063	24 122	12 467	1 339	7 428	89 801
1990	9 215	8 228	1 984	1 074	24 686	12 649	1 409	7 630	92 566
1991	9 549	8 412	2 041	1 085	25 244	12 912	1 450	7 844	95 390
1992	9 871	8 565	2 119	1 096	25 798	13 149	1 491	8 069	98 270
1993	9 997	8 719	2 205	1 107	26 351	13 638	1 532	8 307	101 227
1994	9 767	8 911	2 279	1 118	26 901	14 663	1 575	8 557	104 260
1995	9 656	9 157	2 342	1 129	27 447	15 522	1 618	8 819	107 372
1996	9 855	9 452	2 389	1 139	27 990	15 898	1 661	9 085	110 552
1997	10 103	9 746	2 445	1 150	28 530	16 184	1 704	9 345	113 787
1998	10 356	10 054	2 515	1 160	29 066	16 453	1 746	9 611	117 072
1999	10 613	10 360	2 591	1 169	29 597	16 704	1 787	9 888	120 397
2000	10 874	10 665	2 668	1 179	30 122	16 934	1 826	10 174	123 750
2001	11 134	10 980	2 747	1 190	30 645	17 142	1 863	10 465	127 120
2002	11 393	11 300	2 829	1 200	31 168	17 324	1 897	10 760	130 500
2003	11 651	11 626	2 913	1 210	31 689	17 479	1 927	11 059	133 882

Table 6a. **Population of 57 African Countries, 1950-2003**
(000 at mid-year)

	Reunion	Rwanda	Senegal	Seychelles	Sierra Leone	Somalia	South Africa	Sudan	Swaziland
1950	244	2 439	2 654	33	2 087	2 438	13 596	8 051	277
1951	251	2 486	2 703	33	2 115	2 482	13 926	8 275	284
1952	258	2 535	2 756	33	2 143	2 527	14 265	8 505	290
1953	266	2 587	2 810	34	2 172	2 574	14 624	8 741	297
1954	274	2 641	2 867	35	2 202	2 623	14 992	8 984	304
1955	286	2 698	2 927	36	2 233	2 673	15 369	9 233	311
1956	296	2 759	2 989	38	2 264	2 726	15 755	9 490	319
1957	309	2 822	3 055	38	2 296	2 780	16 152	9 753	327
1958	318	2 889	3 123	39	2 328	2 837	16 558	10 024	335
1959	327	2 959	3 195	40	2 362	2 895	16 975	10 303	343
1960	338	3 032	3 270	42	2 396	2 956	17 417	10 589	352
1961	348	3 046	3 348	43	2 432	3 017	17 870	10 882	361
1962	359	3 051	3 430	44	2 468	3 080	18 357	11 183	370
1963	371	3 129	3 516	45	2 505	3 145	18 857	11 493	380
1964	384	3 184	3 636	47	2 543	3 213	19 371	11 801	389
1965	393	3 265	3 744	48	2 582	3 283	19 898	12 086	399
1966	403	3 358	3 857	49	2 622	3 354	20 440	12 377	410
1967	414	3 451	3 966	50	2 662	3 429	20 997	12 716	421
1968	425	3 548	4 074	51	2 704	3 506	21 569	13 059	432
1969	436	3 657	4 193	53	2 746	3 585	22 157	13 403	443
1970	445	3 769	4 318	54	2 789	3 667	22 740	13 788	455
1971	453	3 880	4 450	56	2 834	3 752	23 338	14 182	467
1972	462	3 992	4 589	57	2 879	3 840	23 936	14 597	480
1973	469	4 110	4 727	58	2 925	3 932	24 549	15 113	493
1974	475	4 226	4 872	59	2 974	4 027	25 179	15 571	507
1975	481	4 357	4 989	61	3 027	4 128	25 815	16 056	521
1976	487	4 502	5 101	62	3 083	4 238	26 468	16 570	536
1977	492	4 657	5 232	63	3 141	4 354	27 130	17 105	551
1978	497	4 819	5 365	64	3 201	4 678	27 809	17 712	568
1979	502	4 976	5 501	65	3 263	5 309	28 506	18 387	588
1980	507	5 139	5 640	66	3 327	5 791	29 252	19 064	611
1981	512	5 311	5 783	68	3 394	5 825	30 018	19 702	631
1982	518	5 510	5 930	68	3 465	5 829	30 829	20 367	650
1983	523	5 705	6 082	69	3 538	6 003	31 664	21 751	673
1984	533	5 868	6 239	70	3 615	6 207	32 523	22 543	697
1985	542	6 023	6 400	71	3 696	6 446	33 406	23 454	722
1986	551	6 186	6 568	71	3 781	6 700	34 156	24 171	751
1987	562	6 375	6 740	72	3 870	6 922	34 894	24 726	779
1988	574	6 584	6 918	72	3 963	6 900	35 640	25 240	817
1989	585	6 781	7 137	73	4 061	6 748	36 406	25 838	852
1990	597	6 962	7 362	73	4 226	6 675	37 191	26 627	885
1991	610	7 150	7 592	74	4 340	6 448	37 924	27 446	926
1992	622	7 328	7 821	75	4 270	6 100	38 656	28 228	963
1993	635	7 489	8 050	76	4 229	6 060	39 271	28 964	992
1994	647	6 441	8 284	76	4 332	6 178	39 762	29 771	997
1995	660	5 723	8 525	77	4 507	6 291	40 256	30 567	1 005
1996	672	6 008	8 774	78	4 633	6 461	40 723	31 307	1 031
1997	685	7 199	9 022	78	4 727	6 634	41 194	32 161	1 057
1998	697	7 159	9 273	78	4 895	6 843	41 658	33 108	1 080
1999	709	7 291	9 527	79	5 053	7 044	42 048	34 085	1 101
2000	721	7 405	9 784	79	5 203	7 253	42 351	35 080	1 120
2001	733	7 532	10 046	80	5 388	7 489	42 573	36 080	1 136
2002	744	7 668	10 311	80	5 565	7 753	42 716	37 090	1 150
2003	755	7 810	10 580	80	5 733	8 025	42 769	38 114	1 161

Table 6a. **Population of 57 African Countries, 1950-2003**
(000 at mid-year)

	Tanzania	Togo	Tunisia	Uganda	Zaire	Zambia	Zimbabwe	6 Country Total	57 Country Total
1950	7 935	1 172	3 517	5 522	13 569	2 553	2 853	1 266	227 333
1951	8 125	1 195	3 583	5 671	13 819	2 611	2 951	1 299	232 068
1952	8 323	1 219	3 648	5 825	14 075	2 672	3 081	1 334	237 008
1953	8 529	1 244	3 713	5 983	14 335	2 734	3 191	1 370	242 086
1954	8 745	1 271	3 779	6 148	14 605	2 800	3 307	1 409	247 273
1955	8 971	1 298	3 846	6 317	14 886	2 869	3 409	1 451	252 759
1956	9 206	1 327	3 903	6 493	15 178	2 941	3 530	1 496	258 409
1957	9 453	1 357	3 951	6 676	15 481	3 016	3 646	1 543	264 222
1958	9 711	1 389	4 007	6 864	15 796	3 094	3 764	1 592	270 231
1959	9 979	1 422	4 075	7 059	16 123	3 173	3 887	1 645	276 454
1960	10 260	1 456	4 149	7 262	16 462	3 254	4 011	1 701	282 919
1961	10 555	1 491	4 216	7 472	16 798	3 337	4 140	1 760	289 385
1962	10 864	1 528	4 287	7 689	17 300	3 421	4 278	1 819	295 977
1963	11 185	1 566	4 374	7 914	17 819	3 508	4 412	1 882	303 251
1964	11 522	1 606	4 468	8 147	18 203	3 599	4 537	1 951	310 725
1965	11 870	1 648	4 566	8 389	18 604	3 694	4 685	2 022	318 478
1966	12 231	1 691	4 676	8 640	19 068	3 794	4 836	2 103	326 534
1967	12 607	1 736	4 787	8 900	19 640	3 900	4 995	2 179	334 945
1968	12 999	1 782	4 894	9 170	20 242	4 009	5 172	2 266	343 591
1969	13 412	1 830	4 996	9 450	20 822	4 123	5 353	2 368	352 457
1970	13 842	1 964	5 099	9 728	21 395	4 252	5 515	2 458	361 168
1971	14 285	2 019	5 198	9 984	21 969	4 376	5 684	2 546	370 534
1972	14 769	2 075	5 304	10 191	22 559	4 506	5 861	2 659	380 026
1973	15 279	2 133	5 426	10 386	23 186	4 643	6 002	2 783	390 034
1974	15 775	2 192	5 556	10 621	23 810	4 785	6 173	2 903	400 314
1975	16 258	2 254	5 704	10 891	24 467	4 924	6 342	2 992	410 827
1976	16 754	2 317	5 859	11 171	25 175	5 067	6 496	3 078	422 188
1977	17 276	2 382	6 005	11 459	25 776	5 217	6 642	3 148	433 995
1978	17 814	2 450	6 136	11 757	26 462	5 371	6 767	3 239	446 294
1979	18 355	2 521	6 280	12 034	27 418	5 532	6 887	3 413	459 413
1980	18 915	2 596	6 443	12 298	28 129	5 700	7 170	3 600	472 721
1981	19 496	2 686	6 606	12 597	28 821	5 885	7 429	3 772	486 060
1982	20 093	2 777	6 734	12 941	29 780	6 101	7 637	3 944	500 253
1983	20 718	2 875	6 860	13 323	30 536	6 339	7 930	4 110	515 235
1984	21 367	2 979	7 185	13 765	31 280	6 565	8 243	4 276	530 353
1985	22 036	3 088	7 362	14 232	32 260	6 783	8 562	4 347	545 742
1986	22 732	3 202	7 545	14 746	33 302	7 026	8 879	4 391	561 280
1987	23 485	3 321	7 725	15 348	34 409	7 268	9 217	4 509	577 158
1988	24 236	3 446	7 895	15 991	35 564	7 483	9 558	4 644	593 250
1989	24 946	3 574	8 053	16 633	36 742	7 683	9 865	4 779	609 818
1990	25 651	3 705	8 207	17 242	37 969	7 876	10 154	4 915	626 814
1991	26 376	3 837	8 364	17 857	39 270	8 068	10 439	5 051	644 889
1992	27 134	3 972	8 523	18 499	40 530	8 262	10 729	5 188	662 410
1993	28 029	3 960	8 680	19 193	41 844	8 452	10 997	5 324	679 567
1994	29 096	4 001	8 831	19 897	43 256	8 641	11 127	5 459	696 273
1995	30 016	4 229	8 972	20 455	45 706	8 827	11 233	5 554	713 856
1996	30 618	4 435	9 105	20 984	46 623	9 010	11 436	5 614	730 822
1997	31 282	4 612	9 234	21 599	47 451	9 206	11 643	5 715	748 865
1998	32 098	4 759	9 359	22 221	48 831	9 397	11 839	5 858	766 842
1999	32 920	4 897	9 479	22 855	50 288	9 590	12 022	6 006	785 235
2000	33 768	5 033	9 593	23 496	51 810	9 799	12 186	6 158	803 311
2001	34 583	5 167	9 705	24 170	53 455	9 986	12 332	6 313	821 088
2002	35 302	5 299	9 816	24 889	55 042	10 149	12 463	6 471	838 720
2003	35 922	5 429	9 925	25 633	56 625	10 307	12 577	6 633	856 261

Table 6a. **Population of 57 African Countries, 1950-2003**
(000 at mid-year)

	Equatorial Guinea	Libya	SãoTomé & Principe	Mayotte + St. Helena + W. Sahara	6 Country Total
1950	211	961	60	34	1 266
1951	214	990	60	36	1 299
1952	217	1 020	60	37	1 334
1953	220	1 052	60	39	1 370
1954	223	1 086	60	40	1 409
1955	226	1 122	60	42	1 451
1956	229	1 161	61	45	1 496
1957	233	1 202	61	47	1 543
1958	237	1 245	62	49	1 592
1959	240	1 290	63	52	1 645
1960	244	1 338	63	55	1 701
1961	248	1 389	64	59	1 760
1962	249	1 442	65	63	1 819
1963	250	1 499	66	67	1 882
1964	252	1 560	67	72	1 951
1965	253	1 624	69	77	2 022
1966	256	1 694	70	83	2 103
1967	260	1 759	71	90	2 179
1968	263	1 834	72	97	2 266
1969	267	1 923	73	105	2 368
1970	270	1 999	74	114	2 458
1971	274	2 077	75	120	2 546
1972	278	2 184	77	121	2 659
1973	271	2 312	78	121	2 783
1974	250	2 451	80	122	2 903
1975	213	2 570	82	128	2 992
1976	191	2 666	84	137	3 078
1977	193	2 722	87	147	3 148
1978	195	2 797	89	158	3 239
1979	221	2 929	92	171	3 413
1980	256	3 065	94	184	3 600
1981	272	3 204	96	199	3 772
1982	285	3 344	99	216	3 944
1983	300	3 485	101	225	4 110
1984	314	3 625	103	233	4 276
1985	325	3 675	106	242	4 347
1986	333	3 700	108	250	4 391
1987	341	3 800	111	258	4 509
1988	350	3 913	114	267	4 644
1989	359	4 027	116	277	4 779
1990	368	4 140	119	288	4 915
1991	378	4 252	123	298	5 051
1992	388	4 365	126	309	5 188
1993	398	4 476	129	321	5 324
1994	408	4 585	133	332	5 459
1995	418	4 654	137	344	5 554
1996	429	4 686	141	357	5 614
1997	440	4 760	146	369	5 715
1998	451	4 875	150	382	5 858
1999	463	4 993	155	395	6 006
2000	474	5 115	160	408	6 158
2001	486	5 241	165	421	6 313
2002	498	5 369	170	434	6 471
2003	510	5 499	176	448	6 633

GDP Levels in Africa

Table 6b. **GDP Levels in 57 African Countries, 1950-2001**
(million 1990 international Geary-Khamis dollars)

	Algeria	*Angola*	*Benin*	*Botswana*	*Burkina Faso*	*Burundi*	*Cameroon*	*Cape Verde*
1950	12 136	4 331	1 813	150	2 076	851	3 279	66
1951	12 221	4 491	1 813	155	2 155	899	3 401	69
1952	12 767	4 660	1 813	159	2 233	927	3 525	71
1953	13 046	4 833	1 762	164	2 314	965	3 653	75
1954	13 811	4 703	1 813	169	2 399	1 018	3 788	76
1955	14 224	5 080	1 813	174	2 489	1 050	3 929	78
1956	15 619	4 985	1 813	179	2 582	1 090	4 073	82
1957	17 391	5 461	1 813	184	2 676	1 132	4 224	81
1958	18 022	5 751	1 880	189	2 777	1 163	4 381	83
1959	21 323	5 777	1 950	195	2 877	1 230	4 542	93
1960	22 780	6 011	2 010	200	2 962	1 249	4 666	100
1961	20 013	6 635	2 075	207	3 080	1 078	4 722	107
1962	15 765	6 444	2 005	213	3 269	1 176	4 867	113
1963	19 928	6 791	2 097	220	3 228	1 224	5 047	120
1964	20 971	7 587	2 240	228	3 302	1 298	5 227	127
1965	22 367	8 194	2 356	235	3 429	1 347	5 332	133
1966	21 287	8 635	2 443	258	3 446	1 409	5 581	140
1967	23 277	9 064	2 467	284	3 749	1 537	5 736	147
1968	25 996	8 947	2 561	313	3 865	1 520	6 109	153
1969	28 484	9 255	2 637	344	3 942	1 501	6 411	160
1970	31 336	9 909	2 692	378	3 950	1 902	6 605	166
1971	28 666	9 943	2 704	448	4 106	2 052	6 801	155
1972	34 685	10 091	2 942	592	4 272	1 831	7 096	148
1973	35 814	10 784	3 011	722	4 045	1 963	7 201	147
1974	37 999	10 242	2 784	873	3 969	1 947	7 523	143
1975	40 705	6 314	2 904	862	3 798	1 966	7 910	147
1976	43 387	5 669	3 029	1 024	3 761	2 121	8 061	147
1977	47 319	5 799	3 199	1 061	4 027	2 383	8 520	148
1978	53 387	6 037	3 301	1 264	4 496	2 357	8 985	164
1979	58 193	6 184	3 565	1 391	4 542	2 404	9 474	182
1980	59 273	6 483	3 901	1 589	4 616	2 594	10 441	249
1981	60 766	6 353	4 122	1 736	4 820	2 877	12 222	271
1982	64 662	6 050	4 566	1 865	4 926	2 865	13 147	279
1983	68 012	5 851	4 366	2 159	4 870	2 954	14 068	306
1984	71 774	5 881	4 713	2 400	4 948	2 951	15 170	317
1985	75 512	5 911	5 068	2 577	5 596	3 295	16 528	345
1986	74 747	5 379	5 182	2 773	6 474	3 421	17 722	355
1987	74 225	5 985	5 104	3 017	6 364	3 562	16 839	380
1988	72 672	6 843	5 258	3 492	6 893	3 694	16 072	392
1989	75 123	6 959	5 144	3 944	6 814	3 747	14 632	413
1990	73 934	7 202	5 347	4 178	6 748	3 879	14 393	430
1991	73 047	7 252	5 598	4 379	7 423	4 073	13 846	283
1992	74 216	7 180	5 822	4 510	7 608	4 101	13 417	231
1993	72 583	5 241	6 026	4 600	7 548	3 859	12 987	434
1994	71 929	5 310	6 291	4 761	7 654	3 716	12 662	463
1995	74 663	5 861	6 581	4 975	7 999	3 445	13 081	499
1996	77 500	6 518	6 942	5 259	8 598	3 156	13 734	532
1997	78 353	7 033	7 338	5 611	9 010	3 169	14 435	573
1998	82 349	7 511	7 675	5 942	9 588	3 320	15 156	615
1999	84 984	7 759	8 037	6 317	10 191	3 287	15 823	668
2000	87 109	7 991	8 503	6 860	10 416	3 284	16 488	713
2001	89 286	8 247	8 928	7 196	11 007	3 362	17 362	734

Table 6b. **GDP Levels in 57 African Countries, 1950-2001**
(million 1990 international Geary-Khamis dollars)

	Central African Rep.	Chad	Comoros	Congo	Côte d'Ivoire	Djibouti	Egypt	Eritrea & Ethiopia	Gabon
1950	972	1 240	83	990	2 977	90	19 288	8 417	1 292
1951	1 008	1 286	88	1 027	3 087	95	19 635	8 652	1 340
1952	1 045	1 333	90	1 064	3 201	98	20 001	8 896	1 389
1953	1 083	1 381	94	1 103	3 317	102	20 349	9 410	1 440
1954	1 123	1 432	99	1 144	3 439	108	20 715	9 410	1 493
1955	1 165	1 485	102	1 186	3 567	111	21 101	9 915	1 548
1956	1 207	1 540	106	1 230	3 698	115	22 104	10 243	1 605
1957	1 252	1 597	110	1 275	3 835	120	23 145	10 167	1 665
1958	1 299	1 657	113	1 323	3 978	123	24 245	10 504	1 727
1959	1 346	1 717	120	1 372	4 123	130	25 402	10 790	1 791
1960	1 358	1 730	130	1 419	4 493	139	26 617	11 346	1 866
1961	1 409	1 753	132	1 465	4 912	150	28 372	11 901	2 090
1962	1 373	1 846	144	1 513	5 130	158	30 263	12 389	2 153
1963	1 369	1 819	174	1 563	5 972	171	32 288	14 031	2 229
1964	1 391	1 773	188	1 616	7 041	182	34 448	14 721	2 268
1965	1 409	1 783	188	1 670	6 886	194	36 724	15 588	2 306
1966	1 420	1 752	208	1 757	7 431	209	36 936	16 194	2 409
1967	1 487	1 764	217	1 850	7 538	224	36 473	16 875	2 508
1968	1 494	1 756	218	1 948	8 714	239	37 052	17 162	2 572
1969	1 565	1 876	221	2 050	9 098	256	39 598	17 801	2 780
1970	1 638	1 912	238	2 158	10 087	327	42 105	18 811	3 020
1971	1 590	1 948	280	2 333	10 593	361	43 861	19 602	3 330
1972	1 557	1 815	258	2 523	11 179	385	44 690	20 604	3 708
1973	1 627	1 726	229	2 727	12 064	412	45 924	21 286	4 086
1974	1 580	1 963	279	2 947	12 412	412	47 680	21 547	5 699
1975	1 609	2 301	219	3 185	12 400	430	52 501	21 580	6 090
1976	1 679	2 267	194	3 199	13 886	468	60 622	22 170	8 487
1977	1 816	2 098	190	2 934	14 541	410	68 530	22 776	6 732
1978	1 848	2 088	197	2 883	15 982	427	73 795	22 523	4 883
1979	1 745	1 640	202	3 323	16 282	444	79 620	23 971	4 814
1980	1 730	1 541	215	3 891	17 539	464	88 223	25 023	4 837
1981	1 757	1 557	226	4 697	18 152	491	91 733	25 536	4 780
1982	1 790	1 640	235	5 072	18 188	513	101 531	25 940	4 685
1983	1 681	1 897	244	5 327	17 479	519	109 343	27 262	4 756
1984	1 803	1 937	252	5 667	16 902	521	116 016	26 698	4 946
1985	1 826	2 361	259	5 412	17 732	521	123 674	24 913	4 846
1986	1 859	2 264	266	5 044	18 262	521	126 933	26 529	4 603
1987	1 812	2 208	277	5 079	17 970	521	130 135	29 021	4 005
1988	1 845	2 551	289	5 089	17 646	521	135 593	29 585	4 086
1989	1 913	2 698	290	5 277	17 542	526	139 663	30 064	4 261
1990	1 982	2 537	294	5 394	16 330	530	143 000	29 593	4 500
1991	1 970	2 801	278	5 523	16 330	533	138 424	28 202	4 775
1992	1 844	2 868	302	5 667	16 297	532	142 992	26 764	4 617
1993	1 850	2 816	311	5 610	16 265	511	145 280	30 350	4 728
1994	1 972	2 971	294	5 301	16 590	506	151 052	30 835	4 903
1995	2 075	2 983	320	5 514	17 768	489	158 065	32 747	5 148
1996	1 919	3 075	316	5 751	19 136	464	165 950	36 219	5 333
1997	2 067	3 204	330	5 716	20 227	461	175 073	37 921	5 637
1998	2 147	3 451	333	5 928	21 198	461	185 115	37 389	5 835
1999	2 225	3 531	340	5 750	21 537	472	196 044	39 633	4 845
2000	2 265	3 566	336	6 221	21 042	475	205 845	41 774	4 753
2001	2 287	3 869	342	6 402	21 063	484	215 109	44 990	4 867

Table 6b. **GDP Levels in 57 African Countries, 1950-2001**
(million 1990 international Geary-Khamis dollars)

	Gambia	Ghana	Guinea	Guinea Bissau	Kenya	Lesotho	Liberia	Madagascar
1950	165	5 943	784	166	3 982	258	869	4 394
1951	174	6 163	831	176	4 851	273	919	4 557
1952	180	6 050	857	187	4 313	281	947	4 724
1953	187	6 888	889	200	4 205	292	984	4 895
1954	197	7 755	941	240	4 695	308	1 039	5 075
1955	203	7 256	972	230	5 050	318	1 073	5 264
1956	211	7 684	1 009	262	5 329	331	1 113	5 457
1957	219	7 933	1 045	279	5 504	343	1 155	5 660
1958	225	7 803	1 077	288	5 563	356	1 188	5 870
1959	238	8 932	1 139	292	5 699	366	1 257	6 086
1960	254	9 591	1 187	309	5 918	393	1 297	6 169
1961	296	9 930	1 265	331	5 775	400	1 328	6 297
1962	292	10 412	1 359	353	6 085	462	1 345	6 442
1963	294	10 774	1 286	369	6 392	511	1 377	6 380
1964	314	11 006	1 370	392	7 013	553	1 447	6 635
1965	348	11 154	1 464	414	7 093	565	1 472	6 604
1966	406	11 166	1 496	436	8 005	562	1 751	6 741
1967	421	11 368	1 543	463	8 419	624	1 740	7 114
1968	427	11 529	1 590	485	9 028	622	1 823	7 597
1969	473	11 939	1 637	513	9 590	631	1 955	7 883
1970	426	12 515	1 694	540	10 291	645	2 083	8 296
1971	475	13 514	1 747	519	10 944	585	2 186	8 621
1972	509	13 109	1 783	552	11 509	697	2 269	8 511
1973	533	13 484	1 861	558	12 107	878	2 212	8 292
1974	638	14 411	1 992	584	12 704	931	2 375	8 459
1975	598	12 616	2 076	630	12 652	855	2 017	8 564
1976	668	12 171	2 280	661	13 162	996	2 096	8 300
1977	701	12 450	2 332	614	14 369	1 172	2 079	8 498
1978	665	13 508	2 394	694	15 663	1 351	2 161	8 274
1979	773	13 163	2 400	708	16 252	1 262	2 257	9 087
1980	697	12 747	2 484	595	17 160	1 351	2 149	9 157
1981	691	12 765	2 499	703	17 555	1 365	2 197	8 366
1982	779	11 879	2 546	745	18 614	1 414	2 134	8 213
1983	685	11 339	2 578	685	18 729	1 292	2 119	8 278
1984	665	12 319	2 651	713	19 056	1 402	2 100	7 975
1985	609	12 943	2 713	752	19 876	1 450	2 071	8 155
1986	641	13 621	2 782	747	21 302	1 479	2 131	8 213
1987	676	14 274	2 870	735	22 569	1 555	2 189	8 393
1988	747	15 077	3 043	765	23 927	1 754	2 189	8 525
1989	799	15 843	3 168	769	25 018	1 947	2 216	8 867
1990	833	16 372	3 304	794	26 093	2 033	2 245	9 210
1991	851	17 240	3 383	834	26 458	2 116	2 281	8 630
1992	889	17 912	3 502	844	26 247	2 214	2 321	8 733
1993	943	18 808	3 673	861	26 352	2 296	2 374	8 917
1994	979	19 429	3 820	889	27 064	2 287	2 426	8 917
1995	945	20 206	3 999	928	28 254	2 575	2 492	9 069
1996	1 003	21 135	4 203	970	29 441	2 819	2 541	9 259
1997	1 052	22 023	4 413	1 024	30 059	2 954	2 555	9 602
1998	1 089	23 058	4 625	736	30 540	2 866	2 580	9 976
1999	1 159	24 073	4 838	795	30 937	2 934	2 623	10 445
2000	1 224	24 963	4 939	870	30 906	3 037	2 667	10 946
2001	1 291	26 012	5 117	872	31 277	3 158	2 712	11 680

Table 6b. GDP Levels in 57 African Countries, 1950-2001
(million 1990 international Geary-Khamis dollars)

	Malawi	Mali	Mauritania	Mauritius	Morocco	Mozambique	Namibia	Niger	Nigeria
1950	913	1 685	467	1 198	13 598	7 084	1 002	2 018	23 933
1951	951	1 747	484	1 267	14 046	7 332	1 033	2 093	25 728
1952	990	1 811	502	1 306	14 509	7 594	1 065	2 170	27 571
1953	1 031	1 879	520	1 356	14 987	7 857	1 106	2 248	28 217
1954	1 074	1 946	539	1 433	15 481	8 041	1 168	2 331	30 299
1955	1 093	2 018	559	1 479	15 991	8 537	1 206	2 418	31 089
1956	1 184	2 093	580	1 535	16 093	8 579	1 251	2 507	30 371
1957	1 233	2 170	601	1 594	16 195	8 770	1 299	2 600	31 615
1958	1 279	2 249	623	1 638	16 299	9 188	1 335	2 697	31 256
1959	1 324	2 333	647	1 733	16 402	9 684	1 412	2 797	32 621
1960	1 360	2 399	698	1 842	16 507	9 918	1 545	2 977	34 081
1961	1 428	2 414	817	2 261	17 085	10 202	1 562	3 100	35 229
1962	1 428	2 428	799	2 278	17 684	10 903	1 783	3 427	37 240
1963	1 403	2 591	750	2 595	18 303	10 513	1 961	3 766	40 734
1964	1 369	2 714	974	2 417	18 944	10 967	2 279	3 776	42 481
1965	1 554	2 753	1 109	2 495	19 608	11 215	2 433	4 061	45 353
1966	1 714	2 869	1 115	2 406	20 700	11 576	2 526	4 010	43 893
1967	1 889	2 964	1 154	2 510	21 853	12 369	2 424	4 029	37 072
1968	1 868	3 075	1 256	2 338	23 071	13 758	2 444	4 061	36 665
1969	1 988	3 060	1 237	2 453	24 356	15 394	2 529	3 940	46 502
1970	2 017	3 248	1 365	2 443	25 713	16 216	2 540	4 061	60 814
1971	2 307	3 361	1 378	2 563	27 154	17 321	2 627	4 291	67 970
1972	2 543	3 535	1 396	2 817	27 807	17 881	2 783	4 069	70 530
1973	2 756	3 449	1 309	3 169	28 800	18 894	2 895	3 377	76 585
1974	2 955	3 365	1 443	3 511	30 351	17 463	3 021	3 671	85 465
1975	3 117	3 831	1 351	3 514	32 385	14 643	3 052	3 570	82 904
1976	3 269	4 352	1 459	4 086	35 950	13 942	3 221	3 595	91 927
1977	3 437	4 648	1 440	4 353	37 711	14 055	3 424	3 873	95 277
1978	3 747	4 524	1 434	4 520	38 808	14 162	3 651	4 394	89 653
1979	3 919	5 612	1 500	4 679	40 584	14 367	3 806	4 709	95 852
1980	3 945	4 953	1 560	4 208	44 278	14 771	3 986	4 937	97 646
1981	3 746	4 787	1 619	4 455	43 054	15 040	4 110	4 995	89 820
1982	3 783	4 512	1 586	4 701	47 203	14 629	4 164	4 935	89 007
1983	3 945	4 711	1 663	4 719	46 930	13 581	4 057	4 844	83 000
1984	4 123	4 918	1 543	4 940	48 894	13 212	4 006	4 025	79 290
1985	4 446	5 029	1 587	5 285	51 955	12 022	4 023	4 095	86 302
1986	4 463	5 348	1 676	5 817	56 023	12 199	4 147	4 283	87 930
1987	4 572	5 449	1 727	6 408	54 762	12 639	4 268	4 130	87 284
1988	4 690	5 440	1 792	6 844	60 367	13 361	4 368	4 362	95 947
1989	4 923	5 995	1 852	7 145	61 748	13 900	4 738	4 368	102 146
1990	5 146	6 040	1 825	7 652	64 082	14 105	4 619	4 289	107 459
1991	5 594	5 986	1 872	8 142	68 504	14 796	4 882	4 396	113 907
1992	5 185	6 488	1 904	8 533	65 764	13 598	5 346	4 110	116 868
1993	5 688	6 333	2 009	9 104	65 106	14 781	5 239	4 168	119 439
1994	5 102	6 498	2 101	9 505	71 877	15 890	5 595	4 335	118 700
1995	5 954	6 952	2 198	9 837	67 133	16 573	5 830	4 447	121 809
1996	6 389	7 251	2 319	10 349	75 323	17 749	6 005	4 599	129 605
1997	6 632	7 737	2 393	10 970	73 566	19 720	6 257	4 727	133 363
1998	6 850	8 116	2 482	11 628	79 339	22 204	6 470	5 219	135 764
1999	7 124	8 660	2 583	12 244	79 259	23 870	6 703	5 188	137 122
2000	7 388	8 981	2 713	12 563	80 052	24 252	6 931	5 115	143 018
2001	7 499	9 115	2 837	13 467	85 255	27 623	7 104	5 504	147 022

Table 6b. **GDP Levels in 57 African Countries, 1950-2001**
(million 1990 international Geary-Khamis dollars)

	Reunion	Rwanda	Senegal	Seychelles	Sierra Leone	Somalia	South Africa	Sudan	Swaziland
1950	485	1 334	3 341	63	1 370	2 576	34 465	6 609	200
1951	512	1 410	3 464	67	1 448	2 724	36 085	6 926	211
1952	528	1 454	3 591	69	1 493	2 810	37 360	7 270	218
1953	549	1 510	3 721	71	1 550	2 915	39 117	7 613	226
1954	580	1 596	3 858	75	1 638	3 083	41 427	7 983	239
1955	598	1 646	4 002	78	1 696	3 183	43 494	8 373	247
1956	621	1 709	4 149	81	1 760	3 301	45 907	9 259	256
1957	645	1 773	4 303	84	1 826	3 425	47 665	9 133	266
1958	663	1 824	4 463	86	1 878	3 520	48 664	9 510	273
1959	701	1 929	4 627	91	1 986	3 726	50 835	10 640	289
1960	756	1 989	4 724	99	2 050	3 775	52 972	10 838	329
1961	796	1 904	4 937	94	2 087	3 956	55 247	10 838	371
1962	859	2 120	5 101	101	2 182	4 130	58 349	11 592	449
1963	925	1 912	5 298	111	2 219	4 290	62 622	11 261	475
1964	1 004	1 673	5 452	116	2 245	3 826	66 827	11 142	545
1965	1 101	1 790	5 656	116	2 405	3 572	70 825	11 896	630
1966	1 170	1 916	5 816	119	2 559	4 079	73 892	11 717	657
1967	1 256	2 051	5 746	119	2 542	4 313	78 959	11 354	719
1968	1 347	2 193	6 107	129	2 791	4 388	82 371	12 048	686
1969	1 477	2 435	5 709	129	3 045	3 840	87 437	12 781	715
1970	1 540	2 702	6 197	139	3 149	4 174	91 986	12 246	926
1971	1 575	2 734	6 187	162	3 120	4 282	96 501	13 092	942
1972	1 757	2 742	6 588	172	3 086	4 717	98 362	12 814	1 057
1973	1 771	2 826	6 217	187	3 180	4 625	102 498	11 783	1 114
1974	1 876	2 959	6 478	190	3 309	3 682	108 254	12 966	1 238
1975	1 838	3 510	6 965	197	3 408	4 960	110 253	14 612	1 282
1976	1 636	3 450	7 587	217	3 305	4 944	112 941	17 302	1 324
1977	1 603	3 629	7 383	234	3 353	6 185	112 734	19 932	1 364
1978	1 730	3 985	7 092	250	3 363	6 500	116 077	19 621	1 399
1979	1 815	4 360	7 590	292	3 554	6 270	120 627	17 586	1 424
1980	1 869	4 892	7 339	284	3 721	6 005	128 416	17 758	1 466
1981	1 913	5 210	7 283	265	3 951	6 482	135 171	18 128	1 566
1982	2 057	5 646	8 388	260	4 019	6 716	134 619	20 421	1 656
1983	2 157	5 984	8 602	255	3 961	6 098	132 172	20 844	1 664
1984	2 181	5 730	8 205	265	4 014	6 306	138 893	19 800	1 698
1985	2 205	5 982	8 515	290	3 904	6 816	137 239	18 557	1 804
1986	2 230	6 309	8 926	297	3 767	7 056	137 307	19 291	1 872
1987	2 248	6 261	9 290	311	3 965	7 409	140 099	19 720	2 031
1988	2 383	6 046	9 765	325	4 072	7 359	145 855	19 952	1 984
1989	2 454	6 168	9 598	343	4 164	7 349	148 888	21 518	2 111
1990	2 694	6 125	10 032	366	4 335	7 231	147 509	19 793	2 154
1991	2 863	5 862	9 992	376	3 988	6 505	146 034	21 179	2 208
1992	2 863	6 248	10 212	402	3 605	5 536	142 967	22 280	2 237
1993	2 863	5 730	9 987	428	3 609	5 536	144 683	22 904	2 310
1994	2 863	2 854	10 277	418	3 735	5 701	149 313	23 362	2 389
1995	2 863	3 858	10 811	420	3 362	5 867	153 942	24 063	2 479
1996	3 012	4 348	11 362	462	2 528	6 048	160 561	25 242	2 576
1997	3 136	4 948	11 930	518	2 083	6 044	164 786	27 766	2 674
1998	3 174	5 388	12 611	548	2 066	6 044	166 054	29 432	2 759
1999	3 240	5 798	13 254	532	1 899	6 151	169 541	31 699	2 856
2000	3 308	6 146	14 022	504	1 971	6 260	175 305	34 773	2 919
2001	3 377	6 557	14 808	463	2 078	6 371	179 162	36 616	2 966

Table 6b. **GDP Levels in 57 African Countries, 1950-2001**
(million 1990 international Geary-Khamis dollars)

	Tanzania	Togo	Tunisia	Uganda	Zaire	Zambia	Zimbabwe	6 Country Total	57 Country Total
1950	3 362	673	3 920	3 793	7 731	1 687	2 000	1 014	203 131
1951	3 786	698	3 963	3 641	8 635	1 795	2 130	1 113	212 653
1952	3 863	723	4 450	3 868	9 424	1 910	2 232	1 186	220 780
1953	3 725	749	4 618	4 039	9 957	2 032	2 424	1 210	228 858
1954	4 028	777	4 720	3 982	10 560	2 161	2 554	1 218	239 781
1955	4 125	806	4 477	4 244	10 970	2 111	2 756	1 476	248 054
1956	4 176	836	4 775	4 479	11 712	2 362	3 148	1 763	258 153
1957	4 277	867	4 579	4 673	12 083	2 465	3 368	1 838	267 612
1958	4 314	899	5 175	4 703	11 735	2 401	3 412	2 014	273 683
1959	4 525	932	4 959	4 942	12 145	2 902	3 596	2 164	288 734
1960	4 710	1 016	5 571	5 177	12 423	3 123	3 762	2 743	301 578
1961	4 657	1 085	6 053	5 124	11 070	3 130	3 956	3 010	308 136
1962	5 080	1 125	5 912	5 332	13 420	3 096	4 016	3 919	320 322
1963	5 400	1 181	6 806	5 943	14 124	3 164	3 976	5 208	343 186
1964	5 695	1 351	7 100	6 394	13 776	3 586	4 326	7 253	361 570
1965	5 901	1 535	7 547	6 535	13 915	4 239	4 608	9 222	381 330
1966	6 657	1 676	7 735	6 941	14 858	4 007	4 678	10 861	392 226
1967	6 926	1 769	7 684	7 312	14 712	4 318	5 068	12 066	400 067
1968	7 282	1 859	8 491	7 498	15 345	4 379	5 168	15 971	420 309
1969	7 417	2 060	8 793	8 325	16 776	4 355	5 812	17 968	453 131
1970	7 847	2 112	9 315	8 450	16 737	4 562	7 072	18 805	490 102
1971	8 177	2 262	10 302	8 700	17 804	4 561	7 692	17 710	512 138
1972	8 725	2 340	12 129	8 757	17 827	4 979	8 342	15 777	530 848
1973	9 007	2 245	12 051	8 704	19 373	4 930	8 594	15 959	549 993
1974	9 216	2 340	13 019	8 719	20 038	5 332	8 810	13 739	575 500
1975	9 693	2 326	13 952	8 541	19 041	5 124	8 890	14 736	582 627
1976	10 386	2 315	15 054	8 606	17 951	5 426	8 816	18 023	621 584
1977	10 678	2 441	15 567	8 738	18 043	5 163	8 108	19 518	647 589
1978	10 987	2 689	16 571	8 260	17 023	5 195	8 338	20 212	663 511
1979	11 122	2 851	17 657	7 350	17 000	5 037	8 338	22 877	694 654
1980	11 216	2 721	18 966	7 100	17 355	5 190	9 288	23 085	725 905
1981	11 092	2 551	20 013	7 373	17 765	5 509	10 454	18 863	733 452
1982	11 236	2 453	19 915	7 980	17 680	5 354	10 726	18 333	756 255
1983	11 186	2 320	20 848	8 571	17 927	5 249	10 896	18 156	761 138
1984	11 465	2 389	22 040	7 843	18 925	5 231	10 688	16 897	777 297
1985	11 438	2 502	23 279	7 999	19 010	5 317	11 430	15 442	801 420
1986	11 811	2 580	22 918	8 025	19 907	5 354	11 732	14 216	818 732
1987	12 413	2 616	24 451	8 533	20 440	5 497	11 588	13 837	831 716
1988	12 937	2 733	24 478	9 148	20 556	5 841	12 672	13 980	865 804
1989	13 371	2 834	25 384	9 815	20 417	5 900	13 498	14 112	892 376
1990	13 852	2 805	27 387	10 206	19 922	6 432	13 766	13 917	904 898
1991	14 143	2 785	28 455	10 308	18 249	6 432	14 523	13 183	911 693
1992	14 228	2 674	30 675	10 628	16 332	6 323	13 216	12 748	912 598
1993	14 398	2 235	31 349	11 520	14 128	6 753	13 388	12 272	921 183
1994	14 628	2 626	32 352	12 257	13 577	5 855	14 165	12 182	941 178
1995	15 155	2 807	33 129	13 716	13 672	5 708	14 193	12 276	969 734
1996	15 837	3 080	35 481	14 895	13 536	6 080	15 669	12 915	1 024 994
1997	15 685	2 928	37 397	15 655	12 777	6 286	16 092	14 302	1 060 213
1998	16 266	2 867	39 192	16 391	12 552	6 167	16 559	14 321	1 099 966
1999	16 835	2 950	41 582	17 637	12 032	6 302	16 443	15 379	1 136 130
2000	17 694	2 894	43 537	18 518	11 286	6 529	15 604	16 413	1 175 890
2001	18 685	2 971	45 714	19 555	10 789	6 849	14 278	18 257	1 222 577

Table 6b. GDP Levels in 57 African Countries, 1950-2001
(million 1990 international Geary-Khamis dollars)

	Equatorial Guinea	Libya	SãoTomé & Principe	Mayotte + St. Helena + W. Sahara	6 Country Total
1950	114	824	49	27	1 014
1951	120	915	49	29	1 113
1952	124	982	49	31	1 186
1953	129	998	49	34	1 210
1954	136	994	51	37	1 218
1955	140	1 251	46	39	1 476
1956	146	1 525	49	43	1 763
1957	151	1 592	49	46	1 838
1958	156	1 755	54	49	2 014
1959	165	1 897	49	53	2 164
1960	182	2 448	55	58	2 743
1961	200	2 688	60	62	3 010
1962	221	3 566	65	67	3 919
1963	252	4 814	70	72	5 208
1964	288	6 812	75	78	7 253
1965	325	8 733	80	84	9 222
1966	339	10 345	86	91	10 861
1967	362	11 515	91	98	12 066
1968	375	15 395	96	105	15 971
1969	364	17 389	101	114	17 968
1970	354	18 222	106	123	18 805
1971	325	17 142	111	132	17 710
1972	284	15 241	109	143	15 777
1973	289	15 410	106	154	15 959
1974	282	13 186	108	163	13 739
1975	276	14 172	116	172	14 736
1976	277	17 438	126	182	18 023
1977	281	18 904	140	193	19 518
1978	306	19 553	149	204	20 212
1979	341	22 155	166	215	22 877
1980	378	22 290	189	228	23 085
1981	387	18 098	137	241	18 863
1982	403	17 502	173	255	18 333
1983	418	17 311	158	269	18 156
1984	528	15 939	145	285	16 897
1985	455	14 529	157	301	15 442
1986	474	13 265	159	318	14 216
1987	502	12 842	156	337	13 837
1988	538	12 927	159	356	13 980
1989	560	13 014	162	376	14 112
1990	576	12 780	166	395	13 917
1991	603	12 013	166	401	13 183
1992	668	11 508	167	405	12 748
1993	710	10 979	169	414	12 272
1994	746	10 836	173	427	12 182
1995	852	10 804	176	444	12 276
1996	1 100	11 160	179	476	12 915
1997	1 884	11 741	181	496	14 302
1998	2 298	11 318	185	520	14 321
1999	3 250	11 397	190	542	15 379
2000	3 773	11 879	196	565	16 413
2001	5 490	11 970	204	593	18 257

Per Capita GDP in Africa

Table 6c. **Per Capita GDP in 57 African Countries, 1950-2001**
(1990 international Geary-Khamis dollars)

	Algeria	Angola	Benin	Botswana	Burkina Faso	Burundi	Cameroon	Cape Verde
1950	1 365	1 052	1 084	349	474	360	671	450
1951	1 347	1 076	1 063	355	487	374	687	455
1952	1 376	1 101	1 043	359	500	379	704	461
1953	1 369	1 126	994	366	512	388	720	467
1954	1 437	1 079	1 002	372	526	402	737	460
1955	1 445	1 148	982	377	539	408	754	463
1956	1 553	1 110	962	383	554	416	771	469
1957	1 693	1 197	941	388	568	425	788	453
1958	1 719	1 241	956	392	583	429	805	449
1959	1 994	1 225	970	399	598	446	822	486
1960	2 088	1 253	978	403	609	444	832	508
1961	1 799	1 396	987	410	626	373	829	525
1962	1 433	1 335	932	415	657	398	840	539
1963	1 768	1 380	952	422	640	408	857	553
1964	1 806	1 510	993	430	646	421	872	564
1965	1 870	1 596	1 020	437	662	426	874	575
1966	1 725	1 660	1 032	473	655	434	898	585
1967	1 824	1 727	1 016	513	701	463	905	594
1968	1 977	1 672	1 029	557	711	448	946	602
1969	2 105	1 691	1 033	601	713	435	973	611
1970	2 249	1 768	1 027	647	702	542	982	619
1971	2 000	1 729	1 006	747	717	572	990	566
1972	2 350	1 713	1 065	954	732	520	1 011	536
1973	2 357	1 791	1 061	1 119	680	556	1 003	529
1974	2 428	1 713	955	1 293	654	543	1 024	512
1975	2 522	1 074	969	1 215	613	537	1 052	525
1976	2 608	955	983	1 370	594	568	1 044	520
1977	2 759	941	1 010	1 344	622	624	1 070	518
1978	3 016	961	1 013	1 519	679	602	1 095	567
1979	3 186	959	1 063	1 591	670	599	1 121	622
1980	3 143	962	1 133	1 738	665	627	1 194	841
1981	3 119	924	1 164	1 827	678	683	1 354	904
1982	3 212	862	1 254	1 891	676	659	1 421	916
1983	3 269	819	1 165	2 110	652	652	1 477	988
1984	3 340	810	1 220	2 259	645	632	1 545	1 009
1985	3 404	799	1 273	2 336	711	685	1 632	1 079
1986	3 272	713	1 263	2 421	802	691	1 695	1 092
1987	3 161	780	1 205	2 538	769	697	1 562	1 148
1988	3 015	877	1 203	2 833	809	699	1 448	1 164
1989	3 039	879	1 140	3 097	774	686	1 285	1 206
1990	2 918	895	1 147	3 183	742	734	1 232	1 231
1991	2 814	880	1 162	3 245	790	755	1 153	797
1992	2 793	848	1 170	3 258	784	749	1 089	639
1993	2 671	603	1 172	3 244	754	690	1 028	1 182
1994	2 590	597	1 185	3 282	743	645	978	1 241
1995	2 632	636	1 200	3 359	754	639	988	1 318
1996	2 677	690	1 226	3 485	787	588	1 014	1 387
1997	2 654	736	1 255	3 659	802	586	1 042	1 475
1998	2 737	771	1 271	3 824	829	605	1 070	1 565
1999	2 773	782	1 290	4 026	857	587	1 093	1 681
2000	2 792	789	1 323	4 348	853	575	1 115	1 777
2001	2 813	797	1 347	4 552	877	576	1 149	1 812

Table 6c. **Per Capita GDP in 57 African Countries, 1950-2001**
(1990 international Geary-Khamis dollars)

	Central African Rep.	Chad	Comoros	Congo	Côte d'Ivoire	Djibouti	Egypt	Eritrea & Ethiopia	Gabon
1950	772	476	560	1 289	1 041	1 500	910	390	3 108
1951	790	486	581	1 315	1 058	1 546	905	394	3 204
1952	809	497	587	1 340	1 075	1 554	900	399	3 302
1953	827	507	598	1 364	1 092	1 575	894	414	3 401
1954	845	518	619	1 388	1 110	1 622	889	407	3 504
1955	864	529	625	1 412	1 127	1 632	885	421	3 611
1956	881	540	635	1 436	1 144	1 651	905	427	3 718
1957	899	552	645	1 459	1 162	1 668	925	416	3 827
1958	917	563	649	1 482	1 179	1 665	947	422	3 939
1959	934	574	671	1 506	1 191	1 711	969	425	4 052
1960	925	569	712	1 523	1 256	1 771	991	439	4 184
1961	943	566	703	1 539	1 328	1 783	1 031	451	4 639
1962	901	586	749	1 553	1 339	1 759	1 074	460	4 725
1963	881	567	887	1 569	1 499	1 774	1 120	511	4 832
1964	878	542	932	1 584	1 697	1 758	1 166	525	4 851
1965	866	533	913	1 599	1 592	1 754	1 213	545	4 860
1966	844	512	984	1 642	1 642	1 761	1 192	554	5 003
1967	860	505	999	1 688	1 589	1 758	1 151	566	5 130
1968	851	491	973	1 732	1 749	1 746	1 146	563	5 176
1969	877	514	963	1 779	1 738	1 742	1 201	571	5 518
1970	896	513	1 009	1 825	1 833	2 069	1 254	591	5 869
1971	851	511	1 154	1 922	1 831	2 142	1 283	603	6 332
1972	815	465	1 032	2 025	1 841	2 150	1 284	620	6 892
1973	837	433	889	2 132	1 899	2 185	1 294	626	7 286
1974	797	481	1 055	2 242	1 874	2 080	1 317	618	9 541
1975	792	550	804	2 342	1 800	2 065	1 421	605	9 399
1976	811	529	692	2 270	1 942	2 154	1 606	606	12 342
1977	860	478	624	2 008	1 960	1 794	1 767	608	9 531
1978	858	464	627	1 904	2 078	1 724	1 844	591	6 723
1979	794	361	624	2 115	2 042	1 687	1 930	622	6 666
1980	771	339	643	2 388	2 123	1 661	2 069	642	6 779
1981	767	335	664	2 778	2 121	1 674	2 076	646	6 543
1982	765	336	675	2 890	2 052	1 676	2 223	641	6 213
1983	705	374	683	2 923	1 903	1 643	2 322	656	6 107
1984	736	378	688	2 981	1 776	1 802	2 390	624	6 143
1985	726	457	691	2 768	1 798	1 758	2 471	573	5 818
1986	727	426	691	2 509	1 787	1 717	2 460	597	5 357
1987	697	401	701	2 458	1 698	1 677	2 465	633	4 546
1988	695	449	712	2 397	1 611	1 597	2 510	624	4 541
1989	701	462	694	2 420	1 544	1 502	2 527	611	4 636
1990	707	421	685	2 408	1 372	1 448	2 522	581	4 795
1991	683	449	630	2 403	1 315	1 420	2 381	530	4 969
1992	622	445	664	2 405	1 276	1 384	2 407	485	4 678
1993	606	422	664	2 323	1 234	1 299	2 394	537	4 664
1994	628	430	610	2 143	1 214	1 257	2 437	532	4 708
1995	648	418	644	2 177	1 259	1 195	2 496	550	4 811
1996	588	417	617	2 220	1 319	1 122	2 565	593	4 851
1997	622	421	625	2 159	1 364	1 103	2 647	606	4 992
1998	635	438	612	2 193	1 402	1 092	2 738	584	5 031
1999	646	434	606	2 085	1 392	1 107	2 838	605	4 068
2000	647	424	581	2 214	1 326	1 103	2 920	624	3 887
2001	642	445	574	2 239	1 297	1 106	2 992	660	3 877

Table 6c. **Per Capita GDP in 57 African Countries, 1950-2001**
(1990 international Geary-Khamis dollars)

	Gambia	Ghana	Guinea	Guinea Bissau	Kenya	Lesotho	Liberia	Madagascar
1950	607	1 122	303	289	651	355	1 055	951
1951	627	1 134	317	306	771	370	1 090	972
1952	632	1 084	322	323	667	375	1 097	992
1953	640	1 202	329	342	633	384	1 113	1 012
1954	660	1 317	343	408	687	399	1 147	1 032
1955	664	1 200	349	389	718	405	1 156	1 052
1956	671	1 236	357	439	736	413	1 170	1 072
1957	678	1 241	363	465	738	422	1 183	1 092
1958	678	1 187	368	476	725	430	1 187	1 112
1959	697	1 321	383	478	720	435	1 223	1 132
1960	722	1 378	392	501	726	458	1 230	1 125
1961	815	1 388	410	532	686	457	1 226	1 126
1962	781	1 416	433	562	701	517	1 209	1 129
1963	762	1 424	402	583	714	560	1 204	1 096
1964	787	1 414	420	642	758	593	1 231	1 116
1965	846	1 393	441	685	743	593	1 218	1 088
1966	955	1 354	442	728	812	577	1 408	1 087
1967	957	1 339	447	771	826	626	1 360	1 123
1968	939	1 318	452	794	857	610	1 384	1 174
1969	1 007	1 325	456	833	881	605	1 442	1 192
1970	879	1 424	463	872	913	604	1 492	1 226
1971	949	1 491	468	833	937	535	1 519	1 246
1972	985	1 401	468	883	949	624	1 530	1 202
1973	997	1 397	478	882	961	769	1 447	1 144
1974	1 157	1 455	502	912	971	797	1 508	1 139
1975	1 050	1 247	512	925	929	715	1 242	1 126
1976	1 134	1 178	551	902	929	814	1 252	1 063
1977	1 152	1 181	552	823	973	936	1 204	1 061
1978	1 058	1 260	555	915	1 018	1 054	1 214	1 007
1979	1 191	1 210	544	918	1 013	962	1 230	1 076
1980	1 039	1 157	551	754	1 028	1 005	1 136	1 055
1981	997	1 142	542	871	1 011	991	1 126	938
1982	1 088	1 042	541	902	1 031	1 001	1 061	895
1983	926	933	535	810	998	893	1 022	878
1984	867	960	525	824	977	944	982	822
1985	765	978	509	849	982	953	939	817
1986	776	989	505	824	1 014	949	937	800
1987	787	1 007	508	793	1 037	974	934	794
1988	838	1 035	525	805	1 063	1 075	905	784
1989	863	1 058	532	790	1 077	1 170	889	792
1990	866	1 063	526	797	1 090	1 201	1 025	799
1991	853	1 089	503	818	1 072	1 232	1 206	728
1992	858	1 100	501	803	1 028	1 272	1 169	715
1993	877	1 121	511	795	1 003	1 304	1 151	709
1994	878	1 125	514	797	1 008	1 286	1 179	689
1995	818	1 144	521	812	1 029	1 435	1 259	680
1996	838	1 171	529	832	1 049	1 560	1 255	674
1997	849	1 196	548	858	1 048	1 623	1 113	678
1998	850	1 227	566	602	1 044	1 566	972	683
1999	876	1 256	574	636	1 038	1 595	882	694
2000	895	1 280	572	681	1 020	1 645	847	706
2001	915	1 311	587	668	1 016	1 705	846	731

Table 6c. **Per Capita GDP in 57 African Countries, 1950-2001**
(1990 international Geary-Khamis dollars)

	Malawi	Mali	Mauritania	Mauritius	Morocco	Mozambique	Namibia	Niger	Nigeria
1950	324	457	464	2 490	1 455	1 133	2 160	813	753
1951	332	465	477	2 540	1 458	1 155	2 176	825	793
1952	339	472	490	2 528	1 460	1 178	2 191	835	832
1953	347	480	504	2 530	1 468	1 199	2 223	846	835
1954	355	488	517	2 587	1 476	1 207	2 292	856	875
1955	354	496	531	2 587	1 483	1 259	2 310	867	877
1956	376	504	545	2 594	1 451	1 242	2 339	877	836
1957	383	513	558	2 613	1 420	1 246	2 370	887	850
1958	388	521	572	2 610	1 389	1 280	2 376	897	821
1959	393	530	586	2 685	1 358	1 323	2 451	907	837
1960	394	535	625	2 777	1 329	1 327	2 616	940	854
1961	404	528	722	3 319	1 341	1 337	2 579	953	862
1962	393	520	697	3 249	1 354	1 400	2 869	1 025	889
1963	376	544	645	3 629	1 367	1 321	3 076	1 096	950
1964	359	558	827	3 283	1 381	1 349	3 486	1 069	967
1965	397	555	928	3 302	1 394	1 351	3 626	1 118	1 007
1966	426	566	920	3 108	1 436	1 364	3 668	1 074	951
1967	456	572	938	3 180	1 480	1 425	3 430	1 049	784
1968	438	581	1 006	2 907	1 524	1 549	3 369	1 028	756
1969	454	566	975	3 006	1 570	1 693	3 396	969	934
1970	449	588	1 059	2 945	1 616	1 743	3 321	971	1 190
1971	501	595	1 051	3 047	1 665	1 816	3 342	997	1 295
1972	537	612	1 047	3 309	1 669	1 823	3 443	919	1 308
1973	567	584	966	3 680	1 694	1 873	3 486	741	1 382
1974	587	556	1 046	4 020	1 751	1 684	3 539	782	1 497
1975	592	619	962	3 969	1 831	1 404	3 473	738	1 407
1976	597	687	1 020	4 551	1 992	1 295	3 559	721	1 511
1977	610	724	988	4 768	2 050	1 263	3 712	754	1 517
1978	647	694	965	4 863	2 069	1 235	3 906	830	1 380
1979	658	848	989	4 943	2 122	1 215	3 986	863	1 426
1980	644	736	1 006	4 367	2 272	1 220	4 089	877	1 402
1981	594	699	1 021	4 550	2 169	1 216	4 159	860	1 246
1982	582	647	978	4 738	2 337	1 162	4 120	824	1 194
1983	589	663	1 001	4 708	2 263	1 063	3 884	783	1 094
1984	597	678	906	4 882	2 296	1 022	3 710	630	1 023
1985	624	679	908	5 173	2 377	920	3 606	622	1 080
1986	604	707	935	5 635	2 499	928	3 593	630	1 073
1987	585	704	938	6 146	2 382	981	3 569	589	1 033
1988	563	690	947	6 504	2 563	1 067	3 478	603	1 101
1989	559	745	956	6 725	2 560	1 115	3 539	588	1 137
1990	558	734	920	7 128	2 596	1 115	3 278	562	1 161
1991	586	712	917	7 505	2 714	1 146	3 366	560	1 194
1992	525	758	898	7 784	2 549	1 034	3 586	509	1 189
1993	569	726	911	8 221	2 471	1 084	3 419	502	1 180
1994	522	729	922	8 502	2 672	1 084	3 553	507	1 138
1995	617	759	939	8 716	2 446	1 068	3 604	504	1 134
1996	648	767	971	9 082	2 691	1 116	3 615	506	1 172
1997	656	794	979	9 541	2 579	1 218	3 671	506	1 172
1998	661	807	987	10 027	2 730	1 350	3 705	543	1 160
1999	671	836	997	10 471	2 678	1 429	3 750	525	1 139
2000	679	842	1 017	10 652	2 658	1 432	3 795	503	1 156
2001	674	830	1 033	11 318	2 782	1 611	3 813	526	1 157

Table 6c. **Per Capita GDP in 57 African Countries, 1950-2001**
(1990 international Geary-Khamis dollars)

	Reunion	Rwanda	Senegal	Seychelles	Sierra Leone	Somalia	South Africa	Sudan	Swaziland
1950	1 989	547	1 259	1 912	656	1 057	2 535	821	721
1951	2 044	567	1 281	2 019	685	1 098	2 591	837	745
1952	2 051	574	1 303	2 050	697	1 112	2 619	855	751
1953	2 067	584	1 324	2 084	714	1 132	2 675	871	762
1954	2 113	604	1 346	2 174	744	1 175	2 763	889	787
1955	2 091	610	1 367	2 164	760	1 191	2 830	907	793
1956	2 098	620	1 388	2 143	777	1 211	2 914	976	803
1957	2 089	628	1 409	2 186	795	1 232	2 951	936	814
1958	2 085	631	1 429	2 200	807	1 241	2 939	949	817
1959	2 142	652	1 448	2 254	841	1 287	2 995	1 033	843
1960	2 239	656	1 445	2 367	856	1 277	3 041	1 024	935
1961	2 288	625	1 475	2 176	858	1 311	3 092	996	1 028
1962	2 394	695	1 487	2 306	884	1 341	3 179	1 037	1 214
1963	2 495	611	1 507	2 458	886	1 364	3 321	980	1 252
1964	2 617	525	1 499	2 488	883	1 191	3 450	944	1 399
1965	2 803	548	1 511	2 435	932	1 088	3 559	984	1 577
1966	2 901	570	1 508	2 434	976	1 216	3 615	947	1 602
1967	3 033	594	1 449	2 381	955	1 258	3 760	893	1 709
1968	3 169	618	1 499	2 522	1 032	1 252	3 819	923	1 588
1969	3 391	666	1 362	2 455	1 109	1 071	3 946	954	1 612
1970	3 463	717	1 435	2 570	1 129	1 138	4 045	888	2 036
1971	3 473	705	1 390	2 910	1 101	1 141	4 135	923	2 015
1972	3 807	687	1 436	3 013	1 072	1 228	4 109	878	2 201
1973	3 774	688	1 315	3 224	1 087	1 176	4 175	780	2 258
1974	3 946	700	1 329	3 203	1 113	914	4 299	833	2 443
1975	3 821	806	1 396	3 251	1 126	1 202	4 271	910	2 462
1976	3 361	766	1 487	3 507	1 072	1 167	4 267	1 044	2 472
1977	3 258	779	1 411	3 691	1 068	1 421	4 155	1 165	2 474
1978	3 480	827	1 322	3 885	1 051	1 390	4 174	1 108	2 462
1979	3 615	876	1 380	4 460	1 089	1 181	4 232	956	2 421
1980	3 686	952	1 301	4 274	1 119	1 037	4 390	931	2 397
1981	3 738	981	1 259	3 914	1 164	1 113	4 503	920	2 481
1982	3 972	1 025	1 415	3 794	1 160	1 152	4 367	1 003	2 548
1983	4 124	1 049	1 414	3 695	1 120	1 016	4 174	958	2 474
1984	4 094	976	1 315	3 799	1 110	1 016	4 271	878	2 437
1985	4 070	993	1 330	4 116	1 056	1 057	4 108	791	2 497
1986	4 045	1 020	1 359	4 163	996	1 053	4 020	798	2 494
1987	4 000	982	1 378	4 335	1 025	1 070	4 015	798	2 607
1988	4 155	918	1 411	4 483	1 028	1 067	4 092	790	2 428
1989	4 193	910	1 345	4 706	1 025	1 089	4 090	833	2 478
1990	4 510	880	1 363	4 984	1 026	1 083	3 966	743	2 434
1991	4 695	820	1 316	5 065	919	1 009	3 851	772	2 384
1992	4 601	853	1 306	5 360	844	908	3 698	789	2 323
1993	4 510	765	1 241	5 656	853	914	3 684	791	2 329
1994	4 423	443	1 241	5 477	862	923	3 755	785	2 395
1995	4 338	674	1 268	5 458	746	933	3 824	787	2 467
1996	4 479	724	1 295	5 960	546	936	3 943	806	2 498
1997	4 579	687	1 322	6 640	441	911	4 000	863	2 531
1998	4 554	753	1 360	6 983	422	883	3 986	889	2 555
1999	4 569	795	1 391	6 741	376	873	4 032	930	2 593
2000	4 588	830	1 433	6 354	379	863	4 139	991	2 606
2001	4 610	871	1 474	5 808	386	851	4 208	1 015	2 610

Table 6c. **Per Capita GDP in 57 African Countries, 1950-2001**
(1990 international Geary-Khamis dollars)

	Tanzania	Togo	Tunisia	Uganda	Zaire	Zambia	Zimbabwe	6 Country Total	57 Country Total
1950	424	574	1 115	687	570	661	701	801	894
1951	466	584	1 106	642	625	688	722	857	916
1952	464	593	1 220	664	670	715	724	889	932
1953	437	602	1 244	675	695	743	760	883	945
1954	461	611	1 249	648	723	772	772	864	970
1955	460	621	1 164	672	737	736	808	1 017	981
1956	454	630	1 223	690	772	803	892	1 179	999
1957	452	639	1 159	700	781	817	924	1 191	1 013
1958	444	647	1 291	685	743	776	906	1 265	1 013
1959	453	656	1 217	700	753	915	925	1 315	1 044
1960	459	698	1 343	713	755	960	938	1 613	1 066
1961	441	728	1 436	686	659	938	956	1 710	1 065
1962	468	736	1 379	694	776	905	939	2 154	1 082
1963	483	754	1 556	751	793	902	901	2 767	1 132
1964	494	841	1 589	785	757	996	953	3 717	1 164
1965	497	932	1 653	779	748	1 147	984	4 560	1 197
1966	544	991	1 654	803	779	1 056	967	5 164	1 201
1967	549	1 019	1 605	822	749	1 107	1 015	5 536	1 194
1968	560	1 043	1 735	818	758	1 092	999	7 048	1 223
1969	553	1 126	1 760	881	806	1 056	1 086	7 589	1 286
1970	567	1 075	1 827	869	782	1 073	1 282	7 652	1 357
1971	572	1 121	1 982	871	810	1 042	1 353	6 956	1 382
1972	591	1 128	2 287	859	790	1 105	1 423	5 934	1 397
1973	590	1 053	2 221	838	836	1 062	1 432	5 734	1 410
1974	584	1 067	2 343	821	842	1 114	1 427	4 732	1 438
1975	596	1 032	2 446	784	778	1 041	1 402	4 925	1 418
1976	620	999	2 569	770	713	1 071	1 357	5 855	1 472
1977	618	1 025	2 592	763	700	990	1 221	6 200	1 492
1978	617	1 098	2 700	703	643	967	1 232	6 241	1 487
1979	606	1 131	2 811	611	620	910	1 211	6 703	1 512
1980	593	1 048	2 944	577	617	911	1 295	6 413	1 536
1981	569	950	3 030	585	616	936	1 407	5 001	1 509
1982	559	883	2 957	617	594	878	1 405	4 648	1 512
1983	540	807	3 039	643	587	828	1 374	4 418	1 477
1984	537	802	3 068	570	605	797	1 297	3 952	1 466
1985	519	810	3 162	562	589	784	1 335	3 552	1 468
1986	520	806	3 038	544	598	762	1 321	3 238	1 459
1987	529	788	3 165	556	594	756	1 257	3 068	1 441
1988	534	793	3 101	572	578	781	1 326	3 010	1 459
1989	536	793	3 152	590	556	768	1 368	2 953	1 463
1990	540	757	3 337	592	525	817	1 356	2 831	1 444
1991	536	726	3 402	577	465	797	1 391	2 610	1 414
1992	524	673	3 599	574	403	765	1 232	2 457	1 378
1993	514	565	3 612	600	338	799	1 217	2 305	1 356
1994	503	656	3 663	616	314	678	1 273	2 232	1 352
1995	505	664	3 692	671	299	647	1 263	2 210	1 358
1996	517	695	3 897	710	290	675	1 370	2 301	1 403
1997	501	635	4 050	725	269	683	1 382	2 503	1 416
1998	507	602	4 188	738	257	656	1 399	2 445	1 434
1999	511	602	4 387	772	239	657	1 368	2 561	1 447
2000	524	575	4 538	788	218	666	1 280	2 665	1 464
2001	540	575	4 710	809	202	686	1 158	2 892	1 489

Table 6c. **Per Capita GDP in 57 African Countries, 1950-2001**
(1990 international Geary-Khamis dollars)

	Equatorial Guinea	Libya	SãoTomé & Principe	Mayotte + St. Helena + W. Sahara	6 Country Total
1950	540	857	820	790	801
1951	561	925	818	816	857
1952	572	963	817	837	889
1953	587	949	817	879	883
1954	610	915	850	915	864
1955	620	1 115	764	920	1 017
1956	636	1 314	806	965	1 179
1957	648	1 325	799	981	1 191
1958	660	1 410	875	991	1 265
1959	687	1 470	784	1 014	1 315
1960	746	1 830	867	1 047	1 613
1961	806	1 936	933	1 053	1 710
1962	887	2 473	995	1 068	2 154
1963	1 006	3 212	1 055	1 074	2 767
1964	1 145	4 366	1 112	1 086	3 717
1965	1 285	5 378	1 165	1 089	4 560
1966	1 322	6 107	1 233	1 097	5 164
1967	1 393	6 545	1 286	1 094	5 536
1968	1 424	8 395	1 337	1 083	7 048
1969	1 364	9 043	1 389	1 084	7 589
1970	1 309	9 115	1 440	1 076	7 652
1971	1 186	8 252	1 483	1 103	6 956
1972	1 023	6 979	1 423	1 187	5 934
1973	1 065	6 664	1 355	1 268	5 734
1974	1 128	5 379	1 356	1 331	4 732
1975	1 294	5 515	1 421	1 348	4 925
1976	1 452	6 540	1 497	1 330	5 855
1977	1 458	6 945	1 613	1 314	6 200
1978	1 572	6 991	1 667	1 291	6 241
1979	1 541	7 565	1 808	1 257	6 703
1980	1 477	7 272	2 009	1 237	6 413
1981	1 424	5 648	1 421	1 209	5 001
1982	1 412	5 234	1 755	1 181	4 648
1983	1 395	4 968	1 567	1 196	4 418
1984	1 679	4 397	1 405	1 222	3 952
1985	1 402	3 953	1 486	1 246	3 552
1986	1 425	3 586	1 470	1 270	3 238
1987	1 472	3 380	1 408	1 308	3 068
1988	1 538	3 303	1 400	1 332	3 010
1989	1 560	3 232	1 391	1 357	2 953
1990	1 564	3 087	1 390	1 374	2 831
1991	1 596	2 825	1 354	1 344	2 610
1992	1 723	2 637	1 326	1 309	2 457
1993	1 785	2 453	1 306	1 291	2 305
1994	1 828	2 363	1 299	1 284	2 232
1995	2 036	2 321	1 284	1 289	2 210
1996	2 563	2 381	1 267	1 334	2 301
1997	4 281	2 467	1 243	1 343	2 503
1998	5 093	2 322	1 232	1 361	2 445
1999	7 025	2 282	1 226	1 372	2 561
2000	7 956	2 322	1 226	1 385	2 665
2001	11 295	2 284	1 236	1 408	2 892

HS–7: The World Economy, 1950–2001

Tables 7a–7c show annual estimates of economic activity in 7 regions and the world for the year 1900, and annually 1950–2001. They aggregate the detailed estimates by country in HS–1 to HS–6 and there are analytical tables showing percentage year–to–year movement in real terms. Three basic ingredients are necessary for these estimates. These are time series on population which we have for 221 countries, time series showing the volume movement in GDP in constant national prices for 179 countries, and purchasing power converters for 99.3 per cent of world GDP in our benchmark year 1990. With these converters we can transform the GDP volume measures into comparable estimates of GDP level across countries for every year between 1950 and 2001. For countries where all three types of measure are available, the estimates of per capita GDP level are derivative. However, to arrive at a comprehensive world total, we need proxy measures of GDP movement for 42 countries, and proxy per capita GDP levels for 48 countries for the year 1990. These proxies collectively represent less than 1 per cent of world output.

a) World Population Movement 1950–2003

There are two comprehensive and detailed estimates of world population which are regularly updated and revised. They both provide annual estimates back to 1950 and projections 50 years into the future. No other source provides such comprehensive detail, length of perspective, or causal analysis of birth and death rates, fertility and migration. Here I have used the latest (October 2002) estimates of the US Bureau of the Census (USBC) for all countries except China, India and Indonesia. In Maddison (2001), I used the USBC 1999 version for 178 countries, OECD sources for 20 countries and Soviet sources for 15 countries. USBC estimates are available at http://www.census.gov/ipc. The United Nations Population Division (UNPD) is the alternative. Its latest estimates, *World Population Prospects: The 2000 Revision*, were prepared in February 2001; the previous version was issued in 1998. The UN shows estimates for quinquennial intervals, but annual country detail is available for purchase on a CD ROM. Table 7a shows my estimates, based mainly on USBC. Table 7* shows UNPD figures with the same regional breakdown. The easiest way to compare the two sources is the ratio of the two alternatives shown in Table 7**. On the world level the differences are minimal, and the regional differences are not very large after 1973. On the country level there are larger differences between the two sources. These are biggest for small countries and the UNPD omits Taiwan. Both sources provide a similar long–term view, showing the fastest demographic momentum in Africa and a general reduction in the pace of growth in the 1990s. Differences are mainly due to use of different sources or conjectures for cases where evidence is poor. It is clear from inspection of the country detail that the USBC takes better account of short–term interruptions due to war, flight of population or natural disasters. Their impact is smoothed by UNPD interpolation between census intervals. One example is the genocide and exodus from Rwanda: USBC shows a 25 per cent fall of population in 1993–5, UNPD 9 per cent. USBC shows a 55 per cent fall in Kuwait in 1991 during the Gulf war, UNPD 2 per cent. USBC shows a 70 per cent fall in Montserrat in 1998 due to volcanic activity, UNPD tapers this decline over several years. In fact, a major objective of the UN is to provide alternative projections of population trends which are of fundamental importance in assessing prospects for its development programmes. USBC is probably more interested in monitoring past and present performance.

b) Movement in Volume of GDP 1950–2001

Table 7–1 shows the coverage of our GDP estimates for five benchmark years since 1820. For 2001 there were direct estimates for 179 countries representing 99.8 per cent of world output with proxies for 42 other countries (mostly very small), for which direct measures were not available (see Tables 1–4, 4–5 and 5–4). Generally speaking the proxies assume per capita GDP movement parallel to the average for other countries in the same region. The total number of countries was bigger in 2001 than 1950, but this was due to the emergence of new states in Eastern Europe and the USSR. The area covered and the degree of reliance on proxies was in fact similar in 1950. Coverage was much more comprehensive than for the nineteenth century.

Table 7-1. **Coverage of World GDP Sample and Proportionate Role of Proxy Measures, 1820-2001**
(GDP in billion international dollars and number of countries)

	1820		1870		1913		1950		2001	
Sample countries										
Western Europe	135.4	(9)	326.9	(14)	898.5	(15)	1 394.8	(20)	7 540.4	(20)
Western Offshoots	12.7	(2)	110.6	(3)	577.2	(3)	1 635.5	(4)	9 156.3	(4)
Eastern Europe and former USSR	6.5	(1)	101.9	(3)	290.9	(3)	694.0	(7)	2 072.0	(27)
Latin America	8.2	(3)	17.5	(6)	101.9	(9)	315.6	(39)	3 078.8	(35)
Asia	383.5	(10)	392.3	(11)	644.6	(17)	969.0	(39)	14 050.4	(39)
Africa	n.a.		n.a.		30.7	(5)	202.1	(54)	1 204.3	(54)
World	546.2	(25)	985.2	(37)	2 543.8	(52)	5 310.9	(163)	37 056.9	(179)
Total GDP including proxy component										
Western Europe	160.1		367.6		902.3	(28)	1 396.2	(29)	7 550.3	(29)
Western Offshoots	13.5		111.5		582.9	(4)	1 635.5	(4)	9 156.3	(4)
Eastern Europe and former USSR	62.6		133.8		367.1	(8)	695.3	(8)	2 072.0	(27)
Latin America	15.0		27.5		119.9	(47)	415.9	(47)	3 087.0	(47)
Asia	412.9		427.0		680.3	(55)	983.7	(57)	14 105.7	(57)
Africa	31.2		45.6		80.9	(57)	203.1	(57)	1 222.6	(57)
World	695.3		1 113.0		2 733.5	(199)	5 329.7	(202)	37 193.9	(221)
Coverage of Sample, per cent of regional and world total										
Western Europe	84.5		98.7		99.6		99.9		99.9	
Western Offshoots	94.2		99.2		99.0		100.0		100.0	
Eastern Europe and former USSR	10.4		76.2		79.2		99.8		100.0	
Latin America	54.5		63.6		85.0		99.9		99.7	
Asia	92.9		91.8		94.8		98.5		99.6	
Africa	0.0		0.0		37.9		99.5		98.5	
World	78.6		88.5		93.1		99.6		99.8	

Measures of GDP volume movement for 1950–2001 are mainly derived from official sources, because of the widespread governmental commitment to their publication, and, from 1953, adherence to the methodology of a standardised system of national accounts (SNA), now endorsed by the EU, IMF, OECD, United Nations, and World Bank (see UN, 1993). Communist countries were an exception. They used the Soviet material product approach (MPS), which exaggerated growth and left out most service activities. Fortunately Kremlinologists (guided by the work of Abram Bergson and Thad Alton) were able to adjust estimates for many of these countries to conform more closely to SNA criteria — see the assessment of their work in Maddison (1995) for Eastern Europe; Maddison (1997) for the USSR; and Maddison (1998) on China. The MPS system has now been abandoned, but there are still residual measurement problems of adjustment to the SNA in the successor countries of the USSR, China, Cuba, North Korea and Vietnam. There are also countries, particularly in Africa, where real GDP estimates are still of low quality, because resources for statistics and trained statisticians are very scarce and in many cases, data collection has been interrupted by war.

For OECD countries, a full set of national accounts statistics, with adjustment to secure comparability, has been published regularly since 1954, with annual data for 1938, and for 1947 onwards. For Eastern Europe official estimates are available in publications of the Economic Commission for Europe (ECE), and adjusted figures by the CIA were published regularly for 1950–90 in the proceedings of the Joint Economic Committee of the US Congress. The Economic Commission for Latin America and the Caribbean (ECLAC) has published detailed national accounts annually since 1950 in its *Statistical Yearbook for Latin America*, with updates in its monthly *ECLAC Notes*. East Asian national accounts are published in detail by the Asian Development Bank in its annual *Key Indicators*. West Asian accounts are published by the Economic and Social Commission for Western Asia (ESCWA) in its annual *National Accounts Studies of the ESCWA Region*. Estimates for African countries 1950–90 were derived mainly from the database of the OECD Development Centre whose *Latest Information on National Accounts of Developing Countries* was published annually from 1969 to 1991. For 1990 onwards, annual GDP movements for virtually all African countries are shown in the IMF *Economic Outlook*.

c) Derivation of 1990 Benchmark Purchasing Power Converters in order to Permit Cross–country Comparison of GDP Levels and Construction of Regional and World Aggregates

In order to make cross–country comparison of GDP levels and aggregate estimates of regional or world totals, we need to convert national currencies into a common unit (numeraire). Table 7–2 shows the derivation of the numeraire for measurement of GDP levels in my benchmark year 1990, which is the interspatial–intertemporal anchor for my comprehensive world estimates. The 1990 cross–section level estimates are merged with the time series for real GDP growth to show GDP levels for all other years. There are four options for deriving GDP converters:

i) Exchange Rates: Conversion of nominal estimates by exchange rates is the simplest option, but exchange rates are mainly a reflection of purchasing power over tradeable items. They may also move erratically because of speculative capital movements or surges of inflation. In poor countries where wages are low, non–tradeable services, like haircuts, government services, building construction, are generally cheaper than in high–income countries, so there is a general tendency for exchange rates to understate purchasing power of their currencies. China is an extreme case. Mr Patten, the last British governor of Hong Kong, stated in an article in the *Economist* newspaper of 4 January 1997 that "Britain's GDP today is almost twice the size of China's". This was an exchange rate comparison. PPP conversion shows British GDP to have been less than a third of China's in 1997. There are very strong reasons for preferring PPP converters which are now available for most of the world economy. Correction for the wide disparity in price levels between countries is a logical interspatial corollary to the use of national GDP deflators to correct for intertemporal changes in the price level. However, there was understandable reluctance on the part of some countries to abandonment of exchange rate comparisons. Although the World Bank made a major contribution to finance work on PPPs, it did not use them for its analytical work because they raise the relative income levels of poor countries substantially compared to their standing in an exchange rate ranking. They feared that this would make them ineligible to borrow from IDA (the cheap loan window of the Bank). For this reason the Bank continued to rank countries by income level in its *Atlas*, by using a three–year moving average of exchange rates.

ii) Purchasing Power Parity (PPP) conversion: This concept was first used by Gustav Cassel in 1918, and crudely implemented by Colin Clark in 1940. A substantial part of Clark's price material was derived from a survey made for the Ford Motor Company, together with his own price comparisons for luxury goods and ILO material on rents in different countries. Much more sophisticated measures have been developed by co–operative research of national statistical offices and international agencies in the past few decades. They have become highly sophisticated comparative pricing exercises involving collection of carefully specified price information on a massive scale by national statistical offices for representative items of consumption, investment goods and government services. The latest OECD exercise for 1999 involved collection of prices for 2 740 items. The OEEC first developed these comparisons of real levels of expenditure and the purchasing parity of currencies in the 1950s for 8 of its member countries and rough proxies for the rest. OECD reactivated this work in 1982 in cooperation with Eurostat (see Michael Ward, 1985). In the meantime Irving Kravis, Alan Heston and Robert Summers set up their International Comparisons Project (ICP) in 1968 and published three major studies in 1975, 1978 and 1982. Their work made major contributions to the methodology of international income comparisons and greatly expanded their coverage. Their last volume covered 34 countries. Their work was taken over by the United Nations Statistical Office which made comparisons for 1980 and 1985. Altogether the two UN comparisons covered 82 countries. There were regional comparisons for some Asian, African and Middle Eastern countries by UN agencies in 1993, but UNSO did not attempt to integrate them. ICP estimation has now been taken over by the World Bank and the next exercise is planned for 2004. The main current activity in this field is by OECD–Eurostat; in 2002 they published a 1999 level comparison for 43 countries.

When the ICP approach was originally developed in OEEC, the main emphasis was on binary comparison. The three most straightforward options were: *i)* a Paasche PPP (with "own" country quantity weights); *ii)* a Laspeyres PPP (with the quantity weights of the numeraire country — the United States); or *iii)*, as a compromise, the Fisher geometric average of the two measures. The corresponding measures of real expenditure levels were *i)* Laspeyres level comparisons based on the prices (unit values) of the numeraire country; *ii)* Paasche level comparisons based on own country prices (unit values); or *iii)* a Fisher geometric average of the two measures. Binary comparisons, e.g. France/US, and UK/US can be linked with the United States as the "star" country. The derivative France–UK comparison will not necessarily produce the same results as direct binary comparison of France and the United Kingdom. Such star system comparisons are not "transitive". However, in studies I made of comparative performance of advanced capitalist countries (Maddison, 1982 and 1991), I preferred to use the Laspeyres level comparison at US prices, because this was the price structure to which the other countries in this group were converging as their productivity and demand patterns approached US levels.

Comparisons can be made transitive if they are done on a "multilateral" rather than a "binary" basis. The Geary–Khamis approach (named for R.S. Geary and S.H. Khamis) is an ingenious method for multilaterising the results which provides transitivity and other desirable properties. It was used by Kravis, Heston and Summers as a method for aggregating ICP results available at the basic heading level. They used it in conjunction with the commodity product dummy (CPD) method (invented by Robert Summers) for filling holes in the basic dataset. I used PPPs of this type for 70 countries representing 93.7 per cent of world GDP in 1990 (see Table 7–2). The Geary–Khamis approach gives a weight to countries corresponding to the size of their GDP, so that a large economy, like the United States, has a strong influence on the results. Eurostat (the statistical office of EU) uses a multilateral method in which all its member countries have an equal weight. This is the EKS technique (named for its inventors, Eltöto, Kovacs and Szulc). For my purpose an equi–country weighting system which treats Luxemburg and Germany as equal partners in the world economy is inappropriate, so I have a strong preference for the Geary–Khamis approach. Fortunately the OECD–Eurostat joint exercise derives both EKS and Geary–Khamis measures — see Maddison (1995), pp. 164–79 for a detailed confrontation of all the binary and multilateral PPPs published up to that time.

iii) Penn World Tables (PWT): For countries not covered by ICP, Summers and Heston devised short–cut estimates. Their latest Penn World Tables (PWT 6.1, October 2002) provide PPP converters for 168 countries. Their estimates for countries which have never had an ICP exercise are necessarily rougher than for those where these exercises are available. For these they use much more limited price information from cost of living surveys (of diplomats, UN officials, and people working abroad for private business) as a proxy for the ICP specification prices. I used PPPs from PWT for 84 countries, 5.6 per cent of world GDP in 1990 (see Table 7–2).

iv) ICOP (International Comparison of Real Output and Productivity): The fourth option is to compare levels of real output (value added) using census of production material on output quantities and prices. Rostas (1948) pioneered this approach for manufacturing. The first study of this type for the whole economy was a binary comparison of the United Kingdom and the United States by Paige and Bombach (1959) published by OEEC. This approach was not used in subsequent ICP comparisons, but I used it in a comparative study of economic growth in 29 countries (*Economic Progress and Policy in Developing Countries,* 1970, Norton, New York). At that time there were no ICP estimates for non–OECD countries. I made estimates of value added and productivity in agriculture, industry and services and total GDP in US relative prices for the 29 countries for 1965. I merged these benchmark estimates to time series of GDP movement in the 29 countries back to 1950, 1938, 1913 and 1870, wherever possible. The basic approach was very similar to that in this volume, although the measures of GDP levels in the benchmark year and the time series for GDP growth were much cruder than they are now. In Maddison (1983) I compared my production–side estimates with those of Kravis, Heston and Summers (1982). I also used the two sets of estimates as benchmarks for merger with time series on economic growth to see what the implications were for comparative levels of performance back to 1820. I concluded provisionally that the ICP approach probably exaggerated service output in the poorer countries, but that an authoritative view on this topic required more careful study on the production side. I therefore set up the ICOP (International Comparison of Output and Productivity) project at the University of Groningen in 1983. The Groningen Growth and Development Centre has produced nearly 100 research memoranda on productivity as well as Ph. D theses on economic growth and levels of performance by Bart van Ark, Tom Elfring, Pierre van der Eng, Andre Hofman, Sompop Manarungsan, Kees van der Meer, Nanno Mulder, Dirk Pilat, Jaap Sleifer and Marcel Timmer. These theses are in the Kuznetsian tradition with fully transparent and complete statistical appendices showing sources and methods of approach (see Maddison and van Ark, 2000). The ICOP programme puts primary emphasis on analysis of labour, capital and joint factor productivity for major sectors of the economy. It was not intended as a rival to IPC, but provides and alternative and complementary approach to the problem of international comparison of GDP levels. So far, the project has covered one or more sectors of the economy for more than 30 countries which together represent more than half of world GDP (see http://www.eco.rug.nl/ggdc/dseries/icop.shtml#top). Recently the scale of its systemic comparative exercises has increased in country coverage and sector detail, in co–operation with international agencies including Euostat, ILO and OECD. The most recent ICOP work was a study for 19 countries, covering more than 30 sectors. These results are a useful crosscheck on the ICP measures and on the validity of my 1990 benchmarks as an anchor for analysis of levels of performance in the past (see HS–8 below).

Table 7-2. **Nature of PPP Converters Used to Estimate GDP Levels in the Benchmark Year 1990**
(billion 1990 Geary-Khamis dollars and number of countries)

	Europe and Western Offshoots		Latin America		Asia		Africa		World	
ICP	15 273	(28)	2 131	(18)	8 017	(24)	0	(0)	25 421	(70)
PWT	59	(3)	71	(14)	524	(16)	891	(51)	1 516	(84)
Proxies	16	(10)	38	(15)	87	(17)	14	(6)	155	(48)
Total	15 349	(41)	2 240	(47)	8 628	(57)	905	(57)	27 122	(202)

Source: The PPP converters used here are the same as those in Maddison (2001) except for 7 African countries.

Europe and Western Offshoots: 99.5 per cent of regional GDP from ICP 6 for 1990; 22 countries from OECD–Eurostat and 6 countries from ECE (see OECD, 1993; ECE, 1994; Maddison, 1995, p. 172 and Maddison, 2001, pp. 189–90); 0.4 per cent of regional GDP (Bulgaria, Cyprus and Malta) from PWT version 5.6; 0.1 per cent from proxy estimates (Albania, Andorra, Channel Isles, Faeroe Isles, Gibraltar, Greenland, Isle of Man, Liechtenstein, Monaco and San Marino).

Latin America: 95.1 per cent of regional GDP (18 countries) from ICP. As there was no Latin America ICP exercise for 1990 or later; I used ICP 3 for 2 countries and ICP 4 for 16 countries updated to 1990 (see Kravis, Heston and Summers, 1982; UN, 1987; and Maddison, 2001, p. 199). Updating involves adjustment for the GDP volume change in the specified country between the reference year and 1990, and for the movement in the US GDP deflator in the same interval. 3.2 per cent of regional GDP (Bahamas, Barbados, Belize, Dominica, Grenada, Guyana, Haiti, Nicaragua, Puerto Rico, St. Kitts Nevis, St. Lucia, St. Vincent, Suriname, Trinidad and Tobago) from PWT version 5.6; 1.7 per cent from proxy estimates (Anguilla, Antigua and Barbuda, Aruba, Bermuda, Cayman Islands, Cuba, French Guyana, Guadeloupe, Martinique, Montserrat, Netherlands Antilles, St. Pierre and Miquelon, Turks and Caicos, Virgin Islands and British Virgin Islands).

Asia: 92.9 per cent of regional GDP (24 countries) from ICP or equivalent. I used ICP 3 for 2 countries, ICP 4 for 5 countries. ICP 5 for 3 countreis and linked Bangladesh and Pakistan to their 1950 level relative to India. All 12 were updated to 1990. OECD estimates were available for Japan and Mongolia for 1990, and I made an estimate for China for 1990 based on Maddison (1998) and Ren (1997). ICP 7 estimates were available from ESCAP(1999) and ESCWA (1997) for 9 countries for 1993 and backdated to 1990 (see Maddison, 2001, pp. 202, 208, 219–20). Backdating involves the same procedure as updating. 6.1 per cent of regional GDP (Bhutan, Burma, Fiji, Iraq, Jordan, Kuwait, Oman, Papua New Guinea, Saudi Arabia, Solomon Islands, Taiwan, Tonga, UAE, Vanuatu, Western Samoa, and Yemen) from PWT version 5.6; 1 per cent of regional GDP from proxy estimates (Afghanistan, American Samoa, Brunei, Cambodia, French Polynesia, Guam, Kiribati, Lebanon, Macao, Maldives, Marshall Islands, Micronesia, New Caledonia, North Korea, Northern Marianas, Palau, Wallis and Futuna.

Africa: 75.8 per cent of regional GDP from PWT 5.6 and 22.7 per cent from PWT 6.1; proxy estimates for 1.5 per cent of regional GDP (Equatorial Guinea, Libya, Mayotte, St. Helena, São Tomé & Principe and Western Sahara); see source note HS–6 and Table 6–11.

d) Alternative Estimates of Movement of World GDP, 1970 onwards

The IMF now makes annual estimates of the growth of world GDP in real terms, available back to 1970. Their preference is for PPP adjustment, but they publish an alternative with exchange rate weights (see IMF, *Economic Outlook*, September 2002, pp. 189–199, which describes their method). Their PPP estimates (with 1996 weights) are derived from ICP. For countries not covered by ICP, they estimate PPPs using a regression technique in which exchange rates are one of the independent variables.

Table 7–3 compares the year–to–year movement of their world aggregate and mine. The IMF measure with PPP weights shows faster growth for 1970–2001 than I do (3.9 per cent a year instead of 3.3 per cent). One would not expect complete concordance as my PPP weights are different and my coverage more complete, but it seems clear that the IMF exaggerates growth. Its measure excludes non–member countries, and makes no proxy estimates for countries where estimation is difficult. Some of these — Afghanistan, Bosnia, Cuba, North Korea, Serbia — have had negative growth. It is clear from their database that they have not adjusted growth estimates for countries which formerly used the Soviet system of national accounts. For China they show GDP growth averaging 8.5 per cent a year for 1970–2001, whereas my adjusted estimate is 6.5 per cent. For Germany for the same period, they show growth averaging 2.2 per cent a year. I show 2.0 per cent as I include East Germany for the whole post–war period. For 1973–2001 they show Russian growth averaging 0.7 per cent and –0.7 for the Ukraine, whereas I have –0.2 per cent for Russia and –1.5 for Ukraine

The Department of Economic and Social Affairs of the United Nations also publishes annual estimates of world GDP, available back to 1980. Their preference is for an aggregate with exchange rate conversion, but they publish an alternative using PPP converters (see *World Economic Survey 2002*, pp. 4, 278–280 and 285). Their PPP weights are for 1995, and are derived from ICP and PWT. It is not clear from the published description how many countries are included, but their world aggregate is probably more comprehensive than that of the IMF. The UN measure shows slower growth than the IMF, and is closer to mine.

Table 7-3. **Annual Change of World GDP, IMF and Maddison Measures, 1970-2001**
(percentage change)

	IMF with Ex. Rate	IMF with PPP	Maddison PPP		IMF with Ex. Rate	IMF with PPP	Maddison PPP
1970	4.6	5.2	5.1	1986	3.3	3.7	3.5
1971	4.3	4.6	4.2	1987	3.7	4.1	3.6
1972	5.0	5.4	4.7	1988	4.5	4.7	4.3
1973	6.4	6.9	6.6	1989	3.7	3.7	3.2
1974	2.2	2.8	2.3	1990	2.7	2.8	2.0
1975	1.5	1.9	1.5	1991	0.7	1.5	1.1
1976	5.0	5.2	4.9	1992	1.0	2.1	2.0
1977	4.2	4.4	4.1	1993	1.0	2.2	2.2
1978	4.5	4.7	4.4	1994	2.9	3.7	3.4
1979	3.7	3.8	3.6	1995	2.8	3.7	3.4
1980	2.5	2.9	2.0	1996	3.3	4.0	3.9
1981	2.0	2.2	1.9	1997	3.5	4.2	3.9
1982	0.6	1.2	1.2	1998	2.2	2.8	2.5
1983	2.9	3.0	2.9	1999	3.1	3.6	3.3
1984	4.8	4.9	4.5	2000	3.9	4.7	4.4
1985	3.5	3.7	3.5	2001	1.1	2.2	1.9

Table 7a. **World Population by Region, 1900 and Annual Estimates 1950-2001**
(000 at mid-year)

	Western Europe	Western Offshoots	Eastern Europe	Former USSR	Latin America	Asia	Africa	World
1900	233 645	86 396	70 993	124 500	64 764	873 324	110 000	1 563 622
1950	304 940	176 458	87 637	179 571	165 938	1 382 447	227 333	2 524 324
1951	307 024	179 667	88 713	182 677	170 411	1 407 689	232 068	2 568 249
1952	308 754	183 025	89 814	185 856	174 975	1 435 439	237 008	2 614 871
1953	310 696	186 273	91 081	188 961	179 664	1 464 409	242 086	2 663 170
1954	312 607	189 819	92 341	192 171	184 563	1 495 497	247 273	2 714 271
1955	314 605	193 395	93 719	195 613	189 673	1 526 707	252 759	2 766 471
1956	316 758	197 027	94 985	199 103	194 935	1 558 727	258 409	2 819 944
1957	318 987	200 936	96 049	202 604	200 395	1 594 212	264 222	2 877 405
1958	321 318	204 541	97 149	206 201	206 069	1 631 177	270 231	2 936 686
1959	323 824	208 165	98 217	209 928	211 951	1 664 717	276 454	2 993 256
1960	326 346	211 671	99 254	213 780	218 029	1 686 796	282 919	3 038 795
1961	329 115	215 357	100 292	217 618	224 157	1 703 409	289 385	3 079 333
1962	332 342	218 807	101 172	221 227	230 450	1 732 716	295 977	3 132 691
1963	335 251	222 128	102 057	224 585	236 957	1 773 645	303 251	3 197 874
1964	338 111	225 410	102 908	227 698	243 648	1 814 092	310 725	3 262 592
1965	340 884	228 454	103 713	230 513	250 474	1 856 366	318 478	3 328 882
1966	343 440	231 351	104 494	233 139	257 370	1 901 303	326 534	3 397 631
1967	345 628	234 132	105 256	235 630	264 339	1 946 533	334 945	3 466 463
1968	347 633	236 710	106 302	237 983	271 430	1 993 844	343 591	3 537 493
1969	349 946	239 293	107 117	240 253	278 670	2 042 155	352 457	3 609 891
1970	352 240	242 290	107 921	242 478	286 007	2 092 954	361 168	3 685 058
1971	354 702	245 500	108 753	244 887	293 427	2 145 665	370 534	3 763 468
1972	356 845	248 287	109 589	247 343	300 900	2 197 174	380 026	3 840 164
1973	358 825	250 841	110 418	249 712	308 399	2 248 260	390 034	3 916 489
1974	360 466	253 386	111 377	252 111	315 957	2 298 349	400 314	3 991 960
1975	361 743	256 071	112 372	254 519	323 524	2 346 352	410 827	4 065 408
1976	362 752	258 622	113 357	256 883	331 109	2 391 522	422 188	4 136 433
1977	363 850	261 274	114 339	259 225	338 791	2 437 228	433 995	4 208 702
1978	364 949	264 036	115 199	261 525	346 493	2 483 253	446 294	4 281 749
1979	366 096	266 918	116 058	263 751	354 326	2 532 444	459 413	4 359 006
1980	367 457	270 106	116 804	265 973	362 069	2 580 468	472 721	4 435 598
1981	368 647	272 975	117 483	268 217	370 057	2 626 665	486 060	4 510 104
1982	369 371	275 785	118 173	270 533	378 204	2 669 803	500 253	4 582 122
1983	369 920	278 403	118 772	273 010	386 279	2 728 669	515 235	4 670 288
1984	370 509	280 908	119 285	275 574	394 193	2 779 117	530 353	4 749 939
1985	371 162	283 494	119 866	278 108	402 110	2 830 331	545 742	4 830 813
1986	372 001	286 181	120 402	280 646	410 248	2 882 699	561 280	4 913 457
1987	372 887	288 928	120 881	283 124	418 470	2 937 328	577 158	4 998 776
1988	374 092	291 768	121 092	285 482	426 758	2 992 532	593 250	5 084 974
1989	375 950	294 843	121 394	287 011	435 097	3 047 760	609 818	5 171 873
1990	377 856	298 304	121 569	289 045	443 276	3 102 638	626 814	5 259 502
1991	379 688	302 265	121 847	290 754	451 387	3 154 008	644 889	5 344 838
1992	381 580	306 337	121 880	292 079	459 512	3 205 102	662 410	5 428 900
1993	383 334	310 340	121 605	292 686	467 639	3 257 972	679 567	5 513 143
1994	384 719	314 108	121 379	292 755	475 790	3 308 981	696 273	5 594 005
1995	385 936	317 858	121 135	292 597	483 957	3 361 948	713 856	5 677 287
1996	387 063	321 620	120 983	292 188	492 093	3 411 457	730 822	5 756 226
1997	388 065	325 459	120 942	291 750	500 150	3 460 624	748 865	5 835 855
1998	388 977	329 239	120 924	291 373	508 094	3 509 481	766 842	5 914 930
1999	389 945	332 994	120 904	291 012	515 916	3 561 961	785 235	5 997 967
2000	391 036	336 601	120 913	290 654	523 612	3 605 017	803 311	6 071 144
2001	392 101	339 838	120 912	290 349	531 213	3 653 504	821 088	6 149 005

Table 7b. **World GDP by Region, 1900 and Annual Estimates 1950-2001**
(million 1990 international Geary-Khamis dollars)

	Western Europe	Western Offshoots	Eastern Europe	Former USSR	Latin America	Asia	Africa	World
1900	675 923	346 869	102 084	154 049	71 810	556 845	66 136	1 973 716
1950	1 396 188	1 635 490	185 023	510 243	415 907	983 737	203 131	5 329 719
1951	1 478 599	1 753 540	195 670	512 566	438 241	1 052 267	212 653	5 643 536
1952	1 532 433	1 821 083	198 236	545 792	453 608	1 139 703	220 780	5 911 635
1953	1 611 339	1 903 763	209 145	569 260	469 286	1 218 405	228 858	6 210 056
1954	1 699 722	1 898 106	218 886	596 910	499 226	1 270 868	239 781	6 423 499
1955	1 805 779	2 032 869	233 857	648 027	530 891	1 330 326	248 054	6 829 803
1956	1 888 452	2 082 376	239 494	710 065	553 553	1 421 380	258 153	7 153 473
1957	1 971 596	2 123 207	257 611	724 470	595 890	1 485 225	267 612	7 425 611
1958	2 018 551	2 111 417	272 635	778 840	625 736	1 581 790	273 683	7 662 653
1959	2 114 619	2 261 993	286 886	770 244	640 912	1 657 765	288 734	8 021 152
1960	2 250 549	2 320 141	304 685	843 434	683 018	1 736 343	301 578	8 439 748
1961	2 370 583	2 374 411	322 781	891 763	715 577	1 744 557	308 136	8 727 808
1962	2 486 946	2 518 521	328 253	915 928	745 383	1 822 562	320 322	9 137 914
1963	2 603 774	2 630 968	344 112	895 016	767 875	1 950 307	343 186	9 535 239
1964	2 761 481	2 785 505	364 518	1 010 727	820 341	2 123 867	361 570	10 228 009
1965	2 877 269	2 962 352	380 016	1 068 117	861 475	2 232 507	381 330	10 763 066
1966	2 983 130	3 151 817	404 452	1 119 932	904 411	2 393 627	392 226	11 349 595
1967	3 088 548	3 234 760	420 645	1 169 422	945 295	2 511 607	400 067	11 770 344
1968	3 252 072	3 389 792	436 444	1 237 966	1 001 954	2 678 075	420 309	12 416 612
1969	3 438 238	3 507 231	449 862	1 255 392	1 066 883	2 935 884	453 131	13 106 621
1970	3 590 948	3 527 862	465 695	1 351 818	1 139 954	3 202 413	490 102	13 768 791
1971	3 711 784	3 647 077	499 790	1 387 832	1 207 908	3 384 521	512 138	14 351 050
1972	3 875 271	3 836 032	524 971	1 395 732	1 285 197	3 584 101	530 848	15 032 152
1973	4 096 456	4 058 289	550 756	1 513 070	1 389 029	3 865 936	549 993	16 023 529
1974	4 185 248	4 067 628	583 528	1 556 984	1 472 124	3 955 086	575 500	16 396 098
1975	4 167 528	4 069 398	604 251	1 561 399	1 516 429	4 143 267	582 627	16 644 898
1976	4 346 755	4 280 195	619 961	1 634 589	1 600 219	4 353 000	621 584	17 456 303
1977	4 471 506	4 459 671	641 681	1 673 159	1 676 380	4 597 844	647 589	18 167 829
1978	4 606 129	4 700 723	662 328	1 715 215	1 748 892	4 873 135	663 511	18 969 933
1979	4 774 306	4 866 597	672 299	1 707 083	1 859 062	5 074 326	694 654	19 648 326
1980	4 849 408	4 878 155	675 819	1 709 174	1 959 670	5 249 683	725 905	20 047 814
1981	4 860 516	5 006 126	667 932	1 724 741	1 971 459	5 466 812	733 452	20 431 038
1982	4 901 367	4 912 862	674 202	1 767 262	1 948 354	5 711 348	756 255	20 671 650
1983	4 990 650	5 103 869	684 326	1 823 723	1 899 531	6 003 271	761 138	21 266 508
1984	5 110 650	5 467 359	705 274	1 847 190	1 971 702	6 354 835	777 297	22 234 307
1985	5 238 333	5 687 354	706 201	1 863 687	2 031 566	6 676 210	801 420	23 004 771
1986	5 385 159	5 875 446	725 733	1 940 363	2 114 454	6 959 604	818 732	23 819 491
1987	5 539 861	6 086 756	721 188	1 965 457	2 180 979	7 360 551	831 716	24 686 508
1988	5 763 264	6 344 832	727 564	2 007 280	2 201 165	7 847 201	865 804	25 757 109
1989	5 960 940	6 560 368	718 039	2 037 253	2 228 826	8 186 232	892 376	26 584 033
1990	6 032 764	6 665 584	662 604	1 987 995	2 239 815	8 627 846	904 898	27 121 506
1991	6 132 879	6 624 976	590 280	1 863 524	2 322 362	8 983 054	911 693	27 428 768
1992	6 202 870	6 813 766	559 611	1 592 084	2 395 423	9 493 542	912 598	27 969 895
1993	6 182 982	6 997 300	550 399	1 435 008	2 477 909	10 007 080	921 183	28 571 861
1994	6 354 335	7 287 292	572 242	1 231 738	2 604 244	10 564 953	941 178	29 555 982
1995	6 506 739	7 488 397	605 392	1 163 401	2 642 483	11 196 934	969 734	30 573 080
1996	6 617 683	7 745 855	628 591	1 125 992	2 734 019	11 879 126	1 024 994	31 756 260
1997	6 791 738	8 071 150	645 039	1 149 255	2 877 534	12 413 389	1 060 213	33 008 319
1998	6 991 426	8 419 092	663 471	1 124 868	2 943 134	12 591 481	1 099 966	33 833 438
1999	7 180 236	8 774 087	675 657	1 171 952	2 950 074	13 079 182	1 136 130	34 967 319
2000	7 430 287	9 110 246	701 746	1 264 526	3 057 092	13 762 085	1 175 890	36 501 872
2001	7 550 272	9 156 267	728 792	1 343 230	3 087 006	14 105 724	1 222 577	37 193 868

Table 7c. World Per Capita GDP by Region, 1900 and Annual Estimates 1950-2001
(1990 international Geary-Khamis dollars)

	Western Europe	Western Offshoots	Eastern Europe	Former USSR	Latin America	Asia	Africa	World
1900	2 893	4 015	1 438	1 237	1 109	638	601	1 262
1950	4 579	9 268	2 111	2 841	2 506	712	894	2 111
1951	4 816	9 760	2 206	2 806	2 572	748	916	2 197
1952	4 963	9 950	2 207	2 937	2 592	794	932	2 261
1953	5 186	10 220	2 296	3 013	2 612	832	945	2 332
1954	5 437	10 000	2 370	3 106	2 705	850	970	2 367
1955	5 740	10 511	2 495	3 313	2 799	871	981	2 469
1956	5 962	10 569	2 521	3 566	2 840	912	999	2 537
1957	6 181	10 567	2 682	3 576	2 974	932	1 013	2 581
1958	6 282	10 323	2 806	3 777	3 037	970	1 013	2 609
1959	6 530	10 866	2 921	3 669	3 024	996	1 044	2 680
1960	6 896	10 961	3 070	3 945	3 133	1 029	1 066	2 777
1961	7 203	11 025	3 218	4 098	3 192	1 024	1 065	2 834
1962	7 483	11 510	3 245	4 140	3 234	1 052	1 082	2 917
1963	7 767	11 844	3 372	3 985	3 241	1 100	1 132	2 982
1964	8 167	12 358	3 542	4 439	3 367	1 171	1 164	3 135
1965	8 441	12 967	3 664	4 634	3 439	1 203	1 197	3 233
1966	8 686	13 624	3 871	4 804	3 514	1 259	1 201	3 340
1967	8 936	13 816	3 996	4 963	3 576	1 290	1 194	3 395
1968	9 355	14 320	4 106	5 202	3 691	1 343	1 223	3 510
1969	9 825	14 657	4 200	5 225	3 828	1 438	1 286	3 631
1970	10 195	14 560	4 315	5 575	3 986	1 530	1 357	3 736
1971	10 465	14 856	4 596	5 667	4 117	1 577	1 382	3 813
1972	10 860	15 450	4 790	5 643	4 271	1 631	1 397	3 914
1973	11 416	16 179	4 988	6 059	4 504	1 720	1 410	4 091
1974	11 611	16 053	5 239	6 176	4 659	1 721	1 438	4 107
1975	11 521	15 892	5 377	6 135	4 687	1 766	1 418	4 094
1976	11 983	16 550	5 469	6 363	4 833	1 820	1 472	4 220
1977	12 289	17 069	5 612	6 454	4 948	1 887	1 492	4 317
1978	12 621	17 803	5 749	6 559	5 047	1 962	1 487	4 430
1979	13 041	18 233	5 793	6 472	5 247	2 004	1 512	4 508
1980	13 197	18 060	5 786	6 426	5 412	2 034	1 536	4 520
1981	13 185	18 339	5 685	6 430	5 327	2 081	1 509	4 530
1982	13 269	17 814	5 705	6 533	5 152	2 139	1 512	4 511
1983	13 491	18 333	5 762	6 680	4 918	2 200	1 477	4 554
1984	13 794	19 463	5 913	6 703	5 002	2 287	1 466	4 681
1985	14 113	20 062	5 892	6 701	5 052	2 359	1 468	4 762
1986	14 476	20 531	6 028	6 914	5 154	2 414	1 459	4 848
1987	14 857	21 067	5 966	6 942	5 212	2 506	1 441	4 939
1988	15 406	21 746	6 008	7 031	5 158	2 622	1 459	5 065
1989	15 856	22 250	5 915	7 098	5 123	2 686	1 463	5 140
1990	15 966	22 345	5 450	6 878	5 053	2 781	1 444	5 157
1991	16 152	21 918	4 844	6 409	5 145	2 848	1 414	5 132
1992	16 256	22 243	4 591	5 451	5 213	2 962	1 378	5 152
1993	16 129	22 547	4 526	4 903	5 299	3 072	1 356	5 182
1994	16 517	23 200	4 715	4 207	5 474	3 193	1 352	5 284
1995	16 860	23 559	4 998	3 976	5 460	3 330	1 358	5 385
1996	17 097	24 084	5 196	3 854	5 556	3 482	1 403	5 517
1997	17 502	24 799	5 333	3 939	5 753	3 587	1 416	5 656
1998	17 974	25 571	5 487	3 861	5 793	3 588	1 434	5 720
1999	18 413	26 349	5 588	4 027	5 718	3 672	1 447	5 830
2000	19 002	27 065	5 804	4 351	5 838	3 817	1 464	6 012
2001	19 256	26 943	6 027	4 626	5 811	3 861	1 489	6 049

Table 7a. **Year–to–Year Percentage Change in World Population, by Region, 1950-2001**

	Western Europe	Western Offshoots	Eastern Europe	Former USSR	Latin America	Asia	Africa	World
1950								
1951	0.7	1.8	1.2	1.7	2.7	1.8	2.1	1.7
1952	0.6	1.9	1.2	1.7	2.7	2.0	2.1	1.8
1953	0.6	1.8	1.4	1.7	2.7	2.0	2.1	1.8
1954	0.6	1.9	1.4	1.7	2.7	2.1	2.1	1.9
1955	0.6	1.9	1.5	1.8	2.8	2.1	2.2	1.9
1956	0.7	1.9	1.4	1.8	2.8	2.1	2.2	1.9
1957	0.7	2.0	1.1	1.8	2.8	2.3	2.2	2.0
1958	0.7	1.8	1.1	1.8	2.8	2.3	2.3	2.1
1959	0.8	1.8	1.1	1.8	2.9	2.1	2.3	1.9
1960	0.8	1.7	1.1	1.8	2.9	1.3	2.3	1.5
1961	0.8	1.7	1.0	1.8	2.8	1.0	2.3	1.3
1962	1.0	1.6	0.9	1.7	2.8	1.7	2.3	1.7
1963	0.9	1.5	0.9	1.5	2.8	2.4	2.5	2.1
1964	0.9	1.5	0.8	1.4	2.8	2.3	2.5	2.0
1965	0.8	1.4	0.8	1.2	2.8	2.3	2.5	2.0
1966	0.7	1.3	0.8	1.1	2.8	2.4	2.5	2.1
1967	0.6	1.2	0.7	1.1	2.7	2.4	2.6	2.0
1968	0.6	1.1	1.0	1.0	2.7	2.4	2.6	2.0
1969	0.7	1.1	0.8	1.0	2.7	2.4	2.6	2.0
1970	0.7	1.3	0.8	0.9	2.6	2.5	2.5	2.1
1971	0.7	1.3	0.8	1.0	2.6	2.5	2.6	2.1
1972	0.6	1.1	0.8	1.0	2.5	2.4	2.6	2.0
1973	0.6	1.0	0.8	1.0	2.5	2.3	2.6	2.0
1974	0.5	1.0	0.9	1.0	2.5	2.2	2.6	1.9
1975	0.4	1.1	0.9	1.0	2.4	2.1	2.6	1.8
1976	0.3	1.0	0.9	0.9	2.3	1.9	2.8	1.7
1977	0.3	1.0	0.9	0.9	2.3	1.9	2.8	1.7
1978	0.3	1.1	0.8	0.9	2.3	1.9	2.8	1.7
1979	0.3	1.1	0.7	0.9	2.3	2.0	2.9	1.8
1980	0.4	1.2	0.6	0.8	2.2	1.9	2.9	1.8
1981	0.3	1.1	0.6	0.8	2.2	1.8	2.8	1.7
1982	0.2	1.0	0.6	0.9	2.2	1.6	2.9	1.6
1983	0.1	0.9	0.5	0.9	2.1	2.2	3.0	1.9
1984	0.2	0.9	0.4	0.9	2.0	1.8	2.9	1.7
1985	0.2	0.9	0.5	0.9	2.0	1.8	2.9	1.7
1986	0.2	0.9	0.4	0.9	2.0	1.9	2.8	1.7
1987	0.2	1.0	0.4	0.9	2.0	1.9	2.8	1.7
1988	0.3	1.0	0.2	0.8	2.0	1.9	2.8	1.7
1989	0.5	1.1	0.2	0.5	2.0	1.8	2.8	1.7
1990	0.5	1.2	0.1	0.7	1.9	1.8	2.8	1.7
1991	0.5	1.3	0.2	0.6	1.8	1.7	2.9	1.6
1992	0.5	1.3	0.0	0.5	1.8	1.6	2.7	1.6
1993	0.5	1.3	-0.2	0.2	1.8	1.6	2.6	1.6
1994	0.4	1.2	-0.2	0.0	1.7	1.6	2.5	1.5
1995	0.3	1.2	-0.2	-0.1	1.7	1.6	2.5	1.5
1996	0.3	1.2	-0.1	-0.1	1.7	1.5	2.4	1.4
1997	0.3	1.2	0.0	-0.1	1.6	1.4	2.5	1.4
1998	0.2	1.2	0.0	-0.1	1.6	1.4	2.4	1.4
1999	0.2	1.1	0.0	-0.1	1.5	1.5	2.4	1.4
2000	0.3	1.1	0.0	-0.1	1.5	1.2	2.3	1.2
2001	0.3	1.0	0.0	-0.1	1.5	1.3	2.2	1.3

Table 7b. **Year–to–Year Percentage Change in World GDP Volume, by Region, 1950-2001**

	Western Europe	Western Offshoots	Eastern Europe	Former USSR	Latin America	Asia	Africa	World
1950								
1951	5.9	7.2	5.8	0.5	5.4	7.0	4.7	5.9
1952	3.6	3.9	1.3	6.5	3.5	8.3	3.8	4.8
1953	5.1	4.5	5.5	4.3	3.5	6.9	3.7	5.0
1954	5.5	-0.3	4.7	4.9	6.4	4.3	4.8	3.4
1955	6.2	7.1	6.8	8.6	6.3	4.7	3.5	6.3
1956	4.6	2.4	2.4	9.6	4.3	6.8	4.1	4.7
1957	4.4	2.0	7.6	2.0	7.6	4.5	3.7	3.8
1958	2.4	-0.6	5.8	7.5	5.0	6.5	2.3	3.2
1959	4.8	7.1	5.2	-1.1	2.4	4.8	5.5	4.7
1960	6.4	2.6	6.2	9.5	6.6	4.7	4.4	5.2
1961	5.3	2.3	5.9	5.7	4.8	0.5	2.2	3.4
1962	4.9	6.1	1.7	2.7	4.2	4.5	4.0	4.7
1963	4.7	4.5	4.8	-2.3	3.0	7.0	7.1	4.3
1964	6.1	5.9	5.9	12.9	6.8	8.9	5.4	7.3
1965	4.2	6.3	4.3	5.7	5.0	5.1	5.5	5.2
1966	3.7	6.4	6.4	4.9	5.0	7.2	2.9	5.4
1967	3.5	2.6	4.0	4.4	4.5	4.9	2.0	3.7
1968	5.3	4.8	3.8	5.9	6.0	6.6	5.1	5.5
1969	5.7	3.5	3.1	1.4	6.5	9.6	7.8	5.6
1970	4.4	0.6	3.5	7.7	6.8	9.1	8.2	5.1
1971	3.4	3.4	7.3	2.7	6.0	5.7	4.5	4.2
1972	4.4	5.2	5.0	0.6	6.4	5.9	3.7	4.7
1973	5.7	5.8	4.9	8.4	8.1	7.9	3.6	6.6
1974	2.2	0.2	6.0	2.9	6.0	2.3	4.6	2.3
1975	-0.4	0.0	3.6	0.3	3.0	4.8	1.2	1.5
1976	4.3	5.2	2.6	4.7	5.5	5.1	6.7	4.9
1977	2.9	4.2	3.5	2.4	4.8	5.6	4.2	4.1
1978	3.0	5.4	3.2	2.5	4.3	6.0	2.5	4.4
1979	3.7	3.5	1.5	-0.5	6.3	4.1	4.7	3.6
1980	1.6	0.2	0.5	0.1	5.4	3.5	4.5	2.0
1981	0.2	2.6	-1.2	0.9	0.6	4.1	1.0	1.9
1982	0.8	-1.9	0.9	2.5	-1.2	4.5	3.1	1.2
1983	1.8	3.9	1.5	3.2	-2.5	5.1	0.6	2.9
1984	2.4	7.1	3.1	1.3	3.8	5.9	2.1	4.6
1985	2.5	4.0	0.1	0.9	3.0	5.1	3.1	3.5
1986	2.8	3.3	2.8	4.1	4.1	4.2	2.2	3.5
1987	2.9	3.6	-0.6	1.3	3.1	5.8	1.6	3.6
1988	4.0	4.2	0.9	2.1	0.9	6.6	4.1	4.3
1989	3.4	3.4	-1.3	1.5	1.3	4.3	3.1	3.2
1990	1.2	1.6	-7.7	-2.4	0.5	5.4	1.4	2.0
1991	1.7	-0.6	-10.9	-6.3	3.7	4.1	0.8	1.1
1992	1.1	2.8	-5.2	-14.6	3.1	5.7	0.1	2.0
1993	-0.3	2.7	-1.6	-9.9	3.4	5.4	0.9	2.2
1994	2.8	4.1	4.0	-14.2	5.1	5.6	2.2	3.4
1995	2.4	2.8	5.8	-5.5	1.5	6.0	3.0	3.4
1996	1.7	3.4	3.8	-3.2	3.5	6.1	5.7	3.9
1997	2.6	4.2	2.6	2.1	5.2	4.5	3.4	3.9
1998	2.9	4.3	2.9	-2.1	2.3	1.4	3.7	2.5
1999	2.7	4.2	1.8	4.2	0.2	3.9	3.3	3.4
2000	3.5	3.8	3.9	7.9	3.6	5.2	3.5	4.4
2001	1.6	0.5	3.9	6.2	1.0	2.5	4.0	1.9

Table 7b. **Year-to-Year Percentage Change in World Per Capita GDP, by Region, 1950-2001**

	Western Europe	Western Offshoots	Eastern Europe	Former USSR	Latin America	Asia	Africa	World
1950								
1951	5.2	5.3	4.5	-1.3	2.6	5.0	2.6	4.1
1952	3.1	1.9	0.1	4.7	0.8	6.2	1.7	2.9
1953	4.5	2.7	4.0	2.6	0.8	4.8	1.5	3.1
1954	4.8	-2.2	3.2	3.1	3.6	2.1	2.6	1.5
1955	5.6	5.1	5.3	6.7	3.5	2.5	1.2	4.3
1956	3.9	0.5	1.0	7.7	1.5	4.6	1.8	2.8
1957	3.7	0.0	6.4	0.3	4.7	2.2	1.4	1.7
1958	1.6	-2.3	4.6	5.6	2.1	4.1	0.0	1.1
1959	3.9	5.3	4.1	-2.9	-0.4	2.7	3.1	2.7
1960	5.6	0.9	5.1	7.5	3.6	3.4	2.1	3.6
1961	4.4	0.6	4.8	3.9	1.9	-0.5	-0.1	2.1
1962	3.9	4.4	0.8	1.0	1.3	2.7	1.6	2.9
1963	3.8	2.9	3.9	-3.7	0.2	4.5	4.6	2.2
1964	5.2	4.3	5.1	11.4	3.9	6.5	2.8	5.1
1965	3.3	4.9	3.4	4.4	2.2	2.7	2.9	3.1
1966	2.9	5.1	5.6	3.7	2.2	4.7	0.3	3.3
1967	2.9	1.4	3.3	3.3	1.8	2.5	-0.6	1.6
1968	4.7	3.7	2.7	4.8	3.2	4.1	2.4	3.4
1969	5.0	2.3	2.3	0.4	3.7	7.0	5.1	3.4
1970	3.8	-0.7	2.7	6.7	4.1	6.4	5.6	2.9
1971	2.6	2.0	6.5	1.7	3.3	3.1	1.9	2.1
1972	3.8	4.0	4.2	-0.4	3.8	3.4	1.1	2.7
1973	5.1	4.7	4.1	7.4	5.5	5.4	0.9	4.5
1974	1.7	-0.8	5.0	1.9	3.4	0.1	2.0	0.4
1975	-0.8	-1.0	2.6	-0.7	0.6	2.6	-1.4	-0.3
1976	4.0	4.1	1.7	3.7	3.1	3.1	3.8	3.1
1977	2.6	3.1	2.6	1.4	2.4	3.6	1.3	2.3
1978	2.7	4.3	2.4	1.6	2.0	4.0	-0.4	2.6
1979	3.3	2.4	0.8	-1.3	3.9	2.1	1.7	1.7
1980	1.2	-0.9	-0.1	-0.7	3.2	1.5	1.6	0.3
1981	-0.1	1.5	-1.7	0.1	-1.6	2.3	-1.7	0.2
1982	0.6	-2.9	0.3	1.6	-3.3	2.8	0.2	-0.4
1983	1.7	2.9	1.0	2.3	-4.5	2.8	-2.3	0.9
1984	2.2	6.2	2.6	0.3	1.7	3.9	-0.8	2.8
1985	2.3	3.1	-0.4	0.0	1.0	3.2	0.2	1.7
1986	2.6	2.3	2.3	3.2	2.0	2.4	-0.7	1.8
1987	2.6	2.6	-1.0	0.4	1.1	3.8	-1.2	1.9
1988	3.7	3.2	0.7	1.3	-1.0	4.6	1.3	2.6
1989	2.9	2.3	-1.6	1.0	-0.7	2.4	0.3	1.5
1990	0.7	0.4	-7.9	-3.1	-1.4	3.5	-1.3	0.3
1991	1.2	-1.9	-11.1	-6.8	1.8	2.4	-2.1	-0.5
1992	0.6	1.5	-5.2	-15.0	1.3	4.0	-2.5	0.4
1993	-0.8	1.4	-1.4	-10.1	1.6	3.7	-1.6	0.6
1994	2.4	2.9	4.2	-14.2	3.3	3.9	-0.3	1.9
1995	2.1	1.5	6.0	-5.5	-0.2	4.3	0.5	1.9
1996	1.4	2.2	4.0	-3.1	1.8	4.6	3.2	2.4
1997	2.4	3.0	2.7	2.2	3.6	3.0	0.9	2.5
1998	2.7	3.1	2.9	-2.0	0.7	0.0	1.3	1.1
1999	2.4	3.0	1.9	4.3	-1.3	2.3	0.9	1.9
2000	3.2	2.7	3.9	8.0	2.1	4.0	1.2	3.1
2001	1.3	-0.5	3.9	6.3	-0.5	1.1	1.7	0.6

Table 7a*. **Alternative UNPD World Population Estimates by Region, 1950-2000**
(000 at mid-year)

	Western Europe	Western Offshoots	Eastern Europe	Former USSR	Latin America	Asia	Africa	World
1950	305 346	181 677	87 673	180 980	167 030	1 375 431	220 888	2 519 025
1951	306 928	184 495	89 008	183 626	171 440	1 404 108	225 634	2 565 238
1952	308 740	187 617	90 307	186 630	176 038	1 431 671	230 526	2 611 528
1953	310 693	190 973	91 574	189 877	180 796	1 458 753	235 583	2 658 249
1954	312 722	194 501	92 809	193 275	185 695	1 485 891	240 822	2 705 716
1955	314 794	198 147	94 014	196 752	190 728	1 513 524	246 257	2 754 214
1956	316 900	201 863	95 184	200 259	195 895	1 541 990	251 899	2 803 991
1957	319 062	205 608	96 318	203 771	201 209	1 571 534	257 757	2 855 260
1958	321 323	209 350	97 410	207 281	206 690	1 602 308	263 838	2 908 200
1959	323 739	213 060	98 456	210 795	212 363	1 634 396	270 146	2 962 955
1960	326 359	216 716	99 451	214 322	218 248	1 667 851	276 686	3 019 633
1961	329 197	220 297	100 394	217 854	224 354	1 702 748	283 464	3 078 307
1962	332 210	223 784	101 290	221 354	230 665	1 739 223	290 486	3 139 011
1963	335 287	227 156	102 149	224 755	237 144	1 777 493	297 763	3 201 746
1964	338 280	230 396	102 984	227 968	243 734	1 817 804	305 307	3 266 473
1965	341 080	233 495	103 808	230 936	250 396	1 860 282	313 125	3 333 121
1966	343 641	236 437	104 624	233 624	257 114	1 904 964	321 237	3 401 640
1967	345 987	239 229	105 434	236 060	263 896	1 951 655	329 644	3 471 903
1968	348 156	241 914	106 242	238 325	270 756	1 999 935	338 319	3 543 647
1969	350 222	244 550	107 055	240 537	277 718	2 049 230	347 225	3 616 536
1970	352 234	247 183	107 875	242 782	284 800	2 099 059	356 340	3 690 271
1971	354 199	249 835	108 703	245 091	291 995	2 149 357	365 655	3 764 836
1972	356 094	252 499	109 540	247 446	299 295	2 200 035	375 204	3 840 112
1973	357 905	255 153	110 391	249 818	306 704	2 250 556	385 056	3 915 583
1974	359 610	257 758	111 263	252 162	314 230	2 300 282	395 306	3 990 612
1975	361 194	260 291	112 160	254 445	321 875	2 348 797	406 026	4 064 789
1976	362 669	262 743	113 083	256 663	329 641	2 395 837	417 236	4 137 873
1977	364 044	265 141	114 026	258 840	337 514	2 441 605	428 928	4 210 098
1978	365 304	267 539	114 964	261 001	345 458	2 486 754	441 103	4 282 122
1979	366 427	270 009	115 868	263 183	353 425	2 532 225	453 754	4 354 891
1980	367 408	272 605	116 714	265 411	361 380	2 578 728	466 871	4 429 118
1981	368 237	275 349	117 489	267 671	369 308	2 626 370	480 450	4 504 874
1982	368 943	278 229	118 195	269 949	377 210	2 675 010	494 482	4 582 017
1983	369 609	281 207	118 841	272 279	385 096	2 724 796	508 941	4 660 769
1984	370 346	284 231	119 445	274 702	392 981	2 775 840	523 797	4 741 343
1985	371 234	287 262	120 019	277 233	400 878	2 828 160	539 016	4 823 802
1986	372 294	290 286	120 572	279 898	408 783	2 881 900	554 594	4 908 327
1987	373 506	293 319	121 092	282 641	416 690	2 936 899	570 508	4 994 655
1988	374 859	296 382	121 543	285 302	424 597	2 992 473	586 684	5 081 841
1989	376 328	299 510	121 876	287 665	432 504	3 047 698	603 029	5 168 610
1990	377 885	302 725	122 060	289 574	440 408	3 101 898	619 477	5 254 027
1991	379 537	306 028	122 079	290 967	448 310	3 154 793	635 996	5 337 710
1992	381 267	309 403	121 954	291 886	456 206	3 206 517	652 604	5 419 837
1993	382 990	312 834	121 739	292 411	464 094	3 257 320	669 345	5 500 733
1994	384 595	316 298	121 512	292 670	471 971	3 307 635	686 288	5 580 970
1995	386 001	319 774	121 329	292 761	479 836	3 357 778	703 487	5 660 967
1996	387 172	323 261	121 211	292 711	487 684	3 407 796	720 952	5 740 787
1997	388 124	326 752	121 143	292 504	495 515	3 457 557	738 675	5 820 270
1998	388 894	330 214	121 103	292 142	503 325	3 506 994	756 680	5 899 353
1999	389 544	333 606	121 055	291 620	511 109	3 562 826	774 991	5 984 752
2000	390 121	336 903	120 970	290 940	518 865	3 604 492	793 627	6 055 918

Table 7a**. **World Population: Confrontation of UNPD and USBC-Maddison Estimates**
(ratio UNPD to USBC-Maddison)

	Western Europe	Western Offshoots	Eastern Europe	Former USSR	Latin America	Asia	Africa	World
1950	1.001	1.030	1.000	1.008	1.007	0.995	0.972	0.998
1951	1.000	1.027	1.003	1.005	1.006	0.997	0.972	0.999
1952	1.000	1.025	1.005	1.004	1.006	0.997	0.973	0.999
1953	1.000	1.025	1.005	1.005	1.006	0.996	0.973	0.998
1954	1.000	1.025	1.005	1.006	1.006	0.994	0.974	0.997
1955	1.001	1.025	1.003	1.006	1.006	0.991	0.974	0.996
1956	1.000	1.025	1.002	1.006	1.005	0.989	0.975	0.994
1957	1.000	1.023	1.003	1.006	1.004	0.986	0.976	0.992
1958	1.000	1.024	1.003	1.005	1.003	0.982	0.976	0.990
1959	1.000	1.024	1.002	1.004	1.002	0.982	0.977	0.990
1960	1.000	1.024	1.002	1.003	1.001	0.989	0.978	0.994
1961	1.000	1.023	1.001	1.001	1.001	1.000	0.980	1.000
1962	1.000	1.023	1.001	1.001	1.001	1.004	0.981	1.002
1963	1.000	1.023	1.001	1.001	1.001	1.002	0.982	1.001
1964	1.000	1.022	1.001	1.001	1.000	1.002	0.983	1.001
1965	1.001	1.022	1.001	1.002	1.000	1.002	0.983	1.001
1966	1.001	1.022	1.001	1.002	0.999	1.002	0.984	1.001
1967	1.001	1.022	1.002	1.002	0.998	1.003	0.984	1.002
1968	1.002	1.022	0.999	1.001	0.998	1.003	0.985	1.002
1969	1.001	1.022	0.999	1.001	0.997	1.003	0.985	1.002
1970	1.000	1.020	1.000	1.001	0.996	1.003	0.987	1.001
1971	0.999	1.018	1.000	1.001	0.995	1.002	0.987	1.000
1972	0.998	1.017	1.000	1.000	0.995	1.001	0.987	1.000
1973	0.997	1.017	1.000	1.000	0.995	1.001	0.987	1.000
1974	0.998	1.017	0.999	1.000	0.995	1.001	0.987	1.000
1975	0.998	1.016	0.998	1.000	0.995	1.001	0.988	1.000
1976	1.000	1.016	0.998	0.999	0.996	1.002	0.988	1.000
1977	1.001	1.015	0.997	0.999	0.996	1.002	0.988	1.000
1978	1.001	1.013	0.998	0.998	0.997	1.001	0.988	1.000
1979	1.001	1.012	0.998	0.998	0.997	1.000	0.988	0.999
1980	1.000	1.009	0.999	0.998	0.998	0.999	0.988	0.999
1981	0.999	1.009	1.000	0.998	0.998	1.000	0.988	0.999
1982	0.999	1.009	1.000	0.998	0.997	1.002	0.988	1.000
1983	0.999	1.010	1.001	0.997	0.997	0.999	0.988	0.998
1984	1.000	1.012	1.001	0.997	0.997	0.999	0.988	0.998
1985	1.000	1.013	1.001	0.997	0.997	0.999	0.988	0.999
1986	1.001	1.014	1.001	0.997	0.996	1.000	0.988	0.999
1987	1.002	1.015	1.002	0.998	0.996	1.000	0.988	0.999
1988	1.002	1.016	1.004	0.999	0.995	1.000	0.989	0.999
1989	1.001	1.016	1.004	1.002	0.994	1.000	0.989	0.999
1990	1.000	1.015	1.004	1.002	0.994	1.000	0.988	0.999
1991	1.000	1.012	1.002	1.001	0.993	1.000	0.986	0.999
1992	0.999	1.010	1.001	0.999	0.993	1.000	0.985	0.998
1993	0.999	1.008	1.001	0.999	0.992	1.000	0.985	0.998
1994	1.000	1.007	1.001	1.000	0.992	1.000	0.986	0.998
1995	1.000	1.006	1.002	1.001	0.991	0.999	0.985	0.997
1996	1.000	1.005	1.002	1.002	0.991	0.999	0.986	0.997
1997	1.000	1.004	1.002	1.003	0.991	0.999	0.986	0.997
1998	1.000	1.003	1.001	1.003	0.991	0.999	0.987	0.997
1999	0.999	1.002	1.001	1.002	0.991	1.000	0.987	0.998
2000	0.998	1.001	1.000	1.001	0.991	1.000	0.988	0.997

HS-8: The World Economy, 1-2001 AD

Tables HS-8 show levels of population, GDP and per capita GDP in 20 countries, 7 regions and the world for eight benchmark years in the past two millennia. There are also 5 analytical tables showing rates of growth and shares of world population and GDP. HS-7 explained the derivation of estimates for 1950–2001. Earlier than this, it is useful to distinguish between estimates for 1820–1950 and those for the centuries before 1820 where the documentation is weaker and the element of conjecture bigger.

Population Movement 1820–1950

For West European countries and Western Offshoots, population estimates for this period are based mainly on censuses dating back to the eighteenth century for Scandinavia and Spain and the early nineteenth for most other countries. The sources are described in HS-1 and HS-2. For Western Europe, annual estimates, adjusted to a midyear basis are shown for all countries back to 1820. For Western Offshoots, they are shown separately for the indigenous population and those of European/African origin at decade intervals for 1820–1870, with annual estimates for the total population thereafter.

For Eastern Europe, annual estimates are shown from 1920. Before the first world–war, these countries were divided between the Austro–Hungarian, Ottoman, Russian and German Empires. Derivation of estimates in the territory corresponding to present boundaries is possible, but they are too rough to warrant presentation on an annual basis. Estimates for the territory of the former USSR are also too rough to warrant annual presentation before 1920. Population sources are described in HS-3.

For Latin America annual estimates are shown back to 1900 for 23 countries. The 1820 and 1870 estimates in Maddison (2001) for the smaller countries are revised and augmented from the *Cambridge History of Latin America*, Engerman and Higman (1997) and other sources cited in HS-4.

For Asia annual estimates are shown from 1913 for the 16 core countries, and for benchmark years 1820, 1850 1870 1890 and 1900. For China, India, Indonesia and Japan annual estimates are shown back to 1870. For other countries there are estimates for benchmark years 1820, 1870, 1900 and 1913. In most cases the sources in HS-5 are the same as in Maddison (2001).

For Africa, the statistical basis is weaker than elsewhere. I show no annual estimates before 1950, but give detail for the sample countries for 1820, 1870 and 1913 in Table 6–10 of HS-6.

Population Change 1–1820 AD

For the centuries before 1820 the most comprehensive evidence is for population and it is of greater proportionate importance for analysis as per capita income growth was much slower then and economic growth was largely extensive.

Demographic changes, e.g. increases in life expectancy, changes in average age which affect labour force participation, changes in the structure of the labour force, are important in providing clues to per capita income development. A striking example is the urbanisation ratio. Thanks to the work of de Vries for Europe and of Rozman for Asia, one can, for some countries, measure the proportion of population living in towns with more than 10 000 inhabitants. In the year 1000, this ratio was virtually zero in Europe (there were only 4 towns with more than 10 000 inhabitants) and in China it was 3 per cent. By 1800 the West European urban ratio was 10.6 per cent, the Chinese 3.8 per cent. When countries are able to expand their urban ratios, it indicates a growing surplus beyond subsistence in agriculture, and suggests that the non–agricultural component of economic activity is increasing. These changing differentials in urban ratios were used to buttress other evidence on per capita progress in China and Europe in Maddison (1998). The Chinese bureaucracy kept population registers which go back more than 2 000 years. These records were designed to assess taxable capacity, and include information on cultivated area and crop production, which was used by Perkins (1969) to assess long run movements in Chinese output per capita. Bagnall and Frier (1994) made brilliant use of fragments of ancient censuses to estimate occupational structure, household size, marriage patterns, fertility and life expectation in Roman Egypt of the third century.

Serious work on historical demography started in the seventeenth century with John Graunt (see Prologue). Modernised techniques and similar types of evidence have been used to make retrospective estimates of population for other European countries for periods before census material was available. Investigations of this character have been carried out by a) the Office of Population Research in Princeton University (established in 1936); b) INED (Institut National des Études Démographiques) founded in the 1950s to exploit family reconstitution techniques developed by Louis Henry; c) the Cambridge Group for the History of Population and Family Structure (established in the 1970s) has carried out a massive research project to reconstitute English population size and structure on an annual basis back to 1541 (Wrigley et al., 1997). This kind of analysis has been sharpened by the application of massive computing power.

Research on Japanese population history has blossomed under the leadership of Akira Hayami and Osamu Saito. Ester Boserup's (1965) analysis of the interaction between demographic pressure, agricultural technology and intensity of labour input in Asia has helped discredit simplistic Malthusian interpretations. There has been a flood of publications on Latin American demography and the shipment of slaves from Africa. As a result of these efforts we are better placed to measure long term changes in world population. The most detailed and best documented are those in McEvedy and Jones (1978). This was the source of my estimates for Africa (see also the masterly analysis of African development in McEvedy, 1995).

Appendix B of Maddison 2001 provided source notes and estimates for 20 countries and 7 regions for benchmark years between the first century and 1700. In this study more country detail is shown for Western Europe, Western Offshoots, Latin America back to 1500 and for Africa back to the first century. There are some changes in the regional totals for Africa (see Table 6–1), but none for other regions.

GDP Growth 1820–1950

Before the second worldwar, only 10 countries had official estimates of national income, assembled without international guidelines to provide comparability. None of these are suitable for our purpose, but there are retrospective official estimates of fairly recent vintage which I used for Austria from 1830, Norway from 1865, Netherlands from 1913, Canada from 1926 and the United States from 1929.

There were non–official estimates in pre–war years. Colin Clark (1940) made a comprehensive survey, but all those he cited have now been superseded. In the past 60 years, work on retrospective national accounts has been undertaken by a large number of scholars who have generally linked their series to official post–war estimates. The initial thrust for these exercises in quantitative economic history was given by Simon Kuznets. His very long career included creation of official US accounts in 1934 and 5 monographs of historical accounts for the United States in 1941–61. These set high standards of scholarship with meticulous and transparent description of sources and methods. These characteristics have permitted succeeding generations of scholars to stand on his shoulders. His persuasive power and influence stemmed from professional integrity and depth of scholarship. He was free from partisanship, open to new ideas and willing to comment sympathetically in detail on the work of others. His influence was reinforced by his style of analysis–use of ideas that could be clearly expressed in literary form, and implemented with relatively simple statistical techniques. He encouraged a band of scholars all over the world to consider that such an enterprise was feasible, exciting, important and rewarding. He encouraged comparable studies for Australia, China, France, Germany, Italy, Japan, Sweden and the United Kingdom. To facilitate this research he helped found the International Association for Income and Wealth in 1947, persuaded the US Social Science Research Council to finance comparative research in other countries, and played a major role in the creation of the Yale Growth Center, which produced basic growth studies for Argentina, Egypt, Korea, Sri Lanka, Taiwan, and the USSR. Between 1953 and 1989 he published 8 volumes containing 70 analytical essays comparing the results which emerged from these quantitative studies and assessing their significance for the study of "modern economic growth". The temporal horizon of this new generation of Kuznetsian scholarship was concentrated on developments since the mid–nineteenth century.

Several university centres are now active in this field, sponsoring their own research and strengthening international networks by holding workshops. Kazushi Ohkawa organised a 14–volume study (1966–1988) of Japanese growth at Hitotsubashi University. The University now has an ambitious comparative project on the quantitative economic history of China, Indonesia, Korea, Taiwan and Vietnam. In the Netherlands, the University of Groningen has been active in this field since 1982. Its Growth and Development Centre has played a major role in international studies of productivity levels and in developing an international database on economic growth. It has published research studies on GDP growth in Brazil, Germany, Indonesia, Japan, Korea, Mexico, the Netherlands, Taiwan, Thailand, and a six–country comparison for Latin America. It maintained close links with Jan Luiten van Zanden's team working on Dutch growth in the University of Utrecht and with the University of Leuven's research on long–run growth in Belgium. It is also linked with the COPPAA group (Comparisons of Output, Productivity and Purchasing Power in Asia and Australia), based in Brisbane, which has carried out a number of studies of comparative performance of economies in the Asia–Pacific region, and was associated with the research of Maddison (1998) on China and Sivasubramonian (2000) on India. Scandinavia has a long history in this field. There have been five rounds of research in Sweden since 1937, and Olle Krantz has made annual estimates of GDP growth since 1800. Riitta Hjerppe supervised a 13 volume study for Finland which was completed in 1989. Svend Aage Hansen produced the second major study of Danish growth in 1974, with annual GDP estimates back to 1818. There is now a Nordic Group, which is revising the Scandinavian historical accounts to enhance their comparability. The International Association for Research in Income and Wealth (IARIW) has held conferences and workshops on measurement of comparative GDP growth and levels of performance, problems of methodology and definition since 1949, and has published its quarterly *Review of Income and Wealth* since 1968. Its membership has always included official statisticians, established scholars working on historical accounts, and younger researchers serving their apprenticeship in this field and has played a major role in developing a standardised approach and extending the range of countries for which studies are available. The European Historical Economics Society (EHES) has also been active in promoting research on quantitative economic history since 1997 when it created the *European Review of Economic History*.

The vitality of recent research activity is clear from Table 8–1 which shows amendments to my estimates since publication of Maddison (2001). The proxy estimates I use for Bulgaria, Poland, Romania and Yugoslavia for 1870 to the 1920s were derived from David Good and Tongshu Ma (1999). Their approach is a variant of that developed originally by Wilfred Beckerman (1966) as a shortcut cross–section technique to measure comparative income levels. Nick Crafts (1983) was the first to use it for diachronic analysis (see Maddison, 1990).

Table 8-1. **Amendments to GDP Estimates in Maddison (2001) for 1820-1950**

Western Europe	Western Offshoots	Eastern Europe and former USSR	Latin America	Asia	Africa
Amendments and New Estimates					
France 1820-70	Australia 1820-70, and 1911-38	Hungary 1870-1900	Cuba 1929-50	Jordan 1820-1950	Algeria 1880–1950
Netherlands 1820-1913			Jamaica 1820-1950	Malaysia 1911-50	Egypt 1886-1950
Portugal 1851-1910			Uruguay 1870-1913	Palestine 1820-1950	Ghana 1891-1950
Spain 1850-1950				Philippines 1902-50	Tunisia 1910-50
Switzerland 1851-1913				Sri Lanka 1820-1950	
				South Korea 1913-50	
				Syria 1820-1950	
				Turkey 1820-1950	
				Vietnam 1820-1950	
Amended and New Proxy Estimates					
Greece 1820-1913	New Zealand 1870-1913	Albania 1870-1950	Caribbean 1820-1950	Arabia 1820-1950	Algeria 1820-80
Switzerland 1820-51, and 1914-24		Bulgaria 1870-1924		Iran 1820-1950	Egypt 1820-86
		Poland 1870-1929		Iraq 1820-1950	Ghana 1820-91
		Romania 1870-1926		Lebanon 1820-1950	Morocco 1820-1920
		Yugoslavia 1870-1912		North Korea 1820-1950	Tunisia 1820-1910
					South Africa 1820-1912

GDP Growth before 1820

Western Europe: Per capita GDP growth rates prior to 1820 in Maddison (2001) are unchanged for Germany, Greece, the Netherlands, Portugal, Spain, Sweden and 13 small territories, but *levels* for 1500–1700 for these countries are affected by the amendments for 1820. In the case of France, the 1700–1820 growth rate is unchanged, but for the second half of the seventeenth century I assume stagnant per capita income because of hunger crises and the depressing influence of more or less continuous warfare, as noted by Boisguilbert and Vauban.

Western Offshoots: There are changes in the "multicultural" per capita GDP estimates 1700–1820 for Australia, Canada and New Zealand, as specified in detail in Tables 2–1 and 2–5; estimates for earlier centuries are unchanged.

Eastern Europe: Per capita GDP growth rates prior to 1820 are unchanged (0.1 percent a year), but the level for 1500–1700 is higher due to use of the Good–Ma proxies for the nineteenth century. There was no significant change for Russia.

Latin America: More detailed scrutiny of the evidence for the Caribbean sugar colonies led to upward revision of their per capita GDP and population levels in 1700–1820. See Table 4–1 for a more detailed sub–regional specification for 1500–1820 than in Maddison (2001).

Asia: GDP estimates for China, India, Indonesia and Japan in Maddison (2001) are unchanged, but I was able to make a more detailed scrutiny for West Asia thanks to recent work by Sevket Pamuk (see Tables 5–6 and 5–8). This raised the 1820 per capita GDP level for this group and its rate of growth 1700–1820. However the level estimates for 1700 and earlier are unchanged.

Africa: I have made more detailed sub–regional conjectures of long–run per capita GDP movement than in Maddison (2001), and presented a detailed analysis of the forces affecting the contours of demographic development. See source note HS–6, and Tables 6–1 and 6–2.

Crosschecking Measures of Comparative Levels of Performance before 1950

In this study, the bulk of the evidence consists of measures of inter–temporal change in GDP volume in individual countries, moving backwards from 2001. These are merged with measures of comparative GDP levels in the reference year 1990 at 1990 prices. The derivation of the inter–spatial estimates is explained in the source notes to HS–7 and in Table 7–2. A more comprehensive survey of the array of level estimates available for years between 1970 and 1990 can be found in Maddison (1995) pp. 162–179. This indicates the range of variance between the results of the successive ICP and PWT rounds and compares the attributes of alternative aggregation procedures (Paasche, Laspeyres, Fisher, EKS and Geary–Khamis). Heston and Summers (1993) compare the GDP growth rates implicit in ICP cross–section estimates of the relative standing of countries at different points of time with direct measures of inter–temporal GDP growth. They do not suggest that deviations between implicit and direct measures cast serious doubt on the latter. But such deviations are obviously a useful crosscheck.

I am satisfied that the 1990 benchmark estimates I used are the best presently available, with the possible exception of those for Eastern Europe and Africa, where the results of the OECD (2002) and PWT 6.1 exercises were too recent to be fully digested here (see Table 6–11). My 1990 benchmark can be subjected to comprehensive review when the World Bank's ICP exercise for 2004 becomes available.

However, updates of the 1990 benchmarks are less important than crosschecks on their validity as measures of relative performance in the distant past. It is clear that patterns of expenditure have changed radically over the long–term (as illustrated by the comparison of British expenditure patterns in 1688 and 1996 in Table 1), and there have also been big changes in relative prices and output structure. Some of these changes may have had a similar impact across countries, but this certainly needs to be investigated.

The most promising crosschecks on my estimates of relative standing in the past have come from binary comparisons of countries which have a significant weight in the world total. Some of these I have done myself, and there are several others which confirm my findings, e. g. those of Broadberry, Toda and van Zanden cited below.

It would also be useful to have ICOP or ICP type multilateral cross–section studies for different points of time in the past. It would not be possible replicate the detail or systemic rigour of modern ICP exercises (prices for more than 2000 items for 200 categories of expenditure), but real wage analysts have accumulated quite a lot of material on price structures which could be mobilised for this purpose. It would be useful and probably feasible to construct such a measure e. g. for 1900 or 1870, using reduced information, on the same lines as PWT estimates for countries where there has been no ICP exercise.

In the absence of such measures, Leandro Prados has made proxy estimates of PPPs and per capita income relatives for benchmark years since 1820, using econometrics, but no information on relative price structures. The results are too shaky to be a serious challenge to my estimates of relative levels in 1820 (see Table 8–2).

There are some authors (Paul Bairoch, Susan Hanley and Kenneth Pomeranz) whose judgement of the relative standing of major Asian countries and Western Europe is very different from mine. I give my reasons for disagreeing with them below.

Finally, I would like to comment on the real wage literature, some of which contradicts my view of West European development over the past few centuries.

a) Confirmatory Crosschecks

i) Stephen Broadberry (1997a): provides the most important of the binary cross–checks because he scrutinises the relative standing of the two successive lead counties (the United Kingdom and the United States) for benchmark years between 1870 and 1990. He found US productivity in manufacturing ahead of the United Kingdom by the middle of the 19th century, whereas I found that US productivity leadership at the aggregate level (GDP per man hour) began several decades later. At first sight these judgements seemed incompatible. As a test, Broadberry (1997a) made an ICOP type analysis of performance in 9 sectors and aggregate GDP in the two countries for 1870–1990 using 1937 value added weights. His results were compatible with my aggregate comparison with 1990 expenditure weights.

Broadberry, 1997b, compared UK and German performance for the same period with 1935 weights. He arrived at a similar confirmatory result, reconciling my estimate of the relative standing of the two countries in terms of aggregate GDP using 1990 expenditure weights, with his aggregate of value added by sector, using 1935 weights.

ii) Yasushi Toda (1990): presented a binary comparison of Japanese and Russian urban consumption levels in 1913 and Japan/USSR in 1975–6. He had a matched sample of 46 items at Japanese and Russian prices for 1913, and 110 items for 1975–6. He found the Japanese real per capita consumption level below that in Russia in 1913 and significantly higher in 1975–6. He had no explicit measure of growth, but the implicit differential in growth rates was very similar to what I found for per capita GDP for this period.

iii) Jan Luiten van Zanden (2003) expressed his concern that distortions may arise in using 1990 benchmarks back to 1820 because of changes in relative price structures. As a test, he compared Dutch growth to his new estimates of Javanese GDP growth for 1815–1880 and made PPP adjustments to compare *levels* of per capita income in the 1820s. He concludes that "in the 1820s per capita GDP in Java was about one third of Dutch per capita GDP" and that my estimates of relative levels of the two economies in 1820 are "by and large correct". He also makes comparative estimates of real wages, food consumption patterns, life expectation, and comparative physical stature of Dutch and Indonesians. These "direct indicators" show a narrower gap. He suggests that the relationship between real wages and average per capita GDP is highly variable and dependent on many factors such as the length of the working year, distribution of income, relative prices etc.

b) Conflicting Interpretations

i) Leandro Prados (2000) offers proxy estimates of per capita GDP levels relative to the United States for 17 benchmark years between 1820 and 1990. For 1880 he shows estimates for 23 countries but the coverage drops to 6 countries in 1820. He restricts the coverage to OECD countries, Argentina and Russia. He makes no use of inter-temporal measures of change in real GDP to estimate past levels of performance, nor does he measure price structures. Instead he backcasts an econometric relationship between purchasing power parity converters and exchange rates which prevailed in 1950-90.

He has 89 ICP or OEEC direct measures of this relationship to support the 155 estimates he shows for 7 reference years from 1950 to 1990 (see his tables 3 and 9). The gaps are filled by a structural equation, which attributes spreads between PPPs and exchange rates to four variables: a) openness of the economies as measured by the ratio of foreign trade (exports and imports) to GDP; b) the ratio of net capital inflows to GDP: *c)* the size of the country in terms of its surface area and population; and *d)* a periphery dummy (in cases where per capita income is less than half of the average level). His cross–section relatives are derived from estimates of these four items for the years he covers, and knowledge of the exchange rates prevailing in those years. With this information he infers the Paasche PPP for a given year in the past for each of the countries. He applies these PPPs to convert estimates of nominal GDP in each country from national currencies into US dollars of the year in question. For years before 1950, he has no ICP or PWT (reduced-information) measures of PPPs. He assumes that the PPP/exchange rate relationships for 1950-1990 are a good guide to the situation in 1820-1938.

He provides two pages of source notes, but shows only his results and none of the basic material on PPPs, his four variables and estimates of nominal GDP. Estimates of variables a and b are likely to be pretty shaky for the early years, and nominal estimates of GDP are often not available. This is the case for his benchmark country, the United States where he derived a nominal value by reflating the real GDP estimates for 1820–1860 with a cost of living and a wholesale price index.

Table 8–2 shows the Prados results for the 6 countries where his estimates go back to 1820. It compares his per capita relatives and mine for 1900 and 1820. It shows my estimates in 1990 international dollars, and his implicit absolute levels, derived by multiplying his relatives by my estimate for the United States. In the bottom panel I compare my estimates of per capita growth with his implicit growth rates. There are very big differences between his relatives and mine for 1820, smaller but appreciable differences for 1900. My growth rates for per capita GDP 1820–1900 are very different from his implicit rates. His growth rate for Australia is much slower than mine, but he shows much faster growth for the four European countries, with France and Denmark growing faster than the United States.

Table 8–2. **Comparison of Maddison Per Capita GDP Levels and Prados' Proxies, 1820–1900**

	Maddison per capita GDP in 1990 int. $	Maddison per capita GDP % of US	Prados per capita GDP % of US	Implicit Prados per capita GDP in 1990 int. $	Maddison nominal per capita GDP % of US	Prados nominal per capita GDP % of US
1820						
Australia	518	41.2	102.2	1 285	n.a.	136.1
United States	1 257	100.0	100.0	1 257	n.a.	100.0
United Kingdom	1 706	135.7	96.5	1 213	n.a.	122.8
Netherlands	1 838	146.2	80.0	1 006	n.a.	95.9
France	1 135	90.3	71.3	896	n.a.	69.0
Denmark	1 274	101.4	51.3	645	n.a.	54.8
1900						
Australia	4 013	98.1	97.6	3 993	104.5	99.3
United States	4 091	100.0	100.0	4 091	100.0	100.0
United Kingdom	4 492	109.8	91.7	3 751	91.9	92.3
Netherlands	3 424	83.7	71.5	2 925	45.6	50.2
France	2 876	70.3	76.8	3 142	52.6	66.6
Denmark	3 017	73.7	66.8	2 733	56.0	59.4
1820–1900 annual average compound growth rate						
Australia	2.59			1.43		
United States	1.49			1.49		
United Kingdom	1.22			1.42		
Netherlands	0.78			1.34		
France	1.17			1.58		
Denmark	1.08			1.82		

Source: Maddison estimates from basic tables, column 5 from Maddison (1991c). Columns 3 and 6 from Prados (2000), Table 9. Col. 4 derived by multiplying my estimate for the United States by Prados' relatives in column 3. The United States is his benchmark country but he does not show his estimate in absolute terms. He shows estimates labelled "Maddison Revised", but I could not see from the description how he derived these and must therefore register a disclaimer. For Australia 1820, he refers to the white population, whereas my estimate includes aborigines (see HS-2 for white population).

ii) Paul Bairoch (1930-1999) was a very prolific quantitative historian, who published many comparative studies of GNP levels, urbanisation and labour force participation. A good deal of his analysis concentrated on the forces making for divergence in the growth of advanced capitalist countries and the third world. He argued (see Bairoch, 1967) that the third world was impoverished by the development process and policies of the rich countries. In Bairoch, 1981, pp 8, 12, 14, he showed the "third world" with a slightly higher average per capita GNP than the "developed countries" in 1750, and slightly lower in 1800. He showed China at more or less the same level as Western Europe in 1800, and Latin America ahead of North America. Bairoch's source notes were frequently cryptic and often cited "personal estimates" he did not publish. They were most exiguous for Asia or Latin America and his results for these continents must therefore be taken with a pinch of salt. The most detailed documentation of his estimates can be found in "Europe's Gross National Product: 1800-1975", *Journal of European Economic History*, Fall 1976. I commented on the quality of these estimates in Maddison (1990), p. 104.

Bairoch's last major work, (*Victoires et Déboires,* Gallimard, Paris, 1997, 3 vols., 2 788 pages) is a massive, comprehensive and fascinating survey of world economic history from 1492 to 1995. It is much less quantitative than most of his other work. He has a very small table P.4 on p. 111 of volume 1 comparing the aggregate per capita GNP performance of the "developed countries" (Europe, Western Offshoots and Japan) and the "third world" (Africa, Asia and Latin America) for 6 benchmark years between 1750 and 1995. As in his earlier work, the third world is credited with a higher level than the developed group in 1750, with minimal progress until after 1950, but he shows no country detail for the third world. Table XII.2 in volume 2, pp. 252–3, presents estimates for each of his 24 "developed countries" for 7 benchmark years from 1800 to 1913. The estimates for Europe are similar to those he presented in 1976 and are in 1960 dollars derived mainly from the OEEC (1958) study of purchasing power, augmented by the proxy PPPs in Beckerman (1966).

To me the most surprising and interesting part of his 1997 study is his discussion of the relative performance and interaction of the European and Asian economies between 1500 and 1800 (pp. 527–645). He suggests that Asia was probably somewhat more advanced than Europe around 1500 and that by the eighteenth century this advantage had disappeared. The Muslim advantage over Europe in the Abbasid caliphate peaked in the 10th century; Chinese superiority had been greatest in the 12th century; the peak for Moghul India was in the 16th century, and that of the Ottoman Empire around 1600. Stagnation or decline followed thereafter, whereas Europe made substantial progress from 1500 to 1800 (see pp. 642–5). This analysis is difficult to reconcile with his earlier position, or the estimates in Table P.4, but it is much nearer to my view of the relative performance of these two parts of the world economy between 1500 and 1800.

iii) Susan Hanley is a demographer and social historian who has concentrated mainly on the economic history of Tokugawa Japan. She is a member of the revisionist school which found evidence to warrant a much more positive view of economic performance from 1600 to the 1860s than that of an earlier generation of scholars. However, she is an unconstrained admirer of Japan, and greatly exaggerates its level of performance in the 1860s. In Hanley (1997) she asserted that "Japanese physical well–being in the 1860s was at least as high as in nineteenth century England". Her evidence for England is pretty flimsy. She admits that Japanese ate virtually no meat, but alleges that this was also the case in mid–nineteenth century England. She alleges that English working class diets in the mid–nineteenth century consisted largely of "bread and margarine" (i.e. at a time before margarine was invented). In fact, we can see from Table 1 (in the Prologue) that already in 1695 only 20 per cent of English food and drink expenditure consisted of bread or things made of meal or flour, and 35 per cent consisted of meat, fish, and dairy products.

In assessing the relative position of two countries at a given point in the past, it is always useful to consider their growth trajectories since that point. The historical accounts of both Japan and the United Kingdom are of high quality. Our basic tables show that per capita income has risen 28–fold in Japan since 1870. In Britain it rose 6–fold. If Hanley's judgement on nineteenth century levels were correct, Japan would now have a gigantic lead over the United Kingdom. In fact the two countries had a similar level of per capita GDP in 2001.

Table 8–3. **The China/West European Dichotomy, 1–2001 AD**

	China	*West Europe*
	Population (million)	
1	59.6	24.7
1000	59.0	25.4
1300	100.0	58.4
1400	72.0	41.5
1500	103.0	57.3
1820	381.0	133.0
1913	437.1	261.0
1950	546.8	304.9
2001	1 275.4	392.1
	Per Capita GDP (1990 int. $)	
1	450	450
1000	450	400
1300	600	593
1400	600	676
1500	600	771
1820	600	1 204
1913	552	3 458
1950	439	4 579
2001	3 583	19 256
	GDP (billion 1990 int $)	
1	26.8	11.1
1000	26.6	10.2
1300	60.0	34.6
1400	43.2	28.1
1500	61.8	44.2
1820	228.6	160.1
1913	241.3	902.3
1950	239.9	1 396.2
2001	4 569.8	7 550.3

Source: HS–1, HS–5, and HS–8 basic tables, Maddison (1998 and 2001).

iv) Kenneth Pomeranz (2000) presents a fascinating comparative picture of Chinese economic performance in the eighteenth and early nineteenth centuries. The comparison is mainly with Western Europe. There are many penetrating insights into the differences between these two areas. His main argument is that both were subject to Malthusian/ecological constraints, that Chinese performance was in many respects better than that of Europe before 1800. He suggests that Western Europe was "a non–too–unusual economy; it became a fortunate freak only when unexpected and significant discontinuities in the late eighteenth and especially nineteenth centuries enabled it to break through the fundamental constraints of energy and resource availability that had previously limited *everyone's* horizons". Pomeranz relies mainly on illustrative evidence and partial indicators of performance to back his judgement. There are only four tables with no attempt at macro–quantification (except for his comparison of life expectancy). He does not provide a chronological profile of development in Europe or China before and beyond his point of comparison. He has one passing reference to Needham, and little discussion of the forces affecting the divergent development of technology in China and Europe. His conclusions are very different from mine. In Maddison (1998) I concluded that Western Europe drew level with China in the fourteenth century and that its average per capita level was twice the Chinese in 1820 (see Table 8–3).

I find Pomeranz's judgements unconvincing. In 1800, the degree of urbanisation was three times higher in Western Europe than in China, the proportion of the population employed in agriculture was a good deal smaller, though the European diet included a much higher proportion of meat and dairy products. Chinese life expectation was two–thirds of that in Western Europe. Pomeranz stresses Western Europe's benefits from international trade, which augmented its supply of food and raw materials from the "ghost acreage" of distant lands. He treats this benefit as if it were a windfall gain. In fact, China turned its back on international trade in the middle of the fifteenth century, and the Ching dynasty forbade settlement on its own ghost acres in Manchuria.

The Pomeranz position is stated with four degrees of nuance. On p. 49 he says "it seems likely that average incomes in Japan, China and parts of southeast Asia were comparable to (or higher than) those in western Europe even in the late eighteenth century." Elsewhere his position is more cautious, and he claims Asian superiority was characteristic only for "core regions". Thus on p. 17, he says "core regions in China and Japan circa 1750 seem to resemble the most advanced parts of western Europe". For China, his core region is the lower Yangtse (which had about 18 per cent of China's population). Here he is on firmer ground, but I think he still exaggerates Chinese performance. Research on Chinese economic history has increased substantially in quantity and quantity in the past two decades. Li (1998) has shown significant advances in productivity and income in the lower Yangtse area during the Ching dynasty. Ma (2003) shows its per capita land tax revenue was about 145 per cent of that for China as a whole in 1753. My estimate of Chinese and West European income levels in 1750 can be derived by interpolating between the estimates for 1700 and 1820 in Table 8c. If Ma's fiscal estimate is taken as a proxy for lower Yangtse per capita income around 1750, it would have been about 870 dollars compared to 1 080 for western Europe as a whole and more than 1 400 for the United Kingdom.

On p. 44, Pomeranz states that "Europeans were not ahead in overall productivity in 1750". This proposition I find completely implausible, because Chinese multi–cropping of rice, intensive water management and rural industry demanded much higher labour inputs, (particularly in the lower Yangtse region) than was the case in Europe. Ester Boserup has stressed increased labour intensity as the Chinese response to land shortage. Pomeranz's obsession with Malthusian constraints leads him to neglect this Chinese–European differential in labour inputs.

Pomeranz, p. 37 suggests that Chinese longevity was "quite comparable" to European. He cites an estimate of Chinese life expectancy of 32 years at age 1 for both sexes combined in Manchuria in 1792–1867 (from Lee and Campbell, 1997). He compares this with the Wrigley and Schofield (1981) estimate of English life expectancy at birth of 37 years for 1600–1749. Following a critique by Razzell, he suggests that Wrigley and Schofield got it wrong and that their figure should be reduced to "somewhere between 31.6 and 34.0", i.e. an average of 32.8. If this were a legitimate correction, it would mean that longevity in England and China were indeed "quite comparable". However, their estimate for England should be adjusted upwards, not downwards. Life expectation at age 1 in eighteenth century England was about 7 years higher than at birth, because 17 per cent of infants died before their first birthday (I am grateful to Jim Oeppen for this information). The Cambridge group rebutted Razzell's critique in their 1997 study (Wrigley, Davies, Oeppen, and Schofield). In Maddison (2001) I compared life expectation in different parts of the world in 1820. The average for Western Europe was 36 years and 24 for Asia at birth.

There are at least four views on the contours of long–run Chinese development and two on West European.

On China, Joseph Needham's view was that its technology gave it a lead over Western Europe from the second century AD. "Chinese evolution represented a slowly rising curve. Running at a higher and sometimes much higher level than Europe between the second and fifteenth centuries". Because of its meritocratic bureaucracy, its precocity in developing printing and the existence of a common written language, best–practice technology was more easily diffused than in Europe (a point stressed by Justin Yifu Lin, 1995). China lost its leadership position because it had no counterpart to Europe's scientific revolution. Needham gave a graphical comparison of the contours of Chinese and European technological development in *Clerks and Craftsmen in China and the West* (1970), p. 414. It is similar in shape to my graph of Chinese and West European per capita GDP in Maddison, 2001, p. 42, except that Needham makes no allowance for Sung exceptionalism.

Mark Elvin's (1973) interpretation is that China made a major advance in the Sung dynasty (960–1280), and had high–level stagnation until the nineteenth century. I think Elvin is correct in stressing the special character of Sung experience. However, he did not attempt macro–quantification, and his qualitative judgement probably implies a bigger leap in the Sung than I find. I think Elvin overstates stagnation after the Sung. Between 1400 and 1820, Chinese population grew significantly faster than that of Western Europe, and its GDP growth was only slightly less than Europe's. China experienced extensive growth, whereas Europe had a mild degree of intensive growth.

My interpretation is a hybrid of Needham and Elvin. It is summarised in quantitative terms in Table 8–3 and in graphical form in Maddison (2001), p. 42.

The least plausible interpretation is that of Kang Chao (1986, pp. 87, 89, 216–220). He suggests that per capita grain output rose by half from the 1st to the 11th century, followed by a millennium of decline, with per capita output falling back to 1st century levels in 1949, because of Malthusian pressure of population on limited land resources. The sources for his estimates are not adequately documented, and their plausibility is not heightened when he throws in supposedly corroborative estimates of real wages which rise (in sheng of grain per person) from 120 in the first century to 800 in 1086 and fall to 12 in 1818!

My view of the contours of West European development is that there was a decline in per capita income after the fall of the Roman Empire, which has no counterpart in China, and a sustained process of slow per capita growth from the eleventh to the early nineteenth century. Thereafter there was a substantial acceleration of growth. The alternative view is that there were centuries of Malthusian torpor followed by an industrial revolution and a sudden take–off. Pomeranz's interpretation involves acceptance of this second view.

v) The Real Wage Literature and its Relation to National Accounts.

The serious study of real wages began with Thorold Rogers (1823–1890). His major works in this field were *A History of Agriculture and Prices in England* (7 vols. 1866–1902) and *Six Centuries of Work and Wages* (1884). Rogers was an active politician, as well as a prolific price historian and professor of political economy in Oxford. He was a Liberal member of parliament (1880–1886) and an advocate of political reform who argued that the condition of English wage earners could be improved by extending the franchise and encouraging trade union activity. Later generations of real wage analysts have generally followed his lead: *a)* adopting a very long–term perspective; *b)* giving almost exclusive emphasis to labour income; *c)* giving substantial attention to price history, *d)* reaching pessimistic conclusions. However, Rogers differed from some of his disciples in two important respects. He was not a Malthusian, and would certainly not have regarded real wages as a proxy for real GDP. For him low wages were the result of exploitation of the labourer by the ruling elite. He made a clear distinction between wage income and national income, as is clear in his citation of Gregory King's estimates of inequality (Rogers, 1884 pp. 463–465). He summarised his position, saying (p. 355) "society may make notable progress in wealth, and wages remain low, ...relatively speaking, the working man of today is not so well off as he was in the fifteenth century"

It is interesting to compare his work with that of his near–contemporary Michael Mulhall (1836–1900). Mulhall was a pioneer in comparative analysis of national income. His main concern was to measure aggregate value added (see Table 3 in the Prologue), whereas Rogers concentrated on one kind of income. Mulhall's temporal horizon was much shorter than that of Rogers, and he was not a social or political reformer. Mulhall's estimates all referred to nominal income, except for the United Kingdom, where he used wheat prices as a crude deflator. Rogers devoted massive effort to price history.

The Rogers–Mulhall dichotomy is interesting because real wage analysis and historical national accounts have continued to tread separate paths. Historical national accountants have progressed well beyond Mulhall. They have developed techniques for measuring real output and real expenditure, and have deflators for the components of these aggregates, but they almost never attempt separate deflation of the components of nominal income (see Maddison, 1995, pp. 120–123). Until recently real wage analysis had not progressed much beyond Rogers. It continued to ignore non–wage income, and used data for a small fraction of wage earners without indicating what proportion of the labour force were covered. National accountants take a macroeconomic view, have developed a standardised system (which defines coverage within clearly defined boundaries of activity) and there are fairly comprehensive crosschecks on consistency. However, their time horizon was, until recently, much shorter than that of real wage analysts.

In the 1920s–40s there was a coordinated European–US research effort with financial support from the International Committee on Price History. Some of the researchers (Beveridge and Posthumus) concentrated on price history, but there was also a substantial effort to measure long–term trends in real wages. It is clear from the account of Cole and Crandall (1964) that they had no guidelines on coverage and methodology. They measured wage rates rather than earnings, without indicating annual hours worked. There was no attempt to determine the relative size of non–wage income. Within the field of wage–income, sample coverage was usually quite small. The validity of the inter–temporal measures was questionable and there were no cross–country comparisons of wage levels. From 1939 to 1968, Jürgen Kuczynski (1904–95) provided a Marxist counterpart, producing 40 volumes on the deteriorating condition of the proletariat under capitalism. At that time there was some interaction with national accountants. Colin Clark (1940) used real wages as a real income proxy for 20 countries. Arthur Bowley (1869–1957) made a considerable effort to incorporate real wage and real income analysis into national accounts.

A third wave of interest in real wages was sparked in 1952–57, when Henry Phelps Brown (1906–94), Sheila Hopkins and other associates produced scholarly articles developing new annual measures of wages and prices in England from 1264 to 1954. (Phelps Brown and Hopkins, 1981) They synthesised the work of the pre–war group (Elsas, Hamilton and Pribram) on Austria, Germany, and Spain, and made new estimates for France. For England, they had daily wage rates for building workers hired by Oxford and Cambridge colleges, Eton school and some other employers in the south of England. For the most part, they had 15 or more quotations a year for craftsmen and 3 for building workers. Between 1500 and 1800 there were 82 years for which they had no wage estimates. They had no data on weekly or annual earnings or days worked. They did not discuss the representativity of their measure. Even if their coverage of building workers is assumed to be adequate, they represented only 5 per cent of the workforce in 1700. People employed in agriculture were 56 per cent of the total and most of them were producing and directly consuming the items which figure in the price index. Many others, such as servants, artisans, the clergy, and the armed forces received an appreciable part of their remuneration in kind. A large part of the working population were thus sheltered from the impact of price rises. In spite of these shortcomings, their findings attracted interest because of the long period they covered and their meticulous scholarship in providing detailed and transparent discussion of sources and methods. As there was no work in historical national accounts for this period, their results were readily accepted.

The conclusions of Phelps Brown and Hopkins were extremely pessimistic. From 1500 to 1800, they suggested that real wages for building workers in southern England fell by 60 per cent. Their results were enthusiastically received by Braudel and Spooner (Cambridge Economic History of Europe, 1967, p. 429). They concluded that "from the late fifteenth century until well into the beginning of the eighteenth century, the standard of living in Europe progressively declined. Before this time, in the fourteenth and fifteenth centuries ...conditions were better". This judgement was easily accepted in France because members of the Annales school were profoundly Malthusian. Le Roy Ladurie's judgement in 1960 was that Languedoc had suffered recurrent and prolonged population setbacks because limited land resources had set rigid limits to agricultural production. His inaugural lecture at the Collège de France in 1973 restated this notion of *l'histoire immobile*. Wilhelm Abel (1978), the German historian, suggested that real living standards fell in Germany from the first half of the fourteenth to the first half of the eighteenth century.

The Phelps Brown analysis was also accepted by Wrigley and Schofield (1981) as a complement to their analysis of English demographic experience from 1541 to 1871. They found it convenient because it was "an approximate guide to fluctuations in the standard of living" in their period (pp. 312–313). They adjusted the results to interpolate gaps (pp. 638–41), they made some judicious comments on its deficiencies, but they took the real wage index to be a representative picture of living standards. In their analysis (pp. 402–412) of the relation between population growth and living standards they concluded that Malthus was right "Before 1800 matters fell out much as Malthus insisted they must..the faster population grew, the lower the standard of living and the grimmer the struggle to exist" A "decisive break" occurred during the industrial revolution. They rejected Boserup's view that "population growth in a pre–industrial economy tended to spark off changes in agricultural techniques which would allow productivity per head in agriculture to be maintained, albeit at the cost of longer hours of work, while at the same time encouraging changes elsewhere in the economy that would lead to a rise in output per head overall".

The Phelps Brown results have now been almost universally rejected as a proxy for the movement of real GDP per capita. Braudel reversed his judgement with characteristic insouciance. In Braudel (1985) p. 314, he stated that there were "clear continuities in European history. The first of these is the regular rise in GNP come hell or high water". Wrigley (1988) concluded his penetrating new analysis thus: "The single most remarkable feature of the economic history of England between the later sixteenth and the early nineteenth century was the rise in output per head in agriculture"(p. 39).

Jan de Vries (1993) joined the attack on the real wage approach. He questioned the representativity of construction worker experience, emphasised the large number of items omitted from the Phelps Brown price index, and contrasted its sombre and stagnant conclusions with his own evidence from probate inventories "All the studies I have examined for colonial New England and the Chesapeake, England and the Netherlands consistently reveal two features. With very few exceptions, each generation of decedents from the mid–seventeenth to the late eighteenth century left behind more and better possessions". He concluded that "economic growth began earlier than previously thought, that the transforming power of industry was felt later than previously thought , and that the century of the Industrial Revolution witnessed no sharp acceleration–not in production, not in consumption". In de Vries (1994) he developed the notion of an "industrious revolution" which is similar to Ester Boserup's (1965) analysis in the Asian context. It helps explain how intensified labour inputs overcame what were previously considered Malthusian constraints.

One reason real wage analysis remained primitive was that historical national accountants and their leading figure, Kuznets, showed no interest in it. Kuznets' (1973, pp. 139–140) speculations on the likely growth of European real per capita GDP between 1500 and 1750 contrasted sharply with the conclusions of Phelps Brown and his disciples, but he made no reference to their work. The two major historians of the national accounting tradition, Studenski (1958) and Stone (1997) made no mention of the real wage literature.

There was a fifth wave of real wage analysis in the past decade. This includes 2 articles on Asia; Feinstein, 1998, is the first rigorous and comprehensive measurement of real earnings of manual workers (1770–1870) by a historical national accountant since Bowley (1900); repair work on the second generation estimates by Robert Allen (2001), and new estimates by Jeffrey Williamson (1995) for 17 countries 1830–1988, which incorporate inter–spatial as well as inter–temporal comparisons.

The articles on Asia break new ground and are discussed below.

Özmucur and Pamuk (2002) present estimates of real wages of building workers in Istanbul for 1489–1914. They find a level in 1820 similar to that at the end of the fifteenth century (with some big dips in between) and about 40 per cent higher by 1910–14. They do not suggest that their measure is a satisfactory proxy for per capita income, but as they have no estimates of the latter before the nineteenth century, they conclude from their evidence that the decline of the Ottoman empire in the sixteenth century was reversed, and it adapted successfully to changing circumstances from the seventeenth to the nineteenth century. Their research is well documented, their conclusions are cautious and Pamuk has also made tentative estimates for of GDP in Turkey and other parts of the Ottoman Empire back to 1820. This study throws new light on a region that has played a significant role in world history for centuries.

Parthasarathi (1998), is a cross–country level comparison of weavers' wages in South India and England in the eighteenth century. He also covers spinners and farm labourers where his evidence is much thinner. He converts weekly wages of weavers in both countries into grain units, assuming a lb of Indian rice equivalent to 1500 calories and a lb of British bread 1000 calories. In Britain weekly earnings of weavers bought 40 to 140 lbs of grain and in South India 65 to 160. He claims that labourers in South India were in a better bargaining position than their English counterparts because they operated as village collectives, appealing to even–handed political authorities in case of dispute. In England legislation prohibited combinations of workers. The article is useful in shaking up conventional views, but is certainly contestable. It may be true that individual workers in England had a weak bargaining position, but it seems likely that in Indian village "collectives" lower castes and untouchables were exploited by the brahmin elite. The sources of his Indian wage estimates are not very clear, and his assumption that British workers got their calories from wheaten loaves bought from bakeries is rather odd. They probably got quite a lot of calories from meat and potatoes, cheese and beer which were not available in south India. A good deal of their bread must have been home–baked.

Chronology

In surveying economic development over the last two millennia in Maddison (2001), it seemed logical to start with the year zero, as official celebrations treated the year 2000 as the beginning of a new millennium. In fact, there is no year zero in the Christian era which begins in AD 1, with I BC as the preceding year. In tables HS–8, I have bowed to convention, and substituted year 1 for year zero. This makes no difference to estimates of growth rates for the first millennium.

It is perhaps useful to consider changes in conventions for measuring time over these two millennia. The Julian calendar, with an average year of 365.25 days was inaugurated by the Roman dictator, Julius Caesar in 46 BC, on the advice of the Alexandrian astronomer Sosigenes. It exaggerated the length of the year by a tiny fraction, and was replaced in the Catholic countries of Europe on October 4th 1582, as decreed in a papal bull of Gregory XIII, on advice from the astronomer Clavius and others. The Gregorian year was a little shorter (averaging of 365.2425 days). 10 days (5–14th October) were dropped from that year to link the two systems. The Protestant countries of Europe started to adopt this calendar in 1700. The last European country to switch was the USSR in 1918.

England and its colonies changed over in 1752. Until then their year began with Lady Day, on 25th March. The British parliament endorsed the change in 1751, stipulating that the year would end on 31st December, and the new Gregorian year would start on 1st January. To complete the transition, 3rd to 13th September were omitted from the 1752 calendar (Wednesday 2nd September being followed by Thursday 14th). The previous anachronistic system meant that anything published from 1st January to 24th March was attributed to the preceding year.

There have also been changes in the dating and denomination of eras. The traditional Roman era began with the foundation of Rome (*ab urbe condita*) which was thought to have been in 753 BC. There was an era of the Emperor Augustus, dating from the battle of Actium in 31BC, and an era of the Emperor Diocletian dating from his accession in 284 AD. The Christian era was first proposed by Dionysius Exiguus in AD 532. He had been asked by Pope John the 1st to provide clear guidelines for calculating the date of Easter. He also suggested the creation of a Christian era to replace that of Diocletian (who martyred Christians). Dionysius believed that Christ was born in 1BC, and that the first year of the new era (anno domini) should be the following year which he called AD 1 (see Richards, pp. 106, 217–8 and 351). There was no symbol for zero in the Roman system of numeration, and the concept of zero as a number did not come to Europe until several centuries later. The Christian era does not seem to have been inaugurated by a papal bull, and did not come into general use until the eleventh century. The first author to use the concept systematically for his chronology was Bede in his *Ecclesiastical History of the English People,* completed in 731. He did not use the term *anno domini,* referring instead to a year in the era as *"anno dominicae incarnationis"*(see Colgrave and Mynors, 1969).

In fact, there is a precedent for starting the Christian era in year zero. Gregory King in his *Notebook,* p. 4, made a comprehensive survey and forecast of world population, using the concept of anno mundi, with continuous numbering since the creation which he assumed had occurred 5630 years before 1695. He provided an alternative numbering system for years before and after Christ, with a dividing point in the year 0. He did not use the terms BC and AD, but distinguished years *ante* and *post Christum.*

Table 8a. **World Population, 20 Countries and Regional Totals, 1-2001 AD**

(000)

	1	1000	1500	1600	1700	1820	1870	1913	1950	1973	2001
Austria	500	700	2 000	2 500	2 500	3 369	4 520	6 767	6 935	7 586	8 151
Belgium	300	400	1 400	1 600	2 000	3 434	5 096	7 666	8 639	9 738	10 259
Denmark	180	360	600	650	700	1 155	1 888	2 983	4 271	5 022	5 353
Finland	20	40	300	400	400	1 169	1 754	3 027	4 009	4 666	5 176
France	5 000	6 500	15 000	18 500	21 471	31 250	38 440	41 463	41 829	52 157	59 658
Germany	3 000	3 500	12 000	16 000	15 000	24 905	39 231	65 058	68 375	78 950	82 281
Italy	7 000	5 000	10 500	13 100	13 300	20 176	27 888	37 248	47 105	54 797	57 845
Netherlands	200	300	950	1 500	1 900	2 333	3 610	6 164	10 114	13 438	15 981
Norway	100	200	300	400	500	970	1 735	2 447	3 265	3 961	4 503
Sweden	200	400	550	760	1 260	2 585	4 169	5 621	7 014	8 137	8 875
Switzerland	300	300	650	1 000	1 200	1 986	2 655	3 864	4 694	6 441	7 283
United Kingdom	800	2 000	3 942	6 170	8 565	21 239	31 400	45 649	50 127	56 210	59 723
12 Country Total	**17 600**	**19 700**	**48 192**	**62 580**	**68 796**	**114 571**	**162 386**	**227 957**	**256 377**	**301 103**	**325 088**
Portugal	500	600	1 000	1 100	2 000	3 297	4 327	5 972	8 443	8 976	10 066
Spain	4 500	4 000	6 800	8 240	8 770	12 203	16 201	20 263	28 063	34 837	40 087
Other	2 100	1 113	1 276	1 858	1 894	2 969	4 590	6 783	12 058	13 909	16 860
Total Western Europe	**24 700**	**25 413**	**57 268**	**73 778**	**81 460**	**133 040**	**187 504**	**260 975**	**304 941**	**358 825**	**392 101**
Eastern Europe	**4 750**	**6 500**	**13 500**	**16 950**	**18 800**	**36 457**	**53 557**	**79 530**	**87 637**	**110 418**	**120 912**
Former USSR	**3 900**	**7 100**	**16 950**	**20 700**	**26 550**	**54 765**	**88 672**	**156 192**	**179 571**	**249 712**	**290 349**
United States	680	1 300	2 000	1 500	1 000	9 981	40 241	97 606	152 271	211 909	285 024
Other Western Offshoots	490	660	800	800	750	1 250	5 847	13 795	24 186	38 932	54 815
Total Western Offshoots	**1 170**	**1 960**	**2 800**	**2 300**	**1 750**	**11 231**	**46 088**	**111 401**	**176 457**	**250 841**	**339 839**
Mexico	2 200	4 500	7 500	2 500	4 500	6 587	9 219	14 970	28 485	57 643	101 879
Other Latin America	3 400	6 900	10 000	6 100	7 550	15 118	31 180	65 965	137 453	250 756	429 334
Total Latin America	**5 600**	**11 400**	**17 500**	**8 600**	**12 050**	**21 705**	**40 399**	**80 935**	**165 938**	**308 399**	**531 213**
Japan	**3 000**	**7 500**	**15 400**	**18 500**	**27 000**	**31 000**	**34 437**	**51 672**	**83 805**	**108 707**	**126 892**
China	59 600	59 000	103 000	160 000	138 000	381 000	358 000	437 140	546 815	881 940	1 275 392
India	75 000	75 000	110 000	135 000	165 000	209 000	253 000	303 700	359 000	580 000	1 023 590
Other Asia	36 600	41 400	55 400	65 000	71 800	89 400	119 792	184 849	392 827	677 613	1 227 630
Total Asia (excluding Japan)	**171 200**	**175 400**	**268 400**	**360 000**	**374 800**	**679 400**	**730 792**	**925 689**	**1 298 642**	**2 139 553**	**3 526 612**
Africa	**16 500**	**32 300**	**46 610**	**55 320**	**61 080**	**74 236**	**90 466**	**124 697**	**227 333**	**390 034**	**821 088**
World	**230 820**	**267 573**	**438 428**	**556 148**	**603 490**	**1 041 834**	**1 271 915**	**1 791 091**	**2 524 324**	**3 916 489**	**6 149 006**

Table 8a. **Rate of Growth of World Population, 20 Countries and Regional Totals, 1-2001 AD**
(annual average coumpound growth rates)

	1-1000	1000-1500	1500-1820	1820-70	1870-1913	1913-50	1950-73	1973-2001
Austria	0.03	0.21	0.16	0.59	0.94	0.07	0.39	0.26
Belgium	0.03	0.25	0.28	0.79	0.95	0.32	0.52	0.19
Denmark	0.07	0.10	0.20	0.99	1.07	0.97	0.71	0.23
Finland	0.07	0.40	0.43	0.81	1.28	0.76	0.66	0.37
France	0.03	0.17	0.23	0.42	0.18	0.02	0.96	0.48
Germany	0.02	0.25	0.23	0.91	1.18	0.13	0.63	0.15
Italy	-0.03	0.15	0.20	0.65	0.68	0.64	0.66	0.19
Netherlands	0.04	0.23	0.28	0.88	1.25	1.35	1.24	0.62
Norway	0.07	0.08	0.37	1.17	0.80	0.78	0.84	0.46
Sweden	0.07	0.06	0.48	0.96	0.70	0.60	0.65	0.31
Switzerland	0.00	0.15	0.35	0.58	0.88	0.53	1.39	0.44
United Kingdom	0.09	0.14	0.53	0.79	0.87	0.25	0.50	0.22
12 Country average	**0.01**	**0.18**	**0.27**	**0.70**	**0.79**	**0.32**	**0.70**	**0.27**
Portugal	0.02	0.10	0.37	0.55	0.75	0.94	0.27	0.41
Spain	-0.01	0.11	0.18	0.57	0.52	0.88	0.94	0.50
Other	-0.06	0.03	0.26	0.88	0.91	1.57	0.62	0.69
Total Western Europe	**0.00**	**0.16**	**0.26**	**0.69**	**0.77**	**0.42**	**0.71**	**0.32**
Eastern Europe	**0.03**	**0.15**	**0.31**	**0.77**	**0.92**	**0.26**	**1.01**	**0.32**
Former USSR	**0.06**	**0.17**	**0.37**	**0.97**	**1.33**	**0.38**	**1.44**	**0.54**
United States	0.06	0.09	0.50	2.83	2.08	1.21	1.45	1.06
Other Western Offshoots	0.03	0.04	0.14	3.13	2.02	1.53	2.09	1.23
Total Western Offshoots	**0.05**	**0.07**	**0.44**	**2.86**	**2.07**	**1.25**	**1.54**	**1.09**
Mexico	**0.07**	**0.10**	-0.04	0.67	1.13	1.75	3.11	2.05
Other Latin America	0.07	0.07	0.13	1.46	1.76	2.00	2.65	1.94
Total Latin America	**0.07**	**0.09**	**0.07**	**1.25**	**1.63**	**1.96**	**2.73**	**1.96**
Japan	**0.09**	**0.14**	**0.22**	**0.21**	**0.95**	**1.32**	**1.14**	**0.55**
China	0.00	0.11	0.41	-0.12	0.47	0.61	2.10	1.33
India	0.00	0.08	0.20	0.38	0.43	0.45	2.11	2.05
Other Asia	0.01	0.06	0.15	0.59	1.01	2.06	2.40	2.15
Total Asia (excl. Japan)	**0.00**	**0.09**	**0.29**	**0.15**	**0.55**	**0.92**	**2.19**	**1.80**
Africa	**0.07**	**0.07**	**0.15**	**0.40**	**0.75**	**1.64**	**2.37**	**2.69**
World	**0.01**	**0.10**	**0.27**	**0.40**	**0.80**	**0.93**	**1.93**	**1.62**

Table 8a. **Share of World Population, 20 Countries and Regional Totals, 1-2001 AD**
(per cent of world total)

	1	*1000*	*1500*	*1600*	*1700*	*1820*	*1870*	*1913*	*1950*	*1973*	*2001*
Austria	0.2	0.3	0.5	0.4	0.4	0.3	0.4	0.4	0.3	0.2	0.1
Belgium	0.1	0.1	0.3	0.3	0.3	0.3	0.4	0.4	0.3	0.2	0.2
Denmark	0.1	0.1	0.1	0.1	0.1	0.1	0.1	0.2	0.2	0.1	0.1
Finland	0.0	0.0	0.1	0.1	0.1	0.1	0.1	0.2	0.2	0.1	0.1
France	2.2	2.4	3.4	3.3	3.6	3.0	3.0	2.3	1.7	1.3	1.0
Germany	1.3	1.3	2.7	2.9	2.5	2.4	3.1	3.6	2.7	2.0	1.3
Italy	3.0	1.9	2.4	2.4	2.2	1.9	2.2	2.1	1.9	1.4	0.9
Netherlands	0.1	0.1	0.2	0.3	0.3	0.2	0.3	0.3	0.4	0.3	0.3
Norway	0.0	0.1	0.1	0.1	0.1	0.1	0.1	0.1	0.1	0.1	0.1
Sweden	0.1	0.1	0.1	0.1	0.2	0.2	0.3	0.3	0.3	0.2	0.1
Switzerland	0.1	0.1	0.1	0.2	0.2	0.2	0.2	0.2	0.2	0.2	0.1
United Kingdom	0.3	0.7	0.9	1.1	1.4	2.0	2.5	2.5	2.0	1.4	1.0
12 Country total	**7.6**	**7.4**	**11.0**	**11.3**	**11.4**	**11.0**	**12.8**	**12.7**	**10.2**	**7.7**	**5.3**
Portugal	0.2	0.2	0.2	0.2	0.3	0.3	0.3	0.3	0.3	0.2	0.2
Spain	1.9	1.5	1.6	1.5	1.5	1.2	1.3	1.1	1.1	0.9	0.7
Other	0.9	0.4	0.3	0.3	0.3	0.3	0.4	0.4	0.5	0.4	0.3
Total Western Europe	**10.7**	**9.5**	**13.1**	**13.3**	**13.5**	**12.8**	**14.7**	**14.6**	**12.1**	**9.2**	**6.4**
Eastern Europe	**2.1**	**2.4**	**3.1**	**3.0**	**3.1**	**3.5**	**4.2**	**4.4**	**3.5**	**2.8**	**2.0**
Former USSR	**1.7**	**2.7**	**3.9**	**3.7**	**4.4**	**5.3**	**7.0**	**8.7**	**7.1**	**6.4**	**4.7**
United States	0.3	0.5	0.5	0.3	0.2	1.0	3.2	5.4	6.0	5.4	4.6
Other Western Offshoots	0.2	0.2	0.2	0.1	0.1	0.1	0.5	0.8	1.0	1.0	0.9
Total Western Offshoots	**0.5**	**0.7**	**0.6**	**0.4**	**0.3**	**1.1**	**3.6**	**6.2**	**7.0**	**6.4**	**5.5**
Mexico			1.7	0.4	0.7	0.6	0.7	0.8	1.1	1.5	1.7
Other Latin America			2.3	1.1	1.3	1.5	2.5	3.7	5.4	6.4	7.0
Total Latin America	**2.4**	**4.3**	**4.0**	**1.5**	**2.0**	**2.1**	**3.2**	**4.5**	**6.6**	**7.9**	**8.6**
Japan	**1.3**	**2.8**	**3.5**	**3.3**	**4.5**	**3.0**	**2.7**	**2.9**	**3.3**	**2.8**	**2.1**
China	25.8	22.1	23.5	28.8	22.9	36.6	28.1	24.4	21.7	22.5	20.7
India	32.5	28.0	25.1	24.3	27.3	20.1	19.9	17.0	14.2	14.8	16.6
Other Asia	15.9	15.5	12.6	11.7	11.9	8.6	9.4	10.3	15.6	17.3	20.0
Total Asia (excl. Japan)	**74.2**	**65.6**	**61.2**	**64.7**	**62.1**	**65.2**	**57.5**	**51.7**	**51.4**	**54.6**	**57.4**
Africa	**7.1**	**12.1**	**10.6**	**9.9**	**10.1**	**7.1**	**7.1**	**7.0**	**9.0**	**10.0**	**13.4**
World	**100.0**	**100.0**	**100.0**	**100.0**	**100.0**	**100.0**	**100.0**	**100.0**	**100.0**	**100.0**	**100.0**

Table 8b. World GDP, 20 Countries and Regional Totals, 1-2001 AD
(million 1990 international Geary-Khamis dollars)

	1	1000	1500	1600	1700	1820	1870	1913	1950	1973	2001
Austria			1 414	2 093	2 483	4 104	8 419	23 451	25 702	85 227	164 851
Belgium			1 225	1 561	2 288	4 529	13 716	32 347	47 190	118 516	214 655
Denmark			443	569	727	1 471	3 782	11 670	29 654	70 032	123 978
Finland			136	215	255	913	1 999	6 389	17 051	51 724	105 298
France			10 912	15 559	19 539	35 468	72 100	144 489	220 492	683 965	1 258 297
Germany			8 256	12 656	13 650	26 819	72 149	237 332	265 354	944 755	1 536 743
Italy			11 550	14 410	14 630	22 535	41 814	95 487	164 957	582 713	1 101 366
Netherlands			723	2 072	4 047	4 288	9 952	24 955	60 642	175 791	347 136
Norway			192	304	450	1 071	2 485	6 119	17 838	44 544	110 683
Sweden			382	626	1 231	3 098	6 927	17 403	47 269	109 794	182 492
Switzerland			411	750	1 068	2 165	5 581	16 483	42 545	117 251	162 150
United Kingdom			2 815	6 007	10 709	36 232	100 180	224 618	347 850	675 941	1 202 074
12 Country Total			**38 459**	**56 822**	**71 077**	**142 693**	**339 104**	**840 743**	**1 286 544**	**3 660 253**	**6 509 723**
Portugal			606	814	1 638	3 043	4 219	7 467	17 615	63 397	143 234
Spain			4 495	7 029	7 481	12 299	19 556	41 653	61 429	266 896	627 733
Other			602	975	1 106	2 110	4 712	12 478	30 600	105 910	269 582
Total Western Europe	**11 115**	**10 165**	**44 162**	**65 640**	**81 302**	**160 145**	**367 591**	**902 341**	**1 396 188**	**4 096 456**	**7 550 272**
Eastern Europe	**1 900**	**2 600**	**6 696**	**9 289**	**11 393**	**24 906**	**50 163**	**134 793**	**185 023**	**550 756**	**728 792**
Former USSR	**1 560**	**2 840**	**8 458**	**11 426**	**16 196**	**37 678**	**83 646**	**232 351**	**510 243**	**1 513 070**	**1 343 230**
United States					527	12 548	98 374	517 383	1 455 916	3 536 622	7 965 795
Other Western Offshoots			800	600	306	951	13 129	65 558	179 574	521 667	1 190 472
Total Western Offshoots	**468**	**784**	**1 120**	**920**	**833**	**13 499**	**111 493**	**582 941**	**1 635 490**	**4 058 289**	**9 156 267**
Mexico			3 188	1 134	2 558	5 000	6 214	25 921	67 368	279 302	722 198
Other Latin America			4 100	2 629	3 788	10 024	21 305	93 950	348 539	1 109 727	2 364 808
Total Latin America	**2 240**	**4 560**	**7 288**	**3 763**	**6 346**	**15 024**	**27 519**	**119 871**	**415 907**	**1 389 029**	**3 087 006**
Japan	**1 200**	**3 188**	**7 700**	**9 620**	**15 390**	**20 739**	**25 393**	**71 653**	**160 966**	**1 242 932**	**2 624 523**
China	26 820	26 550	61 800	96 000	82 800	228 600	189 740	241 344	239 903	740 048	4 569 790
India	33 750	33 750	60 500	74 250	90 750	111 417	134 882	204 242	222 222	494 832	2 003 193
Other Asia	16 470	18 630	31 301	36 725	40 567	52 177	76 994	163 109	363 646	1 388 124	4 908 218
Total Asia (excluding Japan)	**77 040**	**78 930**	**153 601**	**206 975**	**214 117**	**392 194**	**401 616**	**608 695**	**822 771**	**2 623 004**	**11 481 201**
Africa	**7 096**	**13 720**	**19 283**	**23 349**	**25 692**	**31 161**	**45 234**	**79 486**	**203 131**	**549 993**	**1 222 577**
World	**102 619**	**116 787**	**248 308**	**330 982**	**371 269**	**695 346**	**1 112 655**	**2 732 131**	**5 329 719**	**16 023 529**	**37 193 868**

Table 8b. **Rate of Growth of World GDP, 20 Countries and Regional Totals, 1-2001 AD**
(annual average compound growth rates)

	1-1000	1000-1500	1500-1820	1820-70	1870-1913	1913-50	1950-73	1973-2001
Austria			0.33	1.45	2.41	0.25	5.35	2.38
Belgium			0.41	2.24	2.02	1.03	4.08	2.14
Denmark			0.38	1.91	2.66	2.55	3.81	2.06
Finland			0.60	1.58	2.74	2.69	4.94	2.57
France			0.37	1.43	1.63	1.15	5.05	2.20
Germany			0.37	2.00	2.81	0.30	5.68	1.75
Italy			0.21	1.24	1.94	1.49	5.64	2.30
Netherlands			0.56	1.70	2.16	2.43	4.74	2.46
Norway			0.54	1.70	2.12	2.93	4.06	3.30
Sweden			0.66	1.62	2.17	2.74	3.73	1.83
Switzerland			0.52	1.91	2.55	2.60	4.51	1.16
United Kingdom			0.80	2.05	1.90	1.19	2.93	2.08
12 Country Average			**0.41**	**1.75**	**2.13**	**1.16**	**4.65**	**2.08**
Portugal			0.51	0.66	1.34	2.35	5.73	2.95
Spain			0.32	0.93	1.77	1.06	6.60	3.10
Other			0.39	1.62	2.29	2.45	5.55	3.39
Total Western Europe	**-0.01**	**0.29**	**0.40**	**1.68**	**2.11**	**1.19**	**4.79**	**2.21**
Eastern Europe	**0.03**	**0.19**	**0.41**	**1.41**	**2.33**	**0.86**	**4.86**	**1.01**
Former USSR	**0.06**	**0.22**	**0.47**	**1.61**	**2.40**	**2.15**	**4.84**	**-0.42**
United States			0.86	4.20	3.94	2.84	3.93	2.94
Other Western Offshoots			0.34	5.39	3.81	2.76	4.75	2.99
Total Western Offshoots	**0.05**	**0.07**	**0.78**	**4.31**	**3.92**	**2.83**	**4.03**	**2.95**
Mexico			0.14	0.44	3.38	2.62	6.38	3.45
Other Latin America			0.28	1.52	3.51	3.61	5.16	2.74
Total Latin America	**0.07**	**0.09**	**0.23**	**1.22**	**3.48**	**3.42**	**5.38**	**2.89**
Japan	**0.10**	**0.18**	**0.31**	**0.41**	**2.44**	**2.21**	**9.29**	**2.71**
China	0.00	0.17	0.41	-0.37	0.56	-0.02	5.02	6.72
India	0.00	0.12	0.19	0.38	0.97	0.23	3.54	5.12
Other Asia	0.01	0.10	0.16	0.78	1.76	2.19	6.00	4.61
Total Asia (excl. Japan)	**0.00**	**0.13**	**0.29**	**0.05**	**0.97**	**0.82**	**5.17**	**5.41**
Africa	**0.07**	**0.07**	**0.15**	**0.75**	**1.32**	**2.57**	**4.43**	**2.89**
World	**0.01**	**0.15**	**0.32**	**0.93**	**2.11**	**1.82**	**4.90**	**3.05**

Table 8b. **Share of World GDP, 20 Countries and Regional Totals, 1-2001 AD**
(per cent of world total)

	1	1000	1500	1600	1700	1820	1870	1913	1950	1973	2001
Austria			0.6	0.6	0.7	0.6	0.8	0.9	0.5	0.5	0.4
Belgium			0.5	0.5	0.6	0.7	1.2	1.2	0.9	0.7	0.6
Denmark			0.2	0.2	0.2	0.2	0.3	0.4	0.6	0.4	0.3
Finland			0.1	0.1	0.1	0.1	0.2	0.2	0.3	0.3	0.3
France			4.4	4.7	5.3	5.1	6.5	5.3	4.1	4.3	3.4
Germany			3.3	3.8	3.7	3.9	6.5	8.7	5.0	5.9	4.1
Italy			4.7	4.4	3.9	3.2	3.8	3.5	3.1	3.6	3.0
Netherlands			0.3	0.6	1.1	0.6	0.9	0.9	1.1	1.1	0.9
Norway			0.1	0.1	0.1	0.2	0.2	0.2	0.3	0.3	0.3
Sweden			0.2	0.2	0.3	0.4	0.6	0.6	0.9	0.7	0.5
Switzerland			0.2	0.2	0.3	0.3	0.5	0.6	0.8	0.7	0.4
United Kingdom			1.1	1.8	2.9	5.2	9.0	8.2	6.5	4.2	3.2
12 Country total			**15.5**	**17.2**	**19.1**	**20.5**	**30.5**	**30.8**	**24.1**	**22.8**	**17.5**
Portugal			0.2	0.2	0.4	0.4	0.4	0.3	0.3	0.4	0.4
Spain			1.8	2.1	2.0	1.8	1.8	1.5	1.2	1.7	1.7
Other			0.2	0.3	0.3	0.3	0.4	0.5	0.6	0.7	0.7
Total Western Europe	**10.8**	**8.7**	**17.8**	**19.8**	**21.9**	**23.0**	**33.0**	**33.0**	**26.2**	**25.6**	**20.3**
Eastern Europe	**1.9**	**2.2**	**2.7**	**2.8**	**3.1**	**3.6**	**4.5**	**4.9**	**3.5**	**3.4**	**2.0**
Former USSR	**1.5**	**2.4**	**3.4**	**3.5**	**4.4**	**5.4**	**7.5**	**8.5**	**9.6**	**9.4**	**3.6**
United States			0.3	0.2	0.1	1.8	8.8	18.9	27.3	22.1	21.4
Other Western Offshoots			0.1	0.1	0.1	0.1	1.2	2.4	3.4	3.3	3.2
Total Western Offshoots	**0.5**	**0.7**	**0.5**	**0.3**	**0.2**	**1.9**	**10.0**	**21.3**	**30.7**	**25.3**	**24.6**
Mexico			1.3	0.3	0.7	0.7	0.6	0.9	1.3	1.7	1.9
Other Latin America			1.7	0.8	1.0	1.4	1.9	3.4	6.5	6.9	6.4
Total Latin America	**2.2**	**3.9**	**2.9**	**1.1**	**1.7**	**2.2**	**2.5**	**4.4**	**7.8**	**8.7**	**8.3**
Japan	**1.2**	**2.7**	**3.1**	**2.9**	**4.1**	**3.0**	**2.3**	**2.6**	**3.0**	**7.8**	**7.1**
China	26.1	22.7	24.9	29.0	22.3	32.9	17.1	8.8	4.5	4.6	12.3
India	32.9	28.9	24.4	22.4	24.4	16.0	12.1	7.5	4.2	3.1	5.4
Other Asia	16.0	16.0	12.6	11.1	10.9	7.5	6.9	6.0	6.8	8.7	13.2
Total Asia (excl. Japan)	**75.1**	**67.6**	**61.9**	**62.5**	**57.7**	**56.4**	**36.1**	**22.3**	**15.4**	**16.4**	**30.9**
Africa	**6.9**	**11.7**	**7.8**	**7.1**	**6.9**	**4.5**	**4.1**	**2.9**	**3.8**	**3.4**	**3.3**
World	**100.0**	**100.0**	**100.0**	**100.0**	**100.0**	**100.0**	**100.0**	**100.0**	**100.0**	**100.0**	**100.0**

Table 8c. **World Per Capita GDP, 20 Countries and Regional Averages, 1-2001 AD**
(1990 international Geary-Khamis dollars)

	1	1000	1500	1600	1700	1820	1870	1913	1950	1973	2001
Austria			707	837	993	1 218	1 863	3 465	3 706	11 235	20 225
Belgium			875	976	1 144	1 319	2 692	4 220	5 462	12 170	20 924
Denmark			738	875	1 039	1 274	2 003	3 912	6 943	13 945	23 160
Finland			453	538	638	781	1 140	2 111	4 253	11 085	20 344
France			727	841	910	1 135	1 876	3 485	5 271	13 114	21 092
Germany			688	791	910	1 077	1 839	3 648	3 881	11 966	18 677
Italy			1 100	1 100	1 100	1 117	1 499	2 564	3 502	10 634	19 040
Netherlands			761	1 381	2 130	1 838	2 757	4 049	5 996	13 082	21 722
Norway			640	760	900	1 104	1 432	2 501	5 463	11 246	24 580
Sweden			695	824	977	1 198	1 662	3 096	6 739	13 493	20 562
Switzerland			632	750	890	1 090	2 102	4 266	9 064	18 204	22 264
United Kingdom			714	974	1 250	1 706	3 190	4 921	6 939	12 025	20 127
12 Country Average			**798**	**908**	**1 033**	**1 245**	**2 088**	**3 688**	**5 018**	**12 156**	**20 024**
Portugal			606	740	819	923	975	1 250	2 086	7 063	14 229
Spain			661	853	853	1 008	1 207	2 056	2 189	7 661	15 659
Other			472	525	584	711	1 027	1 840	2 538	7 614	15 989
West European average	450	400	**771**	**890**	**998**	**1 204**	**1 960**	**3 458**	**4 579**	**11 416**	**19 256**
Eastern Europe	400	400	**496**	**548**	**606**	**683**	**937**	**1 695**	**2 111**	**4 988**	**6 027**
Former USSR	400	400	**499**	**552**	**610**	**688**	**943**	**1 488**	**2 841**	**6 059**	**4 626**
United States			400	400	527	1 257	2 445	5 301	9 561	16 689	27 948
Other Western Offshoots			400	400	408	761	2 245	4 752	7 425	13 399	21 718
Average Western Offshoots	400	400	**400**	**400**	**476**	**1 202**	**2 419**	**5 233**	**9 268**	**16 179**	**26 943**
Mexico			425	454	568	759	674	1 732	2 365	4 845	7 089
Other Latin America			410	431	502	663	683	1 424	2 536	4 426	5 508
Latin American Average	400	400	**416**	**438**	**527**	**692**	**681**	**1 481**	**2 506**	**4 504**	**5 811**
Japan	400	425	**500**	**520**	**570**	**669**	**737**	**1 387**	**1 921**	**11 434**	**20 683**
China	450	450	600	600	600	600	530	552	439	839	3 583
India	450	450	550	550	550	533	533	673	619	853	1 957
Other Asia	450	450	565	565	565	584	643	882	926	2 049	3 998
Asian average (excl. Japan)	450	450	**572**	**575**	**571**	**577**	**550**	**658**	**634**	**1 226**	**3 256**
Africa	430	425	**414**	**422**	**421**	**420**	**500**	**637**	**894**	**1 410**	**1 489**
World	445	436	**566**	**595**	**615**	**667**	**875**	**1 525**	**2 111**	**4 091**	**6 049**

Table 8b. Rate of Growth of World Per Capita GDP, 20 Countries and Regional Averages, 1-2001 AD
(annual average compound growth rates)

	1-1000	1000-1500	1500-1820	1820-70	1870-1913	1913-50	1950-73	1973-2001
Austria			0.17	0.85	1.45	0.18	4.94	2.12
Belgium			0.13	1.44	1.05	0.70	3.54	1.95
Denmark			0.17	0.91	1.57	1.56	3.08	1.83
Finland			0.17	0.76	1.44	1.91	4.25	2.19
France			0.14	1.01	1.45	1.12	4.04	1.71
Germany			0.14	1.08	1.61	0.17	5.02	1.60
Italy			0.00	0.59	1.26	0.85	4.95	2.10
Netherlands			0.28	0.81	0.90	1.07	3.45	1.83
Norway			0.17	0.52	1.30	2.13	3.19	2.83
Sweden			0.17	0.66	1.46	2.12	3.06	1.52
Switzerland			0.17	1.32	1.66	2.06	3.08	0.72
United Kingdom			0.27	1.26	1.01	0.93	2.42	1.86
12 Country Average			**0.14**	**1.04**	**1.33**	**0.84**	**3.92**	**1.80**
Portugal			0.13	0.11	0.58	1.39	5.45	2.53
Spain			0.13	0.36	1.25	0.17	5.60	2.59
Other			0.13	0.74	1.37	0.87	4.89	2.68
Total Western Europe	**-0.01**	**0.13**	**0.14**	**0.98**	**1.33**	**0.76**	**4.05**	**1.88**
Eastern Europe	**0.00**	**0.04**	**0.10**	**0.63**	**1.39**	**0.60**	**3.81**	**0.68**
Former USSR	**0.00**	**0.04**	**0.10**	**0.63**	**1.06**	**1.76**	**3.35**	**-0.96**
United States			0.36	1.34	1.82	1.61	2.45	1.86
Other Western Offshoots			0.20	2.19	1.76	1.21	2.60	1.74
Total Western Offshoots	**0.00**	**0.00**	**0.34**	**1.41**	**1.81**	**1.56**	**2.45**	**1.84**
Mexico			0.18	-0.24	2.22	0.85	3.17	1.37
Other Latin America			0.15	0.06	1.72	1.57	2.45	0.78
Total Latin America	**0.00**	**0.01**	**0.16**	**-0.03**	**1.82**	**1.43**	**2.58**	**0.91**
Japan	**0.01**	**0.03**	**0.09**	**0.19**	**1.48**	**0.88**	**8.06**	**2.14**
China	**0.00**	0.06	0.00	-0.25	0.10	-0.62	2.86	5.32
India	**0.00**	0.04	-0.01	0.00	0.54	-0.22	1.40	3.01
Other Asia	**0.00**	0.05	0.01	0.19	0.74	0.13	3.51	2.42
Total Asia (excl. Japan)	**0.00**	**0.05**	**0.00**	**-0.10**	**0.42**	**-0.10**	**2.91**	**3.55**
Africa	**0.00**	**-0.01**	**0.00**	**0.35**	**0.57**	**0.92**	**2.00**	**0.19**
World	**0.00**	**0.05**	**0.05**	**0.54**	**1.30**	**0.88**	**2.92**	**1.41**

Select Bibliography

ALDCROFT, D.H. AND A. SUTCLIFFE (eds.) (1999). *Europe in the International Economy: 1500 to 2000*, Elgar, Cheltenham.

ALLEN, R.C. (2001), "The Great Divergence in European Wages and Prices from the Middle Ages to the First World War", *Explorations in Economic History*, 38, pp. 411–447.

BAIROCH, P. (1967), *Diagnostic de l'évolution économique du tiers–monde, 1900–1966*, Gauthiers–Villars, Paris.

BAIROCH, P. (1976), "Europe's Gross National Product: 1800–1975", *Journal of European Economic History*, Fall, pp. 273–340.

BAIROCH, P. (1977), "Estimations du revenu national dans les sociétés occidentales pré–industrielles et au dix–neuvième siècle: propositions d'approches indirectes", *Revue économique*, March, pp. 177–208.

BAIROCH, P. (1997), *Victoires et Déboires*, 3 vols., Gallimard, Paris.

BAIROCH, P. AND M. LEVY–LEBOYER (1981), *Disparities in Economic Development since the Industrial Revolution*, Macmillan, London.

BAGNALL, R.S. AND B.W. FRIER (1994*), The Demography of Roman Egypt*, Cambridge University Press.

BARDET, J.–P. AND J. DUPAQUIER (1997), *Histoire des populations de l'Europe*, Fayard, Paris, 2 vols.

BECKERMAN, W. (1966), *International Comparisons of Real Incomes*, OECD Development Centre, Paris.

BELOCH, J. (1886), *Die Bevölkerung der Griechisch–Römischen Welt*, Duncker and Humblot, Leipzig.

BERGSON, A. (1953), *Soviet National Income and Product in 1937*, Columbia University Press, New York.

BETHELL, L. (1985–6), *The Cambridge History of Latin America*, vols. III and IV, Cambridge University Press.

BOISGUILBERT, P. DE (1696*), La France ruinée sous la règne de Louis XIV par qui et comment*, Marteau, Cologne (author not shown, publisher fictitious, clandestinely printed in Rouen).

BOISGUILBERT, P. DE (1697), *Le détail de la France* (author and publisher not shown).

BOISGUILBERT, P. DE (1966), see INED.

BOOMGAARD, P. (1993), "Economic Growth in Indonesia, 500–1990", *in* SZIRMAI, VAN ARK AND PILAT.

BOOMGAARD, P., see Creutzberg.

BORAH, W. AND S.F. COOK (1963), *The Aboriginal Population of Central Mexico on the Eve of the Spanish Conquest*, University of California, Berkeley.

BORDO, M.D. AND R. CORTÉS–CONDE (2001), *Transferring Wealth and Power from the Old to the New World*, Cambridge University Press.

BOSERUP, E. (1965), *The Conditions of Agricultural Growth*, Allen and Unwin, London.

BOWLEY, A.L. (1900),*Wages in the United Kingdom in the Nineteenth Century*, Cambridge University Press.

BOWLEY, A.L. (1942), *Studies in the National Income*, Cambridge University Press.

BOWMAN A.K. AND E. ROGAN (eds.) (1999), *Agriculture in Egypt from Pharaonic to Modern Times*, Oxford University Press.

BRAUDEL, F. (1985), *Civilization and Capitalism: 15th–18th Century*, vol. 3, Fontana, London.

BRESNAHAN, T.F. AND R.J. GORDON (1997), *The Economics of New Goods*, NBER and University of Chicago Press.

BREWER, J. (1989), *The Sinews of Power: War, Money and the English State, 1688–1783,* Unwin Hyman, London.

BREWER, J. AND R. PORTER (eds.) (1993*), Consumption and the World of Goods*, Routledge, London.

BROADBERRY, S.N. (1997a),"Forging Ahead, Falling Behind and Catching–up: A Sectoral Analysis of Anglo–American Productivity Differences, 1870–1990", *Research In Economic History*, 17, pp. 1–37.

BROADBERRY, S.N. (1997b), "Anglo–German Productivity Differences 1870–1990: A Sectoral Analysis", *European Review of Economic History*, I, pp. 247–267.

BROADBERRY, S.N. (1998), "How did the United States and Germany Overtake Britain? A Sectoral Analysis of Comparative Productivity Levels, 1870–1990", *Journal of Economic History,* June, pp. 375–407.

BUTLIN, N.G. (1983), *Our Original Aggression*, Allen and Unwin, Sydney.

CHALMERS, G. (1802), *An Estimate of the Comparative Strength of Great Britain*, Stockdale, Piccadilly, London.

CHAO, K. (1986), *Man and Land in Chinese History: An Economic Analysis*, Stanford University Press, Stanford.

CHRISTENSEN, J.P., R. HJERPPE, O. KRANTZ AND C.–A. NILSSON (1995),"Nordic Historical National Accounts since the 1880s", *Scandinavian Economic History Review*, XLIII, no. 1.

CIPOLLA, C.M. (1976), *Before the Industrial Revolution: European Society and Economy, 1000–1700*, Norton, New York.

CLARK, C. (1937), *National Income and Outlay*, Macmillan, London.

CLARK, C. (1940), *The Conditions of Economic Progress*, Macmillan, London.

CLARK, C. (1951), *The Conditions of Economic Progress*, second edition, Macmillan, London.

CLARK, C. (1957), *The Conditions of Economic Progress*, third edition, Macmillan, London.

COLE, A.H. AND R. CRANDALL (1964), "The International Scientific Committee on Price History", *Journal of Economic History*, September, pp. 381–388.

COLGRAVE, B. AND R.A.B. MYNORS (eds.) (1969), *Bede's Ecclesiastical History of the English People*, Clarendon Press, Oxford.

COLLINS, J.B. (1995), *The State in Early Modern France*, Cambridge University Press.

COLQUHOUN, P. (1815), *A Treatise on the Wealth, Power, and Resources of the British Empire in Every Quarter of the World*, Mawman, London.

CRAFTS, N.F.R. (1983), Gross National Product in Europe 1870–1910: Some New Estimates", *Explorations in Economic History* (20), pp. 387–401.

CRAFTS, N.F.R. AND C.K. HARLEY (1992), "Output Growth and the British Industrial Revolution: A Restatement of the Crafts–Harley View", *Economic History Review*, November, pp. 703–730.

CREUTZBERG, P. AND P. BOOMGAARD (eds.) (1975–1996), *Changing Economy in Indonesia: A Selection of Statistical Resource Material from the Early 19th century up to 1940*, 16 volumes, Royal Tropical Institute, Amsterdam.

CROSBY, A.W. (1972), *The Columbian Exchange:Biological and Cultural Consequences of 1492*, Greenwood Press, Westport.

CROUZET, F. AND A. CLESSE (eds.) (2003), *Leading the World Economically*, Dutch University Press, The Netherlands.

DAVENANT, C. (1694), *An Essay on Ways and Means of Supplying the War*, (see Whitworth, 1771).

DAVENANT, C. (1699), *An Essay upon the Probable Methods of Making a People Gainers in the Balance of Trade*, (see Whitworth, 1771)

DEANE, P. (1955), "The Implications of Early National Income Estimates for the Measurement of Long–Term Economic Growth in the United Kingdom", *Economic Development and Cultural Change*, pp. 3–38.

DEANE, P. (1955–6), "Contemporary Estimates of National Income in the First Half of the Nineteenth Century", *Economic History Review*, VIII, 3, pp. 339–354.

DEANE, P. (1956–7), "Contemporary Estimates of National Income in the Second Half of the Nineteenth Century", *Economic History Review*, IX, 3, pp. 451–61.

DEANE, P. (1957), "The Industrial Revolution and Economic Growth: The Evidence of Early British National Income Estimates", *Economic Development and Cultural Change*, pp. 159–74.

DEANE, P. (1968), "New Estimates of Gross National Product for the United Kingdom, 1830–1914", *Review of Income and Wealth*, June, pp. 95–112.

DEANE, P. AND W.A. COLE (1964), *British Economic Growth, 1688–1959*, Cambridge University Press.

DENISON, E.F. (1947), "Report on Tripartite Discussions of National Income Measurement", *in Studies in Income and Wealth*, Vol.10, NBER, New York.

DENISON, E.F. (1967), *Why Growth Rates Differ*, Brookings, Washington, D.C.

ECE (ECONOMIC COMMISSION FOR EUROPE) and UN (1994), *International Comparison of Gross Domestic Product in Europe 1990*, New York and Geneva.

ELTIS, D. (1995), "The Total Product of Barbados, 1664–1701", *Journal of Economic History*, June.

ELTIS, D. (1997), "The Slave Economies of the Caribbean: Structure, Perfomance, Evolution and Significance", *in* KNIGHT, pp. 105–137.

ELVIN, M. (1973), *The Pattern of the Chinese Past*, Methuen, London.

ENG, P. VAN DER (1993), *Agricultural Growth in Indonesia Since 1880*, University of Groningen.

ENGERMAN, S.L. AND R.E. GALLMAN (1996–2000), *The Cambridge History of the United States*, 3 vols., Cambridge University Press.

ENGERMAN, S.L. AND B.W. HIGMAN (1997), "The demographic structure of the Caribbean slave societies in the eighteenth and nineteenth centuries" *in* Knight, pp. 45–104.

ESCAP (ECONOMIC COMMISSION FOR ASIA AND THE PACIFIC) (1999), *ESCAP Comparisons of Real Gross Domestic Product and Purchasing Power Parities, 1993*, Bangkok.

ESCWA (ECONOMIC AND SOCIAL COMMISSION FOR WESTERN ASIA) and WORLD BANK (1997), *Purchasing Power Parities: Volume and Price Level Comparisons for the Middle East, 1993*, Beirut.

EUROSTAT (1996), *Comparisons of Price Levels and Economic Aggregates 1993: The Results of 22 African Countries*, Luxembourg.

FEINSTEIN, C.H. (1972), *National Income, Expenditure and Output of the United Kingdom, 1855–1965*, Cambridge University Press.

FEINSTEIN, C.H. (1988),"The Rise and Fall of the Williamson Curve", Journal of Economic History, September, pp. 699–729.

FEINSTEIN, C.H. (1998), "Pessimism Perpetuated: Real Wages and the Standard of Living in Britain during and after the Industrial Revolution", *Journal of Economic History*, September, pp. 625–58.

FOGEL, J.A. (1964), *Railroads and American Economic Growth*, Johns Hopkins University Press, Baltimore.

FRANK, A.G. (1998), *Reorient: Global Economy in the Asian Age*, University of California Press, Berkeley.

GALBRAITH, J.K. *et al.* (1945), *The Effects of Strategic Bombing on the German War Economy*, US Strategic Bombing Survey, Washington, D.C.

GILBERT, M. AND I.B. KRAVIS (1954), *An International Comparison of National Products and Purchasing Power of Currencies*, OEEC, Paris.

GILBERT, M. AND ASSOCIATES (1958), *Comparative National Products and Price Levels*, OEEC, Paris.

GLASS, D.V. (1965), "Two Papers on Gregory King", *in* Glass and Eversley (1965), pp. 159–221.

GLASS, D.V. AND D.E.C. EVERSLEY (eds.) (1965), *Population in History: Essays in Historical Demography*, Arnold, London.

GOITEIN, S.D.F. (1967–93*), A Mediterranean Society: The Jewish Communities of the Arab World as Portrayed in the Documents of the Cairo Geniza*, 6 vols.,University of California Press, Berkeley and Los Angeles.

GOLDSMITH, R.W. (1984), "An Estimate of the Size and Structure of the National Product of the Roman Empire", *Review of Income and Wealth,* September.

GOODY, J. (1971), *Technology, Tradition and the State in Africa*, Oxford University Press.

GRAUNT, J. (1662), *Natural and Political Observations Made Upon the Bills of Mortality*, reprinted in Laslett.

HABIB, I. (1978–9), "The Technology and Economy of Moghul India", *Indian Economic and Social History Review,* vol. XVII, No. 1, pp. 1–34.

HABIB, I. (1995), *Essays in Indian History*, Tulika, New Delhi.

HAIG, B. (2001), *The First Official National Accounting Estimates*, Canberra (processed).

HANLEY, S. (1997), *Everyday Things in Premodern Japan*, University of California, Berkeley.

HANLEY, S.B. AND K. YAMAMURA (1977), *Economic and Demographic Change in Preindustrial Japan, 1600–1868*, Princeton University Press.

HARALDSON, W.C. AND E.F. DENISON, (1945), "The Gross National Product of Germany 1936–44", Special Paper I (mimeographed), *in* GALBRAITH *et al.*

HAYAMI, A. (1986), "Population Trends in Tokugawa Japan 1600–1970", International Statistical Institute Conference.

HESTON, A. AND R. SUMMERS (1993), "What Can be Learned from Successive ICP Benchmark Estimates?" *in* SZIRMAI, VAN ARK AND PILAT (*op. cit.*).

HESTON, A., R. SUMMERS AND B. ATEN (2002), PWT Version 6.1 (CICUP), http:/pwt.econ.upenn.edu).

HJERPPE, R. (1996), *Finland's Historical National Accounts 1860–1994*, University of Jyväskylä, Jyväskylä.

HO, P.T. (1959), *Studies on the Population of China, 1368–1953*, Columbia University Press, New York.

HOFMAN, A.A. (2000), *The Economic Development of Latin America in the Twentieth Century*, Elgar, Cheltenham.

HOPKINS, K. (1980), "Taxes and Trade in the Roman Empire (200 BC–400 AD)", *Journal of Roman Studies*, vol. LXX, pp. 101–25.

IBN KHALDUN (1958), *The Muqqadimah: An Introduction to History*, 3 vols., translated by Franz Rosenthal, Routledge and Kegan Paul, London.

INED (1966), *Pierre de Boisguilbert ou la naissance de l'économie politique,* vol. I, Biographie, correspondance, bibliographies, vol. II, œuvres manuscrites et imprimées, Paris.

JARRETT, H.S. AND J.–N. SARKAR (1949), *'Ain–I–Akbari of Abul Fazl–I–'Allami*, Royal Asiatic Society of Bengal, Calcutta.

JONES, E.L. (1981), *The European Miracle*, Cambridge University Press.

JONES, E.L. (1988), *Growth Recurring: Economic Change in World History*, Clarendon Press, Oxford.

KALDOR, N. (1946), "The German War Economy", *Review of Economic Studies*, vol. XIII, 1.

KING, G. (1696), *Natural and Political Observations and Conclusions upon the State and Condition of England,* reproduced in G.E. Barnett (1936), *Two Tracts by Gregory King*, Johns Hopkins Press, Baltimore.

KING, G. (1697), *Natural and Political Observations and Conclusions upon the State and Condition of England,* manuscript copy of above, interleaved with detailed comments by Robert Harley and King's replies, Manuscript (MS 1458) in National Library of Australia.

KING, G. (1695–70), *Manuscript Notebook*, reproduced in Laslett (1973).

KNIGHT, F.W. (ed.) (1997), *General History of the Caribbean*, vol III, UNESCO, London.

KRAVIS, I.B., A. HESTON AND R. SUMMERS (1978), "Real GDP Per Capita For More Than One Hundred Countries", *Economic Journal,* June.

KRAVIS, I.B., A. HESTON AND R. SUMMERS (1982), *World Product and Income, International Comparisons of Real Gross Product*, Johns Hopkins, Baltimore.

KUZNETS, S. (1948), "Discussion of the New Department of Commerce Income Series", *Review of Economics and Statistics*, August, with reply by Gilbert, Jaszi, Denison and Schwartz, and comment by Kalecki.

KUZNETS, S. (1973), *Population, Capital and Growth: Selected Essays*, Norton, New York.

LAL, D. (1988), *The Hindu Equilibrium*, Oxford University Press.

LAL, D. (1998), *Unintended Consequences*, MIT Press, Cambridge, Mass.

LANDES, D.S. (1969), *The Unbound Prometheus*, Cambridge University Press.

LANDES, D.S. (1998),*The Wealth and Poverty of Nations*, Little, Brown and Company, London.

LARSEN, H. K. (2001), *Convergence? Industrialisation of Denmark, Finland and Sweden 1870–1940*, Finnish Society of Science and Letters, Helsinki.

LASLETT, P. (ed.) (1973), *The Earliest Classics: John Graunt and Gregory King*, Gregg International, London.

LEE, B. AND A. MADDISON (1997), "A Comparison of Output, Purchasing Power and Productivity in Indian and Chinese Manufacturing in the mid–1980s", *COPPAA Paper, No. 5*, Brisbane.

LE ROY LADURIE, E. (1978), "Les comptes fantastiques de Gregory King", *in Le territoire de l'historien*, vol. 1, Gallimard, Paris.

LI, B. (1998), *Agricultural Development in Jiangnan, 1620–1850*, Macmillan, London.

LIN, J.Y. (1995), "The Needham Puzzle: Why the Industrial Revolution did not Originate in China", *Economic Development and Cultural Change*, January.

LINDERT, P.H. AND J.G. WILLIAMSON (1983), "English Workers Living Standards during the Industrial Revolution: A New Look", *Economic History Review*, February, pp. 1–25.

MA, D. (2003), "Modern Economic Growth in the Lower Yangzi: A Quantitative and Historical Perspective", http://aghistory,ucdavis.edu/ma.pdf.

MADDISON, A. (1962), "Growth and Fluctuation in the World Economy, 1870–1960", *Banca Nazionale del Lavoro Quarterly Review,* June.

MADDISON, A. (1969), *Economic Growth in Japan and the USSR*, Allen and Unwin, London.

MADDISON, A. (1970), *Economic Progress and Policy in Developing Countries*, Allen and Unwin, London.

MADDISON, A. (1971), *Class Structure and Economic Growth: India and Pakistan Since the Moghuls*, Allen and Unwin, London.

MADDISON, A. (1982), *Phases of Capitalist Development*, Oxford University Press.

MADDISON, A. (1983), "A Comparison of Levels of GDP Per Capita in Developed and Developing Countries, 1700–1980", *Journal of Economic History*, March, pp. 27–41.

MADDISON, A. (1987a), "Growth and Slowdown in Advanced Capitalist Economies: Techniques of Quantitative Assessment", *Journal of Economic Literature*, June, pp. 649–698.

MADDISON, A. (1987b), "Recent Revisions to British and Dutch Growth, 1700–1870 and their Implications for Comparative Levels of Performance", *in* MADDISON AND VAN DER MEULEN (1987).

MADDISON, A. (1989a), *The World Economy in the Twentieth Century*, Development Centre Studies, OECD, Paris.

MADDISON, A. (1989b), "Dutch Income in and from Indonesia 1700–1938", *Modern Asian Studies*, pp. 645–70.

MADDISON, A. (1990), "Measuring European Growth: the Core and the Periphery", *in* E. AERTS AND N. VALERIO, *Growth and Stagnation in the Mediterranean World,* Tenth International Economic History Conference, Leuven.

MADDISON, A. (1991), *Dynamic Forces in Capitalist Development*, Oxford University Press.

MADDISON, A. (1991*b*), "A Revised Estimate of Italian Economic Growth, 1861–1989", *Banca Nazionale del Lavoro Quarterly Review*, June, pp. 225–41.

MADDISON, A. (1991*c*), *A Long Run Perspective on Saving*, Research Memorandum 443, Institute of Economic Research, University of Groningen (shorter version in *Scandinavian Journal of Economics*, June 1992, pp. 181–96).

MADDISON, A. (1995), *Monitoring the World Economy 1820–1992*, Development Centre Studies, OECD, Paris.

MADDISON, A. (1995*b*) *Explaining the Economic Performance of Nations: Essays in Time and Space*, Elgar, Aldershot.

MADDISON, A. (1995*c*), "The Historical Roots of Modern Mexico: 1500–1940", in Maddison (1995*b*).

MADDISON, A. (1998), *Chinese Economic Performance in the Long Run*, Development Centre Studies, OECD, Paris.

MADDISON, A. (1998*b*), "Measuring the Performance of A Communist Command Economy: An Assessment of the CIA Estimates for the USSR", *Review of Income and Wealth*, September.

MADDISON, A. (1999), Review of Hanley (1997), *Journal of Japanese and International Economies*.

MADDISON, A. (2001), *The World Economy: A Millennial Perspective*, Development Centre Studies, OECD, Paris.

MADDISON, A. (2002), "The Nature of US Economic Leadership: A Historical and Comparative View", *in* O'BRIEN AND CLESSE.

MADDISON, A. (2003), "Growth Accounts, Technological Change, and the Role of Energy in Western Growth" in *Economia e Energia Secc. XIII–XVIII*, Instituto Internazionale di Storia Economica "E. Datini", Prato.

MADDISON, A. (2003), website: http://eco.rug.nl/~Maddison/

MADDISON, A. (2004), *The West and the Rest in the World Economy,* forthcoming.

MADDISON, A. AND ASSOCIATES (1992), *The Political Economy of Economic Growth: Brazil and Mexico*, Oxford University Press, New York.

MADDISON, A. AND B. VAN ARK (1988), *Comparisons of Real Output in Manufacturing,* Policy, Planning and Research Working Papers WPS 5, World Bank, Washington, D.C.

MADDISON, A. AND B. VAN ARK (1989), "International Comparisons of Purchasing Power, Real Output and Labour Productivity: A Case Study of Brazilian, Mexican and US Manufacturing, 1975", *Review of Income and Wealth,* March.

MADDISON, A. AND B. VAN ARK (2000), "The International Comparison of Real Product and Productivity" in MADDISON, PRASADA RAO AND SHEPHERD.

MADDISON, A. AND H. VAN DER MEULEN (eds.) (1987), *Economic Growth in Northwestern Europe: The Last 400 Years*, Research Memorandum 214, Institute of Economic Research, University of Groningen.

MADDISON, A. AND H. VAN DER WEE (eds.) (1994), *Economic Growth and Structural Change: Comparative Approaches over the Long Run*, Proceedings of the Eleventh International Economic History Congress, Milan, September.

MADDISON, A., D.S. PRASADA RAO AND W. SHEPHERD (eds.) (2000), *The Asian Economies in the Twentieth Century*, Elgar, Aldershot.

MADDISON, A. AND G. PRINCE (eds.) (1989), *Economic Growth in Indonesia, 1820–1940*, Foris, Dordrecht.

MANARUNGSAN, S. (1989), *Economic Development of Thailand, 1850–1950*, University of Groningen.

MCEVEDY, C. (1995), *Penguin Atlas of African History*, London.

MCEVEDY, C. AND R. JONES (1978), *Atlas of World Population History*, Penguin, Middlesex.

MᴄNᴇɪʟʟ, W.H. (1963), *The Rise of the West*, University of Chicago Press.

MᴄNᴇɪʟʟ, W.H. (1977), *Plagues and Peoples*, Anchor Books, Doubleday, New York.

MᴄNᴇɪʟʟ, W.H. (1990), "The Rise of the West after Twenty–Five Years", *Journal of World History*, vol. 1, no. 1.

Mᴇᴀᴅᴇ, J. R. ᴀɴᴅ R. Sᴛᴏɴᴇ (1941), "The Construction of Tables on National Income, Expenditure, Savings and Investment", *Economic Journal*, Jun–Sep, pp. 216–33.

Mɪᴛᴄʜᴇʟʟ, B.R. (1975), *European Historical Statistics 1750–1970*, Macmillan, London.

Mɪᴛᴄʜᴇʟʟ, B.R. (1982), *International Historical Statistics: Africa and Asia*, Macmillan, London.

Mɪᴛᴄʜᴇʟʟ, B.R. (1983), *International Historical Statistics: the Americas and Australasia*, Macmillan, London.

Mᴏᴏsᴠɪ, S. (1987), *The Economy of the Moghul Empire c.1595: A Statistical Study*, Oxford University Press, Delhi.

Mᴜʟᴅᴇʀ, N. (2002), *Economic Performance in the Americas*, Elgar, Cheltenham.

Mᴜʟʜᴀʟʟ, M.G. (1880), *The Progress of the World*, Stanford, London.

Mᴜʟʜᴀʟʟ, M.G. (1881), *Balance Sheet of the World for 10 Years 1870–1880*, Stanford, London.

Mᴜʟʜᴀʟʟ, M.G. (1884), *The Dictionary of Statistics*, Routledge, London, 4th edition 1899.

Mᴜʟʜᴀʟʟ, M.G. (1896), *Industries and Wealth of Nations*, Longmans, London.

Nᴇᴇᴅʜᴀᴍ, J. (1954–97), *Science and Civilisation in China*, Cambridge University Press.

Nᴇᴇᴅʜᴀᴍ, J. (1970), *Clerks and Craftsmen in China and the West*, Cambridge University Press.

Nᴏʀᴅʜᴀᴜs, W.D. (1997),"Do Real–Wage Measures Capture Reality? The Evidence of Lighting Suggests Not", *in* Bʀᴇsɴᴀʜᴀɴ ᴀɴᴅ Gᴏʀᴅᴏɴ.

Nᴏʀᴛʜ, D.C. (1990), *Institutions, Institutional Change and Economic Performance*, Cambridge University Press.

Nᴏʀᴛʜ, D.C. ᴀɴᴅ R.P. Tʜᴏᴍᴀs (1973), *The Rise of the Western World*, Cambridge University Press.

O'Bʀɪᴇɴ P.K. ᴀɴᴅ A. Cʟᴇssᴇ (eds.) (2002), *Two Hegemonies: Britain 1846–1914 and the United States 1941–2001*, Ashgate, Aldershot.

OECD (1993), *Purchasing Power Parities and Real Expenditures 1990: GK Results,* Vol. II, Paris.

OECD (2002), *Purchasing Power Parities and Real Expenditures, 1999 Benchmark Year*, Paris.

OECD (2003), *Measuring Productivity Levels–A Reader*, Paris.

Oʜᴋᴀᴡᴀ, K., M. Sʜɪɴᴏʜᴀʀᴀ ᴀɴᴅ M. Uᴍᴇᴍᴜʀᴀ (eds.) (1966–1988), *Estimates of Long–Term Economic Statistics of Japan since 1868*, 14 volumes, Toyo Keizai Shinposha, Tokyo.

Özᴍᴜᴄᴜʀ, S. ᴀɴᴅ S. Pᴀᴍᴜᴋ (2002), "Real Wages and Standards of Living in the Ottoman Empire, 1489–1914", *Journal of Economic History*, June, pp. 293–321.

Pᴀɪɢᴇ, D. ᴀɴᴅ G. Bᴏᴍʙᴀᴄʜ (1959), *A Comparison of National Output and Productivity of the United Kingdom and the United States*, OEEC, Paris.

Pᴀʀᴛʜᴀsᴀʀᴀᴛʜɪ, P. (1998), "Rethinking Wages and Competitiveness in the Eighteenth Century: Britain and South India", *Past and Present*, 158, pp. 79–109.

Pᴇʀᴋɪɴs, D.W. (1969), *Agricultural Development in China, 1368–1968*, Aldine, Chicago.

Pᴇᴛᴛʏ, W. (1997), *The Collected Works of Sir William Petty*, 8 volumes, Routledge/Thoemes Press, London (includes Hull's (1899) collection of Petty's economic writings; E.G. Fitzmaurice's (1895) biography of Petty; Lansdowne's (1927 and 1928) collection of Petty papers and the Southwell–Petty correspondence; Larcom's (1851) edition of Petty's Irish Land Survey, and critical appraisals by T.W. Hutchinson and others).

Pʜᴇʟᴘs Bʀᴏᴡɴ, H. ᴀɴᴅ S.V. Hᴏᴘᴋɪɴs (1981), *A Perspective on Wages and Prices*, Methuen, London.

Pɪʟᴀᴛ, D. (1994), *The Economics of Rapid Growth: The Experience of Japan and Korea*, Elgar, Aldershot.

POMERANZ, K. (2000), *The Great Divergence: China, Europe and the Making of the Modern World Economy*, Princeton University Press, New Jersey.

PRADOS DE LA ESCOSURA, L. (2000), "International Comparisons of Real Product, 1820–1990: An alternative Dataset", in *Explorations in Economic History*, 37 (1), pp1–41.

RAYCHAUDHURI, T. AND I. HABIB (1982), *The Cambridge Economic History of India, c.1200–1750,* vol. I, Cambridge University Press.

RICHARDS, E.G. (1998), *Mapping Time*, Oxford University Press.

REN, R. (1997), *China's Economic Performance in an International Perspective*, Development Centre Studies, OECD, Paris.

RICCIOLI, G.B. (1672), *Geographiae et Hydrographiae Reformatae, Libri Duodecim,* Venice.

ROSENBLAT, A. (1945), *La Poblacion Indigena de America Desde 1492 Hasta la Actualidad*, ICE, Buenos Aires.

ROSTAS, L. (1948), *Comparative Productivity in British and American Industry*, Cambridge University Press, Cambridge.

ROSTOW, W.W. (1960), *The Stages of Economic Growth*, Cambridge University Press.

SHEPHERD, V. AND H. M. BECKLES (eds.) (2000), *Caribbean Slavery in the Atlantic World*, Wiener, Princeton.

SIVASUBRAMONIAN, S. (2000), *The National Income of India in the Twentieth Century*, Oxford University Press, New Delhi.

SIVASUBRAMONIAN, S. (2003), *The Sources of Economic Growth in India 1950–2000*, Oxford University Press, New Delhi.

SMITS, J.P., E. HORLINGS AND J.L. VAN ZANDEN (2000), *Dutch GNP and Its Components, 1800–1913*, Groningen Growth and Development Centre, Monograph Series, No. 5.

SNOOKS, G.D. (1993), *Economics Without Time*, Macmillan, London.

SNOOKS, G.D. (1996), *The Dynamic Society: Exploring the Sources of Global Change*, Routledge, London.

SNOOKS, G.D. (1997), *The Ephemeral Civilisation*, Routledge, London.

STONE, R. (1956), *Quantity and Price Indexes in National Accounts*, OEEC, Paris.

STONE, R. (1961), *Input–Output and National Accounts,* OEEC, Paris.

STONE, R. (1971), *Demographic Accounting and Model Building*, OECD, Paris.

STONE, R. (1997a), "The Accounts of Society"(1984 Nobel Memorial Lecture), *American Economic Review,* December, pp. 17–29.

STONE, R. (1997b), *Some British Empiricists in the Social Sciences 1650–1900*, Cambridge University Press, Cambridge.

STUDENSKI, P. (1958), *The Income of Nations: Theory, Measurement and Analysis: Past and Present*, New York University Press, Washington Square.

SUMMERS, R., I.B. KRAVIS AND A. HESTON (1980), "International Comparison of Real Product and its Composition: 1950–77", *Review of Income and Wealth*, March, pp. 19–66.

SUMMERS R. AND A. HESTON (1988), "A New Set of International Comparisons of Real Product and Prices: Estimates for 130 Countries, 1950–1985", *Review of Income and Wealth*, March, pp. 1–26.

SZIRMAI, A., B. VAN ARK AND D. PILAT (eds.) (1993), *Explaining Economic Growth: Essays in Honour of Angus Maddison*, North Holland, Amsterdam.

THOROLD ROGERS, J.E. (1866–1902), *A History of Agriculture and Prices in England*, 7 vols. Clarendon Press, Oxford.

THOROLD ROGERS, J.E (1884), *Six Centuries of Work and Wages*, Swan Sonnenschein, London.

TODA, YASUSHI (1990), "Catching–up and Convergence: the Standard of Living and the Consumption Pattern of the Russians and the Japanese in 1913 and 1975–1976", paper presented at session C28, 10th World Congress of the International Economic History Association, Leuven, mimeographed.

UN (1987), *World Comparisons of Purchasing Power and Real Product for 1980*, New York.

UN (1993), *System of National Accounts 1993*, Paris (jointly with EU, IMF, OECD and World Bank), earlier versions in 1953 and 1968.

UN (1994), *World Comparisons of Real Gross Domestic Product and Purchasing Power, 1985*, New York.

UN (2001) *World Population Prospects: The 2000 Revision*, vol 1, *Comprehensive Tables,* Population Division, Dept. of Economic and Social Affairs, New York. Annual estimates on CD ROM Disk 2: Extensive Set.

VAUBAN, S. (1707), *La dîme royale* (1992 edition, with introduction by E. Le Roy Ladurie, Imprimerie nationale, Paris).

VRIES, J. DE (1984), *European Urbanization 1500–1800*, Methuen, London.

VRIES, J. DE (1993), "Between Purchasing Power and the World of Goods: Understanding the Household Economy in Early Modern Europe", *in* BREWER AND PORTER (1993).

VRIES, J. DE (1994),"The Industrial Revolution and the Industrious Revolution", *Journal of Economic History,* June, pp. 249–270.

VRIES, J. DE AND A. VAN DER WOUDE (1997), *The First Modern Economy; Success, Failure and Perseverance of the Dutch Economy, 1500–1815*, Cambridge University Press, Cambridge.

WARD, M. (1985), *Purchasing Power Parities and Real Expenditures in the OECD*, OECD, Paris.

WESTERGAARD, H. (1932), *Contributions to the History of Statistics*, King, London (Kelley reprint, 1969).

WHITWORTH, C. (ed.) (1771), *The Political and Commercial Works of Charles Davenant*, 5 vols., London.

WHITE, E.N. (2001), "France and the Failure to Modernise Macroeconomic Institutions", *in* BORDO AND CORTÉS–CONDE.

WILLIAMS, E. (1944), *Capitalism and Slavery*, Russell and Russell, New York.

WILLIAMS, E. (1970), *From Columbus to Castro: The History of the Caribbean 1492–1969*, Deutsch, London.

WILLIAMSON, J.G. (1985),*Did British Capitalism Breed Inequality?* Allen and Unwin, London.

WILLIAMSON, J.G. (1995), "The Evolution of Global Labor Markets since 1930: Background Evidence and Hypotheses", *Explorations in Economic History*, 32, pp. 141–196.

WRIGLEY, E.A. (1988), *Continuity, Chance and Change*, Cambridge.

WRIGLEY, E.A. AND R.S. SCHOFIELD (1981), *The Population History of England 1541–1871*, Arnold, London.

WRIGLEY, E.A., R.S. DAVIES, J.E. OEPPEN AND R.S. SCHOFIELD (1997), *English Population History from Family Reconstitution 1580–1837*, Cambridge University Press, Cambridge.

YOUNG, A. (1794), *Travels During the Years 1787–9 with a View to Ascertaining the Cultivation, Wealth, Resources and National Prosperity of the Kingdom of France*, Richardson, London, (2nd edition).

VAN ZANDEN, J.L. (1999),"Wages and the Standard of Living in Europe, 1500–1800", *European Review of Economic History*, August, pp. 175–198.

VAN ZANDEN, J.L. AND E. HORLINGS (1999), "The Rise of the European Economy 1500–1800", *in* ALDCROFT AND SUTCLIFFE.

VAN ZANDEN, J.L. (2002), "Taking the Measure of the Early Modern Economy: Historical National Accounts for Holland in 1510/14", *European Review of Economic History*, 6, pp. 131–163.

VAN ZANDEN, J.L. (2003), "Rich and Poor before the Industrial Revolution: A Comparison between Java and the Netherlands at the beginning of the 19th Century", *Explorations in Economic History,* 40, pp. 1–23.

VAN ZANDEN, J.L. (forthcoming), "Economic Growth in Java, 1815–1939: Reconstruction of the Historical National Accounts of a Colonial Economy" (http://iisg.nl/research/jvz–reconstruction.pdf).

OECD PUBLICATIONS, 2, rue André-Pascal, 75775 PARIS CEDEX 16
PRINTED IN FRANCE
(41 2003 06 1 P) ISBN 92-64-10412-7 – No. 53197 2003